24Hours

to the Civil Service Exams

Shannon R. Turlington

2nd Edition

THOMSON ™

ARCO

Australia • Canada • Mexico • Singapore • Spain • United Kingdom • United States

An ARCO Book

ARCO is a registered trademark of Thomson Learning, Inc. and is used herein under license by Peterson's.

About The Thomson Corporation and Peterson's

With revenues of US$7.2 billion, The Thomson Corporation (www.thomson.com) is a leading global provider of integrated information solutions for business, education, and professional customers. Its Learning businesses and brands (www.thomsonlearning.com) serve the needs of individuals, learning institutions, and corporations with products and services for both traditional and distributed learning.

Peterson's, part of The Thomson Corporation, is one of the nation's most respected providers of lifelong learning online resources, software, reference guides, and books. The Education Supersite[SM] at www.petersons.com—the Internet's most heavily traveled education resources—has searchable databases and interactive tools for contacting U.S.-accredited institutions and programs. In addition, Peterson's serves more than 105 million education consumers annually.

For more information, contact Peterson's, 2000 Lenox Drive, Lawrenceville, NJ 08648; 800-338-3282; or find us on the World Wide Web at: www.petersons.com/about

ISBN 0-7689-1172-9

Printed in Canada

10 9 8 7 6 5 4 3 2 1   05 04 03

About This Book

Congratulations! You have in your hands the best fast-track civil service exam self-study course available today! *24 Hours to the Civil Service Exams* gives you a structured, step-by-step tutorial program that can help you master all the basics—no matter how limited your study time. In just 24 hour-long lessons, it cuts straight to the essentials, covering all the key points and giving you the practice you need to make each minute count. Even if the test is just days away, this book will help you learn everything it takes to get the high score you want on your civil service exam.

In your very first lesson, you'll get an overview of the civil service job market, including where to get job information and how to apply for federal, state, and municipal jobs. Then you'll take a look at the all-important entry-level exam, examining every test subject and question type. In practically no time, you'll be sailing through confidence-building workshops, practice exercises, and full-length sample exams, sharpening your skills and building your confidence so that when test day comes, you'll be ready!

Who Should Use This Book?

24 Hours to the Civil Service Exams is written for civil service candidates who want to prepare for their exam the smartest way but whose study time is limited. This book is for you if:

- You know that you'll get the most out of a structured, step-by-step tutorial program that takes the guesswork out of test preparation.

- You want to prepare on your own time and at your own pace but don't have time for a preparation program that takes weeks to complete.

- You want a guide that covers all the key points but doesn't waste time on topics you don't absolutely have to know for the test.

- You want to avoid taking risks with this all-important test by relying on those "beat the system" guides that are long on promises but short on substance.

Contents

Introduction

Welcome to *24 Hours to the Civil Service Exams*. By working your way through these pages, you'll get a fast-paced cram course on all the key points you need to know to score high on your Civil Service exam and get the job you want. In just 24 one-hour lessons, you'll review all of the topics and concepts that are tested on Civil Service exams and learn powerful strategies for answering every question type.

How to Use This Book

This book has been designed as a 24-hour teach-yourself training course, complete with examples, workshops, practice exercises, and full-length sample tests. It is expected that you can complete each lesson in about an hour; however, you should work at your own pace. If you think you can complete more than one lesson in an hour, go for it! Also, if you think that you should spend more than one hour on a certain topic, spend as much time as you need.

How This Book Is Organized

Part I, "Start with the Basics," gives you a quick overview of important facts you need to know about the Civil Service job market and the entry-level exam you must take.

You'll learn where to get job information; how to apply for federal, state, and municipal positions; what to expect on the Civil Service test; and how the exam is scored. You'll also get some general test-taking tips that will help you score higher on test day.

Part II, "Learn to Answer Verbal Ability Questions," focuses on the concepts and strategies you'll need to know for the verbal sections of most Civil Service exams. In hours 3–8, you'll cover grammar and usage, spelling, synonyms, sentence completions, verbal analogies, and effective expression as they are tested on Civil Service exams. Then, in hours 9–11, you'll teach yourself reading comprehension, judgment, observation and memory, and mechanical aptitude skills. At the end of each hour, you'll apply what you learned to civil service-type practice exercises.

Part III, "Learn to Answer Clerical Ability Questions," starts in Hour 12 with alphabetizing and filing rules. Then, in hours 13 and 14, you'll examine clerical speed and accuracy tests and typical typing and stenography tests. Here, too, you'll find skill-building practice exercises at the end of each teaching hour.

Part IV, "Learn to Answer Arithmetic Ability Questions," focuses on the arithmetic areas covered on most Civil Service tests. In Hours 15–18, you'll review fractions and decimals, percents, ratio and proportion, graphs and tables, and arithmetic reasoning in preparation for your test. You'll learn strategies for solving each question type, and you'll sharpen your skills by working through practice exercises.

Part V, "Practice with Sample Exams," contains three full-length practice exams that are as close as you can get to the real thing. Take them under timed conditions, and you'll experience just how it feels to take the actual exam. As you finish each exam, check your answers against the Answer Key and read the explanation (Hours 20, 22, and 24) for each question you missed. Once you have finished, you will have completed this entire intensive, superconcentrated preparation program, and you'll be ready to get your best score on your Civil Service test.

Special Features of This Book

This book contains the following special features to help highlight important concepts and information.

A **Note** presents interesting pieces of information related to the surrounding discussion.

A **Tip** offers advice or teaches you an easier way to do something.

A **Caution** advises you about potential problems and helps you steer clear of disaster.

Make Connections tells you where you can find more information on a particular subject elsewhere in the book.

Part I

Start with the Basics

Hour

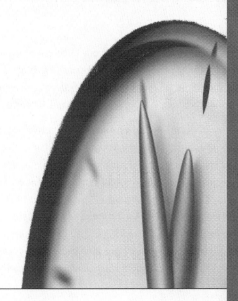

Hour **1**

Civil Service Jobs

What You Will Learn in This Hour

In this hour, you will begin the process of locating a position in civil service. You will discover what jobs are available in federal, state, and municipal government and how to qualify for them. You will also learn how to find job announcements and how to apply for civil service jobs. Here are the goals for this hour:

- Understand various federal jobs and their requirements.
- Learn about state and municipal jobs and their requirements.
- Learn how to obtain job announcements.
- Learn how to apply for civil service jobs.

Federal Employment

The federal government is the nation's largest employer. It employs more than 2.7 million civilian workers in the United States and an additional 130,000

3

civilian workers—half of them U.S. citizens—in U.S. territories and other countries. Government occupations represent nearly every kind of job in private employment, as well as some jobs unique to the federal government, including regulatory inspectors, Foreign Service officers, and Internal Revenue agents.

Many civilian federal employees are employed through the Legislative Branch (Congress, the General Accounting Office, the Government Printing Office, and the Library of Congress) and the Judicial Branch (the Supreme Court and the U.S. Court system). By far the greatest number of federal civilian employees work for the Executive Branch of the government. The Department of Defense, which includes the departments of the Army, Navy, Air Force, and the Marine Corps, is the largest employer with about one million civilian workers. The departments of Agriculture, Health and Human Services, and the Treasury are also big employers. The two largest independent agencies are the U.S. Postal Service and the Veterans Administration.

Note
The headquarters of most government departments and agencies are in Washington, D.C., but only a small percentage of federal employees work there. Federal employees are stationed in all parts of the United States and its territories and in many other countries.

Caution
Alaska, Guam, Hawaii, Puerto Rico, and the Virgin Islands offer very limited federal employment possibilities. Residents receive first consideration for employment in these areas. Other candidates are considered only when no qualified residents are available.

Categories of Federal Jobs

Nearly every occupation in the private sector is also represented in the federal civil service. If you are seeking a career in government service, you will probably be able to put to use the skills you have already acquired. The following are the major categories of federal positions:

- **Professional positions.** These positions require knowledge in a specialized field, usually acquired through college-level or higher education. Positions include engineers, accountants, attorneys, biologists, physicists, and chemists.

1

- **Administrative positions.** Employees in these positions are responsible for overseeing contracts with the private sector and purchasing goods and services needed by the government. Positions include contract specialists, budget analysts, purchasing officers, claims examiners, product control specialists, administrative assistants, personnel officers, and Internal Revenue officers.

- **Investigative and law enforcement positions.** Several government agencies employ police officers or investigators in jobs ranging from guarding property and patrolling borders to highly technical intelligence operations. These agencies include the Department of Justice, State Department, Treasury, Postal Service, Customs Bureau, and Federal Bureau of Investigation.

- **Technical positions.** These positions typically involve support work in a professional or administrative field that is nonroutine in nature, such as computer technicians and electronic technicians.

- **Clerical positions.** There are hundreds of different jobs under the umbrella term "clerical work." Nearly half of the jobs in federal civil service are clerical. Positions include office machine operators, secretaries, stenographers, clerk-typists, mail and file clerks, telephone operators, and workers in computer and related occupations.

- **Labor and mechanical positions.** Most people do not realize that the U.S. government is the largest employer of mechanical, manual, and laboring workers in the country. Positions include mobile equipment operators, mechanics, machine tool and metal workers, maintenance and repair workers, and food preparation and serving workers.

- **Unskilled positions.** Thousands of positions in government service are open to people with no skills or with only a small amount of training. Positions include housekeeping aides, janitors, laundry workers, and mess attendants.

> **Make Connections**
> For more detailed information about different federal positions, duties, and job requirements, turn to Appendix A, "Selected Jobs in the Federal Service."

Specific Programs in the Federal Service

Many federal positions may be entered through special government programs. Normally, experience is not required to qualify, but you may have to take a test that indicates whether you have an aptitude for the occupation. Consider the following special programs as a way to enter civil service:

- **Part-time positions.** Usually 16 to 32 hours per week, part-time positions are available throughout the federal government. Flex-time, job sharing, and nontraditional configurations of the work day and work week are also options for some positions. Check with the personnel office of the specific government agency for more information.

- **Summer employment.** Limited summer work is available for high school, college, law, medical, and dental students throughout the government. Most jobs are in large metropolitan areas. Applications are accepted by individual agencies from December through April 15, and the jobs tend to run from mid-May through September 30.

- **The student career experience.** This work/study program is for high school, vocational/technical school, and college students who are enrolled in school at least part-time. It offers employment in positions directly related to a course of study, which may lead to permanent employment with the agency upon graduation. Interested students should contact their high school counselors, college employment coordinators, or the agency where they would like to work.

- **Student temporary employment.** Part-time student employment does not necessarily have to relate to a course of study. This employment, however, must end when you are no longer enrolled in school at least part time. Again, check with a counselor, employment coordinator, or the agency.

- **The PMI program for Presidential Management Interns.** This program is targeted at graduate students. Only graduate students who expect to receive their degrees by the following June should apply. These students perform high-level work in their fields during the two-year PMI program. Afterward, PMIs may continue in regular federal employment. Interested students must be nominated by the dean of the college or university, or by the chair of their department or graduate program.

Qualifications and Requirements

Jobs in the federal government are in the General Schedule (GS), which assigns grades to jobs according to the difficulty of duties and responsibilities and the knowledge, experience, and skill required. Selection requirements are based on studies of the training, experience, and skills required for successful job performance at the different grade levels.

Job applicants must meet the education and/or experience requirements, show evidence of having the required skills, and pass a job-related written test. Generally, a high school diploma or some previous job experience is all that is needed to qualify for jobs at the entry-level grades. As you gain experience, you become eligible for promotion to higher-level, more specialized jobs. You can also enter the federal government at higher grade levels if you already have the specialized experience or additional education these jobs require.

1

> **Note**
> For most positions, in order to qualify for experience for any grade higher than the entry level, you must have either six months or one year of experience at a comparable level to that of the next-lower grade level. For some positions at GS-11 and lower, experience may have been obtained at two levels below that of the job to be filled. The job announcement provides specific information about the level of experience needed to qualify.

The following educational and experience requirements are typical for various categories of civil service jobs:

- Professional positions require highly specialized knowledge. Typically, you must have a bachelor's degree or higher in a specific field.

- Administrative and managerial positions usually do not require specialized knowledge. A bachelor's degree and/or responsible job experience, however, is required. In general, you begin at the trainee level and learn the duties of the job after being hired.

- Investigative and law enforcement position requirements vary greatly depending on the job. In general, these positions require a bachelor's degree, special training, good physical condition, and/or previous experience.

- Technical and clerical entry-level positions usually require a high school diploma or its equivalent, although junior college or technical school training may enable you to enter the position at a higher level. No additional prior experience or training may be necessary.

- Labor and mechanical positions, particularly those requiring a skilled trade, often require previous experience. Apprenticeships for those with no previous training, however, may be available for some positions.

- Many positions require little or no prior training or experience, including janitors, maintenance workers, and messengers.

> **Note**
> Veterans are entitled to special consideration in hiring. In some cases, veterans are entitled to positions that are not open to the public. In other cases, extra points are added to exam scores, placing veterans at a competitive advantage. Some jurisdictions give surviving spouses of deceased veterans preference. For more information, contact the Veterans Employment Coordinator of the agency where you are seeking employment.

In addition to educational, experience, and skill requirements, there are some general age and physical requirements.

Age

There is no maximum age limit for federal employment. The usual minimum age limit is 18, but high school graduates may apply at 16 for many jobs. If you are younger than 18 and out of school but are not a high school graduate, you may be hired only if you have successfully completed a formal training program or if you have been out of school for at least three months, not counting summer vacation, and school authorities sign a form approving your preference for work instead of additional schooling. The agency that wants to hire you will give you the form.

Caution

Some positions, particularly law enforcement and fire-fighting positions, may have set age limits. Be sure to check the job announcement carefully before applying.

Physical Requirements

You must be physically able to perform the duties of the position, and you must be emotionally and mentally stable. This does not mean that a physical disability will disqualify you, as long as you can do the work efficiently without posing a hazard to yourself or to others. Of course, there are some positions, such as border patrol agent, firefighter, and criminal investigator, that can be filled only by people in top-notch physical condition. Whenever this is the case, the physical requirements are described in detail in the job announcement.

Note

The federal government is the world's largest employer of the physically disabled and has a strong program aimed at their employment. If you have a physical disability, contact the Selective Placement Coordinator at the agency you are interested in for special placement assistance. You should also state the nature of your disability on your application, so special testing arrangements can be made.

Working Conditions and Benefits

More than half of federal civilian employees are paid according to the General Schedule (GS), a pay scale for those in professional, administrative, technical, and clerical jobs and for workers such as guards and messengers. Salaries under the General Schedule are set to reflect pay levels in similar occupations in the private sector.

> **Note**
> GS pay rates are uniform throughout most of the country, although they are adjusted upward in very high cost-of-living regions such as New York City, Los Angeles, and San Francisco. In low-cost areas, the GS pay scale may exceed that of most private-sector workers.

High school graduates with no related work experience usually start in GS-2 jobs, but some who have special skills begin at grade GS-3. Graduates of two-year colleges and technical schools often begin at the GS-4 level. Professional and administrative employees with bachelor's degrees can enter at grades GS-5 or GS-7, depending on experience and academic record. Those who have a master's degree or Ph.D. or equivalent experience may enter at the GS-9 or GS-11 level.

Advancement to higher grades generally depends on ability, work performance, and job openings at higher grade levels. Most agencies fill vacancies by promoting their own employees whenever possible. Promotions are based on increases in responsibility and demonstration of increased experience and skill.

> **Note**
> It is not always necessary to move to a new job in order to advance in grade. Sometimes an employee's work assignments change a great deal in the ordinary course of business—meaning that the job "grows." When that happens, a position classifier determines if the job should be put in a higher grade because of increased difficulty or responsibility.

Most employees receive within-grade pay increases at one-, two-, or three-year intervals if their work is acceptable. (Some managers and supervisors receive increases based on job performance, rather than on time in grade.) Within-grade increases may also be given in recognition of high-quality service.

Federal jobs offer many benefits in addition to pay, including health and life insurance, retirement benefits, and holidays.

Work Hours

The usual government work week is 40 hours. Most government employees work 8 hours per day Monday through Friday. In some cases, the nature of the work may call for a different work week. As in any other business, employees sometimes have to work overtime. If you are required to work overtime, you will either be paid for the extra time or given time off to make up for it.

Training

Training for increased responsibility is often provided on the job, and employees are encouraged to continue their own training. You may participate in individual career development programs and receive job-related training in your own agency, in other agencies, or outside the government (in industrial plants and universities, for example). In addition, the government sponsors some formal training courses and sometimes pays for outside training that is directly related to improving job performance.

Efficiency Counts

Employees are regularly rated on job performance. In most agencies, the ratings are "outstanding," "satisfactory," and "unsatisfactory." Employees with "outstanding" ratings receive extra credit toward retention in case of layoffs. An employee whose rating is "unsatisfactory" may be dismissed or assigned to another position.

Incentive Awards

Government agencies encourage employees to suggest better, simpler, or more economical ways of doing their jobs. They may give a cash award to an employee for a suggestion or invention that results in savings or improved service. They may also reward outstanding job performance or other acts deserving of recognition.

Vacation and Sick Leave

Most federal employees earn annual leave for vacation and other purposes, according to the number of years that they have been in the federal service. Vacation benefits begin at 13 working days a year for most new full-time employees and increase as length of employment increases. Most full-time employees also earn 13 days of sick leave with pay each year, regardless of length of service.

1

Injury Compensation

The government provides generous compensation benefits, including medical care, for employees who suffer injuries in the performance of official duty. Death benefits are also provided if an employee dies because of such injuries.

Group Life Insurance

As a federal employee, you may have low-cost term life insurance without taking a physical examination. Two kinds of insurance are provided: life insurance and accidental death and dismemberment insurance.

Health Benefits

The government sponsors a voluntary health insurance program for federal employees. The program offers a variety of plans to meet individual needs, including basic coverage and major medical protection against costly illnesses. The government contributes part of the cost of premiums, and the employee pays the balance through payroll deductions.

Retirement

The Federal Employees Retirement System (FERS) offers very favorable terms for retirement. Federal employees are covered under a combined Social Security and supplemental retirement program. The government's share of the retirement package is generous, and the employee can contribute to the program to create an even more comfortable retirement. This retirement system gives employees flexibility to move between the private sector and civil service without losing basic retirement benefits.

Holidays

Government workers are entitled to the following 10 regular holidays each year:

- New Year's Day (January 1)
- Martin Luther King Jr.'s Birthday (third Monday in January)
- Presidents' Day (third Monday in February)
- Memorial Day (last Monday in May)
- Independence Day (July 4)
- Labor Day (first Monday in September)
- Columbus Day (second Monday in October)
- Veterans' Day (November 11)
- Thanksgiving Day (fourth Thursday in November)
- Christmas Day (December 25)

> **Note**
> When Inauguration Day falls on a regularly scheduled work day, employees in the Washington metropolitan area get an 11th holiday.

State and Local Government Employment

State and local governments provide a large and expanding source of job opportunities in a variety of fields. More than 11.8 million people work for state and local agencies, and nearly three fourths of these employees work in units of local government, such as counties, municipalities, towns, and school districts.

As with federal employment, nearly every kind of job available in the private sector is also available in state and local employment. Some positions are unique to state and local government, including the following:

- **Public education**. Educational services make up the majority of jobs in state and local government. In addition to teachers, school systems, colleges, and universities employ administrative personnel, librarians, guidance counselors, nurses, dieticians, clerks, and maintenance workers.

- **Health services.** Almost 1.4 million people are employed in health and hospital work, including physicians, nurses, medical laboratory technicians, and hospital attendants.

- **Highway work.** More than 600,000 people work in highway construction and maintenance. Positions include civil engineers, surveyors, equipment operators, truck drivers, concrete finishers, carpenters, and construction workers.

- **Governmental control and finance.** These activities account for about 840,000 employees, including employees in the justice system, tax enforcement, and general administration. Positions include city managers, property assessors, and budget analysts, as well as stenographers and clerks.

- **Law enforcement and fire fighting.** More than 600,000 people work in law enforcement, including not only police officers and detectives but also administrative, clerical, and custodial workers. Local governments employ all of the 300,000 firefighters, many of whom work only part-time.

- **And more.** Other state and local government work can be found in local utilities, transportation, natural resources, public welfare, parks and recreation, sanitation, correction, local libraries, sewage disposal, and housing and urban renewal. These fields require diverse experience, such as economists, electrical engineers, electricians, pipe fitters, clerks, foresters, and bus drivers.

State and local government job requirements, salary scales, and benefits vary from state to state and from municipality to municipality but are comparable to those for federal government employment. Again, applicants must meet the educational and/or experience requirements, show evidence of having the required skills, and pass a job-related written test.

> **Make Connections**
> For more detailed information on the different kinds of state and municipal jobs, including duties and requirements, turn to Appendix B, "Selected State and Municipal Positions."

Obtaining Job Information

A job announcement or an examination announcement is published by a government agency when jobs need to be filled (see Figure 1.1). The announcement lists just about everything you need to know about the job, including requirements, salary, duties, and location. It also says when and where to file for the exam, which application forms must be filled out, and where to get the forms.

> **Caution**
> Most job announcements give a deadline for filing an application. No application mailed past the deadline date will be considered. If the top of the first page of the announcement says "No Closing Date," applications are accepted until all open positions are filled.

> **Tip**
> Look for jobs that are close to home. Local residents usually receive preference in appointments.

Study the job announcement carefully. It will answer many of your questions and help you decide whether you like the position and are qualified for it. The precise duties are described in detail, usually under the heading, Description of Work. Make sure that they come within the range of your experience and ability, and that you meet all the educational, experience, and special requirements listed.

Figure 1.1.

Recruitment Bulletin
Bureau of Land Management

Bulletin Number: CSO-95-06(DEU)

Open: 02-06

Close: 02-27

Publicity Area: CAL/NEVADA

AN EQUAL OPPORTUNITY EMPLOYER: All candidates will receive consideration without regard to race, color, sex, age, religion, national origin, or other non-merit factors.

Public Affairs Specialist

GS-1035-12

Duty Station: Sacramento, California

Number of Vacancies: One or two positions may be filled.

Location: California State Office

        External Affairs Staff

Salary: $43,270 per annum.

Tour of Duty: Permanent Full-Time

Benefits: Entitled to health insurance, life insurance, retirement coverage and annual (vacation) and sick leave

Description of Duties: The position is on the Public Affairs Staff of the Office of the State Director under the immediate direction of the External Affairs Chief. The incumbent is in the capacity of a principal assistant to the Staff Chief on statewide matters related to contacts with Bureau managers and staff and the news media, interest groups, educational groups, and counterparts in government agencies on the national, state and local levels; also for matters related to the Freedom of Information Act. Incumbent is assigned highly controversial issues within many major program areas. Advises and counsels the External Affairs Chief, program managers, staff specialist and other Bureau officials on public affairs policies and procedures as they affect Bureau relationships with the public and media. Identifies issues and actions contained in the Bureau policies, plans and programs that should receive public affairs emphasis and recommends appropriate course of action.

Qualification Requirements: Candidates must have the following length and type of experience:

    One year of specialized experience equivalent to the GS-11 level in the federal service.

Specialized Experience: Experience in or directly related to public affairs and which has equipped the candidate with the particular knowledge, skills and abilities to successfully perform the duties of the position.

1

Basis of Rating: No written test is required. Candidates will be rated on a scale of 70–100 based on the nature, quality and extent of their experience in relation to the duties and requirements of this position and the following ranking factors:

1. Knowledge of issues in ecosystem/multiple-use programs of a natural resource agency.
2. Ability to work with California Congressional delegations and the California legislature.
3. Skill in professional journalistic and public relations in order to prepare all necessary materials and to advice on sensitive issues.
4. Skill in establishing and maintaining effective relations with state and national media, interest groups and other agencies.
5. Ability to organize, plan, and conduct a public affairs initiative project on a state level.
6. Ability to operate personal computers and associated software.

Important Notice: On a separate sheet of paper(s), as a supplement to your application, please provide examples of your experience/education which best describe the extent and level of your ability in each of the above areas. Your application cannot receive proper consideration unless you submit this supplemental information.

Who May Apply: All interested U.S. citizens

How to Apply: Submit the following forms:

1. A resume or the Optional Application for Federal Employment (Form number OF 612). Please indicate the number of this Recruitment Bulletin on your application.
2. Written response to ranking factors.
3. DI-1935, Application Background Survey Form. Submission of this form is strictly voluntary. It is used for statistical purposes only and is not used in the evaluation process.
4. DD-214, if you are claiming 5-point veteran preference.
5. DD-214 and SF-15 if you are claiming 10-point veteran preference. Proof dated within the last 12 months is required to establish 10-point veteran preference.

The required application forms may be obtained by writing or calling the Bureau of Land Management, Branch of Human Resources Management, at the address/phone number given below or by calling the Career America Connection in San Francisco at (415) 744-JOBS (5627) or dialing the electronic bulletin board at (912) 757-3100.

Mail completed forms to:

USDI, Bureau of Land Management
Federal Office Building
2800 Cottage Way, Room E-2845
Sacramento, CA 95825
ATTN: Branch of Human Resources Management
(916) 979-2900

Applications must be received or postmarked by: FEBRUARY 27.

The job announcement also describes the kind of test given for the particular position, so pay close attention to this section. You will learn which areas are covered in the written test and the specific subjects on which questions will be asked. Sometimes sample questions or the method of rating the exam are given. All of this information will be invaluable when preparing for the exam. Sometimes, you will not even have to take an exam; instead, you are rated on education, experience, and past achievements.

Note

By far, the easiest way to get information about job openings throughout the country is to call the Career America Connection at (912) 757-3000. This is a toll call, but it is a 24-hour automated service, so you can hold down costs by calling at night or on the weekend. Allow at least a half-hour to search job categories and geographical areas. The system is equipped to record your name and mailing address so that announcements and forms can be sent to you. If you have a computer with a modem, you can access the same information from an electronic bulletin board by dialing (912) 757-3100.

Learning about Federal Jobs

At one time, federal hiring was a centralized function of the Office of Personnel Management (OPM). This is no longer the case. Now, all hiring is done by the individual agencies.

Tip

If you have Internet access, the OPM Web site provides valuable information, including job announcements, veterans' preferences, online applications, and locations of Federal Job Information Centers. Connect to it at **http://www.opm.gov/**.

If you know which agencies you want to work for, contact them directly to learn about openings and application procedures. At some agencies, you can file an application for future vacancies. Other agencies accept applications only for current or projected openings.

If a federal agency has offices in your area, you will find the telephone number under U.S. Government in the blue pages of your local telephone directory. Ask for the address and phone number of the personnel offices. Visit or call personnel offices and ask for listings or vacancies. If the agency has no office in your area, you may have to call information in the District of Columbia to ask for the telephone number of the personnel office of the agency that you want to reach.

> **Tip**
> Prepare your questions for the personnel office ahead of time to hold down your phone bill.

You can look for a Federal Job Information Center in your area, also listed under U.S. Government in the blue pages. Call the Federal Job Information Center to get automated information or learn where to find job announcements.

Some state employment services maintain computer touch screens, which contain listings of available federal jobs within the state. Other good sources of job announcements include the public library, newspapers, employees of the agency, special publications, college or university placement offices or professors, or professional contacts.

> **Tip**
> Federal, state, and municipal agencies looking for employees frequently contact professional societies, veterans' organizations, unions, and trade associations. Check with any organization to which you belong.

Learning about State and Municipal Jobs

State and municipal governments have developed many ways to make job opportunities known. Check the following places for job announcements:

- The offices of the State Employment Services are administered by the state where they are located, with the financial assistance of the federal government; there are almost 2,000 throughout the country. You will find the address of the one nearest to you in your telephone book.
- The state Civil Service Commission (located in the capital city of your state).
- Some cities, particularly large ones, have a Civil Service Commission as well. It is sometimes called by another name, such as the Department of Personnel, but you should be able to find it in your telephone directory under the listing of city departments.
- City and statewide publications devoted to civil service employees, such as the *Chief-Leader* (published in New York City). Many local newspapers run a section on regional civil service news as well.
- School boards and boards of education, which employ the greatest proportion of all state and local personnel, should be asked directly for information about job openings.

- The municipal building.
- Local libraries.
- College or university placement offices.

> **Tip**
> If you have Internet access, visit the Web site of your state. Many include announcements of job openings in state government, and some enable you to apply electronically. In addition, some state sites connect to county or city sites within the state. You should easily be able to locate your state's Web site by searching for your state in Yahoo (**http://www.yahoo.com/**) or at a similar search site.

How to Apply

The job announcement specifies the application form you should use and where to send for it. Civil service application forms differ little from state to state and locality to locality. The questions, which have been worked out after years of experimentation, are simple and direct, designed to elicit maximum information about you.

> **Tip**
> Sometimes Optional Fields or Options are listed on the front page of the job announcement. These are related positions that can be filled through the same announcement. If you are interested in a position under this heading, you may apply for it simultaneously with the primary position. Just enter the job's title in the Optional Job field on the application.

For most federal jobs, you may submit either the Optional Application for Federal Employment (see Figure 1.2) or a resume that fulfills the requirements set forth in the pamphlet, Applying for a Federal Job (see Figure 1.3).

> **Caution**
> Be sure to include any backup material that is requested on the job announcement with your application, but do not send more than is requested. You can command hiring attention by exactly conforming to requirements.

Figure 1.2.

Optional Application for Federal Employment—OF 612

Form Approved

OMB No. 3206-0219

You may apply for most jobs with a resume, this form, or other written format. If your resume or application does not provide all the information requested on this form and in the job vacancy announcement, you may lose consideration for a job.

1 Job title in announcement _____   2 Grade(s) applying for _____

3 Announcement number _____

4 Last name _____ First and middle names _____   5 Social Security Number _____

6 Mailing address _____   7 Phone numbers (include area code)

   City _____ State _____ ZIP Code _____   Daytime ( ) _____

                                                          Evening ( ) _____

Work Experience

8 Describe your paid and nonpaid work experience related to the job for which you are applying. Do **not** attach job descriptions.

   1) Job title (if Federal, includes series and grade)

   From (MM/YY) _____ To (MM/YY) _____   Salary per _____   Hours per week ____
      $

   Employer's name and address   Supervisor's name and phone number

   _____   _____

   _____   ( ) _____

   Describe your duties and accomplishments

   _____

   _____

   2) Job title (if Federal, include series and grade)

   From (MM/YY) _____ To (MM/YY) _____   Salary per _____   Hours per week ____
      $

   Employer's name and address   Supervisor's name and phone number

   _____   _____

   _____   ( ) _____

   Describe your duties and accomplishments

   _____

   _____

50612-101   NSN 7540-01-351-9178   Optional Form 612 (September 1994)
U.S. Office of Personnel Management

9 May we contact your current supervisor?

YES [   ]   NO [   ] —> If we need to contact your current supervisor before making an offer, we will contact you first.

Education

10 Mark highest level completed.
Some HS [   ]   HS/GED [   ]   Associate [   ]   Bachelor [   ]   Master [   ]   Doctoral [   ]

11 Last high school (HS) or GED school. Give the school's name, city, State, ZIP Code (if known), and year diploma or GED received.

12 Colleges and universities attended. Do **not** attach a copy of your transcript unless requested.

Name City, State, ZIP Code	Total Credits Earned Semester/Quarter	Major(s)	Degree — Year (if any) Received
1)			
2)			
3)			

Other Qualifications

13 **Job-related** training courses (give title and year). **Job-related** skills (other languages, computer software/hardware, tools, machinery, typing speed, etc.). **Job-related** certificates and licenses (current only). **Job-related** honors, awards, and special accomplishments (publications, memberships in professional/honor societies, leadership activities, public speaking, and performance awards). Give dates, but do **not** send documents unless requested.

General

14 Are you a U.S. citizen? **YES** [   ]   **NO** [   ] —> Give the country of your citizenship.

15 Do you claim veteran's preference? **NO** [   ]   **YES** [   ]   —> Mark your claim of 5 or 10 points below.

5 points [   ] —> Attach your DD 214 or other proof   **10 points** [   ] —> Attach an *Application for 10-Point Veterans' Preference* (SF 15) and proof required.

16 Were you ever a Federal civilian employee?   Series _____   Grade _____
From (MM/YY) _____   To (MM/YY) _____
NO [   ]   YES [   ]   —> For highest civilian grade give:

17 Are you eligible for reinstatement based on career or career-conditional Federal status?
NO [   ]   YES [   ]   —> If requested, attach SF 50 proof.

Applicant Certification

18 I **certify** that, to the best of my knowledge and belief, all of the information on and attached to this application is true, correct, complete and made in good faith. I **understand** that false or fraudulent information on or attached to this application may be grounds for not hiring me or for firing me after I begin work, and may be punishable by fine or imprisonment. I **understand** that any information I give may be investigated.

Signature _____   Date Signed _____

Figure 1.3.

Applying for a Federal Job—OF 510

Here's what your resume or application must contain
(in addition to specific information requested in the job vacancy announcement):

Job Information

- Announcement number, and title and grade(s) of the job for which you are applying

Personal Information

- Full name, mailing address *(with ZIP Code)* and day and evening phone numbers *with area code)*
- Social Security Number
- Country of citizenship *(Most Federal jobs require United States citizenship.)*
- Veterans' preference *(See reverse.)*
- Reinstatement eligibility *(If requested, attach SF 50 proof of your career or career-conditional status.)*
- Highest Federal civilian grade held *(Also give job series and dates held.)*

Education

- High school
  Name, city, and state *(ZIP Code if known)*
  Date of diploma or GED
- Colleges and universities
  Name, city, and state *(ZIP Code if known)*
  Majors
  Type and year of any degrees received *(If no degree, show total credits earned and indicate whether semester or quarter hours.)*
- Send a copy of your college transcript only if the job vacancy announcement requests it.

Work Experience

- Give the following information for your paid and nonpaid work experience related to the job for which you are applying *(Do not send job descriptions.)*
  Job title *(include series and grade if Federal job)*
  Duties and accomplishments
  Employer's name and address
  Supervisor's name and phone number
  Starting and ending dates *(month and year)*
  Hours per week
  Salary
- Indicate if we may contact your current supervisor

Other Qualifications

- **Job-related** training courses *(title and year)*
- **Job-related** skills; for example, other languages, computer software/hardware, tools, machinery, typing speed
- **Job-related** certificates and licenses *(current only)*
- **Job-related** honors, awards, and special accomplishments; for example, publications, memberships in professional or honor societies, leadership activities, public speaking, and performance awards *(Give dates but do not send documents unless requested.)*

The Federal Government is an equal opportunity employer

Job Openings

For job information 24 hours a day, 7 days a week, call **912-757-3000**, the U.S. Office of Personnel Management (OPM) automated telephone system. Or, with a computer modem dial **912-757-3100** for job information from an OPM electronic bulletin board. You can also reach the board through the Internet (Telnet only) at FJOB.MAIL.OPM.GOV.

Applicants with Disabilities

You can find out about alternative formats by calling OPM. Select "Federal Employment Topics" and then "People with Disabilities." Or, dial our electronic bulletin board. If you have a hearing disability, **call TDD 912-744-2299.**

How to Apply

Review the list of openings, decide which jobs you are interested in, and follow the instructions given. **You may apply for most jobs with a resume, the Optional Application for Federal Employment, or any other written format you choose.** For jobs that are unique or filled through automated procedures, you will be given special forms to complete. (You can get an *Optional Application* by calling OPM or dialing our electronic bulletin board at the numbers given above.)

What to Include

Although the Federal Government does not require a standard application form for most jobs, we do need certain information to evaluate your qualifications and determine if you meet legal requirements for Federal employment. If your resume or application does not provide all the information requested in the job vacancy announcement and in this flyer, you may lose consideration for a job. Help speed the selection process by keeping your resume or application brief and by sending only the requested material. Type or print clearly in dark ink.

Veterans' Preference in Hiring

- If you served on active duty in the United States Military and were separated under honorable conditions, you may be eligible for veterans' preference. To receive preference if your service began after October 15, 1976, you must have a Campaign Badge, Expeditionary Medal, or a service-connected disability. For further details, call OPM at **912-757-3000**. Select "Federal Employment Topics" and then "Veterans." Or, dial our electronic bulletin board at **912-757-3100**.
- Veterans' preference is not a factor for Senior Executive Service jobs or when competition is limited to status candidates (current or former Federal career or career-conditional employees.)
- To claim a 5-point veterans' preference, attach a copy of your DD-214, *Certificate of Release or Discharge from Active Duty*, or other proof of eligibility.
- To claim a 10-point veterans' preference, attach an SF 15, *Application for 10-Point Veterans' Preference*, plus the proof required by that form.

Other Important Information

- Before hiring, an agency will ask you to complete a *Declaration for Federal Employment* form to determine your suitability for Federal employment and to authorize a background investigation. The agency will also ask you to sign and certify the accuracy of all the information in your application. **If you make a false statement in any part of your application, you may not be hired; you may be fired after you begin work; or you may be fined or jailed.**
- If you are a male over age 18 who was born after December 31, 1959, you must have registered with the Selective Service System (or have an exemption) to be eligible for a Federal job.
- The law prohibits public officials from appointing, promoting, or recommending their relatives.
- Federal annuitants (military and civilian) may have their salaries or annuities reduced. All employees must pay any valid delinquent debts or the agency may garnish their salary.

Tips for Completing the Application

Give the job application serious attention. It is the first important step toward getting the job that you want.

Do

DO make a master copy.
DO make a first draft.
DO use a typewriter or computer.
DO provide a complete employment history.
DO provide a complete educational history.
DO list honors and awards.
DO list special qualifications, experience, and skills.
DO list available professional references.
DO put the job announcement number on all application materials.

Don't

DON'T embroider or falsify any information on the application.
DON'T put employment history or other material into one long paragraph.

DO make a master copy. Do not sign and date it. Instead, make photocopies of it, sign and date them, and send them out. This saves time when applying for more than one position.

DO make a first draft. This is especially important when writing your employment history and other experiences. Rewrite the draft as many times as needed to produce a complete, well-written account. Review your life experiences and make a list of specific on-the-job duties, outside activities, knowledge, and experience that may enhance your qualifications for the position.

DO use a typewriter or computer to fill out the application form. If this is not possible, complete the application neatly and clearly in blue or black ink.

DO provide a complete employment history. Use all the lines allotted to each job and write more on plain white paper if necessary. Be sure to label the attachments with the job announcement number, your birth date, name, and item number. Be specific about what tasks you performed in each job. Do not summarize; explain fully.

> **Tip**
> Note that the application asks you to list your present job first and then the one you had before that one, and so on. Experience acquired more than 15 years ago may be summarized in one block if it is not applicable to the type of position for which you are applying.

DO provide a complete educational history. Include the names of all schools you attended (back to high school), with their locations, the dates you attended, the subjects you studied, the number of classroom or credit hours you earned, the diplomas or degrees you received, and any other pertinent data. Also list in-service workshops, seminars, professional conferences, private study, correspondence courses, military training, leadership orientation, career specialty training, and the like. Again, you may have to add separate sheets to be complete.

> **Tip**
> Only include a college transcript if the job announcement requests one.

DO list honors and awards. Many people are modest about awards—do not be. Honors and awards do not have to be earthshaking to be included. Cite scholarships, safety awards, suggestion awards, community awards and nominations, and election to honorary societies and groups. Include brief excerpts from official or unofficial letters in which your work was praised. Recent awards are usually the most relevant. If you received only a few awards, however, list them all, even if they were presented some years ago.

DO list special qualifications, experience, and skills. Be honest in evaluating your abilities. Even if they do not seem directly related to the position, you should mention any familiarity with a foreign language, computer skills, typing skills, licenses and certificates you have earned, experience with equipment or machines, membership in professional organizations, any material you have written even if unpublished, examples of public speaking, and relevant hobbies. Credit may even be given for unpaid experience or volunteer work on the same basis as on-the-job experience, so be sure to include it.

DO list available, professional references. Use people who know you and who know your work. Make sure that they can be easily reached and include their phone numbers. Do not list people who are out of the country, have no phone, or whose whereabouts are unknown to you. Be sure to ask your references for permission to use their names.

DO put the job announcement number on all application materials. You will find this number on the front of the job announcement. You should also list your name, birth date, and the position on all materials in case they become separated.

DON'T embroider or falsify any information on the application. Your application will be closely checked. If you were ever fired, say so. It is better to state this openly than for the examiner to find out the truth from your former employer.

1

> **Caution**
> You will be asked whether personnel staff may contact your present em-
> ployer. If you say no, it will not affect your employment opportunities, but
> try to provide some form of evaluation or letter of recommendation to
> compensate.

DON'T put employment history or other material into one long paragraph. Aim for a
clear, well-organized presentation. This is especially important if you use more space than
that provided on the application. Break up long descriptions into short sentences and
paragraphs, and use headings. Also, use action verbs and avoid abbreviations or the
passive voice.

> **Tip**
> Include the entire zip code (zip plus four) with addresses on the application.
> It makes you appear efficient.

What to Consider When Completing the Application

Most of the questions on the application form are straightforward, but you should consider
the following carefully:

- **Locations where you are willing to work.** Sometimes, vacancies are available in
  several locations. Consider whether you would accept employment in any location
  or whether you want to work in a specific place, and list all the places where you are
  willing to work.

- **Lowest grade or pay you will accept.** You will not be considered for a job paying
  less than the amount you give in answer to this question. Although the salary is
  clearly stated in the announcement, there may be an earlier opening in the same
  occupation carrying less responsibility and thus a lower entrance salary.

- **Temporary employment.** Temporary positions come up frequently. Willingness to
  accept a temporary assignment can be a good way of getting in the door.

- **Part-time employment.** Part-time work comes up every now and then. Consider
  whether you want to accept a part-time position while waiting for a full-time
  appointment. Again, this can be a good way of getting in the door.

> **Caution**
> You will have to provide proof of citizenship and your Social Security number
> for your application to be considered. Note that many federal jobs require
> U.S. citizenship.

The Hour in Review

1. Federal, state, and local governments are the nation's largest employers, comprising most of the positions found in the private sector, as well as many unique positions.

2. The first step in obtaining a civil service job is looking at the job announcement to discover details about open positions, their requirements, application procedures, and the exam that you will have to take.

3. The second step is to fill out and file the application. Take care to complete the application accurately and honestly, and list all relevant experience and education, because this information is key to consideration for the job.

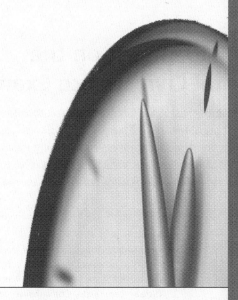

HOUR 2

Overview of the Exams

What You Will Learn in This Hour

Haunted by school day memories, applicants often approach the civil service exam with fear, imagining that someone is going to give them a big list of trick questions to trap them, or that they will have to sit down and laboriously work out the answers to difficult problems. If you have this concept of a government test, change your opinion. In this hour, and in the rest of this book, you will learn exactly what to expect on the civil service exam. Once you do, your fears will vanish. Here are your goals for this hour:

- Learn what to expect on the federal civil service exam.
- Learn what to expect on state and municipal exams.
- Complete the biographical and achievement inventory.
- Learn how to prepare for the exam.
- Learn how the exam is administered and rated.
- Learn how the exam is rated.
- Learn tips and strategies for taking the exam.

What to Expect on the Federal Civil Service Exam

Congress passed the Civil Service Act to ensure that federal employees are hired based on individual merit and fitness. The Civil Service Act provides for competitive exams and the selection of new employees from among the most qualified applicants. Any U.S. citizen may take civil service exams. For most jobs, the agency doing the hiring rates exams to determine which applicants are eligible for the jobs to be filled.

> **Note**
> Some federal jobs are exempt from civil service requirements. Most of these positions, however, are covered by separate merit systems of other agencies, such as the State Department, the Federal Bureau of Investigation, the Nuclear Regulatory Commission, or the Tennessee Valley Authority.

There are two main types of civil service exams: competitive and noncompetitive. In a competitive exam, all applicants for a position compete with each other. The better your score, the better your chance of being appointed. In a noncompetitive exam, each applicant is tested solely to determine qualifications for a given position. You need only pass to become eligible for the job.

The purpose of civil service exams is to identify candidates who have the aptitude and ability to learn the job easily and to do it well. The subjects tested on the exam are closely related to the duties of the position. The written tests for federal occupations measure the verbal, clerical, arithmetic, and any other skills needed for the job. On many clerical exams, for instance, the exam consists of two tests: one measuring verbal ability, and another measuring clerical ability. Test requirements vary depending on the agency and the type of position.

Check the job announcement to confirm the test battery that you will have to take. If the announcement indicates that a written test will be given, you will receive a notice in the mail telling you when and where to report for the test.

> **Tip**
> Pay special attention to the section of the job announcement describing the kind of exam given for the open position. It explains what areas are covered in the written test and lists the specific subjects on which questions will be asked. Sometimes, sample questions are given.

Testing Verbal Ability

Most civil service exams include a section to test verbal ability. The verbal portion of the exam tests you in the following areas:

- Spelling, meaning, and relationship of words.
- Recognition of sentences that are grammatically correct.
- Reading, understanding, and using written material.

These test tasks relate to a variety of job tasks, such as proofreading and correcting typed copy, using instruction manuals, organizing new files of related materials, and carrying out written instructions.

Testing Clerical Ability

The clerical portion of the exam is a test of speed and accuracy on different clerical tasks. Because speed is being measured, this portion of the exam is more heavily timed than other portions. Also, because accuracy is being measured, there is often a penalty for wrong answers, unlike other portions of the exam. You may be tested on any or all of the following areas: alphabetic filing, name and number checking, and typing. Some clerical tests also include a stenography or coding portion.

Testing Arithmetic Ability

Not all exams include an arithmetic section—it depends on the job you are applying for. Many clerical jobs, cashiers, and positions in the manual trades do require some level of arithmetic ability. You may be tested on any of the following:

- Fractions, decimals, and percentages.
- Graphs and tables.
- Ratio and proportion.
- Reasoning problems of various sorts, including work, distance, taxation, and payroll problems.

Other Exam Topics

Depending on the job that you are applying for, you may be tested on other topics. These include general aptitude questions for qualities necessary for the job, and questions testing specific abilities not covered in the clerical portion of the exam. For example, general aptitude questions may measure judgment and communication skills, which are necessary for many jobs. Other subjects are more specific: observation and memory for police officers, firefighters, correction officers, court officers, and similar positions; and mechanical ability for firefighters, custodians, and mechanical workers in many trades.

What to Expect on State and Municipal Exams

Following the lead of the federal government, every state has instituted some form of merit-based hiring procedure. In matters of internal hiring, each state has complete autonomy. No higher authority tells a state which positions must be filled by examination or which exam to use. In the interests of efficiency and fairness in hiring, nearly all states fill positions through civil service exams.

Many states offer their testing services to counties and municipalities as well. Thus, if you qualify on a state-administered exam, you may have your name and ranking listed on any number of eligibility rosters in counties or towns in which you are willing to work. In other states, state testing is only for state positions, and counties and municipalities have their own independent systems.

As testing arrangements vary from state to state, so do procedures and the tests themselves. Because of the differences in state exams, it is not possible to give you the precise information you need for the exam in your state. But many state and municipal exams follow the lead of the federal civil service exam, measuring verbal, clerical, arithmetic, and mechanical abilities, as well as other skills, depending on the job.

> **Note**
> Exam subjects and formats vary the most among law enforcement and correctional exams. By contrast, clerical exams are more limited to the nature of clerical work itself and are more universal.

Biographical and Achievement Inventory

Many federal and state civil service exams conclude with a self-descriptive inventory. This inventory is set up to look like a multiple-choice test and is timed like a test, but it is not a test at all. There are no right or wrong answers. Rather, the examiners are looking for a pattern of achievements, interests, and personality traits that they can compare to the profile of currently active, successful people in the same occupation.

Aside from high school- and college-related questions, you are asked about your likes and dislikes and about the impression that you make on others. There are questions about how you rank yourself with relation to other people, about what your friends think of you, and about the opinions of supervisors or teachers.

> **Caution**
> Do not try to second-guess the testers to give the "right" answer on the biographical and achievement inventory. Internal checks for consistency and honesty are built into the questions. Your best bet is to answer quickly and candidly. Dwelling over the questions is not likely to help.

You cannot really study for this inventory. The only possible preparation is searching old school records to refresh your memory about subjects you studied and your attendance, grades, and extracurricular activities. If you cannot find your records, just answer to the best of your ability.

Preparing for the Exam

Obviously, some schooling is necessary to answer questions in the subjects of reading, spelling, grammar, English usage, and arithmetic. But they demand less schooling than most other subjects employed in testing candidates for particular jobs. Government agencies favor these general test subjects, because they probe a candidate's native intelligence and aptitude for learning how to do a job and succeed in it. The agency does not want to handicap those candidates who have been deprived of a complete education.

Ability questions, such as those testing clerical and mechanical ability, are designed to assess the effects of a specific course of training. These tests assume that applicants have had a specific course of instruction, job apprenticeship, or other relatively uniform experience.

Since aptitude and ability tests overlap, you will clearly benefit from studying the subject matter and learning how to achieve the highest scores on general questions. Experience has shown that it is possible to improve your score, and thus to better demonstrate your aptitude for the job. With the great variety in exams, especially among state and municipal exams, the best preparation is thorough grounding in basic skills and practice with many kinds of exam questions.

The test questions and review materials in this book are based on the requirements given in a variety of job announcements, as well as on questions that have appeared on actual tests. It will be worth your time to try your hand at all the practice questions and sample exams, even if you do not think they will appear on your exam. You want to prepare yourself for whatever type of question you may encounter. In a field of competent applicants, familiarity with different question styles and strategies can give you the competitive edge, a higher score, and an offer of employment.

Any test-taking practice will help in preparation for the exam. In addition, knowing what to expect and familiarity with techniques of effective test-taking should give you the confidence you need to do your best.

Do

DO prepare for the exam.
DO answer all the practice questions.
DO review what you have learned.
DO tailor your study to the subject matter.
DO study alone.
DO keep physically fit.

Don't

DON'T try to learn too much in one study period.
DON'T look at the correct answers before answering the practice questions on your own.

DO prepare for the exam. Do not make the test harder than it has to be by not preparing yourself. You are taking a very important step by reading this book and taking the sample tests. This will help you become familiar with the test and the kinds of questions that you will have to answer. Make a study schedule and stick to it. Regular, daily study is important.

DO answer all the practice questions. Read the sample questions and directions for taking the test carefully. When you take the sample tests, time yourself as you will be timed in the real test. Do not be satisfied with merely the correct answer to each question. Do additional research on the other choices. You will broaden your background and be more adequately prepared for the actual exam.

DO review what you have learned. Once you have studied something thoroughly, review it the next day so that the information will be firmly fixed in your mind.

DO tailor your study to the subject matter. Do not study everything in the same manner. Give special attention to your areas of weakness and to areas that are more likely to be covered on your exam.

DO study alone. You will concentrate better when you work by yourself. Disturbances caused by family and neighbor activities (telephone calls, chit-chat, television programs, etc.) work to your disadvantage. Choose a comfortable, well-lit study spot as far as possible from distractions of family life.

> **Tip**
> Keep a list of questions that you cannot answer and points that you are unsure of to talk over with a friend who is preparing for the same exam. Plan to exchange ideas at a joint review session just before the test.

DO keep physically fit. You cannot retain information well when you are uncomfortable, have headaches, or are tense. Physical health promotes mental efficiency.

DON'T try to learn too much in one study period. If your mind starts to wander, take a short break and then return to your work. Remember that each lesson is designed to be completed in one hour's worth of study time.

DON'T look at the correct answers before answering the practice questions on your own. This can fool you into thinking that you understand a question when you really do not. Try the question on your own first, and then compare your answer with the one given. In a sample test, you are your own grader; you do not gain anything by pretending to understand something that you really do not. Study answer explanations whenever they are supplied, because they may give you extra insights—even into the questions that you answered correctly.

> **Tip**
> The evening before the exam, do something pleasant and go to bed early. On test day, allow the exam to be the main attraction; do not squeeze it in between other activities. Be sure to bring your admission card, ID, and pencils, as instructed. Prepare these the night before so that you are not flustered by a last-minute search. Arrive rested, relaxed, and on time. In fact, plan to arrive a little bit early, and leave plenty of time for traffic tie-ups or other unexpected delays.

How the Exam Is Administered

Civil service exams are generally made up of multiple-choice questions. All multiple-choice tests consist of a question booklet and a separate answer sheet. The question booklet begins with general instructions for taking the test, including the rules and regulations governing your exam, the number of questions, how the exam is timed, and signals used when time is up. Specific directions for different types of questions are explained in the section of the question booklet before each new type of question.

Multiple-choice questions have four or five answer choices lettered (A) through (D) or (E). Each question has one best answer. You must read the question carefully, think, choose the best answer, and blacken the matching lettered circle on the separate answer sheet. If you mark your answer neatly, there is no room for scoring errors in marking a multiple-choice answer sheet. You can be sure of accuracy and objectivity.

In the test room, the examiner will hand out forms for you to fill out and will give you the instructions that you must follow in taking the exam. The examiner will tell you how to fill in the grids on the forms and will explain time limits and timing signals. If you do not understand any of the instructions, ask questions. Do not score less than your best because the examiner did not explain something fully.

> **Caution**
> You must follow the examiner's instructions exactly. Fill in the grids on the forms carefully and accurately. Do not begin until you are told to begin, and stop as soon as the examiner tells you to stop. Do not turn pages until you are told to do so or go back to parts that you have already completed. Any infraction of the rules is considered cheating. Your test paper will not be scored, and you will not be eligible for appointment.

Exam Ratings

Applicants who meet the minimum experience and education requirements and skill levels for the job are given numerical ratings based on their written test scores. You will be notified of your rating by mail. If you pass the exam, you will receive an eligible rating—that is, your name will be placed on a list for appointment, with the highest test scores at the top of the list. Eligible applicants who are not selected for the position are restored to the list for consideration for other openings.

> **Tip**
> If you fail the exam, you can usually take it again as long as applications are being accepted. If you pass but want to improve your score, you can usually retake the test after a year has passed, if the announcement is open at that time.

Once you achieve a rating on a standardized exam, such as a clerical exam, you do not have to take the test again to apply for similar jobs. You also do not have to reestablish that you meet the minimum experience and education requirements or have the required skills. Your rating will expire after a certain period, as indicated on the rating form.

> **Tip**
> Be sure to notify the agency that gave you a rating of address, name, or availability changes. When writing, give your full name, your Social Security number, the title of the job announcement, and the rating you received.

How the Exam Is Scored

The method of rating on all civil service exams is on a scale of 100, with 70 as the usual passing mark. Written tests are most frequently rated by machine. In some written exams, and for rating experience and training, two examiners work independently. In case of a protest about the rating, a third examiner is assigned to rate the exam again. Thus, the chances of error, arbitrary grading, or bias are almost completely eliminated.

On most exams, you get one point for each correct answer. You get no credit for a wrong answer or for a question that you did not answer. Most importantly, you do not lose any credit for a wrong answer. A wrong answer is simply not a right answer. You get no credit, but the wrong answer itself does not work against you.

A few exams or portions of exams do not follow this scoring rule, especially clerical exams that measure accuracy under time pressure. A part of the federal clerical exam penalizes wrong answers, for instance. In some cases, the number of wrong answers is subtracted from the number of right answers. More often, a portion of the wrong answers—usually one fourth—is subtracted from the number of correct answers.

> **Note**
> Not many exams consist of exactly 100 questions. Some contain only 80, others 140 or more. All scores are finally reported on the basis of 100. What this means is that while you get one point for each correct answer, that answer may not be adding exactly one point to your score. The examiners create a confidential formula that converts raw scores (the number you got right) to the final, scaled rating, which determines your ranking on the eligibility list. When an announcement specifies "70 percent required," it refers to the score that is reported after the conversion (and before the addition of veteran's credit).

Rating Nontested Positions

If you applied for a job that did not require a written test, your rating is based on the experience and training you described in your application and on any required supporting evidence. When all this information has been gathered, you will be rated, and the agency will tell you how your qualifications look to the examiners. That is all there is to it, until you are called to the job.

Test-Taking Strategies

When taking the exam, you can employ a number of strategies that will help you complete the test more accurately and quickly and will boost your overall score.

Do

DO read every word of the instructions.

DO read every word of every question.

DO make notes on scratch paper or the question booklet.

DO mark answers carefully and neatly.

DO manage your time.

DO check your answers.

DO guess when wrong answers do not count against you.

Don't

DON'T guess when wrong answers do count against you.

DON'T mark more than one answer for each question.

DON'T skip any questions.

DON'T spend too much time on any one question.

DO read every word of the instructions. Aside from actually knowing the answer, careful reading most influences you choosing the right answer. Misreading of directions causes the greatest damage. For example, if the directions ask you to choose the word that means the opposite of the underlined word, and you choose the word that means the same as the underlined word, you will mark wrong answers for a whole series of questions and do poorly on the exam.

> **Tip**
> If you have time, reread any complicated instructions after you do the first few questions to check that you really do understand them. Whenever you are allowed to, ask the examiner to clarify anything you do not understand.

DO read every word of every question. Careful reading must extend beyond reading of directions to reading of each individual question. Qualifying words like most, least, only, best, probably, definitely, not, all, every, and except make a big difference in determining the correct answer to a specific question.

> **Tip**
> Since reading is so key to success with multiple-choice questions, your preparation should include a lot of attention to reading and reading-based questions. Once you have mastered the techniques of dealing with reading-based questions, you will be well-equipped to tackle all aspects of the civil service exam.

DO make notes on scratch paper or the question booklet. Usually, you are allowed to write in the question booklet. You can put a question mark next to the number of a question at which you took a guess, calculate the answers to math questions, cross out eliminated answer choices, underline key words, or even just doodle in the margins. If you are not permitted to write in the question booklet, you will be issued scratch paper for figuring and writing notes to yourself.

> **Caution**
> When using scratch paper or the question booklet for taking notes, do not forget to mark the final answer on the answer sheet. Only the answer sheet is scored; all other notes are disregarded.

DO mark answers neatly and carefully. The separate answer sheet is the only record of answers that is scored. Blacken your answer space firmly and completely. A correct answer response looks like this:

●

The following are incorrectly marked responses:

The scoring machine might not notice these marks. If the scoring machine does not register your answer, you will not get any credit for it.

> **Caution**
> All of your answers should be in the form of blackened spaces. The machine cannot read English. Do not write any notes in the margins of the answer sheet—they will be disregarded.

DO manage your time. Before you begin, take a moment to plan your progress through the test. Although you are not usually expected to finish all the questions, you should at least get an idea of how much time you need to spend on each question in order to answer them all. For example, if there are 60 questions to answer and you have 30 minutes, you will have about 30 seconds to spend on each question.

DO check your answers. If you finish any part before time is up, use the remaining time to check that each question is answered in the right space and that you marked only one answer for each question. Return to the difficult questions and rethink them. You do not get a bonus for leaving early, so if you finish before time is up, stay until the end of the exam.

> **Tip**
> If you cannot finish any exam part before time is up, do not worry. If you are accurate, you can do well even without finishing. It is even possible to earn a rating of 100 without entirely finishing an exam part if you are very accurate. At any rate, do not let your performance on any one part affect your performance on any other part.

DO guess when wrong answers do not count against you. In most portions of the exam, wrong answers do not take points off your score, so a guess cannot hurt you. The best guess is the educated guess. If you are not sure of the right answer, try to eliminate the obviously wrong answers. If you can narrow the field and guess from among fewer choices, you will raise the odds of guessing right. But even if you have no idea at all, a guess still gives you a chance of getting the question right. Not answering at all ensures that the question will be counted wrong. If you are about to run out of time, mark all the remaining blanks with the same letter. According to the law of averages, you should get some portion of those questions right.

Tip

If you guess, mark the question in the question booklet or write its number on your scratch paper. If you have time after you have completed all the questions, go back and give the marked questions more thought.

DON'T guess when wrong answers do count against you. On some tests, a correct answer gives you one point, a skipped space gives you nothing at all but costs you nothing, and a wrong answer costs you 1/4 point. On this type of test, do not randomly guess—you could hurt your score. (Be sure to keep careful track of skipped questions so you do not mark the wrong lines on your answer sheet). Although you should not make random guesses, an educated guess can still help you on this type of test. Do not rush to fill answer spaces randomly at the end. Instead, work as quickly as possible while concentrating on accuracy until time is called. Then, stop and leave the remaining answers blank.

Tip

Before testing begins, ask what scoring method will be used on your particular exam. You can then guide your guessing procedure accordingly.

DON'T mark more than one answer for each question. If more than one circle for any question is blackened, even if one of the answers is correct, the scoring machine will give no credit for that question. You may change your mind and your answer. When you change an answer, be careful to fully and cleanly erase the first answer. You do not want the machine to misread your choice. Never cross out an answer in favor of a new choice. You must erase, or the machine will read both old and new answers and give you no credit.

DON'T skip any questions. If you mark an answer in the wrong place, it will be scored as wrong. If you notice that you have slipped out of line, you must erase all answers from the point of the error and redo all those questions. Most civil service tests are not heavily speeded, but you do not have the time to waste erasing and reanswering large blocks of questions. Therefore, do not skip any questions or jump around looking for easy questions to answer first. Do not omit a question even if you have no idea of the correct answer. If you are forced to guess so as to answer every question in order, then do so. If you answer every question in order, there should be no chance to slip. (The exception to this rule, of course, is when wrong answers count against you.)

> **Tip**
> Check often to be sure that the question number matches the answer space and that you have not skipped a space by mistake.

DON'T spend too much time on any one question. If you get stuck, do not take the puzzler as a personal challenge. Either guess and mark the question in the question booklet, or skip it entirely, marking the question as a skip and taking care to skip the answer space on the answer sheet. If there is time at the end of the exam portion, you can return and give marked questions another try.

The Hour in Review

1. Federal, state, and municipal exams test abilities required by the job and your aptitude for learning the job. Exams may test verbal, clerical, or arithmetic ability, as well as other skills and aptitudes.

2. Reviewing basic skills and practicing with a variety of questions is the best way to prepare for any civil service exam.

3. Exams are generally multiple-choice and are rated on a 100-point scale, with a passing score of 70 required to be eligible for the position. On most portions of the exam, wrong answers do not count against you.

4. Employing simple test-taking strategies, such as note-taking, time management, and educated guessing, can help you answer more questions accurately and boost your score.

Part II

Learn to Answer
Verbal Ability Questions

HOUR 3

English Grammar and Usage

What You Will Learn in This Hour

Part of the verbal ability portion of the civil service exam tests whether you can recognize incorrect grammar and sentence structure. Getting a high score on this part of the test requires a thorough understanding of the rules of grammar, sentence structure, capitalization, and punctuation. In this hour, you will review those rules and test yourself with practice exercises. Here are your goals for this hour:

- Learn rules of English grammar that you will need to know.
- Learn capitalization and punctuation rules that you will need to know.
- Practice English grammar and usage questions.

Essentials of English Grammar

A strong grasp of the basic rules of English grammar is essential for scoring well on this part of the exam. All of the following rules should be review for you. Study these rules until you are sure you understand them, and recognizing errors in the questions on the exam will come naturally to you.

The Parts of Speech

Review the basic parts of speech:

- A **noun** is a person, place, thing, or idea: teacher, city, desk, democracy.
- **Pronouns** substitute for nouns: he, they, ours, those.
- An **adjective** describes a noun: warm, quick, tall, blue.
- A **verb** expresses action or state of being: yell, interpret, feel, are.
- An **adverb** modifies a verb, adjective, or another adverb: slowly, well, busily.
- **Conjunctions** join words, sentences, and phrases: and, but, or.
- A **preposition** shows position in time or space: in, during, after, behind.

> **Note**
> A phrase is any group of related words that has no subject or predicate and that is used as a single part of speech. Phrases may be built around prepositions, articles, gerunds, or infinitives, but they cannot stand by themselves as sentences.

Noun and Pronoun Rules

The antecedent of the pronoun is the noun to which a pronoun refers. A pronoun must agree with its antecedent in gender, person, and number.

> **Caution**
> The pronoun generally refers to the nearest noun. Make certain that the grammatical antecedent is indeed the intended antecedent. Consider this sentence: Since the mouth of the cave was masked by underbrush, it provided an excellent hiding place. This is incorrect, because "it" refers to underbrush, not the intended antecedent "cave." You may find that the most effective way to clear up an ambiguity is to recast the sentence so the pronoun is not used.

Both pronouns and nouns have three cases:

- **Nominative:** The subject, noun/pronoun of address, or predicate noun/pronoun. Examples of nominative pronouns include *I, he, she, we,* and *they.*

- **Objective:** The direct object, indirect object, or object of a preposition. Examples of objective pronouns include *me, him, her, us,* and *them.*
- **Possessive:** The form that shows possession. Examples of possessive pronouns include *mine, his, hers, ours,* and *theirs.*

There are several rules relating to noun and pronoun case that you should know:

- The subject of a verb is in the nominative case even if the verb is understood and not expressed. Example: They are as old as *we.* (Check your answer by silently finishing off the sentence: *as we are.*)
- Nouns or pronouns connected by a form of the verb to be are always in the nominative case. Example: It is *I.* (Not *me.*)
- *Who* and *whoever* are in the nominative case; *whom* and *whomever* are in the objective case. Examples: The trapeze artist *who* ran away with the clown broke the lion tamer's heart. (*Who* is the subject of the verb *ran.*) Invite *whomever* you wish to accompany you. (*Whomever* is the object of the verb *invite.*)
- The object of a preposition or transitive verb takes a pronoun in the objective case. Example: It would be impossible for *me* to do that job alone. (*Me* is the object of the preposition *for.*)
- Do not use the possessive case when referring to an inanimate object. Incorrect: He had difficulty with the *store's* management. Correct: He had difficulty with the management of the store.
- A noun or pronoun modifying a gerund should be in the possessive case. Example: Is there any criticism of *Arthur's* going? (*Going* is the gerund.)

> **Tip**
> When the first person pronoun is used in conjunction with one or more proper names, confirm the choice of I or me by eliminating the proper names and reading the sentence with the pronoun alone. Consider this sentence: John, George, Marylou, and (me or I) went to the movies last night. By eliminating the names, you can easily see that I went to the movies last night is correct.

Adjective and Adverb Rules

Often, it is unclear whether you should use an adjective or an adverb. Remember that adjectives modify nouns and pronouns, and adverbs modify verbs, adjectives, and other adverbs. Sometimes, context must determine which is used. Consider this sentence: The old man looked angry. In this case, you must use an adjective because you are describing a noun, *the old man*. Consider this sentence: The old man looked *angrily* out the window. Now, you must use an adverb because you are describing a verb, *looked*.

Tip

Adjectives answer the questions, "Which one?" "What kind?" and "How many?" Adverbs answer the questions, "Why?" "How?" "Where?" "When" and "To what degree?"

Place adverbs, clauses, and phrases near the words they modify to prevent confusion. For example, "The man was willing to sell only one horse" is better than "the man was *only* willing to sell one horse," because the adverb *only* modifies the adjective *one*, rather than the verb *was willing*.

Whenever you use a modifier, it must modify something. For example, the sentence, "While away on vacation, the pipes burst," is incorrect. The pipes were not on vacation, so the phrase does not modify anything. A better way to say it is, "While we were on vacation, the pipes burst."

Tip

The best test for the placement of modifiers is to read the sentence literally. If the sentence does not make sense, it is wrong. The meaning of the sentence should be clear to any reader.

Caution

Hardly, scarcely, barely, only, and but (when it means only) are negative words. Do not use another negative in conjunction with any of these words. Incorrect: I can't hardly read the small print. Correct: I can hardly read the small print.

Rules of Sentence Structure

You should know the following basic rules of good sentence structure:

- Every sentence must contain a verb. A group of words without a verb is a sentence fragment, not a sentence.

- Every sentence must have a subject. The subject may be a noun, pronoun, or a phrase functioning as a noun. In commands, however, the subject is usually not expressed but is understood to be *you*.

> **Caution**
> A subordinate clause must never stand alone. It is not a complete sentence, despite the fact that it has a subject and a verb. Subordinate clauses may act as adverbs, adjectives, or nouns. A subordinate adverbial clause is usually introduced by a subordinating conjunction, such as when, while, because, as soon as, if, after, although, as before, since, than, though, until, and unless. Subordinate adjective and noun clauses may be introduced by the pronouns who, which, and that.

Rules of Agreement

The following are sometimes tricky rules of subject-verb agreement and verb tense that you must know:

- A verb should agree in number with the subject of the sentence. Example: Poor study *habits are* the leading cause of unsatisfactory achievement in school.
- A verb should not be made to agree with a noun that is part of a phrase following the subject. Example: *Mount Snow*, one of my favorite ski areas, *is* in Vermont.
- A subject consisting of two or more nouns joined by a coordinating conjunction takes a plural verb. Example: Paul *and* Sue *were* the last to arrive.
- When the conjunctions *or, either/or,* and *neither/nor* are used, the number of the verb agrees with the last subject. Example: Either the cat or the *mice take* charge in the barn.
- The number of the verb is not affected when words introduced by *with, together with, no less than, as well as,* etc. are added to the subject. Example: The *captain,* together with the rest of the team, *was delighted* by the victory celebration.
- In sentences beginning with *there is* and *there are,* the verb agrees with the noun that follows it. Example: There *is not* an unbroken *bone* in her body.
- Statements equally true in the past and the present are usually expressed in the present tense. Example: He said that Venus *is* a planet. (Although he made the statement in the past, the fact remains that Venus is a planet.)
- When expressing a condition contrary to fact or a wish, use the subjunctive form *were*. Example: I wish I *were* a movie star.

> **Caution**
> Each, either, neither, anyone, anybody, somebody, someone, every, everyone, one, no one, and nobody are singular pronouns. Each of these words takes a singular verb and a singular pronoun. Example: Neither likes the pets of the other.

Avoiding Common Errors

The following are common but subtle errors. Train yourself to concentrate on each sentence so that you can recognize errors.

- Comparisons must be logical and complete. Incorrect: Wilmington is larger than any city in Delaware. Correct: Wilmington is larger than any *other* city in Delaware. (Wilmington cannot be larger than itself.)

- Comparisons and other groups must be parallel. Incorrect: She spends all her time eating, asleep, and on her studies. Correct: She spends all her time eating, *sleeping,* and *studying.* (All three verbs are in the same form.)

- Avoid needless shifts in point-of-view—a change within the sentence from one verb tense to another, from one subject or voice to another, or from one person or number to another. Incorrect: Mary especially likes math, but history is also enjoyed by her. (The subject shifts from Mary to history, and the tense shifts from active to passive.) Correct: Mary especially likes math, but she also enjoys history.

- Avoid the *is when* and *is where* constructions. Incorrect: A limerick *is when* a short poem has a catchy rhyme. Correct: A limerick is a short poem with a catchy rhyme.

Other Rules You Must Know

The following list of rules is far from comprehensive. In fact, I have purposely kept it brief so that you can learn every rule and every hint. You will find these rules invaluable for all your writing.

Capitalization Rules

- Capitalize the first word of a sentence.
- Capitalize all proper names.
- Capitalize days of the week, months of the year, and holidays.

> **Caution**
> Do not capitalize the seasons.

- Capitalize the first and all other important words in a title. Example: *The Art of Salesmanship*
- Capitalize common nouns only when they are used as part of proper names. Example: Yesterday I visited *Uncle Charles*, my favorite *uncle*.
- Capitalize the points of the compass only when referring to a specific place or area. Example: Many retired persons spend the winter in the *South*.

> **Caution**
> Do not capitalize the points of the compass when referring to a direction. Example: Many birds fly south in the winter.

- Capitalize languages and specific place names used as modifiers, but do not capitalize any other school subjects. Example: Next year I will study *French,* biology, and *English* literature.
- Capitalize the first word of a direct quotation. Example: Alexander Pope wrote, "*A* little learning is a dangerous thing."

> Caution
> Do not capitalize the first word within quotation marks if it does not begin a complete sentence, as when a direct quotation is broken. Example: "I tore my stocking," she told us, "because the drawer was left open."

Punctuation Rules

Using the Apostrophe

Use an apostrophe in the following situations:

- To indicate possession.

> **Tip**
> When indicating possession, the apostrophe means "belonging to everything to the left of the apostrophe." Use this rule to test for correct placement. For example, childrens' or "belonging to the childrens" is obviously incorrect, while children's or "belonging to the children" is correct. This placement rule applies at all times, even with compound nouns and with entities made up of two or more names. For example, father-in-law's means "belonging to a father-in-law," and Brown and Sons' delivery truck means "delivery truck belonging to Brown and Sons."

- In a contraction in place of the omitted letter or letters. Examples: haven't, we're, class of '85, '70s
- To form plurals of numbers, letters, and phrases referred to as words. Example: The Japanese child pronounced his *l*'s as *r*'s.

Using the Colon

Use a colon in the following situations:

- After a salutation in a business letter. Example: Dear Board Member:
- To separate hours from minutes. Example: The eclipse occurred at *10:36* a.m.

> **Note**
> Use of the colon is optional in the following cases:
> - To introduce a list, especially after an expression like *as follows*.
> - To introduce a long quotation.
> - To introduce a question, such as, "My question is this: Are you willing to punch a time clock?"

Using the Comma

Use a comma in the following situations:

- After the salutation of a personal letter. Example: Dear Mary,
- After the complimentary close of a letter. Example: Cordially yours,
- To set off a noun of address. Example: When you finish your homework, *Jeff*, take out the garbage.
- To set off an appositive—a phrase that follows a noun or pronoun and means the same thing. Example: Mr. Burke, *our lawyer*, gave us some good advice.

- To set off parenthetical expressions—words or phrases that interrupt the flow of the sentence—such as *however, though, for instance,* and *by the way.* Examples: We could not, *however,* get him to agree.

> **Tip**
> Test for placement of commas in a parenthetical expression by reading aloud. If you pause before and after the expression, set it off with commas.

- Between two or more adjectives that equally modify a noun. Example: The *jolly, fat, ruddy* man laughed.

> **Tip**
> If you can add the word *and* between the adjectives without changing the sense of the sentence, use commas.

3

- To separate words, phrases, or clauses in a series. Example: Place *coats, umbrellas, and boots* in the closet.
- To separate a direct quotation from the speaker. Example: She said, "I must leave work on time today."
- After an introductory phrase of five or more words. Example: *Because the prisoner had a history of attempted jailbreaks*, he was guarded heavily.
- After a short introductory phrase whenever the comma would aid clarity. Example: *To Dan*, Phil was a friend as well as brother.

> **Note**
> A comma is not generally used before a subordinate clause that ends a sentence, though in long, unwieldy sentences like this one, use of a comma is optional.

- Before a coordinating conjunction unless the two clauses are very short. Example: The boy wanted to borrow a book from the library, but the librarian would not allow him to take it until he had paid his fines.
- To set off a nonrestrictive adjective phrase or clause—one that can be omitted without changing the meaning of the sentence. Example: Our new sailboat, *which has bright orange sails*, is very seaworthy.

> **Caution**
> A restrictive phrase or clause is vital to the meaning of a sentence and cannot be omitted. Do not set it off with commas. Example: A sailboat without sails is useless.

- If the sentence might be subject to different interpretations without a comma. Examples: My brother Bill is getting married (implying that I have more than one brother). My brother, Bill, is getting married (where Bill is an appositive and presumably the only brother).

- If a pause would make the sentence clearer and easier to read. Incorrect: After all crime must be punished. Correct: After all, crime must be punished.

> **Tip**
> The pause rule is not infallible, but it is your best resort when all other rules governing use of the comma fail you.

Using the Dash

Use a dash in the following situations:

- For emphasis or to set off an explanatory group of words. Example: The tools of his trade—*probe, mirror, cotton swabs*—were neatly arranged on the dentist's tray.

> **Caution**
> Unless the set-off expression ends a sentence, dashes, like parentheses, must be used in pairs.

- To break up a thought. Example: There are five—*remember I said five*—good reasons to refuse their demands.

Using the Hyphen

Use a hyphen in the following situations:

- To divide a word at the end of a line. Always divide words between syllables.
- In numbers from *twenty-one* to *ninety-nine*.

- To join two words serving together as a single adjective before a noun. Example: We left the highway and proceeded on a *well-paved* road.
- With the prefixes *ex-, self-,* and *all-,* and with the suffix *-elect.* Examples: ex-Senator, self-appointed, all-state, Governor-elect
- To avoid ambiguity. Example: After the custodian recovered use of his right arm, he *re-covered* the office chairs.
- To avoid an awkward union of letters. Examples: self-independent, shell-like

Using the Semicolon

Use a semicolon in the following situations:

- To separate a series of phrases or clauses, each of which contains commas. Example: The old gentleman's heirs were Margaret Whitlock, his half-sister; William Frame, companion to his late cousin, Robert Bone; and his favorite charity, the Salvation Army.
- To avoid confusion with numbers. Example: Add the following: *$1.25; $7.50; and $12.89.*

3

Caution

Two main clauses must be separated by a conjunction or by a semicolon, or they must be written as two sentences. A semicolon never precedes a coordinating conjunction. The same two clauses may be written in any one of three ways:
- Autumn had come and the trees were almost bare.
- Autumn had come; the trees were almost bare.
- Autumn had come. The trees were almost bare.

Tip

If you are uncertain about how to use the semicolon to connect independent clauses, write two sentences instead.

Using the Period, Question Mark, and Exclamation Point

- Use a period at the end of a sentence that makes a statement, gives a command, or makes a "polite request" in the form of a question that does not require an answer.

- Use a period after an abbreviation and after the initial in a person's name. Example: Gen. Robert E. Lee

> **Caution**
> Do not use a period after postal service state name abbreviations like AZ or MI.

- Use a question mark after a request for information.

> **Caution**
> A question must end with a question mark even if the question does not encompass the entire sentence. Example: "Daddy, are we there yet?" the child asked.

- Use an exclamation point to express strong feeling or emotion, or to imply urgency. Example: Congratulations! You broke the record.

Using Quotation Marks

Use quotation marks in the following situations:

- To enclose all directly quoted material. Words not quoted must remain outside the quotation marks. Example: "If it's hot on Sunday," she said, "we'll go to the beach."

> **Caution**
> Do not enclose an indirect quote in quotation marks. Example: She said that we might go to the beach on Sunday.

- Around words used in an unusual way. Example: A surfer who "hangs ten" is performing a maneuver on a surfboard, not staging a mass execution.
- To enclose the title of a short story, essay, short poem, song, or article. Example: Robert Louis Stevenson wrote a plaintive poem called "Bed in Summer."

> **Caution**
> Titles of books and plays are not enclosed in quotation marks. They are printed in italics. In handwritten or typed manuscript, underscore titles of books and plays. Example: The song, "Tradition," is from *Fiddler on the Roof.*

Placing Quotation Marks

- Periods and commas always go inside quotation marks. Example: Pornography is sold under the euphemism "adult books."

- Question marks and exclamation points go inside quotation marks if they are part of the quotation. If the whole sentence containing the quotation is a question or exclamation, the punctuation goes outside the quotation marks. Example: What did you really mean when you said "I do"?

- Colons and semicolons always go outside the quotation marks. Example: He said, "War is destructive"; she added, "Peace is constructive."

- When a multiple-paragraph passage is quoted, each paragraph of the quotation must begin with quotation marks, but ending quotation marks are used only at the end of the last quoted paragraph.

> **Note**
> Direct quotations are bound by all the rules of sentence structure. Beware of run-on sentences in divided quotations. Incorrect: "Your total is wrong," he said, "add the column again." Correct: "Your total is wrong," he said. "Add the column again." In the correct example, the two independent clauses form two separate sentences.

Workshop

In this workshop you will review the rules of grammar and usage, because they might be tested on a civil service test.

Practice Exercise

DIRECTIONS: In each of the following questions, there are four sentences. Choose the grammatically incorrect sentence. When you are finished, check your answers in the section immediately following the questions.

1. (A) Everyone at camp must have his medical certificate on file before participating in competitive sports.

   (B) A crate of oranges were sent from Florida for all the children in cabin six.

   (C) John and Danny's room looks as if they were prepared for inspection.

   (D) Three miles is too far for a young child to walk.

2. (A) Being tired, I stretched out on a grassy knoll.

    (B) While we were rowing on the lake, a sudden squall almost capsized the boat.

    (C) Entering the room, a strange mark on the floor attracted my attention.

    (D) Mounting the curb, the empty car crossed the sidewalk and came to rest against a building.

3. (A) Not one in a thousand readers take the matter seriously.

    (B) He was able partially to accomplish his purpose.

    (C) You are not as tall as he.

    (D) The people began to realize how much she had done.

4. (A) In the case of members who are absent, a special letter will be sent.

    (B) The visitors were all ready to see it.

    (C) I like Burns's poem, "To a Mountain Daisy."

    (D) John said that he was sure he seen it.

5. (A) Neither the critics nor the author were right about the reaction of the public.

    (B) The senator depended upon whoever was willing to assist him.

    (C) I don't recall any time when Edgar has broken his word.

    (D) Every one of the campers but John and me is going on the hike.

6. (A) B. Nelson & Co. has a sale on sport shirts today.

    (B) Venetian blinds—called that although they probably did not originate in Venice—are no longer used as extensively as they were at one time.

    (C) He determined to be guided by the opinion of whoever spoke first.

    (D) There was often disagreement as to whom was the better Shakespear-ean actor, Evans or Gielgud.

7. (A) Never before have I seen anyone who has the skill John has when he repairs engines.

    (B) If anyone can be wholly just in his decisions, it is he.

    (C) Because of his friendliness, the new neighbor was immediately accepted by the community.

    (D) Imagine our embarrassment when us girls saw Miss Maltinge sitting with her beau in the front row.

8. (A) The general regarded whomever the colonel honored with disdain.

    (B) Everyone who reads this book will think themselves knights errant on missions of heroism.

    (C) The reason why the new leader was so unsuccessful was that he had fewer responsibilities.

    (D) All the new mechanical devices we have today have made our daily living a great deal simpler, it is said.

9. (A) I can but do my best.

(B) I cannot help comparing him with his predecessor.

(C) I wish that I was in Florida now.

(D) I like this kind of grapes better than any other.

10. (A) Neither Tom nor John was present for the rehearsal.

(B) The happiness or misery of men's lives depends on their early training.

(C) Honor as well as profit are to be gained by these studies.

(D) The egg business is only incidental to the regular business of the general store.

11. (A) The Board of Directors has prepared a manual for their own use.

(B) The company has announced its new policy of advertising.

(C) The jury were out about thirty minutes when they returned a verdict.

(D) The flock of geese creates a health hazard for visitors with allergies.

12. (A) Two-thirds of the building is finished.

(B) Where are Mr. Keene and Mr. Herbert?

(C) Neither the salespeople nor the manager want to work overtime.

(D) The committee was agreed.

13. (A) The coming of peace effected a change in her way of life.

(B) Spain is as weak, if not weaker than, she was in 1900.

(C) In regard to that, I am not certain what my attitude will be.

(D) That unfortunate family faces the problem of adjusting itself to a new way of life.

14. (A) I wondered why it was that the Mayor objected to the Governor's reference to the new tax law.

(B) I have never read *Les Miserables,* but I plan to do so this summer.

(C) After much talk and haranguing, the workers received an increase in wages.

(D) Charles Dole, who is a member of the committee, was asked to confer with commissioner Wilson.

15. (A) Most employees, and he is no exception do not like to work overtime.

(B) The doctor had carelessly left all the instruments on the operating table.

(C) Despite all the power he has, I should still hate to be in his shoes.

(D) I feel bad because I gave such a poor performance in the play tonight.

16. (A) Of London and Paris, the former is the wealthier.

(B) Of the two cities visited, White Plains is the cleanest.

(C) Chicago is larger than any other city in Illinois.

(D) America is the greatest nation, and of all other nations England is the greatest.

17. (A) It was superior in every way to the book previously used.

(B) His testimony today is different from that of yesterday.

(C) The letter will be sent to the United States senate this week.

(D) The flowers smelled so sweet that the whole house was perfumed.

18. (A) When either or both habits become fixed, the student improves.

   (B) When the supervisor entered the room, he noticed that the book was laying on the desk.

   (C) Neither his words nor his action was justifiable.

   (D) A calm almost always comes before a storm.

19. (A) Who did they say won?

   (B) Send whomever will do the work.

   (C) The question of who should be leader arose.

   (D) All the clerks including those who have been appointed recently are required to work on the new assignment.

20. (A) Mrs. Black the supervisor of the unit has many important duties.

   (B) This is the woman whom I saw.

   (C) She could solve even this problem.

   (D) She divided the money among the three of us.

21. (A) He felt deep despair (as who has not?) at the evidence of man's inhumanity to man.

   (B) You will be glad, I am sure, to give the book to whoever among your young friends has displayed an interest in animals.

   (C) When independence day falls on a Sunday, it is officially celebrated on Monday.

   (D) Being a stranger in town myself, I know how you feel.

22. (A) The task of filing these cards is to be divided equally between you and he.

   (B) A series of authentic records of Native American tribes is being published.

   (C) The Smokies is the home of the descendants of this brave tribe.

   (D) Five dollars is really not too much to pay for a book of this type.

23. (A) The game over, the spectators rushed out on the field and tore down the goalposts.

   (B) The situation was aggravated by disputes over the captaincy of the team.

   (C) Yesterday they lay their uniforms aside with the usual end-of-the-season regret.

   (D) It is sometimes thought that politics is not for the high-minded.

24. (A) Consider that the person which is always idle can never be happy.

   (B) Because a man understands a woman does not mean they are necessarily compatible.

   (C) He said that accuracy and speed are both essential.

   (D) Can it be said that the better of the two books is less expensive?

25. (A) Everyone entered promptly but her.

   (B) Each of the messengers were busily occupied.

   (C) At which exit did you leave him?

   (D) The work was not done well.

Answers and Explanations

1. **(B)** The subject of the sentence is *crate*, which takes a singular verb. Correct: A crate of oranges *was* sent from Florida for all the children in cabin six.

2. **(C)** The sentence literally reads as if the strange mark entered the room. A better way to write it would be: *When I entered the room, a strange mark on the floor attracted my attention.*

3. **(A)** The subject of the sentence is one, which takes a singular verb. Correct: Not one in a thousand readers *takes* the matter seriously.

4. **(D)** The verb is in the wrong tense. Correct: John said that he was sure he *had seen* it.

5. **(A)** When two nouns (or pronouns) are joined by the correlative conjunction neither/nor, the verb agrees with the last subject. Correct: Neither the critics nor the author *was* right about the reaction of the public.

6. **(D)** *Who* is the subject of the verb following it, was. Correct: There was often disagreement as to *who* was the better Shakespearean actor, Evans or Gielgud.

7. **(D)** As the subject of the verb saw, the correct word is *we*, not *us*. Correct: Imagine our embarrassment when we girls saw Miss Maltinge sitting with her beau in the front row.

8. **(B)** The sentence switches number in the middle. Correct: Everyone who reads this book will think *himself a knight errant on a mission of heroism.*

9. **(C)** Use the subjunctive, *were*, when stating a wish. Correct: I *wish* that I *were* in Florida now.

10. **(C)** The phrase *as well as profit* does not add to the number of the subject, so the verb should be singular. Correct: Honor as well as profit *is* to be gained by these studies.

11. **(A)** The sentence switches number in the middle (Board of Directors is singular). Correct: The Board of Directors has prepared a manual for *its* own use.

12. **(C)** Because neither/nor is a correlative conjunction, the verb must agree with the nearest noun. Correct: Neither the salespeople nor the manager *wants* to work overtime.

13. **(B)** The comparison is not complete; it needs the addition of the word *as*. Correct: Spain is as weak as, if not weaker than, she was in 1900.

14. **(D)** *Commissioner Wilson* is a specific commissioner, so the *C* must be capitalized. Correct: Charles Dole, who is a member of the committee, was asked to confer with *Commissioner* Wilson.

15. **(A)** Parenthetical expressions must always be enclosed in commas. Correct: Most employees, *and he is no exception,* do not like to work overtime.

16. **(B)** The comparative *er* is used when only two items are being compared; *est*

requires three or more items. Correct: Of the two cities visited, White Plains is the *cleaner*.

17. **(C)** The specific noun *senate* must be capitalized. Correct: The letter will be sent to the United States *Senate* this week.

18. **(B)** The verb *to lay* should be used only when it can be replaced with *to put*; at all other times use a form of the verb *to lie*. Correct: When the supervisor entered the room, he noticed that the book was *lying* on the desk.

19. **(D)** Omitting the clause does not change the meaning of the remaining words, so it is nonrestrictive and should be set off by commas. Correct: All the clerks, *including those who have been appointed recently,* are required to work on the new assignment.

20. **(A)** Appositives should be set off by commas. Correct: Mrs. Black, *the supervisor of the unit,* has many important duties.

21. **(C)** Holidays are always capitalized. Correct: When *Independence Day* falls on a Sunday, it is officially celebrated on Monday.

22. **(A)** Pronouns that are objects of prepositions should be in the objective case. Correct: The task of filing these cards is to be divided equally between you and *him*.

23. **(C)** Because the sentence occurred in the past (*yesterday*), the verb should be in the past tense. Correct: Yesterday they laid their uniforms aside with the usual end-of-the-season regret.

24. **(A)** Use *who* when referring to people and *which* when referring to objects. Correct: Consider that the person *who* is always idle can never be happy.

25. **(B)** *Each* is singular. Correct: Each of the messengers *was* busily occupied.

The Hour in Review

1. Scoring well on the English grammar and usage portion of the verbal ability exam requires an understanding of grammar, capitalization, and punctuation rules.

2. When answering grammar and usage questions, be on the lookout for errors in subject-verb agreement, and verb tense.

3. The best way to quickly recognize grammar and useage errors is to concentrate on each sentence alone.

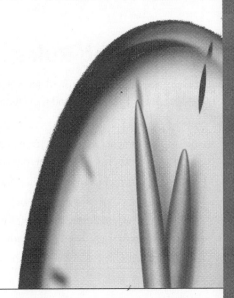

HOUR 4

Spelling

What You Will Learn in This Hour

Spelling questions appear on all civil service exams. Exams for general positions include from 5 to 25 spelling questions among the many different subjects tested. Exams for typists and stenographers may place a much heavier emphasis upon spelling ability. For such positions, some jurisdictions may administer a 90- or 100-question spelling test. Because spelling might be an important part of your civil service exam, you should give a great deal of attention to the rules and strategies outlined in this hour. They will see you through almost any spelling question you may face. Here are your goals for this hour:

- Learn spelling rules that you will need to know.
- Review the kinds of spelling questions that you may have to answer.
- Practice spelling questions.

Essential Spelling Rules

The rules outlined in this section will see you through almost any spelling question that you may face. Study these rules and their most common exceptions. Memorize as many as you can.

- **Rule 1:** i before e except after c or when sounding like ay as in *neighbor* or *weigh*. Exceptions: neither, leisure, foreign, seize, weird, height
- **Rule 2:** If a word ends in y preceded by a vowel, keep the y when adding a suffix. Examples: day, days; attorney, attorneys
- **Rule 3:** If a word ends in y preceded by a consonant, change the y to i before adding a suffix. Examples: try, tried; lady, ladies

> **Caution**
> To avoid double i, retain the y before the suffixes -ing and -ish. Examples: fly, flying; baby, babyish

- **Rule 4:** A silent e at the end of a word is usually dropped before a suffix beginning with a vowel. Examples: dine + ing = dining; locate + ion = location; use + able = usable; offense + ive = offensive

> **Caution**
> Words ending in ce and ge retain e before the suffixes -able and -ous in order to retain the soft sounds of e and g. Examples: peace + able = peaceable; courage + ous = courageous

- **Rule 5:** A silent e is usually kept before a suffix beginning with a consonant. Examples: care + less = careless; late + ly = lately; one + ness = oneness; game + ster = gamester

> **Tip**
> Some exceptions must simply be memorized. Exceptions to rules 4 and 5 are: truly, duly, awful, argument, wholly, ninth, mileage, dyeing, acreage, and canoeing.

- **Rule 6:** A one-syllable word that ends in a *single* consonant preceded by a *single* vowel doubles the final consonant before a suffix beginning with a vowel or y.

Examples: hit, hitting; drop, dropped; big, biggest; mud, muddy. But *help* becomes *helping* because *help* ends in two consonants, and *need* becomes *needing* because the final consonant is preceded by two vowels.

- **Rule 7:** A word with more than one syllable (that accents the *last* syllable and ends in a *single* consonant preceded by a single vowel) doubles the final consonant when adding a suffix beginning with a vowel. Examples: begin, beginner; admit, admitted. But *enter* becomes *entered* because the accent is not on the last syllable.

- **Rule 8:**   A word ending in <u>er</u> or <u>ur</u> doubles the <u>r</u> in the past tense if the word is accented on the *last* syllable. Examples: occur, occurred; prefer, preferred; transfer, transferred

- **Rule 9:**   A word ending in <u>er</u> does not double the <u>r</u> in the past tense if the accent does *not* fall on the last syllable. Examples: answer, answered; offer, offered; differ, differed

- **Rule 10:** When -full is added to the end of a noun to form an adjective, the final <u>l</u> is dropped. Examples: cheerful, cupful, hopeful

- **Rule 11:** All words beginning with *over* are one word. Examples: overcast, overcharge, overhear

- **Rule 12:** All words with the prefix *self* are hyphenated. Examples: self-control, self-defense, self-evident

- **Rule 13:** *Percent* is never hyphenated. It may be written as one word (percent) or as two words (per cent).

> **Note**
> Turn back to the section, "Using the Hyphen," in Hour 3, to review other hyphenation rules. Remember, for instance, that numbers from twenty-one to ninety-nine are hyphenated.

- **Rule 14:** The letter <u>q</u> is always followed by <u>u</u>. Examples: quiz, bouquet, acquire

- **Rule 15:** *Welcome* is one word with one <u>l</u>.

- **Rule 16:** *All right* is always two words; there is no such word as *alright*.

- **Rule 17:** *Already* means prior to some specified time; *all ready* means completely ready. Example: By the time I was *all ready* to go to the play, the bus had *already* left.

- **Rule 18:** *Altogether* means entirely; *all together* means in sum or collectively. Example: There are *altogether* too many people to seat in this room when we are *all together.*

4

- **Rule 19:** *Their* is the possessive of they; *they're* is the contraction for they are; and there is that place. Example: *They're* going to put *their* books over there.
- **Rule 20:** *Your* is the possessive of you; *you're* is the contraction for you are. Example: *You're* certainly planning to leave *your* muddy boots outside.
- **Rule 21:** *Whose* is the possessive of who; *who's* is the contraction for who is. Example: Do you know *who's* ringing the doorbell or *whose* car is in the street?
- **Rule 22:** *Its* is the possessive of it; *it's* is the contraction for it is. Example: *It's* I who put *its* stamp on the letter.

Tip

Develop a personal program for improving your spelling. Think of your own private "devils"—the words that you must look up every time. Everyone has such words. Make a list of these words, correctly spelled. Keep adding to the list right up to exam day, including those words that you miss on the practice exercises. Each day that you have extra study time, type through the list three times. By typing your troublesome words correctly, your hands and fingers will get used to the "feel" of the correct spelling, and your eye will become accustomed to seeing the words correctly spelled. Frequent repetition will embed the correct spellings in your mind.

Answering Spelling Questions

The following exercises illustrate the three most common types of spelling questions found on civil service exams. By studying these examples, you can easily tackle the spelling questions on the actual exam.

One common variety of spelling question looks like this:

DIRECTIONS: In each group of four words, one word is misspelled. Find the misspelled word and mark its letter on your answer sheet.

1. (A) business

    (B) manufacturer

    (C) possibly

    (D) recieved

In this case, you would mark (D) on your answer sheet because recieved is spelled incorrectly. Refer back to rule 1 in the previous section if you are unsure why (D) is incorrect.

A second common spelling question looks like this:

> **DIRECTIONS:** In each group of three words, one word may be misspelled. If you find one word that is incorrectly spelled, mark its letter on your answer sheet. If all the words are spelled correctly, mark (D).

1.   (A) foreign

    (B) acreage

    (C) occurred

In this case, all three words are spelled correctly, so the answer is (D). If you thought one of these words was spelled incorrectly, refer back to spelling rule 1, the exceptions to rule 4, and rule 8 in the previous section.

Or you might run into spelling questions with somewhat more complicated instructions, like this:

> **DIRECTIONS:** Each question consists of three words, any or all of which may be spelled incorrectly. On your answer sheet:

- Mark (A) if *ONLY ONE* word is misspelled.
- Mark (B) if *TWO WORDS* are misspelled.
- Mark (C) if *ALL THREE* words are misspelled.
- Mark (D) if *NO WORDS* are misspelled.

1.   offerred   hopefull   usable

For this question, you would mark (B), because two words are misspelled—the first two. The correct spellings are *offered* (see rule 9) and *hopeful* (see rule 10). If you are unsure why *usable* is correct, refer back to rule 4.

Try another question:

2.   acquire   welcome   per-cent

For this question, you should mark (A) as your answer, because only one word, percent, is misspelled (see rule 13). Look back at rules 14 and 15 to learn why the other two words are spelled correctly.

> **Make Connections**
> If you find this third type of spelling question on your exam, you must be very
> careful to mark the letters of your answers as indicated in the directions.
> Refer to the directions frequently to refresh your memory on which letter
> goes with which answer.

The following spelling exercises will give you practice spotting words that are spelled
incorrectly. The three most common types of spelling questions are included—one in each
set of practice exercises. All of the misspelled words are spelled correctly in the "Answers
and Explanations" section following the practice exercises, and where applicable, the rule
that applies to the misspelled word is given.

> **Tip**
> Sometimes it helps to answer spelling questions by looking away from the
> given choices and writing the word on the margin of your question booklet
> or on your scratch paper. Then, check to see if the spelling you believe is
> correct is given as one of the choices.

Workshop

In this workshop, you will review what you learned this hour by answering the kinds of
spelling questions often used on civil service tests.

Practice Exercise 1

DIRECTIONS: In each group of four words, one is misspelled. Mark the letter of the misspelled
word.

1. (A) hyphen
   (B) index
   (C) office
   (D) diferent

2. (A) corporation
   (B) spindel
   (C) foreign
   (D) material

3. (A) adress
   (B) exactly
   (C) research
   (D) vertical

4. (A) occupation
   (B) accross
   (C) authority
   (D) invoice

5. (A) guardian
    (B) certified
    (C) voucher
    (D) mispelled

6. (A) trustee
    (B) multipal
    (C) promissory
    (D) valuable

7. (A) traveler
    (B) pamphlet
    (C) agencys
    (D) permit

8. (A) automatic
    (B) proportion
    (C) announcement
    (D) municiple

9. (A) recruitment
    (B) mentioned
    (C) optional
    (D) commision

10. (A) responsibility
    (B) disabled
    (C) vetran
    (D) misleading

11. (A) competetive
    (B) review
    (C) erroneous
    (D) license

12. (A) familiarity
    (B) accredited
    (C) payment
    (D) distributer

13. (A) localities
    (B) servise
    (C) central
    (D) occupation

14. (A) offerred
    (B) jogging
    (C) threaten
    (D) throughway

15. (A) vending
    (B) tomorrow
    (C) strangly
    (D) barometer

16. (A) anounce
    (B) local
    (C) grasshopper
    (D) farmer

17. (A) historical
    (B) dustey
    (C) kindly
    (D) humbug

18. (A) current
    (B) comunity
    (C) cement
    (D) calves

19. (A) changeing
    (B) explained
    (C) diameter
    (D) consent

20. (A) sword
    (B) reckord
    (C) signed
    (D) taste

4)

Practice Exercise 2

DIRECTIONS: In each question, one of the words may be spelled incorrectly, or all three may be spelled correctly. If one of the words is spelled incorrectly, mark the letter of this word. If all three words are spelled correctly, mark (D).

1. ✓(A) gratful
   (B) census
   (C) analysis
   (D) none of these

2. (A) installment
   ✓(B) retreive
   (C) concede
   (D) none of these

3. (A) dismissal
   (B) conscientious
   (C) indelible
   ✓(D) none of these

4. ✓(A) percieve
   (B) anticipate
   (C) acquire
   (D) none of these

5. (A) facility
   (B) reimburse
   (C) assortment
   ✓(D) none of these

6. ✓(A) plentifull
   (B) advantageous
   (C) similar
   (D) none of these

7. (A) guarantee
   (B) repel
   (C) ommission
   ✓(D) none of these

8. (A) maintenance
   (B) liable
   (C) announcement
   ✓(D) none of these

9. (A) exaggerate
   (B) seize
   ✓(C) condenm
   (D) none of these

10. ✓(A) pospone
    (B) altogether
    (C) grievance
    (D) none of these

11. (A) argument
    ✓(B) reciept
    (C) complain
    (D) none of these

12. (A) sufficient
    (B) declaim
    (C) visible
    ✓(D) none of these

13. ✓(A) expirience
    (B) dissatisfy
    (C) alternate
    (D) none of these

14. (A) occurred
    (B) noticable
    (C) appendix
    ✓(D) none of these

15. (A) anxious
     (B) guarantee
   ✓ (C) calender
     (D) none of these

16. (A) fundamental
   ✓ (B) dissapear
     (C) accidentally
     (D) none of these

17. (A) guidance
     (B) across
   ✓ (C) carreer
     (D) none of these

18. (A) pamphlet
     (B) always
     (C) commit
   ✓ (D) none of these

19. (A) excessive
   ✓ (B) permited
     (C) appointment
     (D) none of these

20. (A) personnel
     (B) resource
   ✓ (C) colledge
     (D) none of these

Practice Exercise 3

DIRECTIONS: Each question consists of three words, any or all of which may be spelled incorrectly. Beside each question:

- Mark (A) if *ONLY ONE* word is misspelled.
- Mark (B) if *TWO WORDS* are misspelled.
- Mark (C) if *ALL THREE* words are misspelled.
- Mark (D) if *NO WORDS* are misspelled.

A D 1.   professor   satisfactorally   weight
D B 2.   sabbatical   accomplishment   occasionally
   B 3.   associate   bookeeping   carefuly
   B 4.   dictater   beforhand   deceit
   A 5.   accidently   supervisor   efficiently
   D 6.   bureau   manifest   scheduling
   C 7.   auxilary   machinary   distorsion
A D 8.   synthesis   harrassment   exemplify
   B 9.   receiveable   bankrupcy   chronological
   D 10.   facsimile   requisition   liability

B 11.	proxey	pollish	courtesy
A 12.	negotiable	acknowledgment	notarary
B 13.	confidential	typograpfical	memmoranda
B 14.	pertainent	codify	ellimination
A 15.	corrective	performance	clogging

Answers and Explanations

Exercise 1

1. (D) different
2. (B) spindle
3. (A) address
4. (B) across
5. (D) misspelled
6. (B) multiple
7. (C) agencies (see rule 3)
8. (D) municipal
9. (D) commission
10. (C) veteran

11. (A) competitive
12. (D) distributor
13. (B) service
14. (A) offered (see rule 9)
15. (C) strangely (see rule 5)
16. (A) announce
17. (B) dusty
18. (B) community
19. (A) changing (see rule 4)
20. (B) record

Exercise 2

1. (A) grateful (see rule 5)
2. (B) retrieve (see rule 1)
3. (D)
4. (A) perceive (see rule 1)
5. (D)
6. (A) plentiful (see rule 10)
7. (C) omission
8. (D)
9. (C) condemn
10. (A) postpone

11. (B) receipt (see rule 1)
12. (D)
13. (C) experience
14. (B) noticeable (see the exceptions to rule 4)
15. (C) calendar
16. (B) disappear
17. (C) career
18. (D)
19. (B) permitted (see rule 7)
20. (C) college

Exercise 3

1. (**A**) satisfactorally is incorrect; the correct spelling is satisfactorily

2. (**D**) all are correct

3. (**B**) bookeeping and carefuly are incorrect; the correct spellings are bookkeeping and carefully (careful + ly)

4. (**B**) dictater and beforhand are incorrect; the correct spellings are dictator and beforehand

5. (**A**) accidently is incorrect; the correct spelling is accidentally

6. (**D**) all are correct

7. (**C**) all are incorrect; the correct spellings are auxiliary, machinery, and distortion

8. (**A**) harrassment is incorrect; the correct spelling is harassment

9. (**B**) receiveable and bankrupcy are incorrect; the correct spellings are receivable (see rule 4) and bankruptcy

10. (**D**) all are correct

11. (**B**) proxey and pollish are incorrect; the correct spellings are proxy and polish

12. (**A**) notarary is incorrect; the correct spelling is notary

13. (**B**) typograpfical and memmoranda are incorrect; the correct spellings are typographical and memoranda

14. (**B**) pertainent and ellimination are incorrect; the correct spellings are pertinent and elimination

15. (**A**) performence is incorrect; the correct spelling is performance

The Hour in Review

1. Spelling questions appear on most civil service exams.

2. To prepare for spelling questions, memorize as many of the basic spelling rules and exceptions as you can.

3. Also, identify words that give you trouble and study them until the correct spellings are familiar to you.

4. Spelling questions on different civil service exams may appear in different forms, so learn how to answer each type of spelling question.

Hour 5

Synonyms

What You Will Learn in This Hour

Synonym questions test your vocabulary. The best way to prepare for these kinds of questions is to study several examples. Apply the strategies that you will learn in this hour until you are able to answer the majority of the questions correctly. Here are your goals for this hour:

- Learn what a synonym is.
- Learn how to approach synonym questions.
- Learn strategies to use when answering synonym questions.
- Practice synonym questions.

What Are Synonyms?

Two words are *synonyms* if they mean the same thing. In a synonym question, you must pick the word or phrase closest in meaning to the given word. Remember that you are looking for the best match among the choices given, not necessarily a perfect match.

Tip
You may encounter another type of vocabulary question—antonym questions. *Antonyms* are two words that have opposite meanings. In an antonym question, you must choose the word or phrase that most nearly means the *opposite* of the given word. The strategies for tackling antonym questions are similar to those for answering synonym questions, keeping in mind that you are looking for an answer that means the opposite, rather than the closest match. Synonym questions are more commonly found on civil service exams, however, which is why this chapter focuses on them.

Caution
When dealing with vocabulary questions, you must read the directions carefully to determine whether you should choose the opposite of the given word—its antonym—or its closest match—its synonym. Not paying close attention to the directions could result in answering an entire section of the exam incorrectly.

Tackling Synonym Questions

When you are faced with a synonym question, follow these steps to answer the question:

1. Read the question carefully.

2. If you know right away that some of the answer choices are wrong, eliminate them.

3. From the remaining answer choices, select the one that most closely means the same as the given word, even if it is a word that you yourself do not normally use. The correct answer may not be a perfect synonym, but of the choices offered, it is the best fit.

Here is an example of a typical synonym question:

1. FACSIMILE means most nearly

    (A) summary

    (B) exact copy

    (C) list

    (D) artist's sketch

This is a straightforward vocabulary question. The given word is rather difficult, but the choices are not tricky. The correct answer is (B). A *facsimile* is a copy that looks exactly like the original—a photocopy, for instance. The word contains the root *simile*, meaning "like." Choice (C), *list*, has no connection with facsimile. Responses (A), *summary*, and (D), *artist's sketch*, are in a sense copies of something else, but not exact copies.

Here is another example:

2.   FRAUDULENT means most nearly

(A) suspicious

(B) deceptive

(C) unfair

(D) despicable

The answer is (B). The word *fraudulent* means, "characterized by deceit or trickery, especially deliberate misrepresentation." Therefore, *deceptive* is the best synonym. Choice (A), *suspicious*, "sensing that something is wrong without definite proof," could describe a person's reaction to a fraudulent situation. Choices (C), *unfair*, and (D), *despicable*, could both be used to describe a fraudulent act. The basic meanings of these three words, however, are completely different from the meaning of *fraudulent*.

Some tests phrase synonym questions as a sentence. You must then make sure that your answer makes sense in the given sentence and does not change the sentence's meaning. The following is an example of this kind of synonym question:

3.   We had to *terminate* the meeting because a fire broke out in the hall. *Terminate* most nearly means

(A) continue

(B) postpone

(C) end

(D) extinguish

The correct answer is (C). Even if you do not know what *terminate* means, you can eliminate choice (A) because it does not make much sense to say, "We had to *continue* the meeting because a fire broke out in the hall." Choice (B), *postpone*, means "to put off until another time." It makes sense in the given sentence, but it also changes the meaning of the sentence. Choice (D), *extinguish*, is similar in meaning to *terminate* but not as close as *end*. One can extinguish, or "put an end to," a fire but not a meeting.

5

Strategies for Answering Synonym Questions

Answering synonym questions depends largely upon your knowledge of vocabulary. You can apply the following strategies to arrive at the correct answer, if you do not recognize it immediately:

- If you have a general idea about what the word means but are having trouble choosing an answer, try using the word in a short sentence. Then substitute each of the answer choices in the same sentence to see which one seems to fit the sentence best without changing its meaning.

- Try to break the given word into parts to see if the suffix (ending) or the prefix (beginning) gives a clue about its meaning. For example, if you are asked to find the synonym for *previous*, you may remember that the prefix pre- usually means "before." You could use that as a clue to help you choose the correct answer.

You must watch out for traps of logic, though. Study the following example:

1. PERTINENT means most nearly

    (A) relevant

    (B) prudent

    (C) true

    (D) respectful

The correct answer is (A). *Pertinent* means "having some bearing on or relevance to." In the sentence, "Her testimony was pertinent to the investigation," you could put *relevant* in the place of pertinent without changing the meaning. Choice (B), *prudent*, means "careful" or "wise." Although it sounds somewhat like *pertinent*, its meaning is different. Choice (C) may seem possible, because something that is *pertinent* should also be *true*. But watch out. Not everything that is true is pertinent.

Choice (D), *respectful*, is misleading. Its opposite, *disrespectful*, is a synonym for the word *impertinent*. You might logically guess, then, that *respectful* is a synonym for *pertinent*. The best way to avoid a trap like this is to remember how you have seen or heard the word used. You never see *pertinent* used to mean *respectful*.

Workshop

In this workshop, you will apply what you have learned this hour by answering civil service-type synonym questions.

Practice Exercise 1

> **DIRECTIONS:** Select the word or phrase closest in meaning to the given word.

1. RETAIN means most nearly
   - (A) pay out
   - (B) play
   - (C) keep
   - (D) inquire

2. ENDORSE means most nearly
   - (A) sign up for
   - (B) announce support for
   - (C) lobby for
   - (D) renounce

3. INTRACTABLE means most nearly
   - (A) confused
   - (B) misleading
   - (C) instinctive
   - (D) unruly

4. CORRESPONDENCE means most nearly
   - (A) letters
   - (B) files
   - (C) testimony
   - (D) response

5. OBLITERATE means most nearly
   - (A) praise
   - (B) doubt
   - (C) erase
   - (D) reprove

6. LEGITIMATE means most nearly
   - (A) democratic
   - (B) legal
   - (C) genealogical
   - (D) underworld

7. DEDUCT means most nearly
   - (A) conceal
   - (B) withstand
   - (C) subtract
   - (D) terminate

8. MUTILATE means most nearly
   - (A) paint
   - (B) damage
   - (C) alter
   - (D) rebel

9. EGRESS means most nearly
   - (A) extreme
   - (B) extra supply
   - (C) exit
   - (D) high price

10. HORIZONTAL means most nearly
    - (A) marginal
    - (B) in a circle
    - (C) left and right
    - (D) up and down

11. CONTROVERSY means most nearly
    - (A) publicity
    - (B) debate
    - (C) revolution
    - (D) revocation

12. PREEMPT means most nearly
    - (A) steal
    - (B) empty
    - (C) preview
    - (D) appropriate

13. CATEGORY means most nearly
  ✓ (A) class
   (B) adherence
   (C) simplicity
   (D) cataract

14. APATHY means most nearly
   (A) sorrow
  ✓ (B) indifference
   (C) aptness
   (D) sickness

15. TENTATIVE means most nearly
   (A) persistent
   (B) permanent
  ✓ (C) thoughtful
   (D) provisional

16. PER CAPITA means most nearly
   (A) for an entire population
   (B) by income
  ✓ (C) for each person
   (D) for every adult

17. DEFICIENT means most nearly
   (A) sufficient
   (B) outstanding
  ✓ (C) inadequate
   (D) bizarre

18. INSPECT means most nearly
   (A) disregard
  ✓ (B) look at
   (C) annoy
   (D) criticize

19. OPTIONAL means most nearly
  ✓ (A) not required
   (B) infrequent
   (C) choosy
   (D) for sale

20. IMPLIED means most nearly
   (A) acknowledged
   (B) stated
   (C) predicted
  ✓ (D) hinted

Practice Exercise 2

DIRECTIONS: Select the word or phrase closest in meaning to the given word.

1. PRESUMABLY means most nearly
   (A) positively
   (B) helplessly
   (C) recklessly
  ✓ (D) supposedly

2. TEXTILE means most nearly
   (A) linen
  ✓ (B) cloth
   (C) page
  ✓ (D) garment

3. FISCAL means most nearly
   (A) critical
   (B) basic
   (C) personal
  ✓ (D) financial

4. STRINGENT means most nearly
  ✓ (A) demanding
   (B) loud
   (C) flexible
   (D) clear

5. PROCEED means most nearly
   (A) go forward
   (B) parade
   (C) refrain
   (D) resume

6. BROCHURE means most nearly
   (A) ornament
   (B) flowery statement
   (C) breakage
   (D) pamphlet

7. PERMEABLE means most nearly
   (A) penetrable
   (B) durable
   (C) unending
   (D) allowable

8. LIMIT means most nearly
   (A) budget
   (B) sky
   (C) point
   (D) boundary

9. SCRUPULOUS means most nearly
   (A) conscientious
   (B) unprincipled
   (C) intricate
   (D) neurotic

10. STALEMATE means most nearly
   (A) pillar
   (B) deadlock
   (C) maneuver
   (D) work slowdown

11. COMPETENT means most nearly
   (A) inept
   (B) informed
   (C) capable
   (D) caring

12. SOMATIC means most nearly
   (A) painful
   (B) drowsy
   (C) indefinite
   (D) physical

13. OBSTACLE means most nearly
   (A) imprisonment
   (B) hindrance
   (C) retaining wall
   (D) leap

14. REDUNDANT means most nearly
   (A) concise
   (B) reappearing
   (C) superfluous
   (D) lying down

15. SUPPLANT means most nearly
   (A) prune
   (B) conquer
   (C) uproot
   (D) replace

16. HAPHAZARD means most nearly
   (A) devious
   (B) without order
   (C) aberrant
   (D) risky

17. COMMENSURATE means most nearly
   (A) identical
   (B) of the same age
   (C) proportionate
   (D) measurable

18. ACCELERATE means most nearly
   (A) drive fast
   (B) reroute
   (C) decline rapidly
   (D) speed up

5

19. PURCHASED means most nearly

   (A)   charged

   (B)   bought

   (C)   ordered

   (D)   supplied

20. ZENITH means most nearly

   (A)   depths

   (B)   astronomical system

   (C)   peak

   (D)   solar system

Answers

Practice Exercise 1

If you miss any of the questions, look up the given word in a dictionary and study how the correct answer relates to the given word.

1.	C	11.	B
2.	B	12.	D
3.	D	13.	A
4.	A	14.	B
5.	C	15.	D
6.	B	16.	C
7.	C	17.	C
8.	B	18.	B
9.	C	19.	A
10.	C	20.	D

Practice Exercise 2

If you miss any of the questions, look up the given word in a dictionary and study how the correct answer relates to the given word.

1.	D	7.	A
2.	B	8.	D
3.	D	9.	A
4.	A	10.	B
5.	A	11.	C
6.	D	12.	D

13.	B	17.	C
14.	C	18.	D
15.	D	19.	B
16.	B	20.	C

The Hour in Review

1. Synonym questions test your vocabulary by asking you to choose an answer that is closest in meaning—but not necessarily an exact match for—a given word.

2. Answer synonym questions by first eliminating the answers that obviously do not match and then by examining the remaining answers to find the closest fit.

3. One way to tackle synonym questions is to use the given word in a sentence, then replace it with your answer—making sure that the meaning of the sentence does not change.

4. Another way to tackle synonyms is to break the given word down and look for clues in its prefix, suffix, or root.

5

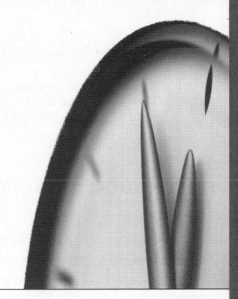

Hour 6

Sentence Completions

What You Will Learn in This Hour

Sentence completion questions are more complex than synonym questions. They test not only your knowledge of basic vocabulary, but also your ability to understand what you read. While studying individual words may be helpful, the best way to prepare for this type of question is to read a lot. A dictionary will tell you what a word means; reading will teach you how it is actually used. Here are your goals for this hour:

- Learn what sentence completions are.
- Learn how to approach a sentence completion question.
- Practice sentence completion questions.

What Are Sentence Completions?

In a sentence completion question, you are given a sentence or long passage in which something has been left blank. A number of words or phrases are suggested to fill that blank. You must select the word or phrase that will best complete the meaning of the passage as a whole.

> **Tip**
> Although more than one answer may make sense, the best choice will be the one that is most exact, appropriate, or likely, considering the information given in the sentence or passage.

Tackling Sentence Completion Questions

Follow these steps to answer a sentence completion question:

1. Read the question carefully, looking at all the answer choices.

2. Eliminate any answer choices that are obviously wrong.

3. Of the remaining choices, select the one that best completes the meaning of the sentence or passage given.

4. To check yourself, read the sentence or passage through again, putting your answer in the blank.

The following example shows you how to follow these steps in answering a sentence completion question:

1. Trespassing on private property is _____ by law.

   (A) proscribed

   (B) warranted

   (C) prescribed

   (D) eliminated

First, eliminate any choices that are obviously wrong. Choice (B), *warranted*, may remind you of a warrant for arrest, which might be the result of trespassing; *warranted*, however, means "justified," which would make the given sentence obviously untrue. Choice (C), *prescribed*, means "recommended"; like *warranted*, it makes nonsense out of the given sentence.

Now, select the best answer from the remaining choices and insert it into the blank to be sure that it makes sense in the given sentence. Choice (D), *eliminated*, is a likely choice, but it doesn't fit the sentence; the law may be intended to eliminate trespassing, but it can never be completely successful in doing so. Therefore, the most likely and thus the correct answer is (A), *proscribed*.

> **Caution**
> Watch out for words that look alike but have different meanings, such as
> *proscribed* and *prescribed* in the previous example. Read each answer choice
> carefully so that you will not fall for this trap.

Try another example question:

2. Despite the harsh tone of her comments, she did not mean to _____ any criticism
    of you personally.

    (A) infer

    (B) aim

    (C) comply

    (D) imply

You can eliminate choice (C), *comply*, which means "obey" and makes no sense in the
context. Choice (B), *aim*, is more likely, but it doesn't work in the sentence as given. You
might say, "She did not mean to aim any criticism *at* you," but you would not normally
say, "She did not mean to aim any criticism *of* you."

The correct answer is (D), *imply*, which means "suggest indirectly." Be careful of choice
(A), *infer*; this word is often confused with *imply*. *Infer* means, "conclude from reasoning
or implication." A speaker implies, a listener infers.

> **Tip**
> Sentence completion questions often contain clue words that help you
> determine the missing word:
>
> • **Contrast words** tell you that the missing word should contrast with
>   another idea stated in the sentence: *although; despite; though; but;
>   however; rather than; not; yet; instead of.*
>
> • **Support words** tell you that the missing word is supported by another part
>   of the sentence: *and; for; furthermore; also; because; so.*
>
> • **Summary words** tell you that the missing word summarizes an idea already
>   stated in the sentence: *as a result; finally; in conclusion; on the whole.*
>
> • **Cause-and-effect words** tell you that the missing word is an effect of a
>   cause stated in the sentence, or vice versa: *consequently; so that; thus;
>   since; if; therefore; accordingly.*

6

Try the following question:

3.   The department's _____ does not allow for unlimited copying by all the instructors in the program. Each instructor can be reimbursed for copying expenses only up to ten dollars.

(A) paperwork

(B) staff

(C) organization

(D) budget

Since the concern here is with money, the correct answer is (D), *budget*. A budget puts limits on spending. Choices (A), *paperwork*, and (B), *staff*, aren't appropriate to the meaning of the passage. Choice (C), *organization*, is barely possible, but only because it is so vague. *Budget* both makes sense and is much more exact.

Tip

If you are having trouble finding the correct answer, look for clues in the overall subject of the sentence. In the previous example, the sentence was primarily about money, so you can assume that the answer is a word that relates to money — *budget*.

Tackle one more example question:

4.   If the company offered a settlement commensurate with the damages sustained, the couple would _____ their right to a hearing.

(A) cancel

(B) ensure

(C) waive

(D) assert

The correct answer is (C), *waive*, which means "forego" or "give up." One *waives* something to which one is entitled, such as a right. Choice (A), *cancel*, is similar in meaning but is not used in this way. One can cancel a hearing but not a right. Choice (B), *ensue*, may mislead you by its similarity to sue. The sentence does imply that the couple is suing or planning to sue the company for damages of some sort. However, *ensue* simply means "follow as a result" and so makes no sense in this context. Choice (D), *assert*, here means the opposite of *waive*. One can assert a right, but the meaning of the first part of the sentence makes this choice unlikely.

Workshop

In this workshop, you will practice the skills you learned this hour by answering the kinds of sentence completion questions used on many civil service tests.

Practice Exercise

DIRECTIONS: Each of the following sentences or passages contains a blank. Select the word or phrase that will best complete the meaning of the sentence or passage as a whole.

1. He was the chief _____ of his uncle's will. After taxes he was left with an inheritance worth close to twenty thousand dollars.

    (A) exemption

    (B) pensioner

    ✓ (C) beneficiary

    (D) contestant

2. In view of the extenuating circumstances and the defendant's youth, the judge recommended _____.

    (A) conviction

    (B) a defense

    (C) a mistrial

    ✓ (D) leniency

3. The basic concept of civil service is that where a public job exists, all those who possess the _____ shall have an opportunity to compete for it.

    (A) potential

    (B) contacts

    ✓ (C) qualifications

    (D) credits

4. They would prefer to hire someone fluent in Spanish since the neighborhood in which the clinic is located is _____ Hispanic.

    (A) imponderably

    (B) sparsely

    (C) consistently

    ✓ (D) predominantly

5. The lover of democracy has an _____ toward totalitarianism.

    ✓ (A) antipathy

    (B) attitude

    (C) empathy

    (D) idolatry

6. The candidate's _____ was carefully planned; she traveled to six cities and spoke at nine rallies.

    (A) pogrom

    ✓ (B) itinerary

    (C) adjournment

    (D) apparition

7. _____ recommendations are generally more constructive than vague complaints or blanket praise.

   (A) Justified

   (B) Nebulous

   (C) Sweeping

   ✓ (D) Specific

8. In the face of an uncooperative Congress, the Chief Executive may find himself _____ to accomplish the political program to which he is committed.

   ✓ (A) impotent

   (B) equipped

   (C) neutral

   (D) contingent

9. The authorities declared an _____ on incoming freight because of the trucking strike.

   (A) impression

   (B) immolation

   ✓ (C) embargo

   (D) opprobrium

10. The information we have available on that question is _____: The form, scope, and reliability of the documents vary tremendously.

   (A) essential

   (B) homogenous

   (C) heterogeneous

   ✓ (D) minimal

11. The _____ on the letter indicated that it had been mailed in Minnesota three weeks previously.

   (A) address

   (B) stamp

   ✓ (C) postmark

   (D) envelope

12. The television ads _____ an unprecedented public response. Sales skyrocketed and within a few months the brand name had become a household word.

   (A) boosted

   (B) promised

   ✓ (C) elicited

   (D) favored

13. The chairman submitted a _____ for the new equipment, but it will not be delivered for two weeks.

   ✓ (A) requisition

   (B) reason

   (C) proposal

   (D) plea

14. With all his courtroom experience, the attorney was able to pry very little information out of the _____ witness.

   (A) cooperative

   ✓ (B) recalcitrant

   (C) reactionary

   (D) testifying

15. Although for years substantial resources had been devoted to alleviating the problem, a satisfactory solution remained _____.

    (A) costly

    (B) probable

    ✓ (C) elusive

    (D) esoteric

16. The local police department will not accept for _____ a report of a person missing from his residence if such residence is located outside of the city.

    (A) foreclosure

    (B) convenience

    ✓ (C) investigation

    (D) control

17. The consumer group is optimistic about the _____ of the new regulations on the industry's safety standards.

    (A) incision

    ✓ (B) effect

    (C) affectation

    (D) input

18. The mayor sent a letter _____ our invitation and commending us on our work; she regrets that she will be unable to attend the opening ceremonies due to a prior commitment.

    (A) rebuffing

    (B) reconsidering

    (C) returning

    ✓ (D) acknowledging

19. His wealth of practical experience and his psychological acuity more than _____ his lack of formal academic training.

    (A) concede to

    (B) comprise

    ✓ (C) compensate for

    (D) educate for

20. Suffering from _____, she was forced to spend almost all her time indoors.

    (A) claustrophobia

    ✓ (B) agoraphobia

    (C) anemia

    (D) ambivalence

21. The treaty cannot go into effect until it has been _____ by the Senate.

    (A) considered

    (B) debated

    ✓ (C) ratified

    (D) shelved

22. You will have to speak to the head of the agency; I am not _____ to give out that information.

    (A) willing

    ✓ (B) authorized

    (C) programmed

    (D) happy

23. When new individuals have proved their capability and reliability, they ought to achieve journeyman status in the company _____.

    (A) intrinsically

    ✓ (B) permanently

    (C) automatically

    (D) decisively

24. The object may be _____ but the plan as presented is far from practicable.
    (A) compensatory
    (B) laudable
    (C) precarious
    (D) subversive

25. You must _____ a copy of your latest federal income tax return before your loan application can be considered.
    (A) surrender
    (B) replicate
    (C) supplement
    (D) submit

Answers and Explanations

1. **(C)** Because the subject received a benefit from his uncle's will, *beneficiary* fits the sentence best.

2. **(D)** The words, "extenuating circumstances" and "youth" should tip you off that the judge will be merciful, or recommend *leniency*.

3. **(C)** As you learned earlier in this book, you must have the *qualifications* for the job.

4. **(D)** The cause-and-effect clue "since" tells you that the second part of the sentence is the cause of the first part. If the neighborhood is *predominantly*, or "mostly," Hispanic, then clinic workers there would need to speak Spanish.

5. **(A)** Totalitarianism is the opposite of democracy, so someone who loves democracy would naturally feel *antipathy*, or "a strong feeling of distaste" toward totalitarianism.

6. **(B)** The words "planned" and "traveled" suggest that the best answer is *itinerary*, which means "a planned route on a journey."

7. **(D)** The word "than" contrasts the last part of the sentence with the first part; therefore, you should choose an answer that means the opposite of vague — *specific*.

8. **(A)** In this case, *impotent* means "powerless"; if Congress is uncooperative, the President is probably powerless.

9. **(C)** The words "because of" are a cause-and-effect clue. If truckers are on strike, then there is no one to bring in the freight, so there must be an *embargo*, or "prohibition," of it.

10. **(C)** None of the choices fit the sentence as well as *heterogeneous*.

11. **(C)** The only thing that can indicate when and where a letter was mailed is the *postmark*.

12. **(C)** *Elicited* means "brought out" or "provoked"; the ads brought out an unprecedented response, as indicated by the following sentence.

13. **(A)** In a business context, the correct term is *requisition*, or "a formal request for."

14. **(B)** Since the witness gave very little information, he is obviously *recalcitrant*, or "stubbornly resistant to authority."

15. **(C)** The word "although" contrasts the two parts of the sentence; therefore, the best answer is *elusive* — the solution to the problem evaded all the attempts to find it.

16. **(C)** Since the sentence is about the police, *investigation* is the best choice.

17. **(B)** The best choice is *effect*, or "result." Be careful of *affectation*, which looks like *effect* but actually means, "artificial behavior designed to impress others."

18. **(D)** The mayor did *acknowledge*, or "recognize," the invitation. Since she politely declined, she did not *rebuff*, *return*, or *reconsider* the invitation.

19. **(C)** *Compensate for*, or "make up for," best fits the sentence.

20. **(B)** Someone who has *agoraphobia* has a fear of open spaces, so she would need to stay inside. Watch out for *claustrophobia* —a fear of close spaces—which is the opposite of the correct answer.

21. **(C)** When the members of the Senate ratify a treaty, they approve it; they may *debate* or *consider* it first, but the treaty cannot go into effect until it is approved.

22. **(B)** The best answer is *authorized*— "permitted" or "allowed"; the speaker may be *willing* or *happy* to give out the information, but still cannot because he's not allowed by his superior, the head of the agency.

23. **(C)** The word "when" implies that the second part of the sentence—the effect—should happen as soon as the first part—the cause—occurs; in other words, it should happen *automatically*.

24. **(B)** The word "but" contrasts the first part of the sentence with the second part; the best fit is *laudable*, or "deserving praise."

25. **(D)** *Submit*, or "give," best fits the meaning of the sentence.

6

The Hour in Review

1. Sentence completion questions test your knowledge of vocabulary and your ability to form logical sentences.

2. The answer of a sentence completion question is the one that best fits the information given in the entire sentence or passage.

3. To determine the answer to a sentence completion question, look for clues in the given sentence, such as contrast, support, or cause-and-effect words, the overall meaning, or any other words that lead to the answer.

HOUR 7

Verbal Analogies

What You Will Learn in This Hour

Verbal analogies test your understanding of word meanings and your ability to grasp relationships between words and ideas. There are various classifications of relationships, such as similarity (or synonyms), opposition (or antonyms), cause and effect, and sequence. Here are your goals for this hour:

- Learn what verbal analogies are.
- Learn how to approach verbal analogy questions.
- Practice verbal analogy questions.

What Are Verbal Analogy Questions?

A verbal analogy question has four terms in two pairs. You are given the first complete pair, which establishes the relationship. You must then choose a pair of words whose relationship is *most* similar to the relationship in the given pair.

One type of verbal analogy question gives the first pair of words and the first half of the second pair, followed by a list of possible matches. This kind of question looks like this:

1.   CLOCK is to TIME as THERMOMETER is to

The four answer choices are all single words. You must choose the one that completes a relationship with thermometer that is analogous to the relationship between clock and time.

Or you may just be given the first pair of words, and then a selection of paired terms from which you must find the one that implies the same relationship as the given pair. This kind of question looks like this:

1.   CLOCK : TIME ::

The four answer choices are all pairs of words. You must choose the pair that has an analogous relationship to the relationship between clock and time.

Tackling Verbal Analogy Questions

To answer these questions, look at the given pair of words and decide what the relationship between the words is. Then choose the answer that has the most similar relationship to the given pair of words. Follow these steps:

1.   Read each question carefully.

2.   Establish what the correct relationship is between the two terms in the given pair.

3.   Study the selection of possible answers carefully and eliminate any that do not share the same relationship as the given pair.

4.   Read the remaining choices through again, this time substituting the key relationship word from the sample pair (CLOCK measures TIME, THERMOMETER measures TEMPERATURE).

Try this question:

1.   SPEEDOMETER is to POINTER as WATCH is to

(A) case

(B) hands

(C) dial

(D) numerals

First consider what a *pointer* is used for on a *speedometer*. It indicates speed at a particular moment. A *watch* uses *hands* (choice B) for the same general function, that is, to indicate something at a particular moment. In this case, the hands indicate time. Choice (A), *case*, is incorrect because the watch case has nothing to do with this function. Choices (C), *dial*, and (D), *numerals*, are wrong because although the dial and the numbers have to do with indicating time, they don't perform the specific function of indicating something at any one particular moment.

> **Tip**
> Remember to choose the correct answer because it is an analogous relation-ship, not because it is on the same subject as the given pair of words.

Try another sample question:

2.   WINTER is to SUMMER as COLD is to

   (A) wet

   (B) future

   (C) warm

   (D) freezing

Winter and *summer* are opposites, so you should look for an answer choice that means the opposite of cold. The correct answer is (C), warm.

Now, try the other kind of verbal analogy:

3.   SPELLING : PUNCTUATION ::

   (A) pajamas : fatigue

   (B) powder : shaving

   (C) bandage : cut

   (D) biology: physics

Spelling and *punctuation* are parts of the mechanics of English. Biology and physics are parts of the field of science. Therefore, the pair of words with the most analogous relation-ship to the given pair is answer choice (D).

> **Tip**
> In this type of question, it may help to substitute the colons with words when you read the question in your head. You would read the previous example like this: "Spelling *is* to punctuation *as* _____ *is* to _____."

7

Workshop

In this workshop, you'll get plenty of practice with the kinds of analogy questions commonly used on civil service tests.

Practice Exercise 1

DIRECTIONS: In each question, the first two words have a certain relationship to each other. Select the letter of the word that is related to the third word in the same way that the first two words are related.

1. ORATION is to CHAT as BANQUET is to
   (A) festival
   (B) party
   (C) wedding
   ✓(D) snack

2. INCLEMENT is to CLEAR as PERTINENT is to
   (A) pert
   (B) cloudy
   ✓(C) irrelevant
   (D) perceptive

3. WHEAT is to FLOUR as GRAPE is to
   (A) vintage
   (B) vine
   ✓(C) wine
   (D) fruit

4. COMMON is to IRON as RARE is to
   (A) steak
   (B) crowd
   (C) humor
   ✓(D) diamond

5. VICTORY is to CONTEST as KNOWLEDGE is to
   (A) professor
   (B) test
   (C) degree
   ✓(D) study

6. DIAGNOSIS is to ANALYSIS as THESIS is to
   (A) antithesis
   ✓(B) research
   (C) paper
   (D) college

7. MARE is to FILLY as KING is to
   (A) throne
   ✓(B) prince
   (C) queen
   (D) kingdom

8. ARMY is to RECRUIT as RELIGION is to
   (A) priest
   (B) worshipper
   ✓(C) convert
   (D) acolyte

9. OPULENCE is to LUXURY as
    POVERTY is to

    ✓ (A) penury

    — (B) misery

    (C) charity

    (D) hunger

10. WILL is to CODICIL as CONSTITU-
    TION is to

    (A) preamble

    ✓ (B) amendment

    (C) law

    (D) independence

Practice Exercise 2

DIRECTIONS: In each question, the two capitalized words have a certain relationship to each other. Select the letter of the pair of words that are related in the same way as the two capitalized words.

1. INTIMIDATE : FEAR ::

    (A) maintain : satisfaction

    ✓ (B) astonish : wonder

    (C) sooth : concern

    (D) feed: hunger

2. STOVE: KITCHEN ::

    (A) window : bedroom

    ✓ (B) sink : bathroom

    (C) television : living room

    (D) trunk : attic

3. CELEBRATE : HAPPINESS ::

    (A) announce : birthday

    (B) report : injury

    ✓ (C) lament : sorrow

    (D) face : penalty

4. MARGARINE : BUTTER ::

    (A) cream : milk

    (B) lace : cotton

    ✓ (C) nylon : silk

    (D) egg : chicken

5. NEGLIGENT : REQUIREMENT ::

    (A) careful : position

    ✓ (B) remiss : duty

    (C) cautious : injury

    (D) cogent : task

6. GAZELLE : SWIFT ::

    (A) horse : slow

    (B) wolf : hungry

    ✓ (C) swan : graceful

    (D) elephant : gray

7. IGNOMINY : DISLOYALTY ::

    ✓ (A) acclaim : heroism

    (B) castigation : praise

    (C) death : victory

    (D) approbation : consecration

8. SATURNINE : MERCURIAL ::

    (A) Saturn : Venus

    (B) Apennines : Alps

    (C) redundant : wordy

    ✓ (D) allegro : adagio

7

9. ORANGE : MARMALADE ::
    (A) potato : vegetable
    (B) jelly : jam
    ✓ (C) tomato : ketchup
    (D) cake : picnic

10. BANISH : APOSTATE ::
    (A) reward : traitor
    ✓ (B) welcome : ally
    (C) remove : result
    (D) avoid : truce

11. CIRCLE : SPHERE ::
    ✓ (A) square : cube
    (B) balloon : jet plane
    (C) heaven : hell
    (D) wheel : orange

12. OPEN : SECRETIVE ::
    (A) mystery : detective
    (B) tunnel : toll
    ✓ (C) forthright : wily
    (D) better : best

13. AFFIRM : HINT ::
    (A) say : deny
    (B) assert : convince
    (C) confirm : reject
    ✓ (D) charge : insinuate

14. THROW : BALL ::
    (A) kill : bullet
    ✓ (B) shoot : gun
    (C) question : answer
    (D) hit : run

15. SPEEDY : GREYHOUND ::
    (A) innocent : lamb
    (B) animate : animal
    (C) voracious : tiger
    ✓ (D) sluggish : sloth

16. TRIANGLE : PYRAMID ::
    ✓ (A) cone : circle
    (B) corner : angle
    (C) rectangle : box
    (D) pentagon : quadrilateral

17. IMPEACH : DISMISS ::
    (A) arraign : convict
    (B) exonerate : charge
    ✓ (C) imprison : jail
    (D) plant : reap

18. EMULATE : MIMIC ::
    (A) slander : defame
    ✓ (B) praise : flatter
    (C) aggravate : promote
    (D) complain : condemn

19. HAND : NAIL ::
    ✓ (A) paw : claw
    (B) foot : toe
    (C) head : hair
    (D) ear : nose

20. SQUARE : DIAMOND ::
    (A) cube : sugar
    ✓ (B) circle : ellipse
    (C) innocence : jewelry
    (D) pentangle : square

Answers and Explanations

Practice Exercise 1

1. **(D)** An *oration* is a far more elaborate form of speech than a *chat*; a *banquet* is a far more elaborate form of meal than a *snack*.

2. **(C)** *Inclement* is the opposite of *clear*; *pertinent* is the opposite of *irrelevant*.

3. **(C)** *Flour* comes from *wheat*; *wine* comes from the *grape*.

4. **(D)** A characteristic of *iron* is that it is *common*; a characteristic of a *diamond* is that it is *rare*.

5. **(D)** A *contest* results in *victory*; *study* results in *knowledge*.

6. **(B)** *Diagnosis* comes after careful *analysis*; a *thesis* comes after thorough *research*.

7. **(B)** The *mare* is a parent of a *filly*; the *king* is a parent of a *prince*.

8. **(C)** A *recruit* is new to the *army*; a *convert* is new to a *religion*.

9. **(A)** *Opulence* is the same as *luxury*; *poverty* is the same as *penury*.

10. **(B)** The purpose of a *codicil* is to change a *will*; the purpose of an *amendment* is to change the *constitution*.

Practice Exercise 2

1. **(B)** To *intimidate* is to inspire *fear*; to *astonish* is to inspire *wonder*.

2. **(B)** A *stove* is often part of a *kitchen*; a *sink* is often part of a *bathroom*.

3. **(C)** To *celebrate* is to react with *happiness*; to *lament* is to react with *sorrow*.

4. **(C)** *Margarine* is a manufactured substitute for *butter*; *nylon* is a manufactured substitute for *silk*.

5. **(B)** Someone *negligent* doesn't fulfill a *requirement*; someone *remiss* doesn't fulfill his *duty*.

6. **(C)** A *gazelle* moves *swiftly*; a *swan* moves *gracefully*.

7. **(A)** One falls into *ignominy* if he shows *disloyalty*; one gains *acclaim* if he shows *heroism*.

8. **(D)** *Saturnine* and *mercurial* are antonyms; so are *allegro* and *adagio*.

9. **(C)** *Marmalade* is made from *oranges*; *ketchup* is made from *tomatoes*.

10. **(B)** An *apostate* is *banished* (sent away); an *ally* is *welcomed* (brought in).

11. **(A)** A *circle* is a type of *sphere*; a *square* is a type of *cube*.

12. **(C)** *Open* is the opposite of *secretive*; *forthright* is the opposite of *wily*.

13. **(D)** When you *affirm*, you are direct; when you *hint*, you are indirect. When you *charge*, you are direct; when you *insinuate*, you are indirect.

14. **(B)** One *throws* a *ball* and one *shoots* a *gun*.

7

15. **(D)** A *greyhound* is proverbially *speedy*; on the other hand, a *sloth* is proverbially *sluggish*.

16. **(C)** A *triangle* is a three-sided plane figure; a *pyramid* is a three-sided solid figure. A *rectangle* is a four-sided plane figure; a *box* is a four-sided solid figure.

17. **(A)** To *impeach* is to charge or challenge; if the impeachment proceedings are successful, the charged person is *dismissed*. To *arraign* is to call into court as a result of accusation; if the accusation is proved correct, the arraigned person is *convicted*.

18. **(B)** To *emulate* is to imitate another person's good points; to *mimic* is to imitate another person. To *praise* is to speak well of another person; to *flatter* is to praise another person.

19. **(A)** For people, the thin substance at the end of the *hands* are called *nails*; for animals, the horny sheaths at the end of the *paws* are called *claws*.

20. **(B)** A *diamond* is a partially compressed *square*; an *ellipse* is a partially compressed *circle*.

The Hour in Review

1. Verbal analogy questions test your knowledge of vocabulary and your ability to detect logical relationships between words.

2. The best answer to a verbal analogy question is the pair of words whose relationship is most similar to the relationship between the given pair of words.

3. To answer a verbal analogy question, first determine the relationship between the given pair of words, and then choose the pair of words that best fits that relationship.

HOUR 8

Effective Expressions

What You Will Learn in This Hour

Because language is a living, active thing, your grasp of correct and effective expression is best measured by a type of question that tests a multitude of grammatical skills. Effective expression questions draw upon your practical ability to discern and correct errors in grammar. Here are your goals for this hour:

- Learn what effective expression questions test.
- Learn how to approach effective expression questions.
- Practice effective expression questions.

What Is Being Tested?

Effective expression questions test the entire range of grammatical skills, including knowledge of correct grammar, spelling, word usage, and sentence formation. They also test reading comprehension and writing skills. Everything that you have learned so far will come into play when answering these questions. Even if you do not find effective expression questions on your civil service exam, studying the questions in this hour will be a great help in preparing for the entire verbal ability portion of the exam.

Make Connections

Before answering any of the practice questions, it will be helpful to turn back to Hour 3 and review the rules of grammar. If you have time, quickly review the spelling rules listed in Hour 4 as well.

Tackling Effective Expression Questions

In the effective expression portion of the exam, you are presented with a long passage. Some portions of the passage are underlined and numbered. Corresponding to each numbered portion are three different ways of saying the same thing. You must choose the answer that is the best way to phrase the expression.

Follow these steps to answer an effective expression question:

1. Read through the passage quickly to determine the sense of the passage.

2. Return to the first underlined portion.

3. Choose the best answer from the following criteria:

   • If you feel that there is an error in grammar, sentence structure, punctuation, or word usage in the underlined portion, mark the correct choice from the answers given.

   • If the underlined portion appears to be correct, but you believe that one of the alternatives would be more effective, mark that choice.

   • If you feel that the underlined portion is correct and the most effective choice, mark answer choice (A), NO CHANGE.

4. After answering quickly and to the best of your knowledge, go on to the next underlined portion.

8

Try a sample question:

If a <u>person were to try</u> stripping the

           1

disguises from actors while they play a

scene upon the stage, showing to the

audience <u>there real looks</u> and the

           2

faces they were <u>born with. Would</u>

           3

not such a one spoil the whole play?

Destroy the illusion and <u>any play was</u>

           4

<u>ruined.</u>

1. (A) NO CHANGE
    (B) Person were to try
    (C) Person was to try
    (D) person was to try

2. (A) NO CHANGE
    (B) their real looks
    (C) there Real Looks
    (D) their "real looks"

3. (A) NO CHANGE
    (B) born to—would
    (C) born. Would
    (D) born with, would

4. (A) NO CHANGE
    (B) any Play was ruined
    (C) any play is ruined?
    (D) any play is ruined.

In this example, the correct answers are:

1. (**A**) The passage is correct as shown; therefore, NO CHANGE is the best selection.
2. (**B**) The possessive pronoun is spelled *their*.
3. (**D**) The comma corrects the sentence fragment.
4. (**D**) The present tense *is* is consistent with the present tense *destroy*.

> **Tip**
> Remember to look for the best, most effective answer. Even if the underlined portion of the passage is technically correct, it may not be the best way to phrase the expression.

Workshop

In this workshop, you will try your hand at correcting three passages similar to the ones you will find on civil service tests.

Practice Exercise

DIRECTIONS: In each of the following passages, some portions are underlined and numbered. Corresponding to each numbered portion are three different ways of saying the same thing. If you feel that an underlined portion is correct and is stated as well as possible, mark letter (A), NO CHANGE. If you feel that there is an error in the underlined portion or if one of the alternatives would be more effective, choose the correct answer.

Passage I

The standardized educational or

psychological <u>tests, that are</u> widely

               1

used to aid in selecting, classifying,

assigning, or <u>promoting students,</u>

               2

employees, and military personnel have

been the target of recent attacks in

books, magazines, and <u>newspapers</u>

<u>that are printed every day.</u> The target is

               3

wrong, for in attacking the tests, critics

1. (A) NO CHANGE
    (B) tests that are
    (C) tests, which are
    (D) tests; which are

2. (A) NO CHANGE
    (B) promoting of students
    (C) promotion of students
    (D) promotion for students

3. (A) NO CHANGE
    (B) the daily press
    (C) newspapers that are
        published daily
    (D) the daily newspaper press

8

<u>revert attention from</u> the fault that
                4

<u>lays with illinformed</u> or incompetent
                5

users. The tests themselves are merely

<u>tools; with</u> characteristics that can be
        6

<u>assessed reasonably precise</u> under
                7

specified conditions. Whether the results

will be valuable, meaningless, or even

misleading <u>are dependent partly upon</u>
                8

the tool itself but largely upon the user.

4. (A) NO CHANGE
    (B) revert attention to
    (C) divert attention from
    (D) avert attention from

5. (A) NO CHANGE
    (B) lies with poorly-informed
    (C) lays with poor-informed
    (D) lies with ill-informed

6. (A) NO CHANGE
    (B) tools with
    (C) tools, possessed of
    (D) tools; whose

7. (A) NO CHANGE
    (B) assessed as to its reason-
        able precision
    (C) assessed reasonably and
        with precision
    (D) assessed with reasonable
        precision

8. (A) NO CHANGE
    (B) is dependent partly upon
    (C) depend partly upon
    (D) depends partly upon

Passage II

The forces that generate conditions

conducive to crime and <u>riots, are</u>

<u>stronger</u> in urban communities

     9

9. (A) NO CHANGE
     (B) rioting, are stronger
     (C) riots are more strong
     (D) riots are stronger

<u>then in rural areas.</u> Urban living is

     10

10. (A) NO CHANGE
     (B) then in rural communities
     (C) than in rural areas
     (D) then they are in the country

more anonymous <u>living, it</u> often

     11

11. (A) NO CHANGE
     (B) living. It
     (C) living; which
     (D) living. Because it

releases the individual from community

restraints more common in <u>tradition,</u>

     12

12. (A) NO CHANGE
     (B) traditional oriented
        societies
     (C) traditionally, oriented
        societies
     (D) tradition-oriented societies

<u>oriented societies.</u> <u>But</u> more

     13

13. (A) NO CHANGE
     (B) Moreover
     (C) Therefore
     (D) Besides

freedom from constraints and controls

also provides greater freedom to deviate.

In the more impersonalized, <u>formally,</u>

<u>controlled</u> urban society regulatory

     14

14. (A) NO CHANGE
     (B) formally controlled
     (C) formalized controlled
     (D) formally-controlled

orders of conduct are often directed by

distant bureaucrats. The police are

strangers <u>which execute</u> these

15

prescriptions on, at worst, an alien sub-

community and, at best, an <u>anonymous</u>

<u>and unknown</u> set of subjects. Minor

16

offensives in a small town or village are

often handled <u>without resort to</u> official

17

police action. As disputable as such

action may seem to be, <u>you will find it</u>

<u>results</u> in fewer recorded violations of

18

the law compared to the city.

Passage III

Human beings are born with a desire to

<u>communicate with</u> other human

19

beings, they satisfy this desire in many

20

ways. A smile communicates

<u>a friendly feeling,</u> a clenched

21

15. (A) NO CHANGE
     (B) they execute
     (C) executing
     (D) who conduct executions of

16. (A) NO CHANGE
     (B) anonymously unknown
     (C) anonymous
     (D) anonymous, unknown

17. (A) NO CHANGE
     (B) without their having to
         resort to
     (C) without needing
     (D) outside the limits of

18. (A) NO CHANGE
     (B) they say it results
     (C) you will say, "It results
     (D) it nonetheless results

19. (A) NO CHANGE
     (B) communicate to
     (C) communicate about
     (D) communicate

20. (A) NO CHANGE
     (B) beings. They
     (C) beings; and they
     (D) beings—who

21. (A) NO CHANGE
     (B) a friendly, feeling;
     (C) friendship,
     (D) a friendly feeling;

8

fist anger; tears, sorrow. From the first

22

days of life, <u>pain and hunger are</u>

23

<u>expressed by baby's</u> by cries and

actions. Gradually they add expressions

of pleasure and <u>smiling</u> for a familiar

24

face. Soon they begin to reach out

<u>for picking up.</u>

25

<u>Those people who are human beings</u>

26

 also use words to communicate.

Babies eventually learn the

language of <u>there</u> parents. If the

27

parents speak English, the baby will

learn to speak English. If the parents

22. (A) NO CHANGE
     (B) fist an angry feeling,
     (C) fist, anger,
     (D) fist, angriness,

23. (A) NO CHANGE
     (B) babies express pain or
         hunger
     (C) a baby's pain or hunger are
         expressed
     (D) pain and hunger is
         expressed by babies

24. (A) NO CHANGE
     (B) smiled
     (C) smiles
     (D) he may smile

25. (A) NO CHANGE
     (B) to pick up
     (C) and pick up
     (D) to be picked up

26. (A) NO CHANGE
     (B) (BEGIN new paragraph)
         Those people who are
         human beings
     (C) (BEGIN new paragraph)
         Human being babies
     (D) (BEGIN new paragraph)
         Human beings

27. (A) NO CHANGE
     (B) their
     (C) they're
     (D) OMIT

speak Spanish, <u>a Spanish-speaking baby</u>

28

will result. An <u>American baby</u> who is

29

taken from his natural parents and

brought up by foster parents who speak

Chinese, Urdu, Swahili, or any other

language <u>will talk</u> the language of the

30

people around him instead of English.

28.   (A) NO CHANGE
        (B) their baby will speak
            Spanish.
        (C) the baby will learn spanish.
        (D) there baby will speak
            Spanish.

29.   (A) NO CHANGE
        (B) American Baby
        (C) american baby
        (D) american-born baby

30.   (A) NO CHANGE
        (B) will be speaking
        (C) will speak
        (D) will talk of

Answers and Explanations

1.   **(B)** The phrase following *tests* is an essential part of this sentence and should not be set off by commas.

2.   **(A)** This is correct.

3.   **(B)** The three words *the daily press* say everything that is said by the other, more wordy choices.

4.   **(C)** *Divert*, meaning "to turn from one course to another," is the most appropriate choice. *Revert* means "to return" and *avert* means "to turn away or prevent."

5.   **(D)** The present tense of the verb *to lie*, meaning "belonging to," is required here.

6.   **(B)** It is not necessary to separate the prepositional phrase from the rest of the sentence.

7.   **(D)** This is the clearest and least-awkward choice.

8.   **(D)** The subject of the verb here is implied—the subject is actually the significance of the results. Thus, a singular verb is needed, and choice (D) gives the only singular verb construction that is spelled correctly.

9.   **(D)** Do not use a comma to separate a subject and a verb (except when the subject contains a nonessential clause, an appositive, or another phrase that is set off by two commas).

10.   **(C)** *Than*, a conjunction, is used after the comparative degree of an adjective or adverb. Then, an adverb, means "at that time" or "next."

11. **(B)** To correct this run-on sentence, it is necessary to add a period after *living*. Beginning the next sentence with *Because* creates a sentence fragment, rather than a complete sentence.

12. **(D)** Use a hyphen in unit modifiers immediately preceding the word or words modified. *Tradition-oriented* is a unit modifier.

13. **(A)** *But* is correct to indicate a contrasting idea. *Moreover* and *besides* mean "in addition to what has been said." *Therefore* means "for that reason."

14. **(B)** Do not use punctuation between the terms of a unit modifier when the first term is an adverb modifying the second term.

15. **(C)** The participle *executing*—meaning "carrying out," not "putting to death"—is the correct word for this sentence. *Which* refers to things, not to people. Choice (B) creates a run-on sentence.

16. **(C)** *Anonymous* means "unknown."

17. **(A)** This is the most concise and correct way to make this statement.

18. **(D)** As written, this sentence illustrates a needless shift in subject (from *action* to *you*), which results in a dangling modifier.

19. **(A)** This is correct.

20. **(B)** As written, this is a run-on sentence. To correct it, add a period after *beings* and start a new sentence with *They*.

21. **(D)** Use a semicolon to separate sentence parts of equal rank if one or more of these parts is subdivided by commas.

22. **(C)** Use a comma to indicate the omission of a word or words. This phrase actually means "a clenched fist (communicates) anger."

23. **(B)** Avoid the shift from the active to the passive voice. The possessive *baby's* is incorrectly substituted for the plural *babies*.

24. **(C)** *And* is used to connect similar grammatical elements, in this case the noun *expressions* and the noun *smiles*.

25. **(D)** The present infinitive is correct, because the action of the infinitive is present or future in relation to the action of the finite verb *begin*.

26. **(D)** The introduction of a new topic—the use of words to communicate—indicates the need for a new paragraph. *Human beings* are people, and so the phrase *Those people who are* is unnecessary.

27. **(B)** The possessive pronoun needed here is *their*. *There* refers to place, and *they're* is a contraction for "they are."

28. **(B)** A comparison is being drawn between English- and Spanish-speaking families. The two sentences that form the comparison should be parallel in structure. *Spanish* is a proper noun and must begin with a capital letter.

29. **(A)** *American* is a proper noun and should be capitalized; *baby* is merely a noun and needs no capital letter.

30. **(C)** *Speak* the *language* is idiomatically correct.

The Hour in Review

8

1. Effective expression questions test many skills: grammar, vocabulary, spelling, sentence formation, reading comprehension, and writing.

2. In effective expression questions, the correct answer is the one that best expresses the phrase or sentence; even if two or more answers are technically correct, only one will be the most effective answer.

3. Reviewing what you have already learned—grammar rules, spelling rules, vocabulary, and sentence completions—is the best way to study for effective expression questions.

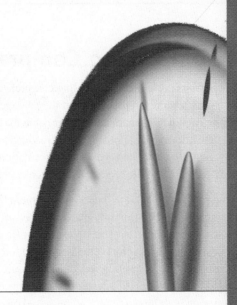

HOUR 9

Reading Comprehension

What You Will Learn in This Hour

It might seem that reading comprehension is adequately tested in the civil service exam itself. Without being able to read and understand not only the complex sets of directions, but also the tricky questions posed on some tests, you can't do well on the exam. Nonetheless, most civil service exams also test your ability to read a passage, understand the point being made, and answer questions based on what is said in the passage. This hour will teach you strategies for answering those kinds of reading comprehension questions. Here are your goals for this hour:

- Learn the types of reading-based questions found on civil service exams.
- Learn how to approach reading comprehension questions.
- Learn strategies for improving reading comprehension.
- Practice reading comprehension questions.

Kinds of Reading Comprehension Questions

Some exams present classic reading comprehension questions that provide a passage and then ask questions on the details of the passage and, perhaps, on its meaning. Other exams require candidates to indicate proper behavior based on their reading of printed procedures and regulations. Still another type of reading-based question requires candidates to reason and choose the next steps based on information presented in a passage. There are nearly as many variations of the reading-based question as there are test makers.

In the past few years, the federal government has introduced a new style of reading comprehension question into many of its exams. The reading selection itself is very short, and it is followed by only one question. At first glance, the task is deceptively simple. However, the paragraph is often dense with information and difficult to absorb. The question may be phrased in a circular, oblique, or negative fashion. Total concentration is needed for answering this type of reading question. You will get the opportunity to practice on both this type of reading-based question and on the classic reading comprehension question at the end of the hour.

Most often, you will be given a reading passage and then asked to answer a series of questions based on the passage. The following are the most common kinds of questions asked:

- **Question of fact or detail.** You may have to mentally rephrase or rearrange, but you should find the answer stated in the body of the passage.

- **Best title or main idea.** The answer may be obvious, but the incorrect choices to the "main idea" question are often half-truths that are easily confused with the main idea. They may misstate the idea, omit part of the idea, or even offer a supporting idea quoted directly from the text. The correct answer is the one that covers the largest part of the selection.

- **Interpretation.** This type of question asks you what the selection means, not just what it says. On police examples, questions based on definitions of crimes fall into this category, for example.

- **Vocabulary.** Some civil service reading passages directly or indirectly ask the meanings of certain words used in the passage.

- **Inference.** This is the most difficult type of reading comprehension question. It asks you to go beyond what the passage says and predict what might happen next. Your answer must be based on the information in the passage and your own common sense, but not on any other information that you may have about the subject.

> **Note**
> Don't worry if you're unfamiliar with the subject discussed in the reading selection. You don't need to have any knowledge about the subject of the passage because the answer to the question is always given in the passage itself.

Tackling Reading Comprehension Questions

Success with reading-based questions depends on more than reading comprehension. You must also know how to draw the answers from the reading selection and be able to distinguish the best answer from a number of answers that all seem to be good ones, or from a number of answers that all seem to be wrong.

To answer a reading comprehension question, follow these steps:

1. Read the questions—not the answer choices, just the questions themselves—before you read the passage. The questions will alert you to look for certain details, ideas, and points of view in the passage. Underline key words in the questions to help direct your attention as you read.

2. Skim the passage rapidly to get an idea of its subject matter, its organization, and the point being made. If key words or ideas pop out at you, underline them, but don't consciously search out details at this point.

3. Now read the selection again carefully with comprehension as your main goal. Give attention to details and point of view. Underline important words.

4. Return to the questions and read the first question carefully. Determine exactly what is being asked.

5. Read all the answer choices. Don't rush to choose the first answer that might be correct.

6. Eliminate choices that clearly conflict with the paragraph.

7. If you still have two or more choices left, look for the specific section of the passage that covers the information given in each of the choices.

8. Compare the facts carefully until you can eliminate the remaining incorrect choices.

9. Don't spend too much time on any one question. If looking back at the passage doesn't help you find the answer, choose from among the remaining answers and move on to the next question.

> **Tip**
> Be alert for hints as to what the author of the passage thinks is important. Phrases such as "note that," "of importance is," and "do not overlook" give clues to what the writer is stressing.

> **Caution**
> A major cause of error on reading comprehension questions is misreading questions, so read each question carefully and be sure that you understand what it's asking. Watch for negative or all-inclusive words that can greatly affect your answer, like "always," "never," "all," "only," "every," "absolutely," "completely," "none," "entirely," and "no."

Improving Reading Comprehension

Before you begin to devote attention to strategies for dealing with reading-based questions, give some thought to your reading habits and skills. How well do you read? Do you concentrate? Do you get the point on your first reading? Do you notice details?

Between now and test day, resolve to improve your reading concentration and comprehension. Your daily newspaper provides excellent material to practice reading comprehension skills. Here are some tips for using your newspaper to improve your reading comprehension:

- Make a point of reading all the way through any article that you begin. Don't be satisfied with the first paragraph or two.

- Read with a pencil in hand. Underline details and ideas that seem to be crucial to the meaning of the article. Notice points of view, arguments, and supporting information.

- When you finish the article, summarize it for yourself. Do you know the purpose of the article? The main idea presented? The attitude of the writer? The points over which there is controversy? Did you find certain information lacking?

- Skim back over your underlinings. Did you focus on important words and ideas? Did you read with comprehension?

As you repeat this process day after day, you'll find that your reading will become more efficient. You will read with greater understanding and will get more from your newspaper.

> **Caution**
> Avoid inserting your judgments into your answers. Even if you disagree with the author or even if you spot a factual error in the passage, you must answer based on what is stated or implied in the passage.

Workshop

In this workshop, you'll apply the strategies you learned in this hour to a variety of reading comprehension passages and questions.

Practice Exercise

> **DIRECTIONS:** Answer each question on the basis of the information stated or implied in the accompanying reading passage.

Passage 1

The recipient gains an impression of a business letter before beginning to read the message. Facts that give a good first impression include margins and spacings that
(5) are visually pleasing, formal parts of the letter that are correctly placed according to the style of the letter, copy that is free of errors, and transcript that is even and clear. The problem for the typist is how to
(10) produce that first, positive impression of her work.

There are several general rules that a typist can follow when she wishes to prepare a properly spaced letter on a sheet of
(15) letterhead. The width of a letter should ordinarily not be less than four inches, nor more than six inches. The side margins should also have a proportionate relation to the bottom margin, as well as the space

(20) between the letterhead and the body of the letter. Usually the most appealing arrangement is when the side margins are even, and the bottom margin is slightly wider than the side margins. In some offices,
(25) however, a standard line length is used for all business letters, and the typist then varies the spacing between the date line and the inside address according to the length of the letter.

1. The best title for the preceding paragraph is

(A) "Writing Office Letters."

(B) "Making Good First Impressions."

(C) "Judging Well-Typed Letters."

(D) "Proper Spacing for Office Letters."

2.   Which of the following might be considered the way that people quickly judge the quality of a business letter?

(A) by measuring the margins to see if they are correct

✓ (B) by looking at the placement of elements in the letter for overall visual appeal

(C) by scanning the body of the letter for meaning

(D) by checking for misspelled names in the letter

3.   What would definitely be undesirable as the average line length of a typed letter?

(A) four inches

(B) five inches

(C) six inches

✓ (D) seven inches

4.   When the line length is kept standard, the secretary

(A) does not have to vary the spacing at all because this also is standard.

✓ (B) adjusts the spacing between the date line and inside address for different lengths of letters.

(C) uses the longest line as a guideline for spacing between the date line and inside address.

(D) varies the number of spaces between the lines.

Passage 2

Cotton fabrics treated with XYZ Process have features that make them far superior to any previously known flame-retardant-treated cotton fabrics.

(5)   XYX Process-treated fabrics endure repeated laundering and dry cleaning; they are glow-resistant as well as flame-resistant; when exposed to flames or intense heat they form tough, pliable, and protective
(10)   chars; they are inert physiologically to persons handling or exposed to the fabric; they are only slightly heavier than untreated fabrics and are susceptible to further wet and dry finishing treatments. In
(15)   addition, the treated fabrics exhibit little or no adverse change in feel, texture, and appearance and are shrink-, rot-, and mildew-resistant. The treatment reduces strength only slightly. Finished fabrics
(20)   have "easy care" properties in that they are wrinkle-resistant and dry rapidly.

5.   It is most accurate to state that the author in the preceding selection presents

✓ (A) facts but reaches no conclusion concerning the value of the process.

(B) a conclusion concerning the value of the process and facts to support that conclusion.

(C) a conclusion concerning the value of the process unsupported by facts.

(D) neither facts nor conclusions, but merely describes the process.

6.   Of the following articles, which is the XYZ Process most suitable for?

(A) nylon stockings

(B) woolen shirt

(C) silk tie

✓ (D) cotton bedsheet

9

7. Of the following aspects of the XYZ Process, which is not discussed in the preceding selection?

    (A) costs

    (B) washability

    (C) wearability

    (D) the human body

8. The main reason for treating a fabric with XYZ Process is to

    (A) prepare the fabric for other wet and dry finishing treatment.

    (B) render it shrink-, rot-, and mildew-resistant.

    (C) increase its weight and strength.

    (D) reduce the chance that it will catch fire.

9. Which of the following would be considered a minor drawback of the XYZ Process?

    (A) It forms chars when exposed to flame.

    (B) It makes fabrics mildew-resistant.

    (C) It adds to the weight of fabrics.

    (D) It is compatible with other finishing treatments.

Passage 3

Language performs an essentially social function. It helps us communicate and achieve a great measure of concerted action. Words are signs that have signifi-
(5) cance by convention, and the people who do not adopt the conventions simply fail to communicate. They do not "get along," and a social force arises that encourages them to achieve the correct associations.

(10) By "correct" we mean as used by other members of the social group. Some of the vital points about language are brought home to an English visitor to America, and vice versa, because our vocabularies are
(15) nearly the same, but not quite.

10. As defined in the preceding selection, usage of a word is "correct" when it is

    (A) defined in standard dictionaries.

    (B) used by the majority of persons throughout the world who speak the same language.

    (C) used by a majority of educated persons who speak the same language.

    (D) used by other persons with whom we are associating.

11. The author is concerned primarily with the

    (A) meaning of words.

    (B) pronunciation of words.

    (C) structure of sentences.

    (D) origin and development of language.

12. The main language problem of an English visitor to America stems from the fact that an English person

    (A) uses some words that have different meanings for Americans.

    (B) has different social values than the Americans.

    (C) has had more exposure to non-English speaking persons than Americans have had.

    (D) pronounces words differently from the way Americans do.

Passage 4

Since almost every office has some contact with data-processed records, a senior stenographer should have some understanding of the basic operations of
(5) data processing. Data-processing systems now handle about one-third of all office paperwork. On punched cards, magnetic tape, or on other mediums, data are recorded before being fed into the compu-
(10) ter for processing. A machine such as the keypunch is used to convert the data written on the source document into the coded symbols on punched cards or tapes. After data has been converted, it must be
(15) verified to guarantee absolute accuracy of conversion. In this manner, data becomes a permanent record that can be read by electronic computers that compare, store, compute, and otherwise process data at
(20) high speeds.

One key person in a computer installation is a programmer, the man or woman who puts business and scientific problems into special symbolic languages that can
(25) be read by the computer. Jobs done by the computer range all the way from payroll operations to chemical process control, but most computer applications are directed toward management data. About half of
(30) the programmers employed by business come to their positions with college degrees; the remaining half are promoted to their positions without regard to education from within the organization on the basis
(35) of demonstrated ability.

13. The best title for the preceding selection is

(A) "The Stenographer as Data Processor."

(B) "The Relation of Keypunching to Stenography."

(C) "Understanding Data Processing."

(D) "Permanent Office Records."

14. A senior stenographer should understand the basic operations of data processing because

(A) almost every office today has contact with data-processed records by computer.

(B) any office worker may be asked to verify the accuracy of data.

(C) most offices are involved in the production of permanent records.

(D) data can be converted into computer language by typing on a keypunch.

15. The data that the computer understands is most often expressed

(A) as a scientific programming language.

(B) as records or symbols punched on tape, cards, or other mediums.

(C) as records on cards.

(D) as records on tape.

16. Computers are used most often to handle

(A) management data.

(B) problems of higher education.

(C) the control of chemical processes.

(D) payroll operations.

17. Computer programming is taught in many colleges and business schools. The preceding selection implies that programmers in industry

(A) must have professional training.

(B) need professional training to advance.

(C) must have at least a college education to do adequate programming tasks.

(D) do not need college education to do programming work.

18. Data to be processed by computer should be

(A) recent.

(B) complete.

(C) basic.

(D) verified.

Passage 5

The modern conception of the economic role of the public sector (government), as distinct from the private sector, is that every level of government is a link
(5) in the economic process. Government's contribution to political and economic welfare must, however, be evaluated not merely in terms of its technical efficiency, but also in the light of its acceptability to
(10) a particular society at a particular state of political and economic development. Even in a dictatorship, this principle is formally observed, although the authorities usually destroy the substance by presuming to
(15) interpret to the public its collective desires.

19. The paragraph best supports the statement that

(A) it is not true that some levels of government are not links in the economic process.

(B) all dictatorships observe the same economic principles as other governments.

(C) all links in the economic process are levels of government.

(D) the contributions of some levels of government do not need to be evaluated for technical efficiency and acceptability to society.

(E) no links in the economic process are institutions other than levels of government.

Passage 6

All property is classified as either personal property or real property, but not both. In general, if something is classified as personal property, it is transient and
(5) transportable in nature, while real property is not. Things such as leaseholds, animals, money, and intangible and other moveable goods are examples of personal property. Permanent buildings and land,
(10) on the other hand, are fixed in nature and are not transportable.

20. The paragraph best supports the statement that

(A) if something is classified as personal property, it is not transient and transportable in nature.

(B) some forms of property are considered to be both personal property and real property.

(C) permanent buildings and land are real property.

(D) permanent buildings and land are personal property.

(E) tangible goods are considered to be real property.

Answers and Explanations

1. **(D)** The best title for any selection is the one that takes in all the ideas presented without being too broad or too narrow. Choice (D) provides the most inclusive title for this passage. A look at the other choices shows you why. Choice (A) can be eliminated because the passage discusses typing a letter, not writing one. Although the first paragraph states that a letter should make a good first impression, the passage is clearly devoted to the letter, not the first impression, so choice (B) can be eliminated. Choice (C) puts the emphasis on the wrong aspect of the typewritten letter. The passage concerns how to prepare a properly spaced letter, not how to judge one.

2. **(B)** Both placement of elements and visual appeal are mentioned in the first paragraph as ways to judge the quality of a typed letter. The first paragraph states that the margins should be "visually pleasing" in relation to the body of the letter, but that doesn't imply margins of a particular measure, so choice (A) is incorrect.

3. **(D)** This answer comes from the information provided in the second paragraph, that the width of a letter "should not be less than four inches, nor more than six inches." According to this rule, seven inches is an undesirable line length.

4. **(B)** The answer to this question is stated in the last sentence of the passage. When a standard line length is used, the typist "varies the spacing between the date line and the inside address according to the length of the letter." The passage offers no support for any other choice.

5. **(B)** This is a combination main idea and interpretation question. If you cannot answer this question readily, reread the passage. The author clearly thinks that the XYZ Process is terrific and says so in the first sentence. The rest of the selection presents a wealth of facts to support the initial claim.

6. **(D)** At first glance, you might think that this is an inference question requiring you to make a judgment based upon the few drawbacks of the process. Closer reading, however, shows you that there is no contest for the correct answer here. This is a simple question of fact. The XYZ Process is a treatment for cotton fabrics.

7. **(A)** Your underlinings should help you with this question of fact. Cost is not mentioned; all other aspects of the XYZ Process are. If you are having trouble finding mention of the effect of the XYZ Process on the human body, look up *inert* and *physiologically* in the dictionary.

8. **(D)** This is a main idea question. You must distinguish between the main idea and the supporting and incidental facts.

9. **(C)** Obviously a drawback is a negative feature. The selection mentions only two negative features. The treatment reduces strength slightly, and it makes fabrics slightly heavier than untreated fabrics. Only one of these negative features is offered among the answer choices.

10. **(D)** The answer to this question is stated in the next-to-last sentence of the passage.

11. **(A)** This main idea question is an easy one to answer. You should have readily eliminated all the wrong choices.

12. **(A)** This is a question of fact. The phrasing of the question is quite different from the phrasing of the last sentence, but the meaning is the same. You may have found this reading selection more difficult to absorb than some of the others, but you should have had no difficulty answering this question by eliminating the wrong answers.

13. **(C)** Choosing the best title for this passage is not easy. Although the senior stenographer is mentioned in the first sentence, the passage isn't really concerned with stenographers or with their relationship to keypunching—eliminate choices (A) and (B). Permanent office records are mentioned in the passage, but only along with other equally important uses for data processing—eliminate choice (D). When in doubt, the most general title is usually correct.

14. **(A)** This is a question of fact. Any one of the answer choices could be correct, but the answer is given almost verbatim in the first sentence. Take advantage of answers that are handed to you.

15. **(B)** This is a question of fact, but it's a tricky one. The program language is a symbolic language, not a scientific one. Reread carefully and eliminate choice (A). Choice (B) includes more of the information in the selection than either choice (C) or (D) and thus is the best answer.

16. **(A)** This is a question of fact. The answer is stated in the next-to-last sentence.

17. **(D)** Remember, you are answering the questions based on the information given in the passage. In spite of any information you may have to the contrary, the last sentence of the passage states that half the programmers employed in business achieved their positions by moving up from the ranks without regard to education.

18. **(D)** Judicious underlining proves very helpful in finding the correct answer to this question buried in the middle of the passage. Since any one of the answers might be correct, the way to deal with this question is to skim the underlined words in the passage, eliminate those that aren't mentioned, and choose the appropriate answer.

19. **(A)** This answer can be inferred from the first sentence of the paragraph, which states that "every level of government is a link in the economic process." It can be deduced that its contradictory statement, "some levels of government are not links in the economic process," cannot be true. Choice (B) isn't supported by the paragraph because it goes beyond the information given. The third sentence of the paragraph states that a dictatorship observes (at least formally) one of the same principles as other governments. It cannot be concluded from this that dictatorships observe more than this one principle in common with other governments.

Choices (C) and (E) represent incorrect interpretations of the information given in the first sentence, which states that "every level of government is a link in the economic process." You can't infer from this statement that "all links in the economic process are levels of government," only that some are. We know that the category "all levels of government" is contained in the category "links in the economic process," but we don't know if links in the economic process exist that are not levels of government. In regard to choice (E), it cannot be inferred that "no links in the economic process are institutions other than levels of government," because that would be the same as saying that all links in the economic process are levels of government.

Choice (D) isn't supported by the passage because the second sentence implies that the contributions of *all* levels of government must be evaluated for technical efficiency and acceptability to society. There is nothing to suggest that the contributions of some levels of society do *not* need to be evaluated.

Note that in this question, the correct answer follows from one sentence in the paragraph, the first sentence. The rest of the paragraph presents additional information about the public sector and its effects on society that is relevant to the discussion but not necessary to make the inference. Part of your task is to understand what you read and then to discern which conclusions follow logically from statements in the passage. Consequently, you will find some questions necessitate the use of all or most of the statements presented in the paragraph, while others, such as this one, require only one statement to infer the correct answer.

20. (**C**) The answer can be inferred from information contained in the first, second, and fourth sentences. The first sentence is a disjunction; that is, it presents two mu-

tually exclusive alternatives—"all property is classified as either personal property or real property, but not both." The second sentence states that "if something is classified as personal property, it is transient and transportable in nature." The fourth sentence states that "permanent buildings and land…are fixed in nature and are not transportable." You can conclude that, since permanent buildings and land are not transient and transportable in nature, they are not personal property. In view of the disjunction in the first sentence, it can be seen that they must be real property.

Choice (A) is incorrect because it contradicts the information presented in the second sentence. Choice (B) is incorrect because it contradicts the first sentence, which states that "all property is classified as either personal property or real property, but not both."

Choice (D) contradicts the information presented in the second and fourth sentences. The second sentence states that "if something is classified as personal property, it is transient and transportable in nature." The fourth sentence indicates that permanent buildings and land don't have these qualities. Therefore, you can conclude that they are not personal property.

Choice (E) seems to be derived from the third sentence, which says that intangible goods are examples of personal property. However, you can't conclude from this statement that tangible goods are real property. In fact, the third sentence gives examples of tangible goods that are personal property.

The Hour in Review

1. Reading comprehension questions can take many forms; based on a passage, you might be asked to find the main idea, answer fact-based questions, make inferences, or interpret the meaning.

2. If you approach a reading selection logically, skim it for meaning and then read it closely for comprehension, underlining key points. You will be able to answer the questions based on the selection more quickly and accurately.

3. When answering reading-based questions, read the questions carefully and look for clues that can help you arrive at the correct answer.

4. You can start improving your reading comprehension in preparation for the exam by practicing reading and underlining key points in the newspaper articles that you read.

9

HOUR 10

Testing Judgment, Communication, Observation, and Memory Skills

What You Will Learn in This Hour

Civil service exams identify those candidates who have the aptitude to learn the job easily and do it well. Depending on the position that you are applying for, you may be asked to answer exam questions that fall outside the standard verbal ability questions. These questions are designed to assess your judgment, communication, observation, and memory skills, which may be necessary for many government positions such as police officers, firefighters, correction officers, court officers, and the like. In this hour, you will learn about these kinds of questions and practice answering them. Here are your goals for this hour:

- Learn how to answer judgment questions.
- Learn how to answer communication questions.
- Learn how to answer observation and memory questions.

Answering Judgment Questions

Good judgment is a necessary skill for many positions in federal, state, and local government. Even the entry-level employee who works under close supervision has occasions when he or she must rely on his or her own good judgment in dealing with an emergency situation—or in choosing priorities when there is no supervisor to consult. Almost all multiple-choice civil service exams include some questions designed to measure judgment, either directly or indirectly. For test-taking purposes, judgment is defined as a process of combining knowledge and understanding with common sense.

To recognize judgment questions and understand how to answer them, try the following practice exercises. You must read the passage and choose the best answer for the question asked. The correct answers and explanations of those answers follow the set of practice questions.

Caution
Even though judgment questions resemble reading comprehension questions, they are different in that you must choose the best answer based on your accumulated knowledge and common sense. The answer will not necessarily be given in the reading selection. Clues to the correct answer, however, may be found in the reading passage, so reading comprehension will play a large part in answering judgment questions correctly.

Practice Judgment Questions

1. Decisions about handcuffing or restraining inmates are often up to the correction officers involved. An officer is legally responsible for exercising good judgment and for taking necessary precautions to prevent harm both to the inmate involved and to others. In which one of the following situations is handcuffing or other physical restraint most likely to be needed?

    (A) An inmate seems to have lost control of his senses and is banging his fists repeatedly against the bars of his cell.

    (B) During the past two weeks, an inmate has deliberately tried to start three fights with other inmates.

    (C) An inmate claims to be sick and refuses to leave his cell for a scheduled meal.

    (D) During the night, an inmate begins to shout and sing, disturbing the sleep of other inmates.

2.   While you are working on a routine assignment, a coworker asks you to help her
for a few minutes so that she can complete an assignment that has top priority
and must be completed immediately. Of
the following, the best action for you to
take should be to

(A) tell her to find somebody who does
not look busy and ask that person for
help.

(B) tell her you will help her as soon as
you complete your own work.

(C) help her to complete her assignment
and then go back to your work.

(D) tell her that your work is as important to you as her work is to her, and
continue to work on your own assignment.

3.   A police officer stationed along the route
of a parade has been ordered not to allow
cars to cross the route while the parade is
in progress. An ambulance driver on an
emergency run attempts to drive an ambulance across the route while the parade
is passing. Under these circumstances, the
officer should

(A) ask the driver to wait while the officer calls headquarters and obtains a
decision.

(B) stop the parade long enough to per-
mit the ambulance to cross the street.

(C) direct the ambulance driver to the
shortest detour available, which will
add at least ten minutes to the run.

(D) hold up the ambulance in accordance
with the order.

4.   An office worker frequently complains to
the building custodian that her office is
poorly lighted. The best action for the
building custodian to follow is to

(A) ignore the complaints because they
come from a habitual crank.

(B) inform the worker that illumination
is a fixed item built into the building
originally and evidently is the result
of faulty planning by the architect.

(C) request a licensed electrician to install
additional ceiling lights.

(D) investigate for faulty illumination features in the room, such as dirty lamp
globes and incorrect lamp wattage.

5.   Suppose that one of your neighbors walks
into the police precinct where you are an
administrative aide and asks you to make
100 photocopies of a flyer he intends to
distribute in the neighborhood. Of the following, what action should you take in this
situation?

(A) Pretend that you do not know the person and order him to leave the building.

(B) Call a police officer and report the
person for attempting to make illegal
use of police equipment.

(C) Tell the person that you will make the
copies when you are off duty.

(D) Explain that you cannot use police
equipment for non-police work.

10

6. A police officer, walking a beat at 3 a.m., notices heavy smoke coming out of a top-floor window of a large apartment building. Out of the following, the action the officer should take first is to

   (A) make certain that there really is a fire.
   (B) enter the building and warn all the occupants of the apartment building.
   (C) attempt to extinguish the fire before it gets out of control.
   ✓ (D) call the fire department.

7. An elevator inspector on routine inspection for the Building Department notices a number of dangerous situations in the basement of the building she is in. Of the following conditions that she notices, which is the most dangerous and should be reported immediately?

   ↙ (A) Gas is leaking from a broken pipe.
   (B) The sewer pipe is broken.
   (C) Water is seeping into the basement.
   (D) The basement is unlighted.

8. There are times when an employee of one city department should notify and seek assistance from employees of another department. A parking enforcement agent is checking meters on a busy one-way street. Of the following situations he notices, which should he report immediately?

   (A) A rat runs out of a building and into the storm sewer across the street.
   ↙ (B) A wire is dangling over the sidewalk, giving off sparks.
   (C) A car is parked directly in front of a hydrant.
   (D) Two men are sitting on the front steps of a building sharing a marijuana joint.

Answers and Explanations

1. (**A**) The inmate who repeatedly bangs his fists against the bars of his cell is in immediate danger of causing himself bodily harm. The inmate must be restrained. The other inmates require attention, and their situations must be dealt with, but they do not require physical restraint.

2. (**C**) There are a number of points to take into consideration: Your own task is described as routine; the coworker's assignment is described as one that has top priority; and the coworker has asked for only a few minutes of your time. If you were involved in "rush" work yourself, you might refuse to help until you had finished your own task, but under these circumstances, help get the priority work done.

A side benefit to be considered here is maintaining a good relationship with the coworker, so that you, too, may request assistance at some time when your job demands it.

3. (**B**) Without any knowledge of police rules, common sense dictates that saving of lives is the number 1 priority. An ambulance on an emergency run is on a mission to save a life. Lifesaving takes precedence over the desire for an uninterrupted parade, despite the officer's prior orders.

4. (**D**) The repeated complaints may be quite legitimate if the lighting problem has not been corrected. Do not dismiss the office worker as a "crank." The custodian should

check out the fixtures personally before calling in an electrician. Costs can be held down by having house staff perform those tasks for which they are qualified.

5. **(D)** Where calm, reasoned explanation is offered as an answer choice, it is nearly always the correct answer. There is no need to be impolite or hostile to the neighbor. He may not even realize that he is asking you to do something that is not permitted. He will respect you for obeying the rules.

6. **(D)** A police officer is a police officer and not a firefighter. Eliminate choices (A) and (C) at once. It is the job of the firefighters to ascertain whether or not there really is a fire and to put it out. Since the building is a large one and fires spread rapidly, the practical move is to call the fire department immediately rather than running through the building alone trying to rouse all the occupants. Firefighters will have greater manpower to do this efficiently and are trained in nighttime rousing procedures.

7. **(A)** Leaking gas can be ignited, causing a fire. If a large amount of gas collects in the basement and is ignited, an explosion and fire are likely. This is the greatest hazard. The broken sewer pipe and the water seepage can create health hazards and should be reported and repaired, but these corrections do not represent the same emergency situations as the gas leak. An unlit basement is also a safety hazard, but is even less of an emergency.

8. **(B)** The most urgent hazard is that caused by the sparking wire. A quick call to the Police Department will get the area sealed off and a repair crew to attend to the wire. The Health Department could be notified of rodents in the building, but pest infestation is a chronic problem rather than an emergency. The parking enforcement agent can ticket the illegally parked car. The two men sharing one joint pose no immediate danger.

10

Answering Communication Skill Questions

No one works entirely alone. Every person must at times communicate information to someone else. The communication may be in the form of written memos or reports, or it may be oral. No matter what form the communication takes, it must be clear and readily understood. It must convey all necessary information in a usable form.

Most city civil service exams include some measure of a candidate's ability to organize and communicate information. Where the communication is likely to be oral, such as a telephone call to a central post, communication questions offer a set of facts and ask how you would best organize those facts into a clear and accurate report. The following practice questions will help you answer this type of question, which measures your oral communication skills. The correct answers and explanations follow the practice questions.

> **Note**
> Grammar and English usage questions, such as those found in Hour 3 and Hour 8, also measure communication skills. These questions often appear on exams for positions that require written communication skills.

Practice Communication Skill Questions

1. Police Officer Franks arrives at the scene of a frame, two-family house in Brooklyn and observes flames leaping from the door onto the porch. A woman on the sidewalk gives him a description of a man she saw running from the house just before she noticed the fire. The information is:

    - Place of Occurrence: 1520 Clarendon Road, Brooklyn
    - Time of Occurrence: 6:32 a.m.
    - Type of Building: two-family frame dwelling
    - Event: fire, suspected arson
    - Suspect: male, white, approx. 6-ft, wearing blue jeans
    - Witness: Mary Smith of 1523 Clarendon Road, Brooklyn

    Officer Franks is about to radio an alert for the suspect. Which of the following expresses the information *most clearly and accurately?*

    (A) At 6:32 a.m., Mary Smith of 1523 Clarendon Road, Brooklyn, saw a white male wearing approximately 6-ft blue jeans running from the building across the street.

    (B) A white male wearing blue jeans ran from the house at 1520 Clarendon Road at 6:32 a.m. Mary Smith saw him.

    (C) At 6:32 a.m., a 6-ft white male wearing blue jeans ran from a burning two-family frame structure at 1520 Clarendon Road, Brooklyn. He was observed by a neighbor, Mary Smith.

    (D) A two-family frame house is on fire at 1520 Clarendon Road in Brooklyn. A white male in blue jeans probably did it. Mary Smith saw him run.

2. A woman runs to the token clerk at the platform of the subway station to report that her purse was just snatched. She gives the following information to the token clerk:

- Time of Occurrence: 1:22 a.m.

- Place of Occurrence: uptown-bound platform, 59th Street Station, 7th Avenue line

- Victim: Juana Martinez

- Crime: purse-snatching

- Description of Suspect: unknown, fled down steps to lower platform

The token clerk is about to call for assistance from the transit police. Which of the following expresses the information *most clearly and accurately?*

(A) Juana Martinez had her purse snatched on the subway platform at 59th Street Station. She did not see him.

(B) A purse was just snatched by a man who ran down the steps. This is the 7th Avenue token booth at 59th Street Station. Her name is Juana Martinez.

(C) It is 1:22 a.m. The person who snatched Juana Martinez' purse is downstairs at 59th Street Station.

(D) This is the 59th Street Station, uptown-bound 7th Avenue token booth. A Juana Martinez reports that her purse was just snatched by a man who fled down the steps to a lower platform.

10

Answers and Explanations

1. **(C)** This statement tells what happened, where, and when. It gives a brief description of the suspect and identifies the witness. Choices (A) and (B) neglect to mention the fire; choice (D) omits the height of the suspect, which is an important fact, and does not identify the relationship of the witness for later questioning if necessary.

2. **(D)** This statement gives the precise location, the event, and a direction in which the suspect might be traced. Since the statement says that the event just occurred, the time is irrelevant. The recipient of the message knows to move quickly. Choice (A) does not give enough details to be of use. Choice (B) makes a disjointed statement. Choice (C) makes a flat statement that is not necessarily true; the purse-snatcher may have exited by another route.

Observation and Memory Questions

Some government positions, such as firefighter, police officer, and corrections officer, require good observation and memory skills. Civil service exams for these and related positions may include questions that measure these skills. Typically, you are presented with a picture and are allowed to study it for a short period of time. Then, the picture is covered, and you must answer questions based on what you remember of the details that you observed in the picture.

The following exercises will help you practice for this type of question. You will need a kitchen timer so that you can correctly time the time period allowed for studying the picture.

> **Tip**
> If you miss several of the following questions, then you should practice developing your observation and memory skills. Have a friend or family member compose similar questions for you to practice with.

Practice Exercises

DIRECTIONS: You will have three minutes to study the following picture, to note details about people, time and place, and activities. Then you will have to answer five questions about the picture without looking back at the picture.

Figure 10.1.

Answer questions 1 to 5 on the basis of the picture. Cover the picture with your hand or a piece of paper. Do not look at the picture again.

1.   The teller is
     (A) wearing a striped tie
     ✓(B) wearing glasses
     (C) making change
     (D) left-handed

2.   The man wearing a hat is also
     (A) handing money to the teller
     (B) wearing a bow tie
     (C) talking to another man in the line
     ✓(D) smoking a pipe

3.   The teller's name is
     (A) R. Smith
     (B) T. Jones
     (C) T. Smith
     ✓(D) R. Jones

4.   The woman in the dark dress is
     (A) carrying a handbag
     ✓(B) wearing gloves
     (C) holding a hat
     (D) third in line

5.   The time of day is
     (A) early morning
     ✓(B) around noon
     (C) mid-afternoon
     (D) late afternoon

10

Answers

1. B
2. D
3. D
4. B
5. B

The Hour in Review

1. Many civil service exams include a selection of judgment questions that assess your ability to deal with emergency situations and to order priorities.

2. Oral communication questions test your ability to organize facts into a coherent, accurate report; written communication questions test your knowledge of English grammar and usage.

3. Observation and memory skills are necessary for many law enforcement positions. To test these skills, the civil service exam may ask you to observe the details of a picture and answer questions based on what you remember from the picture.

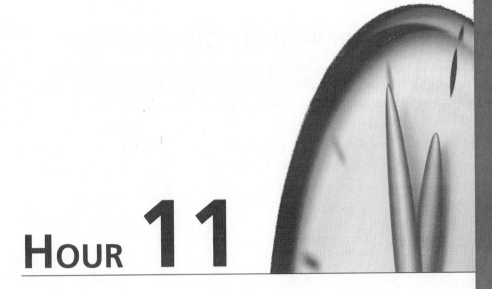

HOUR 11

Mechanical Aptitude

What You Will Learn in This Hour

A civil service exam is designed to identify candidates who have the aptitude and ability to learn the job easily and do it well. Some positions require specific testing to determine whether you have the aptitude and ability to do that particular job. For example, the civil service exam for firefighters, custodians, and mechanical workers in many trades may include questions that test your mechanical aptitude. In this hour, you will find examples of mechanical aptitude questions, so you will be prepared if they appear on your civil service exam. Here are your goals for this hour:

- Learn what is tested by mechanical aptitude questions.
- Practice mechanical aptitude questions.

What Mechanical Aptitude Questions Test

Mechanical aptitude questions are useful in predicting success in jobs that require the ability to operate, service, or maintain machinery. Frequently, these questions draw upon your acquired knowledge through education, prior work experience, and what you have learned on your own.

Depending on the position that you are applying for, mechanical aptitude questions may test any or all of the following skills and aptitudes:

- Knowledge of tools and their uses.
- Knowledge of shop practices.
- Knowledge of electronics information.
- Knowledge of automotive information.
- Knowledge of maintenance work.
- Your inherent feeling for machinery.
- Your mechanical experience.

Make Connections

Civil service exams that have a mechanical aptitude portion often include arithmetic questions that test your ability to solve reasoning problems and perform basic computations in typical shop situations. Turn to Part IV of this book to learn how to answer arithmetic ability questions.

Workshop

In this workshop, you will try your hand at the kinds of mechancal aptitude questions that appear most often on civil service tests.

Practice Exercise

DIRECTIONS: Read each question carefully. Select the best answer from the choices given.

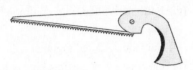

1. The saw shown above is used mainly to cut

   (A) plywood.

   ✓ (B) odd-shaped holes in wood.

   (C) along the grain of the wood.

   (D) across the grain of the wood.

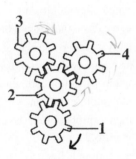

2. Four gears are shown in the figure above. If Gear 1 turns as shown, then which of the following gears are turning in the same direction?

   (A) 2 and 3.

   (B) 2 and 4.

   ✓ (C) 3 and 4.

   (D) 2, 3, and 4.

3. After brakes have been severely over-heated, what should be checked?

   (A) Water condensation in brake fluid

   ✓ (B) Glazed brake shoes

   (C) Wheels out of alignment

   (D) Crystallized wheel bearings

4. The tool shown above is used for

   (A) pressure lubricating.

   (B) welding a steel plate.

   (C) drilling small holes in tight places.

   (D) holding small parts for heat treating.

5. When working on live 600-volt equipment where rubber gloves might be damaged, an electrician should

   (A) work without gloves.

   (B) carry a spare pair of rubber gloves.

   (C) reinforce the fingers of the rubber gloves with rubber tape.

   (D) wear leather gloves over the rubber gloves.

6. Concrete is usually made by mixing

   (A) only sand and water.

   ✓ (B) only cement and water.

   (C) lye, cement, and water.

   (D) rock, sand, cement, and water.

7.   The tool used to locate a point directly below a ceiling hook is a

(A) plumb bob.

(B) line level.

(C) transit.

(D) drop gauge.

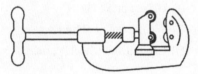

8.   The tool above is a

(A) marking gauge.

(B) knurling tool.

(C) thread cutter.

(D) pipe cutter.

9.   A "pinch bar" is used for

(A) joining.

(B) leveling.

(C) prying.

(D) tightening.

10.   When marking wood, an allowance of $\frac{1}{16}$" to $\frac{1}{8}$" should be made to allow for

(A) drying of the wood.

(B) absorption of water by the wood.

(C) the width of the saw.

(D) knots in the wood.

11.   The primary function of a power-driven sabresaw is to

(A) cut angles.

(B) saw heavy wood stock.

(C) cut curves in flat wood.

(D) make perfectly straight cuts.

12.   The best electrical connection between two wires is obtained when

(A) the insulations are melted together.

(B) all insulation is removed and the wires are bound together with friction tape.

(C) both are wound on a common binding post.

(D) they are soldered together.

13.   If every time a washing machine is started the circuit breaker must be reset, the best solution would be to

(A) oil the motor in the washer.

(B) replace the circuit breaker.

(C) tape the breaker switch closed.

(D) repair the timing mechanism.

14.   One use of a coaxial cable is to

(A) ground a signal.

(B) pass a signal from the set to the antenna of a mobile unit.

(C) carry the signal from a ballast tube.

(D) carry grid signals in high-altitude areas.

15.   A black gummy deposit in the end of the tail pipe of an automobile indicates that

(A) the automobile "burns" oil.

(B) there is probably a leak in the exhaust manifold.

(C) the timing is late.

(D) there are leaks in the exhaust valves.

16.   Of the following, the most important reason for not letting oily rags accumulate in an open storage bin is that they

(A) may start a fire by spontaneous combustion.

(B) will drip oil onto other items in the bin.

(C) may cause a foul odor.

(D) will make the area messy.

17. The best tool to use to make a hole in a con-
crete floor for a machine hold-down bolt is a
   (A) counterboring tool.
   (B) cold chisel.
   (C) drift punch.
   (D) star drill.

18. The best reason for overhauling a machine
on a regular basis is
   (A) that overhauling is easier to do when
       done often.
   (B) to minimize breakdowns of the ma-
       chine.
   (C) to make sure that the machine is prop-
       erly lubricated.
   (D) to make sure that employees are fa-
       miliar with the machine.

19. The best method to employ in putting out
a gasoline fire is to
   (A) use a bucket of water.
   (B) smother it with rags.
   (C) use a carbon dioxide extinguisher.
   (D) use a carbon tetrachloride extin-
       guisher.

20. What would be the most probable cause
if an automobile has a weak spark at the
plugs, "turns over" very slowly, and has
dim headlights?
   (A) Weak battery
   (B) Faulty condenser
   (C) Faulty ignition cable
   (D) Worn contact breaker points

21. A miter box is used
   (A) for locating dowel holes in two pieces
       of wood to be joined together.
   (B) to hold a saw at a fixed angle while
       sawing.
   (C) to hold a saw while sharpening its
       teeth.
   (D) to clamp two pieces of wood together
       at 90 degrees.

22. The nominal voltage of the "D" size dry-
cell battery used in common hand-held
flashlights is most nearly
   (A) 1 volt.
   (B) 1.5 volts.
   (C) 2.0 volts.
   (D) 2.5 volts.

23. The purpose of a water trap in a plumbing
drainage system is to
   (A) prevent the leakage of water.
   (B) prevent freezing of the pipes.
   (C) block off sewer gases.
   (D) reduce the water pressure in the sys-
       tem.

24. Gaskets are commonly used between the
flanges of large pipe joints to
   (A) make a leak-proof connection.
   (B) provide for expansion.
   (C) provide space for assembly.
   (D) adjust for poor alignment.

25. To prevent damage to an air compres-
sor, the air coming into the compressor
is usually
   (A) cooled.
   (B) heated.
   (C) expanded.
   (D) filtered.

11

Answers and Explanations

1. **(B)** The compass saw is used to cut odd-shaped holes in wood.

2. **(C)** Gear 1 turns clockwise; Gear 2 turns counterclockwise; Gears 3 and 4 turn clockwise.

3. **(B)** Overheating the brake shoe will cause the brake material to glaze and become slippery. Slippery brakes are dangerous because they take longer to stop a car.

4. **(B)** The tool is a welding torch used in making a metal joint. Welding is generally done with material made of steel.

5. **(D)** Leather gloves offer the best protection over the rubber gloves. The leather can withstand severe conditions before it will tear. The rubber acts as insulation.

6. **(D)** Rock, sand, cement, and water are used to make concrete.

7. **(A)** A plumb bob is used in this situation.

8. **(D)** The tool is a pipe cutter.

9. **(C)** The "pinch bar" is used for prying.

10. **(C)** You must make an allowance for the width of the saw.

11. **(C)** The sabresaw is used to cut curves in flat wood.

12. **(D)** Soldering obtains the best electrical connection.

13. **(B)** In this situation, you should replace the circuit breaker.

14. **(B)** A coaxial cable can be used to pass a signal from the set to the antenna of a mobile unit.

15. **(A)** This situation indicates that the automobile is "burning" oil.

16. **(A)** The most important reason not to let the oily rags accumulate in the bin is to prevent a fire.

17. **(D)** The best tool to use is a star drill.

18. **(B)** The best reason to regularly overhaul a machine is to prevent breakdowns.

19. **(C)** Using a carbon dioxide extinguisher is the best way to put out a gasoline fire.

20. **(A)** This situation indicates a weak battery in the automobile.

21. **(B)** Use a miter box to hold a saw at a fixed angle while sawing.

22. **(B)** "D" size dry-cell batteries are most nearly 1.5 volts.

23. **(C)** The water trap blocks off sewer gases.

24. **(A)** Gaskets are used to make a leak-proof connection.

25. **(D)** The air is usually filtered.

The Hour in Review

1. Mechanical aptitude questions are often found on Civil Service exams for positions that require work with machinery.

2. Mechanical aptitude questions can test a wide range of mechanical knowledge, including knowledge of tools, automobile repair, electronics, and shop practices.

3. Often, mechanical aptitude questions test the mechanical knowledge that you have previously acquired through work experience, school training, and on your own.

11

Part III

Learn to Answer
Clerical Ability Questions

Hour

Hour 12

Alphabetizing and Filing

What You Will Learn in This Hour

Alphabetizing names and filing them correctly is an important skill for office workers of all kinds. If you are applying for a clerical position, you can be sure that alphabetizing and filing questions will appear on the clerical ability portion of your civil service exam. These questions may also be included on exams for other office positions. In this hour, you'll learn the rules of alphabetic filing that these questions test. Here are your goals for this hour:

- Learn alphabetizing rules that you'll need to know.
- Learn the different kinds of alphabetizing and filing questions.
- Practice alphabetizing and filing questions.

Rules of Alphabetic Filing

The most important rule for putting names in alphabetical order is to consider each letter in the complete name in strict alphabetical order, exactly as it appears, starting with the last name for individuals. However, there are some specific rules that you should understand, and these can differ for names of people and names of organizations. The following sections outline all the rules that you should know to score well on this portion of the clerical ability exam.

Names of Individuals

The following rules apply to the alphabetizing of people's names:

- The names of individuals are filed in strict alphabetical order, first according to last name, then according to first name or initial, and finally according to middle name or initial. For example, *George Allen* comes before *Edward Bell*, and *Leonard P. Reston* comes before *Lucille B. Reston*.

- When last names and first initials are the same, the one with the initial comes before the one with the name written out. For example, *A. Green* comes before *Agnes Green*.

- When first and last names are the same, the name without a middle initial comes before the one with a middle name or initial. For example, *John Doe* comes before both *John A. Doe* and *John Alan Doe*.

- When first and last names are the same, the name with a middle initial comes before the one with a middle name beginning with the same initial. For example, *Jack R. Hertz* comes before *Jack Richard Hertz*.

> **Tip**
> In regard to the last three rules, all you need to remember is this: Nothing comes before something, and less comes before more. The same rule applies to the alphabetizing of business and organization names.

- Prefixes like *De*, *O'*, *Mac*, *Mc*, and *Van* are filed exactly as written and treated as part of the names they come before. Ignore apostrophes for purposes of filing. For example, *Robert O'Dea* comes before *David Olsen*, and *Gladys McTeague* comes before *Frances Meadows*.

- Foreign names are filed as spelled. Prefixes are not considered separately. Likewise, foreign language articles (such as *le*, *La*, *Les*, and *El*), whether they begin with a lowercase or capital letter, are considered part of the name with which they appear. For example, *Carl Da Costa* is filed before *Ugo D'Agnota*.

- Hyphenated surnames are indexed as though the hyphen joins the two parts, making one. Thus, *Amadeus Lyttonet* is filed before *John Lytton-Strachey*.

- Abbreviated names are treated as if they are spelled out. For example, *Chas.* is filed as *Charles*, and *Thos.* is filed as *Thomas*.

- Titles and designations, such as Dr., Mr., Prof., Jr., or II, are given last consideration in filing.

Names of Businesses

The following rules apply to the alphabetizing of business names:

- The names of organizations, institutions, and buildings are filed according to the order in which each word in the name appears, *except* where these names include the full names of individuals.

- When business names include the full names of individuals, the business names are filed using the rules for filing individual names. For example, *Edward Rice and Sons, Ltd.* is filed as *Rice, Edward, and Sons Ltd.*

- When *the*, *of*, *and*, or an apostrophe are parts of a business name, they are disregarded for purposes of filing.

- Names that include numerals should be filed as if the numerals were spelled out. Thus, *10th Street Bootery* is filed as *Tenth Street Bootery*.

- When the same names appear with different addresses, arrange them alphabetically according to town or city, considering state only when town or city names are duplicated. Example: *American Tobacco Co., Norfolk, VA; American Tobacco Co., Quincey, IL; American Tobacco Co., Quincey, MA.*

- Abbreviations are alphabetized as though the words were spelled out. Thus, *Indus. Bros. of America* is filed as *Industrial Brothers of America*.

- Hyphenated firm names are treated as separate words. For example, *Oil-O-Match Heating Co.* is filed before *Oilimatic Heating Co.*

- Compound geographic names written as separate words are always treated as separate words. For example, *West Chester* comes before *Westchester*.

- Bureaus, boards, offices, and government departments are filed under the names of the chief governing body. For example, *Bureau of the Budget* would be filed as if written *Budget, Bureau of the.*

Kinds of Alphabetizing and Filing Questions

There are four different kinds of alphabetizing and filing questions, and any of these may appear on your civil service exam. Therefore, you should read the directions closely and make certain that you mark your answers exactly as specified. Let's take a look at an example of each kind of question.

One type is a simple alphabetizing question. All you have to do is insert the given word into its correct alphabetical position in the list of words and choose the letter of the word it precedes. Try an example:

1.   BIOGRAPHY

   (A) bible

   (B) bibliography

   (C) bilge

   (D) biology

The correct answer is (**D**). Biography should be filed *before* biology.

Another kind of alphabetizing question tests your knowledge of the rules for filing names of individuals. You are given a name, followed by four names in proper alphabetic order. The spaces between the names are lettered. You must mark the space where the given name should be filed. Try an example:

2.   Kessler, Neilson

   (A)-

   Kessel, Carl

   (B)-

   Kessinger, D. J.

   (C)-

   Kessler, Karl

   (D)--

   Kessner, Lewis

   (E)-

The correct answer is (D). According to the rules for alphabetizing names of individuals, when the last names are the same, you should alphabetize by the first name. Thus, *Neilson* falls after *Karl.*

A third type of question tests your ability to alphabetize both individual and business names. One name in a group of names is bold. You must determine where this name should be filed in the entire group: mark (A) if it should be first, mark (B) if it should be second, mark (C) if it should be third, and mark (D) if it should be fourth. Try a question of this type:

3.   Albert Brown

       James Borenstein

       Frieda Albrecht

       Samuel Brown

You should mark (D). The correctly alphabetized group would look like this: Albrecht, Frieda; Borenstein, James; Brown, Albert; **Brown, Samuel**. Because the bold name is fourth in the group, (D) is the correct answer.

The final kind of alphabetizing question also tests your ability to file individual and business names. You are given a group of four names, and you must select the name that would be *third* if the group were correctly alphabetized. Here's an example:

4.   (A) Herbert Restman

       (B) H. Restman

       (C) Harry Restmore

       (D) H. Restmore

The answer is (**D**). The correctly alphabetized group would look like this: Restman, H.; Restman, Herbert; Restmore, H.; Restmore, Harry. Choice (D), *H. Restmore*, falls third in this group.

Tip
When answering the third and fourth types of alphabetizing questions, it's helpful to write out the group of names in alphabetical order in your test booklet or on your scratch paper.

12

Caution
As you can see from the previous examples, the directions for alphabetizing and filing questions can be complicated. Read the directions carefully before answering any questions, and make sure that you understand what you must mark as the correct answer. It's a good idea to go back and reread the directions after answering a few questions.

Workshop

In this workshop, you'll apply what you learned this hour by practicing with every type of alphabetizing and filing question commonly used on civil service tests.

Practice Exercise 1

DIRECTIONS: Each question consists of a CAPITALIZED word that is to be filed correctly among the alphabetized words listed. Choose the word *after* where the given word should be filed.

1. CATHOLIC
   (A) catacombs
   (B) catalogs
   (C) catechisms
   ✓ (D) cattle

2. DRAMA
   ✓ (A) drawing
   (B) Drayton
   (C) Dreyfus
   (D) drugs

3. INQUISITION
   (A) industry
   ✓ (B) insurance
   (C) international
   (D) interne

4. LUGUBRIOUS
   (A) Lucretius
   ✓ (B) lumber
   (C) Luther
   (D) Lutheran

5. OCEANIC
   (A) occult
   ✓ (B) Ohio
   (C) Oklahoma
   (D) optics

6. ENGLAND
   (A) engineering
   ✓ (B) English
   (C) engraving
   (D) entomology

7. IRRIGATION
   (A) Ireland
   (B) Irish
   (C) iron
   ✓ (D) Irving

8. MARINE
   (A) Margolin
   ✓ (B) marketing
   (C) Mary
   (D) Maryland

9. PALEONTOLOGY
   (A) Pacific
   (B) painting
   ✓ (C) Palestine
   (D) paltry

10. ASIATIC
    (A) ascetic
    ✓ (B) assyriology
    (C) astronomy
    (D) astrophysics

Practice Exercise 2

DIRECTIONS: In each of the following questions, you are given a name, followed by four names in proper alphabetic order. The spaces between the names are lettered. Decide where the given name belongs in the alphabetic series, and mark the letter of the space.

1. Eatley, Mary
   (A)-
      Eagin, John
   (B)-
      Eagley, Robert
   ✓(C)-
      Ebert, Jack
   (D)-
      Eckert, Wallace
   (E)-

2. Pinch, Nathaniel
   (A)-
      Payne, Briscoe
   (B)-
      Pearlman, Abe
   ✓(C)-
      Pincus, Harry
   (D)-
      Pollaci, Angelina
   (E)-

3. Raphan, Max
   (A)-
      Rankin, H.
   ✓(B)-
      Rappan, Sol
   (C)-
      Rascoll, Jon
   (D)-
      Rich, Harold
   (E)-

4. Schwartz, H.
   (A)-
      Scavone, John
   ✓(B)-
      Schwartz, Harry
   (C)-
      Seiden, Burt
   (D)-
      Shields, Vera
   (E)-

5. Hakim, Wm.
   (A)-
      Hakiel, R.
   (B)-
      Hakim, Louis
   (C)-
      Hakim, M.
   ✓(D)-
      Halabi, Joe
   (E)-

6. Horn, Sol
   (A)-
      Hormel, Max
   (B)-
      Horn, Harold
   (C)-
      Horn, Irving
   ✓(D)-
      Hornbeck, J. W.
   (E)-

12

7. Krommes, Selma

(A)-

Kromolitz, J.

(B)-

Kromowitz, L.

(C)-

Kromwitz, Abe

(D)-

Kron, Harold

(E)-

8. Melzer, Max

(A)-

Meltz, Lena

(B)-

Meltzer, Abe

(C)-

Meltzer, Alex

(D)-

Melzner, L.

(E)-

9. Nesbitt, Carl

(A)-

Nesbiet, Jerry

(B)-

Nesbitt, Al

(C)-

Nesbitt, Gloria

(D)-

Nesci, Jas.

(E)-

10. Perron, Homer

(A)-

Perrin, Larry

(B)-

Perron, Lewis

(C)-

Perrone, James

(D)-

Perrotta, Chas.

(E)-

Practice Exercise 3

DIRECTIONS: Consider each group of names as a unit. Determine where the name printed in **boldface** would be if the names in the group were correctly alphabetized. If the name in **boldface** is first, mark (A); if second, mark (B); if third, mark (C); and if fourth, mark (D).

D 1. Hugh F. Martenson
3   A. S. Martinson
2   Albert Martinsen
4   **Albert S. Martinson**

C 2. Arthur Roberts
3   **James Robin**
2   J. B. Robin
4   Arnold Robinson

C 3. **Eugene Thompkins**
4   Alice Thompson
1   Arnold G. Thomas
2   B. Thomas

A 4. Albert Green
     Wm. Greenfield
1   **A. B. Green**
     Frank E. Green

B 5. Dr. Francis Karell
2   **John Joseph Karelsen, Jr.**
3   John J. Karelson, Sr.
4   Mrs. Jeanette Kelly

A 6. Norman Fitzgibbons
4   Charles F. Franklin
1   **Jas. Fitzgerald**
3   Andrew Fitzsimmons

C 7. **Chas. R. Connolly**
2   Frank Conlon
     Charles S. Connolly
1   Abraham Cohen

B 8. **The 5th Ave. Bus Co.**
1   The Baltimore and Ohio Railroad
3   3rd Ave. Elevated Co.
7   Pennsylvania Railroad

A 9. The Jane Miller Shop
1   **Joseph Millard Corp.**
3   John Muller & Co.
4   Jean Mullins, Inc.

B 10. **Anthony Delaney**
1   A. De Landri
     A. M. D'Elia
4   Alfred De Monte

12

Practice Exercise 4

> **DIRECTIONS:** Each question consists of four names. For each question, select the one of the four names that should be *third* if the four names were arranged in alphabetical order in accordance with the rules for alphabetical filing.

1. (A) Elm Trading Co.
   (B) El Dorado Trucking Corp.
   (C) James Eldred Jewelry Store
   (D) Eldridge Printing, Inc.

2. (A) Fifth Avenue Book Shop
   (B) Mr. Wm. A. Fifner
   (C) 52nd Street Association
   (D) Robert B. Fiffner

3. (A) Timothy Macalan
   (B) Fred McAlden
   (C) Tomas MacAllister
   (D) Mrs. Frank McAllen

4. (A) Peter La Vance
   (B) George Van Meer
   (C) Wallace De Vance
   (D) Leonard Vance

5. (A) 71st Street Theater
   (B) The Seven Seas Corp.
   (C) 7th Ave. Service Co.
   (D) Walter R. Sevan and Co.

6. (A) Dr. Chas. D. Peterson
   (B) Miss Irene F. Petersen
   (C) Lawrence E. Peterson
   (D) Prof. N. A. Petersen

7. (A) Edward La Gabriel
   (B) Marie Doris Gabriel
   (C) Marjorie N. Gabriel
   (D) Mrs. Marian Gabriel

8. (A) Adam Dunn
   (B) E. Dunn
   (C) A. Duncan
   (D) Edward Robert Dunn

9. (A) Paul Moore
   (B) William Moore
   (C) Paul A. Moore
   (D) William Allen Moore

10 (A) George Peters
   (B) Eric Petersen
   (C) G. Peters
   (D) E. Petersen

Answers and Explanations

Practice Exercise 1   ## Practice Exercise 2

1. D   1. C
2. A   2. C
3. B   3. B
4. B   4. B
5. B   5. D
6. B   6. D
7. D   7. A
8. B   8. D
9. C   9. C
10. B   10. B

Practice Exercise 3

For this exercise, the correct answers and alphabetization of the group are given.

1. **(D)** Martenson, Hugh F.; Martinsen, Albert; Martinson, A. S.; **Martinson, Albert S.**

2. **(C)** Roberts, Arthur; Robin, J. B.; **Robin, James**; Robinson, Arnold

3. **(C)** Thomas, Arnold G.; Thomas, B.; **Thompkins, Eugene**; Thompson, Alice

4. **(A) Green, A. B.**; Green, Albert; Green, Frank E.; Greenfield, Wm.

5. **(B)** Karell, Francis, Dr.; **Karelsen, John Joseph, Jr.**; Karelson, John J., Sr.; Kelly, Jeanette, Mrs.

6. **(A) Fitzgerald, Jas.**; Fitzgibbons, Norman; Fitzsimmons, Andrew; Franklin, Charles F.

7. **(C)** Cohen, Abraham; Conlon, Frank; **Connolly, Chas. R.**; Connolly, Charles S.

8. **(B)** Baltimore and Ohio Railroad, The; **5th (Fifth) Ave. Bus Co., The**; Pennsylvania Railroad; 3rd (Third) Ave. Elevated Co.

9. **(A) Millard, Joseph, Corp.**; Miller, Jane Shop, The; Muller, John & Co.; Mullins, Jean, Inc.

10. **(B)** De Landri, A.; **Delaney, Anthony**; D'Elia, A. M.; De Monte, Alfred

12

Practice Exercise 4

For this exercise, the correct answers and alphabetization of the group are given.

1. **(D)** El Dorado Trucking Corp.; Eldred, James Jewelry Store; Eldridge Printing, Inc.; Elm Trading Co.

2. **(A)** Fiffner, Robert B.; Fifner, Wm. A., Mr.; Fifth Avenue Book Shop; 52nd (Fifty-second) Street Association

3. **(B)** Macalan, Timothy; MacAllister, Thomas; McAlden, Fred; McAllen, Frank, Mrs.

4. **(D)** De Vance, Wallace; La Vance, Peter; Vance, Leonard; Van Meer, George

5. **(C)** Sevan, Walter R. and Co.; Seven Seas Corp., The; 7th (Seventh) Ave. Service Co.; 71st (Seventy-first) Street Theater

6. **(A)** Petersen, Irene F., Miss; Petersen, N. A., Prof.; Peterson, Chas. D., Dr.; Peterson, Lawrence E.

7. **(C)** Gabriel, Marian, Mrs.; Gabriel, Marie Doris; Gabriel, Marjorie N.; La Gabriel, Edward

8. **(B)** Duncan, A.; Dunn, Adam; Dunn, E.; Dunn, Edward Robert

9. **(B)** Moore, Paul; Moore, Paul A.; Moore, William; Moore, William Allen

10. **(D)** Peters, G.; Peters, George; Petersen, E.; Petersen, Eric

The Hour in Review

1. When alphabetizing names of individuals, consider each letter in the complete name in strict alphabetical order, exactly as it appears. Consider the last name first, then the first name or initial, and finally the middle name or initial.

2. When alphabetizing names of businesses or organizations, consider each letter in the complete name, according to the order in which the words appear. There are exceptions, however, such as when the name includes a person's full name or an insignificant article.

3. Many kinds of alphabetizing and filing questions may appear on your civil service exam, so it is crucial to read the directions carefully and follow them exactly.

HOUR 13

Clerical Speed and Accuracy

What You Will Learn in This Hour

Most clerical ability tests require you to demonstrate speed and accuracy. Unlike verbal ability questions, clerical speed and accuracy questions are closely timed, and wrong answers do count against you. The most common type of speed and accuracy question is the comparison question, which asks you to compare names and numbers and find mistakes. You may also find coding questions on your exam, which require you to correctly use a letter-to-number code. In this hour, you'll learn how to tackle both kinds of clerical speed and accuracy questions. Here are your goals for this hour:

- Review of strategies for answering timed questions.

- How to answer comparison questions.

- How to answer coding questions.

Answering Timed Questions

Generally, time is a crucial factor in comparison questions. You'll probably find that there are more questions than you can answer in the time allowed. Since accuracy is of prime importance, you should follow these rules:

Do

DO work steadily until time is called.

Don't

DON'T rush beyond your ability to focus on words and numbers.
DON'T guess.
DON'T randomly answer the remaining questions when time is called.

Tests of clerical speed and accuracy put such a premium on accuracy that the scoring formula is sometimes "score equals the correct answers minus the wrong answers." Don't allow the fear of making errors to slow you down so that you plod along and answer very few questions; speed is also important. However, you must work steadily until time is called and then stop promptly.

> **Caution**
> Part of clerical accuracy is accuracy in reading directions. Each of the practice exercises in this hour is governed by a different set of instructions. Read the directions slowly and carefully. Time spent getting the directions straight is not wasted.

Comparison Questions

In comparison questions, you are given several sets of names or numbers. You must quickly compare them to find which is different or inaccurate. Comparison tests are the chief measure of clerical speed and accuracy in use today. Lots of practice with various forms of comparison questions should improve your skills in this area.

Strategies for Answering Comparison Questions

In answering comparison questions, look for differences in one area at a time. If you narrow your focus to compare only short numbers, abbreviations, or just the words, you're more likely to notice differences and less apt to see what you expect to see rather than what is actually printed on the page.

Start with length of line, number of digits, middle initials, or small words. Once you spot *any difference* at all, you know that the two items being compared are different. If, while concentrating on one area, you happen to catch a difference in another area, consider the items to be different and go on to the next comparison. A system may be useful, but don't stick to it slavishly.

The best way to read names, numbers, and addresses being compared is to read exactly what you see and to sound out words by syllables. For example:

- If you see *St*, read "es-tee" not "street."

- If you see *NH*, read "en-aitch" not "New Hampshire."

- If you see *1035*, read "one-zero-three-five" not "one thousand thirty-five."

- Read *sassafras* as "sas-sa-fras."

Psychologists have discovered that the human mind always tries to complete a figure. If you read "Pky" as "Parkway," you'll probably read "Pkwy" as "Parkway" and never notice the difference between the two. Your mind will complete the word without allowing you to focus on the letters. If, however, you read the abbreviation as an abbreviation, you'll notice that the two are different.

Finally, trust yourself. Once you've decided that the two items being compared are exactly alike, stick with your decision. Never look back and recheck two items.

13

Workshop: Comparisons

Here's your chance to practice answering the three types of comparison questions most commonly used on civil service tests. Answers and explanations follow the last exercise.

Practice Exercise 1

> **DIRECTIONS:** Each question lists four names or numbers. The names or numbers may or may not be exactly the same. Compare the four names or numbers in each question, and mark your answer as follows:
> - Mark (A) if all four names or numbers are DIFFERENT.
> - Mark (B) if TWO of the names or numbers are exactly the same.
> - Mark (C) if THREE of the names or numbers are exactly the same.
> - Mark (D) if all FOUR names or numbers are exactly the same.

B 1.   W.E. Johnston
       W.E. Johnson
       W.E. Johnson
       W.B. Johnson

D 2.   Vergil L. Muller
       Vergil L. Muller
       Vergil L. Muller
       Vergil L. Muller

B 3.   5261383
       5263183
       5263183
       5623183

A 4.   Atherton R. Warde
       Asheton R. Warde
       Atherton P. Warde
       Athertin P. Warde

D 5.   8125690
       8126690
       8125609
       8125609

B 6.   E. Owens McVey
       E. Owen McVey
       E. Owen McVay
       E. Owen McVey

B 7.   Emily Neal Rouse
       Emily Neal Rowse
       Emily Neal Roose
       Emily Neal Rowse

C 8.   Francis Ramsdell
       Francis Ransdell
       Francis Ramsdell
       Francis Ramsdell

D 9.   2395890
       2395890
       2395890
       2395890

D 10. 1926341
       1962341
       1963241
       1926341

Practice Exercise 2

DIRECTIONS: Each question gives the name and identification number of an employee. You are to choose the *one* answer that has exactly the same identification number and name as those given in the question.

1. 176823   Katherine Blau
   (A) 176823   Catherine Blau
   (B) 176283   Katherine Blau
   (C) 176823   Katherine Blau
   (D) 176823   Katherine Blaw

2. 673403   Boris T. Frame
   (A) 673403   Boris P. Frame
   (B) 673403   Boris T. Frame
   (C) 673403   Boris T. Fraim
   (D) 673430   Boris T. Frame

3. 498832   Hyman Ziebart
   (A) 498832   Hyman Zeibart
   (B) 498832   Hiram Ziebart
   (C) 498832   Hyman Ziebardt
   (D) 498832   Hyman Ziebart

4. 506745   Barbara O'Dey
   (A) 507645   Barbara O'Day
   (B) 506745   Barbara O'Day
   (C) 506475   Barbara O'Day
   (D) 506745   Barbara O'Dey

5. 344223   Morton Sklar
   (A) 344223   Morton Sklar
   (B) 344332   Norton Sklar
   (C) 344332   Morton Sklaar
   (D) 343322   Morton Sklar

6. 816040   Betsy B. Voight
   (A) 816404   Betsy B. Voight
   (B) 814060   Betsy B. Voight
   (C) 816040   Betsy B. Voight
   (D) 816040   Betsey B. Voight

7. 913576   Harold Howritz
   (A) 913576   Harold Horwitz
   (B) 913576   Harold Howritz
   (C) 913756   Harold Horwitz
   (D) 913576   Harald Howritz

8. 621190   Jayne T. Downs
   (A) 621990   Janie T. Downs
   (B) 621190   Janie T. Downs
   (C) 622190   Janie T. Downs
   (D) 621190   Jayne T. Downs

9. 004620   George McBoyd
   (A) 006420   George McBoyd
   (B) 006420   George MacBoyd
   (C) 006420   George McBoid
   (D) 004620   George McBoyd

10. 723495   Alice Appleton
    (A) 723495   Alice Appleton
    (B) 723594   Alica Appleton
    (C) 723459   Alice Appleton
    (D) 732495   Alice Appleton

13

Practice Exercise 3

> **DIRECTIONS:** Each of the following questions consists of three sets of names and name codes. In each question, the two names and name codes on the same line are supposed to be *exactly* the same. Look carefully at each set of names and codes, and mark your answer as follows:
> - (A) if there are mistakes in all THREE sets
> - (B) if there are mistakes in TWO of the sets
> - (C) if there are mistakes in only ONE set
> - (D) if there are NO MISTAKES in any of the sets

1. Macabe, John N.   V 53162   Macade, John N.   V 53162
   Howard, Joan S.   J 24791   Howard, Joan S.   J 24791
   Ware, Susan B.   A 45068   Ware, Susan B.   A 45968

2. Powell, Michael C.   78537 F   Powell, Michael C.   78537 F
   Martinez, Pablo J.   24435 P   Martinez, Pablo J.   24435 P
   MacBane, Eliot M.   98674 E   MacBane, Eliot M.   98674 E

3. Fitz-Kramer Machines Inc.   259090   Fitz-Kramer Machines Inc.   259090
   Marvel Cleaning Service   482657   Marvel Cleaning Service   482657
   Donato, Carl G.   637418   Danato, Carl G.   687418

4. Martin Davison Trading Corp.   43108 T   Martin Davidson Trading Corp.   43108 T
   Cotwald Lighting Fixtures   76065 L   Cotwald Lighting Fixtures   70056 L
   R. Crawford Plumbers   23157 C   R. Crawford Plumbers   23157 G

5. Fraiman Engineering Corp.   M4773   Friaman Engineering Corp.   M4773
   Neuman, Walter B.   N7745   Neumen, Walter B.   N7745
   Pierce, Eric M.   W6304   Pierce, Eric M.   W6304

6. Constable, Eugene   B 64837   Comstable, Eugene   B 64837
   Derrick, Paul   H 27119   Derrik, Paul   H 27119
   Scalsi Office Furniture   R 36742   Scalsi Office Furniture   R 36742

7. Hernando Delivery Service Co.   D 7456   Hernando Delivery Service Co.   D 7456
   Barettz Electrical Supplies   N 5392   Barettz Electrical Supplies   N 5392
   Tanner, Abraham   M 4798   Tanner, Abraham   M 4798

8. Kalin Associates   R 38641   Kaline Associates   R 38641
   Sealey, Robert E.   P 63533   Sealey, Robert E.   P 63553
   Scalsi Office Furniture   R 36742   Scalsi Office Furniture   R 36742

9. Janowsky, Philip M.   742213   Janowsky, Philip M.   742213
   Hansen, Thomas H.   934816   Hanson, Thomas H.   934816
   L. Lester and Son Inc.   294568   L. Lester and Son Inc.   294568

10. Majthenyi, Alexander	P 4802	Majthenyi, Alexander	B 4802
Prisco Pools, Inc.	W 3641	Frisco Pools, Inc.	W 3641
DePaso, Nancy G.	X 4464	DePaso, Nancy G.	X 4464

Answers and Explanations

Practice Exercise 1

1. **(B)** The second and third names are the same.

2. **(D)** All four names are the same.

3. **(B)** The second and third numbers are the same.

4. **(A)** All the names are different.

5. **(B)** The third and fourth numbers are the same.

6. **(B)** The second and fourth names are the same.

7. **(B)** The second and fourth names are the same.

8. **(C)** The first, third, and fourth names are the same.

9. **(D)** All four numbers are the same.

10. **(B)** The first and fourth numbers are the same.

Practice Exercise 2

1. C
2. B
3. D
4. D
5. A

6. C
7. B
8. D
9. D
10. A

Practice Exercise 3

1. **(B)** There are mistakes in the first and third sets.

2. **(D)** There are no mistakes.

3. **(C)** There are mistakes in the third set.

4. **(A)** There are mistakes in all three sets.

5. **(B)** There are mistakes in the first and second sets.

6. **(B)** There are mistakes in the first and second sets.

7. **(D)** There are no mistakes.

8. **(B)** There are mistakes in the first and second sets.

9. **(C)** There is a mistake in the second set.

10. **(B)** There are mistakes in the first and second sets.

13

Answering Coding Questions

The most common variety of coding questions found on civil service exams consists of a coding table (which need not be memorized) and a series of questions that requires you to demonstrate your understanding of the use of the code and your ability to follow directions in answering the questions. From one exam to another, the chief variations in coding questions tend to be in the number of digits and letters in each question line and in the directions. The best way to learn how to answer coding questions is to practice with some examples.

Workshop: Coding

In this workshop, you'll try your hand at answering typical civil service coding questions. Answers and explanations follow the last exercise.

Practice Exercise 1

DIRECTIONS: Each letter should be matched with its number in accordance with the following table:

Letter	P	S	B	O	Q	K	A	M	E	Y
Number	0	1	2	3	4	5	6	7	8	9

For each question, compare each line of letters and numbers carefully to see if each letter is matched correctly to its corresponding number. Mark your answer according to the number of lines in which all the letters and numbers are matched correctly:

- Mark (A) if NONE of the lines is matched correctly.
- Mark (B) if only ONE of the lines is matched correctly.
- Mark (C) if TWO of the lines are matched correctly.
- Mark (D) if all THREE lines are matched correctly.

1. SEOB   1732
    YMQA   9756
    BEPM   2806

2. AOSY   6319
    EKQM   8547
    YBOP   9230

3. QABS   3621
    PKEO   0583
    SEYO   1983

4. AQOB   6432
    YSAP   9061
    BAKM   2657

5. SBOK   1234
    YEAQ   9854
    MPES   7081

Practice Exercise 2

> **DIRECTIONS:** Each question contains three lines of letters and numbers. The numbers in each line should correspond with the code letters in this table:
>
> | Code Letter | M | Q | O | H | B | C | I | N | Y | V |
> |---|---|---|---|---|---|---|---|---|---|---|
> | Number | 0 | 1 | 2 | 3 | 4 | 5 | 6 | 7 | 8 | 9 |
>
> In some of the lines below, an error exists in the coding. Compare the numbers and letters in each question very carefully. Mark your answers according to the number of lines in which you find an error as follows:
> - Mark (A) if only ONE line contains an error.
> - Mark (B) if TWO lines contain errors.
> - Mark (C) if all THREE lines contain errors.
> - Mark (D) if NONE of the lines contains an error.

1. BCMHIOB   4503624
    VYBQNCO   8941752
    MHBCNIV   0345869

2. HYVNOQM   3987210
    NCOMHYQ   7520481
    QBCHIYN   1463687

3. MHBNYQO   0347812
    CONBMYH   5274083
    QBHNOMV   1430279

Answers and Explanations

Practice Exercise 1

1. **(A)** None of the lines is matched correctly. In the first set, *E* is incorrectly matched with *7*. In the second set, *Q* is incorrectly matched with *5*. In the third set, *M* is incorrectly matched with *6*.

2. **(D)** All three lines are matched correctly.

3. **(B)** Only the second set is matched correctly. In the first set, *Q* is incorrectly matched with *3*. In the third set, *E* is incorrectly matched with *9*, and *Y* is incorrectly matched with *8*.

4. **(C)** The first and third sets are matched correctly. In the second set, *S* is incorrectly matched with *0*, and *P* is incorrectly matched with *1*.

5. **(B)** Only the last set is matched correctly. In the first set, *K* is incorrectly matched with *4*. In the second set, *A* is incorrectly matched with *5*.

13

Practice Exercise 2

1. **(B)** The first line contains no errors. On the second line, *V* is incorrectly coded as *8*, and *Y* is incorrectly coded as *9*. On the third line, *N* is incorrectly coded as *8*.

2. **(C)** All three lines contain errors. In the first line, *Y* is incorrectly coded as *9*, and *V* is incorrectly coded as *8*. In the second line, *H* is incorrectly coded as *4*. In the third line, *C* is incorrectly coded as *6*.

3. **(A)** The first and second lines contain no errors. In the third line, *N* is incorrectly coded as *0*, and *M* is incorrectly coded as *7*.

The Hour in Review

1. Clerical speed and accuracy questions are closely timed and wrong answers do count against you. Therefore, you must adjust your scoring strategies for this portion of the exam.

2. When answering comparison questions, the best strategy is to examine small areas of the items being compared until you find an error.

3. Coding questions test your ability to understand a letter-to-number code and quickly spot errors in coding.

4. The directions for all clerical speed and accuracy questions are complex and require careful reading to score answers accurately.

HOUR 14

Typing and Stenography Tests

What You Will Learn in This Hour

The clerical portion of some civil service exams may include either a typing or stenography test, or both. The typing test, which is more common, is often a pass/fail measure of a minimum typing speed and accuracy required for the position that you're applying for. The best way to prepare for typing and stenography tests is to practice the skills that you've already acquired through job experience, a training course, or in school. This hour will show you what to expect from stenography and typing tests on the civil service exam and will provide practice exercises. Here are your goals for this hour:

- Practice for the typing test.
- Practice for the stenography test.

The Typing Test

Nearly every applicant for any U.S. job must take a typing test. Most often the typing test is merely a qualifying test; you must pass the test in order to be hired, but your score doesn't count toward your final score on the entire exam. You must simply prove that you know how to type to a minimum speed and accuracy standards.

For jobs in which typing is a very important skill, the typing test may be competitively scored. In those cases, the score on the typing test is part of the overall civil service exam score and affects hiring decisions.

In the typing test, you're faced with a single task: copying material exactly as it is presented. You must demonstrate how rapidly you can do so and with what degree of accuracy.

What to Expect on the Typing Test

The typing test consists of a passage that you must copy exactly as it is presented to you. You'll have a specified length of time in which to type, and your score will be based upon the number of words per minute that you type within that time and upon the number of errors that you make.

You'll also be given a practice exercise before the test itself. The practice exercise, usually about 10 lines in length, enables you to warm up and to make certain that your typewriter is functioning properly. It is not scored.

The test may be administered on a computer or on a standard typewriter. You'll get a chance to turn the typewriter on and off and to check the preset margins and tabs to be sure that they are accurate. You shouldn't need to make any adjustments on the supplied typewriter.

How the Typing Test Is Scored

The length of the typing test varies from one governmental jurisdiction to the other. Most typing tests last five minutes. The minimum performance standards also vary. For some positions, a minimum speed of 30 words per minute (wpm) is adequate; for others 35 wpm, 40 wpm, or even greater speeds are required. Likewise, the number of errors permitted varies according to jurisdiction and the position for which you're applying.

> **Note**
> Once the minimum words-per-minute requirement is met, accuracy counts twice as much as speed.

The basic principles in charging typing errors are as follows:

- WORD or PUNCTUATION MARK incorrectly typed or in which there was an erasure. (An error in spacing that follows an incorrect word or punctuation mark is not further charged.)
- SERIES of consecutive words omitted, repeated, inserted, transposed, or erased. (A charge is made for errors within such series, but the total charge cannot exceed the number of words.)
- LINE or part of a line typed over other material, typed with all capitals, or apparently typed with the fingers on the wrong keys.
- CHANGE from the MARGIN where most lines are begun by the candidate or from the PARAGRAPH INDENTION most frequently used by the candidate.

> **Note**
> Because corrections on a computer are quick and clean, the attitude toward errors may be more relaxed when the test is given on a computer than when it is given on a typewriter. Nonetheless, accuracy remains a consideration, along with speed.

Strategies for Taking the Typing Test

Assuming that you already know how to type, the best preparation for any typing test is typing. Choose any material at all and practice copying it line for line, exactly as you see it. As on the actual typing test, spell, capitalize, punctuate, and begin and end lines exactly as they appear on the page that you're copying. Try to balance yourself to meet speed requirements while maintaining a very high level of accuracy.

> **Tip**
> When you practice, try to keep your typing error-free. Then try to increase your speed. Use an accurate signal timer or have a friend or relative time you.

14

Practice Typing Test

DIRECTIONS: Type the copy exactly as it is given below. Spell, space, begin and end each line, paragraph, punctuate, and capitalize precisely as shown. Make no erasures, insertions, or other corrections. Errors are penalized whether they are erased or otherwise corrected. Keep on typing even though you detect an error in your copy. If you finish typing the passage before the time limit is up, simply double-space once and start typing from the beginning of the passage. If you fill up one side of the paper, turn it over and continue typing on the other side.

TIME: 5 minutes

Line Count

1   In the field of public administration in the narrow and more
technical sense, significant trends are observable. These are
3   closely related to the efficiency movement in modern business
and the new social background of administrative activity. The
5   new movement involves larger administrative areas, consolidation
of authority at all levels, central control over subordinate authori-
7   ties in the region, a professional personnel, and the application of
new technical devices to the rationalization of the service. These
9   movements are especially apparent in the states and in the special
fields of health, highways, education, and finance. Consolidation
11   is also seen in the cities, both under the council mayor and the
council manager forms of government.
13   The federal government has established an important form of
administrative control by means of grants-in-aid. At the same
15   time, an important relationship has been developed in the
cooperative exchange of administrative services between the
17   federal government and the states and to a more limited extent
between the states and localities. The continuing involvement of
19   federal agencies in these matters is a significant indicator of this
new policy. It augurs well for the future.

EACH TIME YOU REACH THIS POINT, DOUBLE SPACE ONCE
AND BEGIN AGAIN.

TYPING SPEED ATTAINED: _____ words per minute

NUMBER OF ERRORS: _____

The Stenography Test

Only stenographer competitors take a stenography test. You will be expected to take
dictation at the rate of 80 words per minute. You must then consult your notes to fill in the
missing words of a transcript from an alphabetic word list. The sample stenography test
given in this section shows the length of the dictated material and will help you prepare if
your exam includes a stenography test.

To take the practice stenography test, sit down with your pencil and notebook, and hand
this book to a friend or family member. Have that person dictate the passage to you. Each
pair of lines is dictated in 10 seconds. Your friend should dictate periods, but not commas,
and should read the exercise with the expression that the punctuation indicates. Have your
friend use a watch with a second hand to read the sentences at the proper speed.

Sample Stenography Test

DIRECTIONS: Exactly on a minute start dictating. Finish reading each line at the
number of seconds indicated below.

I realize that this practice dictation	
is not a part of the examination	10 sec.
proper and is not to be scored. (Period)	
When making a study of the private	20 sec.
pension structure and its influence on	
turnover, the most striking feature is its	30 sec.
youth. (Period) As has been shown, the time	
of greatest growth began just a few years	40 sec.
ago. (Period) The influence that this	
growth has had on the labor market and	50 sec.
worker attitudes is hard to assess,	
partly because the effects have not yet fully	1 min.
evolved and many are still in the	
growing stage. (Period) Even so, most pension	10 sec.

14

plans began with much more limited gains

than they give now. (Period) For example,   20 sec.

as private plans mature they grant

a larger profit and a greater range of gains to   30 sec.

more workers and thereby become more

important. (Period) Plans that protect accrued pension   40 sec.

credits are rather new and are being

revised in the light of past trends. (Period)   50 sec.

As informal and formal information on pension

plans spreads, the workers become more   2 min.

aware of the plans and their provisions

increase. (Period) Their impact on employee attitudes   10 sec.

and decisions will no doubt become

stronger. (Period) Each year, more and more workers   20 sec.

will be retiring with a private pension,

and their firsthand knowledge of the benefits to   30 sec.

be gained from private pensions will spread

to still active workers. (Period) Thus, workers   40 sec.

may less often view pensions as just

another part of the security package   50 sec.

based on service and more often

see them as unique benefits. (Period)   3 min.

> **DIRECTIONS:** The following transcript and word list is taken from the previous dictation. Many words have been omitted from the transcript. Compare your notes with it. When you come to a blank space in the transcript, decide what word (or words) belongs there. Look for the missing word in the word list. Notice which letter (A, B, C, or D) is printed beside the word. Write that letter in the blank. (B) is written in blank 1 to show how you are to record your choice. Write (E) if the exact answer is not in the word list. You may also write the word (or words) or the shorthand for it, if you wish. The same choice may belong in more than one blank.

Alphabetic Word List

Write (E) if the answer is not listed.

a — (D)

attitudes — (C)

be — (B)

been — (C)

began — (D)

being — (A)

completely — (A)

examination — (A)

examine — (B)

examining — (D)

feat — (A)

feature — (C)

full — (B)

fully — (D)

greater — (D)

grow — (B)

growing — (C)

had — (D)

has — (C)

has been — (B)

has had — (A)

has made — (A)

in — (C)

in part — (B)

influence — (A)

labor — (C)

main — (B)

make — (A)

making — (B)

market — (B)

markets — (D)

marking — (D)

never — (B)

not — (D)

over — (C)

part — (C)

partly — (D)

pension — (C)

14

practical — (C)   to — (D)

practice — (B)   to be — (C)

private — (D)   trial — (A)

proper — (C)   turn — (D)

section — (D)   turnover — (B)

so — (B)   values — (A)

still — (A)   yet — (C)

structure — (D)

Transcript

I realize that this <u>B</u> dictation is __ a __ of the __ __ and is __ __

                        1   2   3   4 5   6 7

scored. When __ a __ of the __ __ __ and its __ on __, the most

                8   9   10 11 12   13   14

striking __ is its youth. As __ shown, the time of __ growth began just a few

      15   16   17

years ago. The __ that this growth __ on the labor __ and worker __ is hard

         18   19   20   21

to assess, __ because the effects have not yet __ evolved and many are __ in the

      22   23   24

__ stage.

25

Answers and Explanations

1. (B) practice (filled in for you)
2. (D) not
3. (C) part
4. (A) examination
5. (C) proper
6. (D) not
7. (C) to be
8. (B) making
9. (E) study (not given)
10. (D) private
11. (C) pension
12. (D) structure
13. (A) influence

14. (B) turnover
15. (C) feature
16. (B) has been
17. (E) greatest (not given)
18. (A) influence
19. (A) has had
20. (B) market
21. (C) attitudes
22. (D) partly
23. (D) fully
24. (A) still
25. (C) growing

The Hour in Review

1. Many clerical positions require you to demonstrate that you can meet minimum typing accuracy and speed standards by taking a typing test. Often, the test is not competitively scored.

2. If typing skill is important to the position that you're applying for, the typing test may be competitively scored. In that case, accuracy is most important, once you meet the minimum speed requirement.

3. Stenography tests are only given on civil service exams for stenographer positions. You must demonstrate that you can take dictation at the standard rate and correctly transcribe your notes.

14

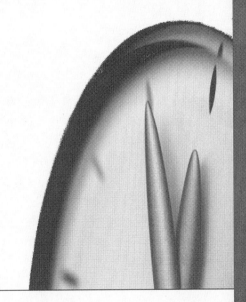

Part IV

Learn to Answer Arithmetic Ability Questions

HOUR **15**

Fractions and Decimals

What You Will Learn in This Hour

The clerical ability portion of the Civil Service exam may include many kinds of arithmetic questions. Depending on the position for which you're applying, arithmetic ability questions may also be asked on exams that aren't for clerical positions. In this and the next few hours, you'll review the kinds of arithmetic questions most commonly found on civil service exams. We'll start with arithmetic problems involving fractions and decimals. Here are your goals for this hour:

- Learn to answer problems involving fractions and mixed numbers.
- Learn to answer problems involving decimals.

Fractions and Mixed Numbers

Before going over the rules for solving arithmetic problems involving fractions and mixed numbers, let's review what fractions and mixed numbers are:

- A **fraction** is part of a unit. The two parts of the fraction are the numerator and the denominator. In the fraction $\frac{3}{4}$, 3 is the numerator and 4 is the denominator. In any fraction, the numerator is being divided by the denominator. So in the previous example, 3 is being divided by 4.

- A **mixed number** is an integer together with a fraction, such as $2\frac{3}{5}$. The integer is the integral part, and the fraction is the fractional part.

- An **improper fraction** is one in which the numerator is equal to or greater than the denominator, such as $\frac{19}{6}$, $\frac{25}{4}$, or $\frac{10}{10}$.

> **Note**
> In a fraction problem, the whole quantity is 1, which can be expressed by a fraction in which the numerator and denominator are the same number. For example, if a problem involves $\frac{1}{8}$ of a quantity, the whole quantity is $\frac{8}{8}$, or 1.

Rules to Know

If you understand the rules outlined in this section, you'll be able to solve any arithmetic problem that involves fractions and mixed numbers. Study the rules and example problems, and be sure that you understand each rule before moving on to the practice exercises.

Converting Mixed Numbers and Improper Fractions

It's often helpful to convert mixed numbers to improper fractions to solve fraction problems. Follow these steps:

1. Multiply the denominator of the fraction by the integer.
2. Add the numerator to this product.
3. Place this sum over the denominator.

To change $3\frac{4}{7}$ to an improper fraction, for example, follow these steps:

1. 7 (denominator) × 3 (integer) = 21
2. 21 (product) + 4 (numerator) = 25
3. The answer is $\frac{25}{7}$.

To convert an improper fraction to a mixed number, reverse the steps:

1. Divide the numerator by the denominator. The quotient, disregarding the remainder, is the integral part of the mixed number.

2. Place the remainder, if any, over the denominator. This is the fractional part of the mixed number.

Change $\frac{36}{13}$ to a mixed number:

1. 36 (numerator) ÷ 13 (denominator) = 2 with a remainder of 10

2. The answer is $2\frac{10}{13}$.

Reducing Fractions

The numerator and denominator of a fraction can be changed by dividing both by the same number, without affecting the value of the fraction. This process is called reducing the fraction. A fraction that has been reduced as much as possible is said to be in lowest terms.

For example, the value of the fraction $\frac{3}{12}$ is not altered if both the numerator and denominator are divided by 3, resulting in $\frac{1}{4}$. Likewise, if $\frac{6}{30}$ is reduced to lowest terms (by dividing both numerator and denominator by 6), the result is $\frac{1}{5}$.

Note
The numerator and denominator of a fraction can also be multiplied by the same number without affecting the value of the fraction.

Tip
To arrive at the final answer to a problem, reduce fractions as far as possible, and change improper fractions to mixed numbers.

Adding Fractions

Fractions can't be added unless the denominators are all the same. To convert all fractions to the same denominator, you must first find the lowest common denominator.

The lowest common denominator (LCD) is the lowest number that can be divided evenly by all the given denominators. If no two of the given denominators can be divided by the same number, the LCD is the product of all the denominators.

To find the LCD when two or more of the given denominators can be divided by the same number, follow these steps:

1. Write down all the denominators.

2. Select the smallest number (other than 1) by which two or more of the denominators can be divided evenly.

3. Divide the denominators by this number, copying down those that cannot be divided evenly. Write this number to one side.

4. Repeat this process, writing each divisor to one side until there are no longer any denominators that can be divided evenly by the same number.

5. Multiply all the divisors to find the LCD.

To find the LCD of $\frac{1}{5}$, $\frac{1}{7}$, $\frac{1}{10}$, and $\frac{1}{14}$, follow these steps:

1. Write down the denominators: 5, 7, 10, 14

2. 10 and 14 can be divided by 2: 5, 7, 5, 7

3. 5 and 5 can be divided by 5: 1, 7, 1, 7

4. 7 and 7 can be divided by 7: 1, 1, 1, 1

5. None of the remainders can be divided any further. Multiply the divisors: $2 \times 5 \times 7 = 70$

70 is the lowest common denominator.

Tip
If two fractions have the same denominator, the one with the larger numerator is the *greater* fraction. If two fractions have the same numerator, the one with the larger denominator is the *smaller* fraction. To compare fractions with different numerators and denominators, change them to equivalent fractions by finding the LCD.

Now that you know how to find the LCD, you can add any fractions by following these steps:

1. Find the LCD of the denominators.

2. Convert each fraction to an equivalent fraction with the LCD as its denominator.

3. Add all the numerators and place this sum over the common denominator.

4. Reduce the answer as far as possible. Change improper fractions to mixed numbers.

Add $\frac{1}{4}$, $\frac{3}{10}$, and $\frac{2}{5}$:

1. Find the LCD; your answer should be 20.
2. Convert each fraction to one having a denominator of 20: $\frac{1}{4} \times \frac{5}{5} = \frac{5}{20}$;
   $\frac{3}{10} \times \frac{2}{2} = \frac{6}{20}$; $\frac{2}{5} \times \frac{4}{4} = \frac{8}{20}$
3. Add all the numerators: $5 + 6 + 8 = 19$
4. Place the sum over the common denominator: $\frac{19}{20}$. This is not an improper fraction and it cannot be reduced, so it is the final answer.

> **Tip**
> If the problem contains any mixed numbers, add the fractions first, and then add the integers. You don't need to convert the mixed numbers to improper fractions.

Subtracting Fractions

In subtraction, as in addition, the denominators must be the same. Follow these steps to subtract fractions:

1. Find the LCD of the two fractions.
2. Convert both fractions to equivalent fractions with the LCD as the denominator.
3. Subtract the numerator of the second fraction from the numerator of the first, and place this difference over the LCD.
4. Reduce the fraction, if possible, and convert improper fractions to mixed numbers.

> **Tip**
> When subtracting mixed numbers, it may be necessary to "borrow," so that the fractional part of the first term is larger than the fractional part of the second term. Otherwise, subtract the fractions and integers separately.

Subtract $16\frac{4}{5}$ from $29\frac{1}{3}$:

1. Find the LCD: $5 \times 3 = 15$.
2. Convert both fractions to ones with the LCD: $29\frac{5}{15} - 16\frac{12}{15}$.
3. Note that $\frac{5}{15}$ is less than $\frac{12}{15}$. Borrow 1 from 29, which is equivalent to $\frac{15}{15}$, and add this to the fraction: $28\frac{20}{15} - 16\frac{12}{15}$.
4. Subtract the numerators and the integers. The answer is $12\frac{8}{15}$.

Multiplying Fractions

Fractions don't need to have the same denominators to be multiplied. Follow these steps to multiply fractions:

1. Change the mixed numbers, if any, to improper fractions.
2. Multiply all the numerators.
3. Multiply all the denominators.
4. Place the product of the numerators over the product of the denominators.
5. Reduce, if possible, and convert improper fractions to mixed numbers.

Multiply $\frac{2}{3} \times 2\frac{4}{7} \times \frac{5}{9}$:

1. Convert $2\frac{4}{7}$ to an improper fraction: $\frac{18}{7}$.
2. Multiply the numerators and denominators, and put the products on top of each other: $\frac{2}{3} \times \frac{18}{7} \times \frac{5}{9} = \frac{180}{189}$.
3. Reduce as much as possible: $\frac{180}{189} \div \frac{9}{9} = \frac{20}{21}$.

Note

A whole number has an understood denominator of 1. To multiply a whole number by a mixed number, first multiply the fractional part of the mixed number by the whole number, and then the integral part of the mixed number; then add both products. For example, to multiply $23\frac{3}{4}$ by 95, first multiply $\frac{3}{4}$ by $\frac{95}{1}$, then multiply 23 by 95, and then add the results of each. You should get $2256\frac{1}{4}$.

Tip

Dividing a numerator and a denominator by the same number in a multiplication problem, or canceling, can facilitate multiplication. In the problem $\frac{4}{7} \times \frac{5}{6}$, the numerator 4 and the denominator 6 can both be divided by 2: $\frac{2}{7} \times \frac{5}{3} = \frac{10}{21}$.

Dividing Fractions

To divide two fractions, multiply one fraction by the other's reciprocal. The reciprocal of a fraction is its invert; for example, the reciprocal of $\frac{3}{8}$ is $\frac{8}{3}$. Since every whole number has an understood denominator of 1, the reciprocal of a whole number has 1 as the numerator and the whole number as the denominator; for example, the reciprocal of 5 is $\frac{1}{5}$.

Follow these steps to divide two fractions:

1.   Convert all mixed numbers, if any, to improper fractions.

2.   Invert the second fraction, and multiply the two.

3.   Reduce the answer, if possible. Convert improper fractions to mixed numbers.

Divide $\frac{2}{3}$ by $2\frac{1}{4}$:

1.   Convert $2\frac{1}{4}$ to an improper fraction: $\frac{9}{4}$.

2.   Invert the second fraction and multiply the two: $\frac{2}{3} \div \frac{9}{4} = \frac{2}{3} \times \frac{4}{9}$.

3.   The answer is $\frac{8}{27}$.

Tip

A complex fraction has a fraction as the numerator and/or the denominator,

such as $\frac{\frac{2}{3}}{\frac{5}{14}}$. To clear (or simplify) a complex fraction, divide the numerator by

the denominator and reduce.

Tackling Fraction Problems

Most fraction problems can be arranged in the form, "What fraction of a number is another number?" This form contains three important parts: the fractional part; the number following "of"; and the number following "is." Follow these rules to find the answer:

- If the fraction and the "of" number are given, multiply them to find the "is" number. For example, if asked, "What is $\frac{3}{4}$ of 20?" rewrite the question as "$\frac{3}{4}$ of 20 is what number?" Then multiply $\frac{3}{4}$ (the fraction) by 20 (the "of" number) to get $\frac{60}{4}$, which can be reduced to 15.

- If the fraction and the "is" number are given, divide the "is" number by the fraction to find the "of" number. For example, if asked, "$\frac{4}{5}$ of what number is 40?" divide 40 (the "is" number) by $\frac{4}{5}$ (the fraction) to get $\frac{200}{4}$, which can be reduced to 50.

- To find the fraction when the other two numbers are known, divide the "is" number by the "of" number. For example, if asked, "What part of 12 is 9?" divide 9 (the "is" number) by 12 (the "of" number). The answer is $\frac{9}{12}$, which can be reduced to $\frac{3}{4}$.

Workshop: Fractions

In this workshop, you'll apply what you learned about fractions to the kind of fraction problems you might find on a civil service test. Answers and explanations follow Exercise 2.

Practice Exercise 1

DIRECTIONS: Each question has four suggested answers. Select the correct one.

1. Reduce to lowest terms: $\frac{60}{108}$.

   (A) $\frac{1}{48}$

   (B) $\frac{1}{3}$

   (C) $\frac{5}{9}$

   (D) $\frac{10}{18}$

2. Change $\frac{27}{7}$ to a mixed number.

   (A) $2\frac{1}{7}$

   ✓(B) $3\frac{6}{7}$

   (C) $6\frac{1}{3}$

   (D) $7\frac{1}{2}$

3. Find the LCD of $\frac{1}{6}$, $\frac{1}{10}$, $\frac{1}{18}$, and $\frac{1}{21}$.

   (A)   160

   (B)   330

   (C)   630

   (D)   1260

4. Add $16\frac{3}{8}$, $4\frac{4}{5}$, $12\frac{3}{4}$, and $23\frac{5}{6}$.

   (A) $57\frac{91}{120}$

   (B) $57\frac{1}{4}$

   (C)   58

   (D)   59

5. Subtract $27\frac{5}{14}$ from $43\frac{1}{6}$.

   (A)   15

   (B)   16

   (C) $15\frac{8}{21}$

   (D) $15\frac{17}{21}$

6. Multiply $17\frac{5}{8}$ by 128.

   (A)   2200

   (B)   2305

   (C)   2356

   (D)   2256

7. Divide $1\frac{2}{3}$ by $1\frac{1}{9}$.

   (A) $\frac{2}{3}$

   (B) $1\frac{1}{2}$

   (C) $1\frac{23}{27}$

   (D)   6

Practice Exercise 2

DIRECTIONS: Each question has four suggested answers. Select the correct one.

1. The number of half-pound packages of tea that can be weighed out of a box that holds $10\frac{1}{2}$ pounds of tea is

    (A)   5

    (B) $10\frac{1}{2}$

    (C) $20\frac{1}{2}$

    (D)   21

2. If each bag of tokens weighs $5\frac{3}{4}$ pounds, how many pounds do three bags weigh?

    (A) $7\frac{1}{4}$

    (B) $15\frac{3}{4}$

    (C) $16\frac{1}{2}$

    (D) $17\frac{1}{4}$

3. During one week, a man traveled $3\frac{1}{2}$, $1\frac{1}{4}$, $1\frac{14}{24}$, and $2\frac{3}{8}$ miles. The next week he traveled $\frac{1}{4}$, $\frac{3}{8}$, $\frac{9}{16}$, $3\frac{1}{16}$, $2\frac{5}{8}$, and $3\frac{3}{16}$ miles. How many more miles did he travel the second week than the first week?

    (A) $1\frac{7}{8}$

    (B) $1\frac{1}{2}$

    (C) $1\frac{3}{4}$

    (D)   1

4. A certain type of board is sold only in lengths of multiples of two feet. The shortest board sold is 6 feet and the longest is 24 feet. A builder needs a large quantity of this type of board in $5\frac{1}{2}$-foot lengths. For minimum waste, the lengths to be ordered should be

    (A)   6 feet

    (B)   12 feet

    (C)   22 feet

    (D)   24 feet

5. A man spent $\frac{15}{16}$ of his entire fortune in buying a car for $7500. How much money did he possess?

    (A) $6000

    (B) $6500

    (C) $7000

    (D) $8000

6. The population of a town was 54,000 in the last census. It has increased $\frac{2}{3}$ since then. Its present population is

    (A)   18,000

    (B)   36,000

    (C)   72,000

    (D)   90,000

7. If one-third of the liquid contents of a can evaporates on the first day, and three-fourths of the remainder evaporates on the second day, the part of the original contents remaining at the close of the second day is

(A) $\frac{5}{12}$

(B) $\frac{7}{12}$

(C) $\frac{1}{6}$

(D) $\frac{1}{2}$

8. A car is run until the gas tank is $\frac{1}{8}$ full. The tank is then filled to capacity by putting in 14 gallons. The capacity of the gas tank of the car is

(A)   14 gal.

(B)   15 gal.

(C)   16 gal.

(D)   17 gal.

Answers and Explanations

Practice Test 1

1. **(C)** Divide the numerator and denominator by 12 to get $\frac{5}{9}$.

2. **(B)** Divide the numerator (27) by the denominator (7) to get 3 with a remainder of 6; the answer is $3\frac{6}{7}$.

3. **(C)** You can divide the denominators by 2, 3, 3, 5, and 7. Multiply these divisors to find 630.

4. **(A)** The LCD is 120, so the mixed numbers convert to $16\frac{45}{120} + 4\frac{96}{120} + 12\frac{90}{120} + 23\frac{100}{120}$. Add the numerators and the integers: $55\frac{331}{120}$. Change the improper fraction to a mixed number: $57\frac{91}{120}$.

5. **(D)** The LCD is 42, so the mixed numbers convert to $43\frac{7}{42} - 27\frac{15}{42}$. "Borrow" to make the first numerator greater than the second: $42\frac{49}{42} - 27\frac{15}{42}$. Subtract the integers and numerators: $15\frac{34}{42}$. Reduce: $15\frac{17}{21}$.

6. **(D)** Convert $17\frac{5}{8}$ to an improper fraction: $\frac{141}{8}$. Multiply the numerators and denominators: $\frac{141}{8} \times \frac{128}{1} = \frac{18048}{8}$. Reduce: 2256.

7. **(B)** Convert the mixed numbers to improper fractions: $\frac{5}{3} \div \frac{10}{9}$. Invert the second fraction and multiply: $\frac{5}{3} \times \frac{9}{10} = \frac{45}{30}$. Reduce: $\frac{3}{2}$. Convert to a mixed number: $1\frac{1}{2}$.

Practice Exercise 2

1. **(D)** Divide $10\frac{1}{2}$ pounds by $\frac{1}{2}$ pound:
   $\frac{21}{2} \div \frac{1}{2} = \frac{21}{2} \times \frac{2}{1} = \frac{42}{2} = 21.$

2. **(D)** Multiply $5\frac{3}{4}$ pounds by 3:
   $\frac{23}{4} \times \frac{3}{1} = \frac{69}{4} = 17\frac{1}{4}.$

3. **(A)** For the first week, the LCD is 16; add all the fractions to get $8\frac{3}{16}$ miles. For the second week, the LCD is 16; add all the fractions to get $10\frac{1}{16}$ miles. Subtract $8\frac{3}{16}$ from $10\frac{1}{16}$. "Borrow" to make the first numerator greater than the second: $9\frac{17}{16} - 8\frac{3}{16} = 1\frac{14}{16}$. Reduce to $1\frac{7}{8}$.

4. **(C)** Consider each choice. Each 6-foot board yields one $5\frac{1}{2}$-foot board with $\frac{1}{2}$ foot waste. Each 12-foot board yields two $5\frac{1}{2}$-foot boards with 1 foot waste ($2 \times 5\frac{1}{2} = 11$; $12 - 11 = 1$). Each 24-foot board

   yields four $5\frac{1}{2}$-foot boards with 2 feet waste ($4 \times 5\frac{1}{2} = 22$; $24 - 22 = 2$). Each 22-foot board yields four $5\frac{1}{2}$-foot boards with no waste ($4 \times 5\frac{1}{2} = 22$ exactly). So 22 feet is the best choice.

5. **(D)** $\frac{15}{16}$ of the fortune is $7500. Therefore, the fortune is $7500 \div \frac{15}{16}$ or $8000.

6. **(D)** The increase equals $\frac{2}{3}$ of 54,000. Therefore, the increase is $\frac{2}{3} \times \frac{54000}{1}$ or 36,000. The present population is 54,000 + 36,000 or 90,000.

7. **(C)** On the first day, $\frac{1}{3}$ evaporates and $\frac{2}{3}$ remains. On the second day, $\frac{3}{4}$ of $\frac{2}{3}$ evaporates, and $\frac{1}{4}$ of $\frac{2}{3}$ remains. The amount remaining is $\frac{1}{4} \times \frac{2}{3}$ or $\frac{1}{6}$ of the original contents.

8. **(C)** $\frac{7}{8}$ of capacity equals 14 gal. Therefore, the capacity is $14 \div \frac{7}{8}$ or 16 gal.

Decimals

A decimal is actually a fraction, the denominator of which is understood to be a power of 10. The number of digits, or places, after a decimal point determines which power of 10 the denominator is. If there is one digit, the denominator is 10; if there are two digits, the denominator is 100, and so on. For example, $.3 = \frac{3}{10}$, $.57 = \frac{57}{100}$, and $.643 = \frac{643}{1000}$.

> **Note**
> Adding zeros after a decimal point doesn't change the value of the decimal:
> .7 = .70 = .700.

> **Tip**
> Convert a mixed number containing a decimal to a fraction by dividing the mixed number by the power of 10 indicated by its number of decimal places. The fraction doesn't count as a decimal place. To convert .25 $\frac{1}{3}$ to a fraction, for example, divide 25 $\frac{1}{3}$ by 100.

Rules to Know

Study the rules outlined in this section to learn how to solve any arithmetic problem that involves decimals. Be sure that you understand the rules before moving on to the practice problems.

Adding and Subtracting Decimals

Decimals are added and subtracted in the same way as whole numbers. However, decimal points must be kept in a vertical line to determine the place of the decimal point in the answer:

$$
\begin{array}{r}
2.3100 \\
.0370 \\
4.0000 \\
+\ 5.0017 \\
\hline
11.3487
\end{array}
\qquad
\begin{array}{r}
15.3000 \\
-\ 4.0037 \\
\hline
11.2963
\end{array}
$$

Multiplying Decimals

Decimals are multiplied the same way as whole numbers. The number of decimal places in the product equals the sum of the decimal places in the multiplicand and the multiplier. If there are fewer places in the product than this sum, then a sufficient number of zeros must be added in front of the product to equal the number of places required, and the decimal point is placed in front of the zeros. For example, 2.372 (three decimal places) × .012 (three decimal places) = .028464 (six decimal places).

> **Tip**
> A decimal can be multiplied by a power of 10 by moving the decimal point to the *right* as many places as indicated by the power: .235 ×10 = 2.35.

Dividing Decimals

There are four types of division involving decimals:

- When the dividend only is a decimal, the division is the same as that of whole numbers; the number of decimal places in the answer must equal that in the dividend: $12.864 \div 32 = .402$.

- When the divisor only is a decimal, the decimal point in the divisor is omitted and as many zeros are placed to the right of the dividend as there are decimal points in the divisor: $211{,}327 \div 6.817 = 211{,}327{,}000 \div 6817 = 31{,}000$.

- When both divisor and divided are decimals, the decimal point in the divisor is omitted, and the decimal point in the dividend is moved to the right as many decimal places as there are in the divisor. If there aren't enough places in the dividend, zeros must be added to make up the difference: $2.62 \div .131 = 2620 \div 131 = 20$.

- When neither the divisor nor the dividend is a decimal, the problem may still involve decimals. This occurs when the dividend is a smaller number than the divisor, and when you must work out a division to a certain number of decimal places. In either case, write in a decimal point after the dividend, add as many zeros as necessary, and then divide: $7 \div 50 = 7.00 \div 50 = .14$.

> **Tip**
> A decimal can be divided by a power of 10 by moving the decimal to the *left* as many places as indicated by the power. If there aren't enough places, add zeros in front of the number to make up the difference: .4 ÷ 10 = .04.

Converting Fractions to Decimals

A fraction can be changed to a decimal by dividing the numerator by the denominator and working out the division to as many decimal points as required. For example, to change $\frac{5}{11}$ to a decimal of two places, divide 5.00 by 11, which equals $.45\frac{5}{11}$.

Because decimal equivalents of fractions are often used, it's helpful to be familiar with the most common conversions (the decimal values have been rounded to the nearest ten-thousandth):

$\frac{1}{2} = .5$

$\frac{1}{3} = .3333$

$\frac{2}{3} = .6667$

$\frac{1}{4} = .25$

$\frac{3}{4} = .75$

$\frac{1}{5} = .2$

$\frac{1}{8} = .125$

Workshop: Decimals

Here you'll have a chance to apply what you have just learned to a variety of civil service test questions. Answers and explanations for these questions follow Exercise 2.

Practice Exercise 1

DIRECTIONS: Each question has four suggested answers. Select the correct one.

1. Add 37.03, 11.5627, 3.4005, 3423, and 1.141.
    - (A)   3476.1342
    - (B)   3500
    - (C)   3524.4322
    - (D)   3424.1342

2. Subtract 4.64324 from 7.
    - (A)   3.35676
    - (B)   2.35676
    - (C)   2.45676
    - (D)   2.36676

3. Multiply 27.34 by 16.943.
    - (A)   463.22162
    - (B)   453.52162
    - (C)   462.52162
    - (D)   462.53162

4. How much is 19.6 divided by 3.2 carried out to three decimal places?
    - (A)   6.125
    - (B)   6.124
    - (C)   6.123
    - (D)   5.123

5. What is $\frac{5}{11}$ in decimal form (to the nearest hundredth)?
    - (A)   .44
    - (B)   .55
    - (C)   .40
    - (D)   .45

6.   What is $.64\frac{2}{3}$ in fraction form?

(A) $\frac{97}{120}$

(B) $\frac{97}{150}$

(C) $\frac{97}{130}$

(D) $\frac{98}{130}$

7.   What is the difference between $\frac{9}{8}$ and $\frac{3}{5}$ expressed decimally?

(A)   .525

(B)   .425

(C)   .520

(D)   .500

Practice Exercise 2

DIRECTIONS: Each question has four suggested answers. Select the correct one.

1.   A boy saved up $4.56 the first month, $3.82 the second month, and $5.06 the third month. How much did he save altogether?

(A) $12.56

(B) $13.28

(C) $13.44

(D) $14.02

2.   The diameter of a certain rod is required to be 1.51 ± .015 inches. The rod would not be acceptable if the diameter measured

(A)   1.490 inches

(B)   1.500 inches

(C)   1.510 inches

(D)   1.525 inches

3.   After an employer figures out an employee's salary of $190.57, he deducts $3.05 for Social Security and $5.68 for pension. What is the amount of the check after these deductions?

(A) $181.84

(B) $181.92

(C) $181.93

(D) $181.99

4.   If the outer diameter of a metal pipe is 2.84 inches and the inner diameter is 1.94 inches, the thickness of the metal is

(A)   .45 inches

(B)   .90 inches

(C)   1.94 inches

(D)   2.39 inches

5. A boy earns $20.56 on Monday, $32.90 on Tuesday, and $20.78 on Wednesday. He spends half of all that he earned during the three days. How much has he left?

    (A) $29.19
    (B) $31.23
    (C) $34.27
    (D) $37.12

6. To the nearest cent, the total cost of $3\frac{1}{2}$ pounds of meat at $1.69 a pound and 20 lemons at $.60 a dozen will be

    (A) $6.00
    (B) $6.40
    (C) $6.52
    (D) $6.92

7. A reel of cable weighs 1279 pounds. If the empty reel weighs 285 pounds and the cable weighs 7.1 pounds per foot, the number of feet of cable on the reel is

    (A)   220
    (B)   180
    (C)   140
    (D)   100

8. To the nearest cent, 345 fasteners at $4.15 per hundred will cost

    (A) $.14
    (B) $1.43
    (C) $14.32
    (D) $143.20

Answers and Explanations

Practice Exercise 1

1. (A) 3476.1342. Line up the decimal points one under the other before adding.

2. (B) 2.35676. Add a decimal point and five zeros to the 7 before subtracting.

3. (A) 463.22162. Because two decimal places are in the multiplicand and three decimal places are in the multiplier, there should be five decimal places in the product.

4. (A) Omit the decimal point in the divisor by moving it one place to the right. Move the decimal point in the dividend one place to the right and add three zeros in order to carry your answer out to three decimal places: $196.000 \div 32 = 6.125$.

5. (D) Divide the numerator by the denominator: $5.000 \div 11 = .45$ to the nearest hundredth.

6. (B) Divide by the power of 10 indicated by the number of decimal places. (The fraction doesn't count as a decimal place.) $64\frac{2}{3} \div 100 = \frac{97}{150}$.

7. (A) Convert each fraction to a decimal and subtract to find the difference: $\frac{9}{8} = 1.125$; $\frac{3}{5} = .60$; $1.125 - .60 = .525$.

Practice Exercise 2

1. **(C)** Add the savings for each month: $13.44.

2. **(A)** The rod may have a diameter of 1.495 inches to 1.525 inches: 1.51 + .015 = 1.525; 1.510 – .015 = 1.495. Therefore, 1.490 in. is not acceptable.

3. **(A)** Add to find the total deductions: $3.05 + $5.68 = $8.73. Subtract total deductions from salary to find the amount of the check: $190.57 – $8.73 = $181.84.

4. **(A)** The difference of the two diameters equals the total thickness of the metal on both ends of the inner diameter. Find the difference of the two diameters, and then divide by 2: 2.84 - 1.94 = .90; .90 ÷ 2 = .45 in. (the thickness of the metal).

5. **(D)** Add the daily earnings to find the total earnings: $20.56 + $32.90 + $20.78 = $74.24. Divide the total earnings by 2 to find what he has left: $74.24 ÷ 2 = $37.12.

6. **(D)** Find the cost of $3\frac{1}{2}$ pounds of meat: $1.69 × 3.5 = $5.92 (to the nearest cent). Find the cost of 20 lemons: .60 ÷ 12 = $.05 (for one lemon); $.05 × 20 = $1.00 (for 20 lemons). Add the cost of the meat and the cost of the lemons: $5.92 + $1.00 = $6.92.

7. **(C)** Subtract the weight of the empty reel from the total weight to find the weight of the cable: 1279 pounds – 285 pounds = 994 pounds. Each foot of cable weighs 7.1 pounds; therefore, to find the number of feet of cable on the reel, divide 994 by 7.1 = 140.

8. **(C)** Each fastener costs $4.15 ÷ 100 = $.0415. 345 fasteners cost 345 × .0415 = $14.32 (rounded to the nearest cent).

The Hour in Review

1. Understanding the rules for adding, subtracting, multiplying, and dividing fractions will make it a simple matter to solve arithmetic problems involving fractions. Remember to reduce the answer as much as possible and convert improper fractions to mixed numbers.

2. Often, the phrasing of a fraction problem provides a clue as to whether the two given numbers must be divided or multiplied to find the answer.

3. Decimals are fractions where the denominator is some power of 10, as determined by the placement of the decimal point.

4. Adding, subtracting, multiplying, and dividing decimals is the same as for whole numbers, except you must pay attention to the placement of the decimal point in the answer.

HOUR 16

Percents, Ratio, and Proportion

What You Will Learn in This Hour

Percent, ratio, and proportion problems are commonly found on civil service exams, usually in the form of word problems. These types of problems build on what you already know about solving problems involving fractions and decimals, so review the rules in Hour 15 if you're having trouble. Here are your goals for this hour:

- Solving problems involving percents.
- Solving problems involving ratios and proportions.

Percents

The percent symbol (%) means "parts of a hundred." Some problems require you to express a fraction or a decimal as a percent. In other problems, you must convert a percent to a fraction or decimal to perform the calculations.

Rules to Know

Often, percent problems require you to change a fraction, mixed number, or decimal to a percent, and vice versa, so it's important to understand the following rules for making these conversions.

Converting Decimals to Percents

Follow these steps to change a whole number or decimal to a percent:

1.   Multiply the number by 100.
2.   Affix a % sign to the product.

To change 3 to a percent, for example, multiply 3 by 100 and affix a percent sign: 300%. To change .67 to a percent, multiply .67 by 100 and affix a percent sign: 67%.

> **Tip**
> To convert a percent to a decimal or whole number, divide the percent by 100. For example, .5% equals .005. You can then convert the resulting decimal to a fraction, if necessary.

Converting Fractions to Percents

Follow these steps to change a fraction or mixed number to a percent:

1.   Multiply the fraction or mixed number by 100.
2.   Reduce, if possible, and convert improper fractions to mixed numbers.
3.   Affix a % sign to the result.

Change $4\frac{2}{3}$ to a percent:

1.   Multiply $4\frac{2}{3}$ by 100: $\frac{14}{3} \times 100 = \frac{1400}{3}$.

2.   Convert the improper fraction to a mixed number: $466\frac{2}{3}$.

3.   Affix a percent sign: $466\frac{2}{3}\%$.

Some fraction-percent equivalents are used so frequently that it's helpful to be familiar with them:

$$\frac{1}{25} = 4\%$$

$$\frac{1}{20} = 5\%$$

$$\frac{1}{10} = 10\%$$

$$\frac{1}{5} = 20\%$$

$$\frac{1}{4} = 25\%$$

$$\frac{1}{2} = 50\%$$

$$\frac{3}{4} = 75\%$$

Tip

To convert a fractional percent to a fraction, divide the fractional percent by 100 and reduce, if possible. For example, $\frac{3}{4}\% \div 100 = \frac{3}{400}$. You can then convert the resulting fraction to a decimal, if necessary.

Tackling Percent Problems

Most percent problems involve three quantities:

- the rate (R), which is followed by a percent sign
- the base (B), which follows the word "of"
- the amount of percentage (P), which usually follows the word "is"

Depending on which two quantities you know, you can easily find the third quantity by following a formula:

- If the rate and the base are known, then $P = R \times B$.
- If the rate and the percentage are known, then $B = \frac{P}{R}$.
- If the percentage and the base are known, then $R = \frac{P}{B}$.

Try an example of each kind of problem:

1.   Find 15% of 50.

In this problem, you know the rate (15%) and the base (50). To find the percentage, multiply 15% by 50: $.15 \times 50 = 7.5$.

2.   7% of what number is 35?

In this problem, you know the rate (7%) and the percentage (35). To find the base, divide 35 by 7%: $35 \div .07 = 500$.

3.   There are 96 men in a group of 150 people. What percent of the group are men?

Here you know the base (150) and the amount, or percentage (96). To find the rate, divide 96 by 150: $96 \div 150 = .64$ or 64%.

Tip
In all percent problems, the whole is always 100%. Knowing this, you can often deduct a solution to a problem. If a problem involves 10% of a quantity, the rest of the quantity is 90%; if a quantity has been decreased by 15%, the new amount is 85% of the original quantity; or if a quantity has been increased by 5%, the new amount is 105% of the original quantity.

Workshop: Percents

In this workshop, you'll apply what you have learned about percents to the kinds of problems you might face on a civil service test. Answers and explanations to these questions follow Exercise 2.

Practice Exercise 1

DIRECTIONS: Each question has four suggested answers. Select the correct one.

---

1. 10% written as a decimal is

    (A)   1.0
    (B)   0.01
    (C)   0.001
    (D)   0.1

2. What is 5.37% in fraction form?

    (A) $\frac{537}{10,000}$

    (B) $5\frac{37}{10,000}$

    (C) $\frac{537}{1000}$

    (D) $5\frac{37}{100}$

3. What percent of $\frac{5}{6}$ is $\frac{3}{4}$?

    (A)   75%
    (B)   60%
    (C)   80%
    (D)   90%

4. What percent is 14 of 24?

    (A) $62\frac{1}{4}\%$

    (B) $58\frac{1}{3}\%$

    (C) $41\frac{2}{3}\%$

    (D) $33\frac{3}{5}\%$

5. 200% of 800 equals

    (A)   2500
    (B)   16
    (C)   1600
    (D)   4

16

Practice Exercise 2

DIRECTIONS: Each question has four suggested answers. Select the correct one.

1. If John must have a mark of 80% to pass a test of 35 items, the number of items he may miss and still pass the test is
   (A)   7
   (B)   8
   (C)   11
   (D)   28

2. The regular price of a TV set that sold for $118.80 at a 20% reduction sale is
   (A) $148.50
   (B) $142.60
   (C) $138.84
   (D) $95.04

3. A circle graph of a budget shows the expenditure of 26.2% for housing, 28.4% for food, 12% for clothing, 12.7% for taxes, and the balance for miscellaneous items. The percent for miscellaneous items is
   (A)   31.5
   (B)   79.3
   (C)   20.7
   (D)   68.5

4. Two dozen shuttlecocks and four badminton rackets are to be purchased for a playground. The shuttlecocks are priced at $.35 each and the rackets at $2.75 each. The playground receives a discount of 30% from these prices. The total cost of this equipment is
   (A) $7.29
   (B) $11.43
   (C) $13.58
   (D) $18.60

5. A piece of wood weighing 10 ounces is found to have a weight of 8 ounces after drying. The moisture content was
   (A)   25%
   (B) $33\frac{1}{3}\%$
   (C)   20%
   (D)   40%

6. A bag contains 800 coins. Of these, 10 percent are dimes, 30 percent are nickels, and the rest are quarters. The amount of money in the bag is
   (A)   less than $150
   (B)   between $150 and $300
   (C)   between $301 and $450
   (D)   more than $450

7. Six quarts of a 20% solution of alcohol in water are mixed with four quarts of a 60% solution of alcohol in water. The alcoholic strength of the mixture is
   (A)   80%
   (B)   40%
   (C)   36%
   (D)   72%

8. A man insures 80% of his property and pays a $2\frac{1}{2}\%$ premium amounting to $348. What is the total value of his property?
   (A) $17,000
   (B) $18,000
   (C) $18,400
   (D) $17,400

9. A clerk divided his 35-hour workweek as
    follows: $\frac{1}{5}$ of his time was spent in sort-
    ing mail; $\frac{1}{2}$ of his time in filing letters;
    and $\frac{1}{7}$ of his time in reception work. The
    rest of his time was devoted to messenger
    work. The percent of time spent on mes-
    senger work by the clerk during the week
    was most nearly

    (A)   6%
    (B)   10%
    (C)   14%
    (D)   16%

10. In a school in which 40% of the enrolled
    students are boys, 80% of the boys are
    present on a certain day. If 1152 boys are
    present, the total school enrollment is

    (A)   1440
    (B)   2880
    (C)   3600
    (D)   5400

16

Answers and Explanations

Practice Exercise 1

1. **(D)** $10\% \div 100 = 0.1$

2. **(A)** $5.37\% \div 100 = .0537 = \frac{537}{10,000}$

3. **(D)** Base (number following "of") = $\frac{5}{6}$; percentage (number following "is") = $\frac{3}{4}$;
    rate = percentage ÷ base = $\frac{3}{4} \div \frac{5}{6} = \frac{9}{10} = .9 = 90\%$

4. **(B)** Base (number following "of") = 24; percentage (number following "is") = 14;
    rate = percentage ÷ base = $14 \div 24 = .58\frac{1}{3} = 58\frac{1}{3}\%$

5. **(C)** Percentage = 200; base = 800; rate = percentage x base = $2.00 \times 800 = 1600$

Practice Exercise 2

1. **(A)** He must answer 80% of 35 correctly. Therefore, he can miss 20% of 35. 20% of 35
    (percentage) = .20 (rate) × 35 (base) = 7.

2. **(A)** Since $118.80 represents a 20% reduction, $118.80 equals 80% of the regular price. The
    regular price (base) = $118.80 (percentage) ÷ 80% (rate) = 118.80 ÷ .80 = $148.50.

3. **(C)** All the items in a circle graph total 100%. Add the figures given for housing, food,
    clothing, and taxes: 26.2 + 28.4 + 12 + 12.7 = 79.3%. Subtract this total from 100% to find
    the percent for miscellaneous items: 100 – 79.3 = 20.7%.

4. **(C)** The price of the shuttlecocks: 24 × $.35 = $8.40. The price of the rackets: 4 × $2.75 = $11.00. The total price: $8.40 + $11.00 = $19.40. The discount is 30%, and 100% minus 30% equals 70%. So the actual cost is 70% of $19.40: .70 (rate) × 19.40 (base) = $13.58 (percentage).

5. **(C)** Subtract the weight of the wood after drying from the original weight of the wood to find the amount of moisture in the wood: $10 - 8 = 2$ ounces of moisture in the wood. The moisture content (rate) equals 2 ounces (percentage) divided by 10 ounces (base): $2 \div 10 = .2 = 20\%$.

6. **(A)** Find the number of each kind of coin: 10% of 800 = .10 × 800 = 80 dimes; 30% of 800 = .30 × 800 = 240 nickels; 60% of 800 = .60 × 800 = 480 quarters. Find the value of the coins: 80 dimes = 80 × .10 = $8.00; 240 nickels = 240 × .05 = $12.00; 480 quarters = 480 × .25 = $120.00; $8.00 + $12.00 + $120.00 = $140.00. So, there is less than $150 in the bag.

7. **(C)** The first solution contains 20% of 6 quarts of alcohol; the alcohol content is .20 × 6 = 1.2 quarts. The second solution contains 60% of 4 quarts of alcohol; the alcohol content is .60 × 4 = 2.4 quarts. The mixture contains 1.2 + 2.4 = 3.6 quarts alcohol, and 6 + 4 = 10 quarts liquid. So the alcoholic strength of the mixture (rate) = 3.6 (percentage) ÷ 10 (base) = 36%.

8. **(D)** $2\frac{1}{2}\%$ or 2.5% of the insured value = $348; the insured value (base) = 348 (percentage) ÷ 2.5% (rate): 348 ÷ .025 = $13,920. The insured value ($13,920) is 80% of the total value; the total value (base) = $13,920 (percentage) ÷ 80% (rate): 13,290 ÷ .80 = $17,400.

9. **(D)** The workweek is 35 hours long. $\frac{1}{5} \times 35 = 7$ hours sorting mail; $\frac{1}{2} \times 35 = 17\frac{1}{2}$ hours filing; $\frac{1}{7} \times 35 = 5$ hours reception. $7 + 17\frac{1}{2} + 5 = 29\frac{1}{2}$ hours accounted for. $35 - 29\frac{1}{2} = 5\frac{1}{2}$ hours left for messenger work. The percentage time spent on messenger work (rate) = $5\frac{1}{2}$ (percentage) ÷ 35 (base) = $\frac{11}{70} = 15\frac{5}{7}$ = most nearly 16%.

10. **(C)** 80% of the boys equals 1152; the total number of boys (base) = 1152 (percentage) ÷ 80% (rate) = 1152 ÷ .80 = 1440 boys. 40% of the students = 1440, so the total number of students (base) = 1440 (percentage) ÷ 40% (rate) = 1440 ÷ .40 = 3600 students.

Ratio and Proportion

Ratio and proportion questions have long been a popular type of arithmetic problem given on civil service exams. This section will help you understand the rules governing ratio and proportion problems.

Solving Ratio Problems

A ratio expresses the relationship between two (or more) quantities in terms of numbers. The mark used to indicate ratio is the colon (:) and is read "to." For example, the ratio 2:3 is read "2 to 3."

A ratio also represents division. Therefore, any ratio of two terms can be written as a fraction, and any fraction can be written as a ratio. For example, $3{:}4 = \frac{3}{4}$.

Follow these steps to solve problems in which the ratio is given:

1.   Add the terms in the ratio.

2.   Divide the total amount that is to be put into a ratio by this sum.

3.   Multiply each term in the ratio by this quotient.

For example, the sum of $360 is to be divided among three people according to the ratio 3:4:5. How much does each one receive?

1.   Add the terms in the ratio: $3 + 4 + 5 = 12$.

2.   Divide the total amount to be put into the ratio by this sum: $\$360 \div 12 = \$30$.

3.   Multiply each term in the ratio by this quotient: $\$30 \times 3 = \$90$; $30 \times 4 = \$120$; $\$30 \times 5 = \$150$.

The money is divided thus: $90, $120, and $150.

> **Tip**
> To simplify any complicated ratio of two terms containing fractions, decimals, or percents, you only need to divide the first term by the second. Reduce the answer to its lowest terms, and write the fraction as a ratio. For example,
> simplify the ratio $\frac{5}{6}{:}\frac{7}{8} ; \frac{5}{6} \div \frac{7}{8} = \frac{20}{21} = 20{:}21$.

Solving Proportion Problems

A proportion indicates the equality of two ratios. For example, $2{:}4 = 5{:}10$ is a proportion. This is read, "2 is to 4 as 5 is to 10." The two outside terms are the extremes (2 and 10), and the two inside terms are the means (4 and 5).

> **Note**
> Proportions are often written in fractional form. For example, the proportion
> $2{:}4 = 5{:}10$ can be written as $\frac{2}{4} = \frac{5}{10}$.

In any proportion, the product of the means equals the product of the extremes. If the proportion is in fractional form, the products can be found by cross-multiplication. For example, in the proportion $\frac{2}{4} = \frac{5}{10}$, $4 \times 5 = 2 \times 10$.

Many problems in which three terms are given and one term is unknown can be solved using proportions. To solve such problems, follow these steps:

1. Formulate the proportion very carefully according to the facts given. (If any term is misplaced, the solution will be incorrect.) Any symbol can be written in place of the missing term.

2. Determine by inspection whether the means or the extremes are known. Multiply the pair that has both terms given.

3. Divide this product by the third term given to find the unknown term.

Try this example problem:

1. The scale on a map shows that 2 centimeters represents 30 miles of actual length. What is the actual length of a road that is represented by 7 centimeters on the map?

In this problem, the map lengths and the actual lengths are in proportion; that is, they have equal ratios. If m stands for the unknown length, the proportion is $\frac{2}{7} = \frac{30}{m}$. As the proportion is written, m is an extreme and is equal to the product of the means, divided by the other extreme: $m = 7 \times 30 \div 2 = 210 \div 2 = 105$. Therefore, 7 cm. on the map represents 105 miles.

Workshop: Ratio and Proportion

Here's your chance to practice what you have just learned with a variety of test-type problems. Answers and explanations follow Exercise 2.

Practice Exercise 1

DIRECTIONS: Each question has four suggested answers. Select the correct one.

1. The ratio of 24 to 64 is
    (A)   8:3
    (B)   24:100
    (C)   3:8
    (D)   64:100

2. The Baltimore Ravens won 8 games and lost 3. The ratio of games won to games played is
    (A)   8:11
    (B)   3:11
    (C)   8:3
    (D)   3:8

3.   The ratio of $\frac{1}{4}$ to $\frac{3}{5}$ is

   (A)   1 to 3

   (B)   3 to 20

   (C)   5 to 12

   (D)   3 to 4

4.   If there are 16 boys and 12 girls in a class, the ratio of the number of girls to the number of children in the class is

   (A)   3 to 4

   (B)   3 to 7

   (C)   4 to 7

   (D)   4 to 3

5.   259 is to 37 as

   (A)   5 is to 1

   (B)   63 is to 441

   (C)   84 is to 12

   (D)   130 is to 19

16

Practice Exercise 2

DIRECTIONS: Each question has four suggested answers. Select the correct one.

1.   Two dozen cans of dog food at the rate of three cans for $1.45 would cost

   (A) $10.05

   (B) $11.20

   (C) $11.60

   (D) $11.75

2.   A snapshot measures $2\frac{1}{2}$ inches by $1\frac{7}{8}$ inches. It is to be enlarged so that the longer dimension will be four inches. The length of the enlarged shorter dimension will be

   (A) $2\frac{1}{2}$ inches

   (B)   3 inches

   (C) $3\frac{3}{8}$ inches

   (D)   none of these

3.   Men's white handkerchiefs cost $2.29 for three. The cost per dozen handkerchiefs is

   (A) $27.48

   (B) $13.74

   (C) $9.16

   (D) $6.87

4.   A certain pole casts a shadow 24 feet long. Another pole 3 feet high casts a shadow 4 feet long. How high is the first pole, given that the heights and shadows are in proportion?

   (A)   18 feet

   (B)   19 feet

   (C)   20 feet

   (D)   21 feet

5. The actual length represented by $3\frac{1}{2}$ inches on a drawing having a scale of $\frac{1}{8}$ inch to the foot is

    (A)   3.75 ft.

    (B)   28 ft.

    (C)   360 ft.

    (D)   120 ft.

6. Aluminum bronze consists of copper and aluminum, usually in the ratio of 10:1 by weight. If an object made of this alloy weighs 77 pounds, how many pounds of aluminum does it contain?

    (A)   7.7

    (B)   7.0

    (C)   70.0

    (D)   62.3

7. It costs 31 cents a square foot to lay vinyl flooring. To lay 180 square feet of flooring, it will cost

    (A) $16.20

    (B) $18.60

    (C) $55.80

    (D) $62.00

8. If a per diem worker earns $352 in 16 days, the amount that he will earn in 117 days is most nearly

    (A) $3050

    (B) $2575

    (C) $2285

    (D) $2080

9. Assuming that on a blueprint, $\frac{1}{8}$ inch equals 12 inches of actual length, the actual length in inches of a steel bar represented on the blueprint by a line $3\frac{3}{4}$ inches long is

    (A) $3\frac{3}{4}$

    (B)   30

    (C)   450

    (D)   360

10. A, B, and C invested $9000, $7000, and $6000, respectively. Their profits were to be divided according to the ratio of their investments. If B uses his share of the firm's profit of $825 to pay a personal debt of $230, how much will he have left?

    (A) $30.50

    (B) $32.50

    (C) $34.50

    (D) $36.50

Answers and Explanations

Practice Exercise 1

1. **(C)** The ratio 24 to 64 can be written 24:64, or $\frac{24}{64}$. In fraction form, the ratio can be reduced to $\frac{3}{8}$, or 3:8.

2. **(A)** The number of games played was $3 + 8 = 11$. The ratio of games won to games played is 8:11.

3. **(C)** $\frac{1}{4} : \frac{3}{5} = \frac{1}{4} \div \frac{3}{5} = \frac{5}{12} = 5:12$

4. **(B)** There are $16 + 12 = 28$ children in the class. The ratio of number of girls to number of children is 12:28, which can be reduced to 3:7.

5. **(C)** The ratio $\frac{259}{37}$ reduces by 37 to $\frac{7}{1}$. The ratio $\frac{84}{12}$ also reduces to $\frac{7}{1}$. Therefore, $\frac{259}{37} = \frac{84}{12}$ is a proportion.

Practice Exercise 2

1. **(C)** The number of cans is proportional to the price. Let p represent the unknown price: $\frac{3}{24} = \frac{1.45}{p}$. $p = 1.45 \times 24 \div 3 = 34.80 \div 3 = \$11.60$.

2. **(B)** Let s represent the unknown shorter dimension: $\frac{2\frac{1}{2}}{4} = \frac{1\frac{7}{8}}{s}$. $s = 4 \times 1\frac{7}{8} \div 2\frac{1}{2} = \frac{15}{2} \div 2\frac{1}{2} = $ 3 inches.

3. **(C)** If p is the cost per dozen (12), the proportion is: $\frac{3}{12} = \frac{2.29}{p}$. $p = 12 \times 2.29 \div 3 = \$9.16$.

4. **(A)** If f is the height of the first pole, the proportion is: $\frac{f}{24} = \frac{3}{4}$. $f = 24 \times 3 \div 4 = 18$ ft.

5. **(B)** If y is the unknown length, the proportion is: $\frac{3\frac{1}{2}}{\frac{1}{8}} = \frac{y}{1}$. $y = 3\frac{1}{2} \times 1 \div \frac{1}{8} = 28$ ft.

6. **(B)** Because only two parts of a proportion are known (77 is the total weight), the problem must be solved by the ratio method. The ratio of 10:1 means that if the alloy were separated into equal parts, 10 of those parts would be copper and 1 would be aluminum, for a total of 11 parts. $77 \div 11 = 7$ pounds per part. The alloy has 1 part aluminum: $7 \times 1 = 7$ pounds aluminum.

7. **(C)** The cost (c) is proportional to the number of square feet: $\frac{.31}{c} = \frac{1}{180}$. $c = .31 \times 180 \div 1 =$ $55.80.

8. **(B)** The amount earned is proportional to the number of days worked. If a is the unknown amount, the proportion is: $\frac{\$352}{a} = \frac{16}{117}$. $a = 352 \times 117 \div 16 = \$2575$.

9. **(D)** If n is the unknown length, the proportion is: $\frac{\frac{1}{8}}{3\frac{3}{4}} = \frac{12}{n}$. $n = 12 \times 3\frac{3}{4} \div \frac{1}{8} = 360$.

10. **(B)** The ratio of investment is: 9000:7000:6000 or 9:7:6. $9 + 7 + 6 = 22$. Each share of the profit is $825 \div 22 = \$37.50$. B's share of the profit is $7 \times 37.50 = \$262.50$. The amount B has left is $262.50 \div \$230.00 = \$32.50$.

The Hour in Review

1. A percent refers to the number of parts in a hundred; often, you must convert percents to equivalent fractions or decimals to solve percent problems.

2. Percent problems generally provide two quantities, and you must find the missing third; memorizing the formulas for finding the missing quantity based on what is given is the best way to tackle these problems.

3. Ratios represent the relationship between numbers and can be written as a fraction; solving problems in which a ratio is given is a matter of following a simple formula.

4. A proportion indicates the equality of two ratios; when one number in a ratio is missing, you can use the rules of proportions to find it.

Graphs and Tables

What You Will Learn in This Hour

Two kinds of arithmetic problems found on the civil service exam involve visual elements (i.e., graphs and tables). These questions have become very widely used on exams. Once you understand what you're looking at, arriving at the answer is often a matter of simple arithmetic. Here are your goals for this hour:

- Learn to answer questions involving graphs.
- Learn to answer questions involving tables or tabular completion questions.

Graphs

A graph is a picture that illustrates comparisons and trends in statistical information. This section will prepare you to see the "complete picture" in a graph and supply the correct answers based on the data. The following are the most commonly used graphs:

- Bar graphs
- Circle graphs
- Line graphs
- Pictographs

Understanding Bar Graphs

Bar graphs compare various quantities using either horizontal or vertical bars. Each bar may represent a single quantity or may be divided to represent several quantities.

See Figure 17.1 for an example of a bar graph. The questions following the graph are typical of the kinds of questions found on the civil service exam.

Figure 17.1. Municipal Expenditures, Per Capita

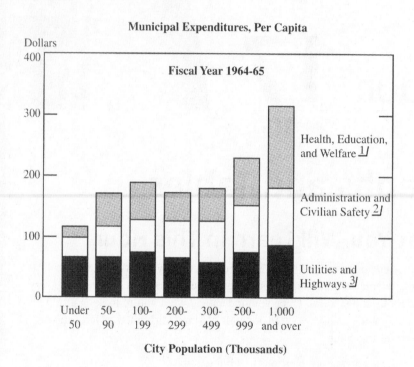

1] Public welfare, education, hospitals, health, libraries, and housing
     and urban renewal
2] Police and fire protection, financial administration, general control,
     general public buildings, interest on general debt, and other.
3] Highways, sewage, sanitation, parks and recreation, and utilities.
     Source: department of commerce.

1.   What was the approximate municipal expenditure per capita in cities having
      populations of 200,000 to 299,000?

The middle bar represents cities having populations from 200,000 to 299,000. This bar reaches about halfway between 100 and 200. Therefore, the per capita expenditure is approximately $150.

2.   Which cities spent the most per capita on health, education, and welfare?

The bar for cities having populations of 1 million and over has a larger striped section than the other bars. Therefore, those cities spent the most.

3.   Of the three categories of expenditures, which was least dependent on city size?

The expenditures for utilities and highways, the darkest part of each bar, varied least as city size increased.

Understanding Line Graphs

Line graphs illustrate trends, often over a period of time. A line graph may include more than one line, with each line representing a different item. Study the line graph in Figure 17.2 and try answering the questions following the graph.

Figure 17.2. The graph indicates the number of citations issued for various offenses at five-year intervals from 1960 to 1980.

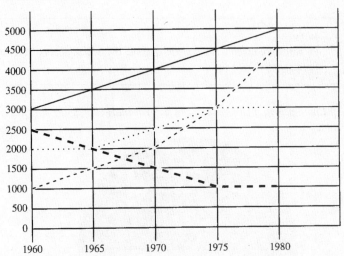

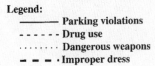

Legend:
———— Parking violations
- - - - - Drug use
. . . . Dangerous weapons
— — · Improper dress

1. Over the 20-year period, which offense shows an average rate of increase of more than 150 citations per year?

Drug use citations increased from 1000 in 1960 to 4500 in 1980. The average increase over the 20-year period is $\frac{3500}{20} = 175$.

2. Over the 20-year period, which offense shows a constant rate of increase or decrease?

A straight line indicates a constant rate of increase or decrease. Of the four lines, the one representing parking violations is the only straight one.

3. Which offense shows a total increase or decrease of 50% for the full 20-year period?

Dangerous weapons citations increased from 2000 in 1960 to 3000 in 1980, an increase of 50%.

Understanding Circle Graphs

Circle graphs show the relationship of various parts of a quantity to each other and to the whole quantity. Each part of a circle graph is called a sector.

> **Note**
> Percents are often used in circle graphs. The 360 degrees of the circle represents 100%.

Figure 17.3. The following graph shows how the federal budget of $300.4 billion was spent.

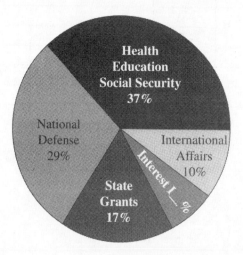

Study the circle graph in Figure 17.3 and answer the questions following the graph.

　1.　What is the value of I?

There must be a total of 100% in a circle graph. The sum of the other sections is: 17% + 29% + 37% + 10% = 93%. Therefore, I equals 100% – 93% = 7%.

　2.　How much money was actually spent on national defense?

29% × $300.4 billion = $87.116 billion or $87,116,000,000.

　3.　How much more money was spent on state grants than on interest?

17% – 7% = 10%; 10% × $300.4 billion = $30.04 billion or $30,040,000,000.

Understanding Pictographs

Pictographs compare quantities using symbols. Each symbol represents a given number of a particular item. Take a look at the pictograph in Figure 17.4 and answer the questions following the graph.

Figure 17.4 Number of new houses built in XYZ town 1965–1980.

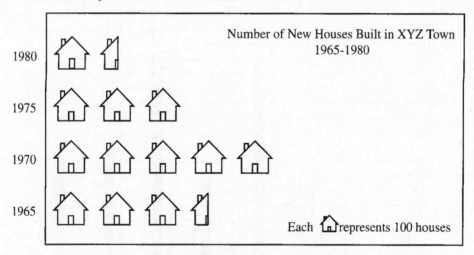

　1.　How many more new houses were built in 1970 than in 1975?

There are two more symbols for 1970 than for 1975. Each symbol represents 100 houses. Therefore, 200 more houses were built in 1970.

　2.　How many new houses were built in 1965?

There are $3\frac{1}{2}$ symbols shown for 1965: $3\frac{1}{2} \times 100 = 350$ houses.

　3.　In which year were half as many houses built as in 1975?

In 1975, 3 × 100 = 300 houses were built. Half of 300, or 150 houses, were built in 1980.

Workshop: Graphs

In this workshop, you'll practice with the kind of graph questions most commonly used on civil service tests. Answers and explanations follow the last question.

Practice Exercise

DIRECTIONS: Each question has four suggested answers. Select the correct one.

Questions 1–4 refer to the following graph:

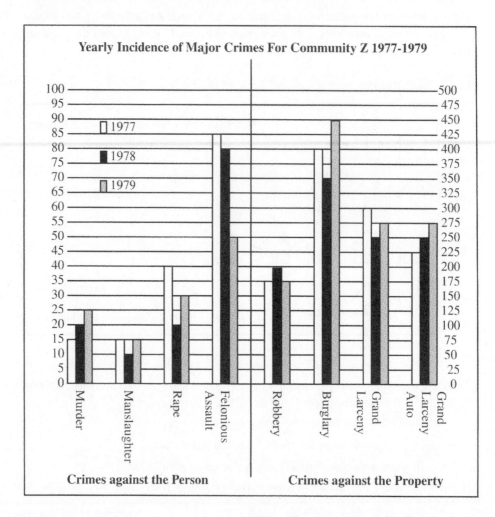

1. In 1979, the incidence of which of the following crimes was greater than in the previous two years?

    (A) Grand larceny

    (B) Murder

    (C) Rape

    (D) Robbery

2. If the incidence of burglary in 1980 had increased over 1979 by the same number as it had increased in 1979 over 1978, then the average for this crime for the four-year period from 1977 to 1980 would be most nearly

    (A) 100

    (B) 400

    (C) 425

    (D) 440

3. The graph on page 218 indicates that the percentage increase in grand larceny auto from 1978 to 1979 was

    (A) 5%

    (B) 10%

    (C) 15%

    (D) 20%

4. Which of the following cannot be determined because there is not enough information in the above graph to do so?

    (A) For the three-year period, what percentage of all "Crimes Against the Person" involved murders committed in 1978?

    (B) For the three-year period, what percentage of all "Major Crimes" was committed in the first six months of 1978?

    (C) Which major crimes followed a pattern of continuing yearly increases for the three-year period?

    (D) For 1979, what was the ratio of robbery, burglary, and grand larceny crimes?

17

Questions 5–7 refer to the following graph:

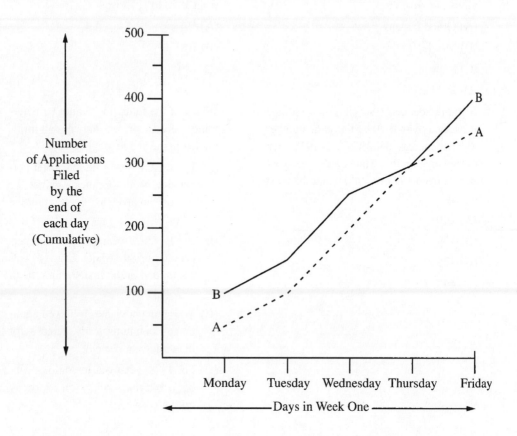

In the graph above, the lines labeled "A" and "B" represent the cumulative progress in the work of two file clerks, each of whom was given 500 consecutively numbered applications to file in the proper cabinets over a five-day workweek.

5. The day during which the largest number of applications was filed by both clerks was

    (A) Monday.

    (B) Tuesday.

    (C) Wednesday.

    (D) Friday.

6. At the end of the second day, the percentage of applications still to be filed was

    (A) 25%

    (B) 50%

    (C) 66%

    (D) 75%

7.   Assuming that the production pattern is
     the same the following week as the week
     shown in the chart, the day on which Clerk
     B will finish this assignment will be

     (A) Monday.

     (B) Tuesday.

     (C) Wednesday.

     (D) Friday.

Questions 8–11 refer to the following graphs:

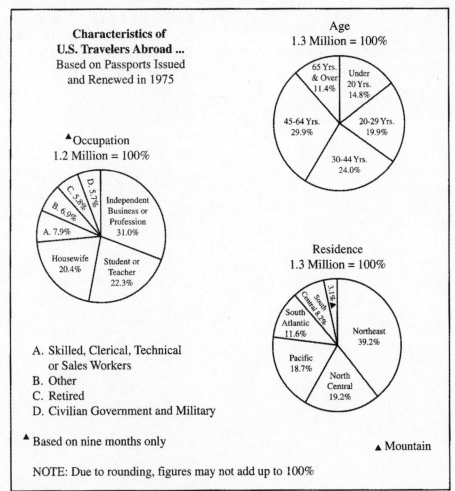

**Characteristics of
U.S. Travelers Abroad ...**
Based on Passports Issued
and Renewed in 1975

▲Occupation
1.2 Million = 100%

Independent
Business or
Profession
31.0%

D. 5.7%
C. 5.8%
B. 6.9%
A. 7.9%

Housewife
20.4%

Student or
Teacher
22.3%

A. Skilled, Clerical, Technical
    or Sales Workers
B. Other
C. Retired
D. Civilian Government and Military

▲ Based on nine months only

NOTE: Due to rounding, figures may not add up to 100%

Age
1.3 Million = 100%

65 Yrs.
& Over
11.4%

Under
20 Yrs.
14.8%

45-64 Yrs.
29.9%

20-29 Yrs.
19.9%

30-44 Yrs.
24.0%

Residence
1.3 Million = 100%

South
Central 8.2%

3.1% ▲

South
Atlantic
11.6%

Northeast
39.2%

Pacific
18.7%

North
Central
19.2%

▲ Mountain

17

8. Approximately how many persons aged 29 or younger traveled abroad in 1975?

(A) 175,000

(B) 245,000

(C) 385,000

(D) 450,000

9. Of the people who did not live in the Northeast, what percent came from the North Central states?

(A) 19.2%

(B) 19.9%

(C) 26.5%

(D) 31.6%

10. The fraction of travelers from the four smallest occupation groups is most nearly equal to the fraction of travelers

(A) under age 20, and 65 and over, combined.

(B) from the North Central and Mountain states.

(C) between 45 and 64 years of age.

(D) from the Housewife and Other categories.

11. If the South Central, Mountain, and Pacific sections were considered as a single classification, how many degrees would its sector include?

(A) 30°

(B) 67°

(C) 108°

(D) 120°

Questions 12–15 refer to the following graph:

**Vechicles Crossing
the Hudson Bridge**

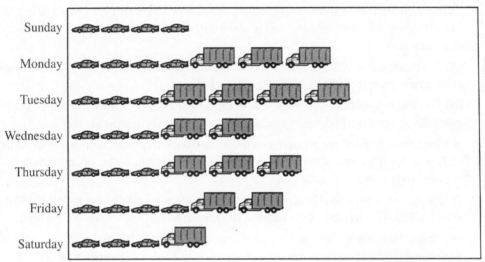

Each symbol represents 500 vehicles

Passenger car

Truck

12. What percent of the total number of vehicles on Wednesday were cars?

   (A) 30%

   (B) 60%

   (C) 20%

   (D) 50%

13. What was the total number of vehicles crossing the bridge on Tuesday?

   (A) 7

   (B) 700

   (C) 1100

   (D) 3500

14. How many more trucks crossed on Monday than on Saturday?

   (A) 200

   (B) 1000

   (C) 1500

   (D) 2000

15. If trucks paid a toll of $1.00 and cars paid a toll of $.50, how much money was collected in tolls on Friday?

   (A) $400

   (B) $600

   (C) $2000

   (D) $2500

Answers and Explanations

1.   **(B)** The incidence of murder increased from 15 in 1977 to 20 in 1978 to 25 in 1979.

2.   **(D)** The incidence of burglary in 1977 was 400; in 1978, it was 350; and in 1979, it was 450. The increase from 1978 to 1979 was 100. An increase of 100 from 1979 gives 550 in 1980. The average of 400, 350, 450, and 550 is: $400 + 350 + 450 + 550 = 1750 \div 4 = 437.5$, which rounds up to 440.

3.   **(B)** The incidence of grand larceny auto went from 250 in 1978 to 275 in 1979, an increase of 25. The percent increase is $25 \div 250 = .10 = 10\%$.

4.   **(B)** This graph gives information by year, not month. It's impossible to determine from the graph the percentage of crimes committed during the first six months of any year.

5.   **(C)** For Clerks A and B, the greatest increase in the cumulative totals occurred from the end of Tuesday until the end of Wednesday. Therefore, the largest number of applications was filed on Wednesday.

6.   **(D)** By the end of Tuesday, Clerk A had filed 100 applications and Clerk B had filed 150, for a total of 250. This left 750 of the original 1000 applications: $750 \div 1000 = .75 = 75\%$.

7.   **(B)** During Week One, Clerk B filed 100 applications on Monday, 50 on Tuesday, 100 on Wednesday, 50 on Thursday, and 100 on Friday. If he follows this pattern, he will file 50 on the Monday of Week Two, for a total of 450, and the remaining 50 during Tuesday.

8.   **(D)** 20 – 29 yrs. = 19.9%; under 20 yrs. = 14.8%; $19.9\% + 14.8\% = 34.7\%$; $34.7\% \times 1.3$ million = .4511 million = 451,100, which rounds down to 450,000.

9.   **(D)** $100\% - 39.2\% = 60.8\%$ did not live in the Northeast. 19.2% lived in the North Central states. $19.2 \div 60.8 =$ approximately .316 or 31.6%.

10.   **(A)** The four smallest groups of occupation: $7.9 + 6.9 + 5.8 + 5.7 = 26.3$. Age groups under 20 and over 65: $14.8 + 11.4 = 26.2$. Therefore, these two groups are most nearly equal.

11.   **(C)** South Central: 8.2%; Mountain: 3.1%; Pacific: 18.7%; $8.2 + 3.1 + 18.7 = 30.0\%$; $30\% \times 360° = 108°$.

12.   **(B)** There are five vehicle symbols, of which three are cars: $3 \div 5 = 60\%$.

13.   **(D)** On Tuesday, there were $3 \times 500 = 1500$ cars and $4 \times 500 = 2000$ trucks. The total number of vehicles was 3500.

14.   **(B)** The graph shows two more truck symbols on Monday than on Saturday. Each symbol represents 500 trucks, so there were $2 \times 500 = 1000$ more trucks on Monday.

15.   **(C)** On Friday there were $4 \times 500 = 2000$ cars and $2 \times 500 = 1000$ trucks; car tolls: $2000 \times \$.50 = \$1000$; truck tolls: $1000 \times \$1.00 = \$1000$; total tolls: $\$1000 + \$1000 = \$2000$.

Tabular Completions

Tabular completion questions are the newest type of arithmetic question to appear on the civil service exam. Numerically, these are among the easiest questions. The arithmetic involved is entirely restricted to addition and subtraction. The numbers may be large, but the process itself is simple.

Answering Tabular Completion Questions

The difficulty of answering tabular completion questions lies in choosing which numbers to add or subtract. The tables demand careful reading.

In answering these questions, you must first determine which entries combine to create each total and subtotal. If you're unclear as to how a number is arrived at, you may have to look at a completed column to determine how certain figures were arrived at. Then move over into the column with the unknown that you're seeking, and calculate it by combining the appropriate entries.

Both the reasoning process involved and the actual calculations are important to success with these questions, but concentration and care should enable you to master them. Practice will help.

17

Workshop: Tabular Completions

This workshop will give you plenty of practice with the kind of tabular completion questions you are most likely to find on civil service tests. Answers and explanations follow the last question.

Practice Exercise

DIRECTIONS: These questions are based on information presented in tables. You must calculate the unknown values by using the known values given in the table. In some questions, the exact answer will not be given as one of the response choices. In such cases, you should select choice (E), "none of the above."

Questions

TABLE FOR QUESTIONS **1 – 5:**

LOCAL GOVERNMENT EXPENDITURES OF FINANCES: **1979** TO **1982**
(IN MILLIONS OF DOLLARS)

Item	1979	1980	1981	1982	Total Percent*
Expenditures	I	432,328	485,174	520,966	100.0
Direct General Expenditures	326,024	367,340	405,576	IV	83.2
Utility and Liquor Stores	30,846	II	43,016	47,970	9.2
Water and electric	20,734	24,244	28,453	31,499	6.0
Transit and others	10,112	11,947	14,563	16,471	3.2
Insurance Trust Expenditures	23,504	28,797	36,582	39,466	V
Employee retirement	12,273	14,008	III	17,835	3.4
Unemployment compensation	11,231	14,789	20,887	21,631	4.2

*Rounded to one decimal place

1. What is the value of I in millions of dollars?
   (A) 380,374
   (B) 377,604
   (C) 356,870
   (D) 349,528
   (E) None of the above

2. What is the value of II in millions of dollars?
   (A) 338,543
   (B) 64,988
   (C) 53,041
   (D) 40,744
   (E) None of the above

3. What is the value of III in millions of dollars?
   (A) 57,469
   (B) 52,277
   (C) 20,887
   (D) 15,695
   (E) None of the above

4. What is the value of IV in millions of dollars?
   (A) 472,996
   (B) 433,530
   (C) 425,026
   (D) 134,807
   (E) None of the above

5. What is the percent value of V?
   (A) 7.6
   (B) 7.4
   (C) 6.7
   (D) 3.3
   (E) None of the above

TABLE FOR QUESTIONS 6 – 10:

REVENUE OF ALL GOVERNMENTS BY SOURCE AND LEVEL OF GOVERNMENT FISCAL YEAR 1981

(IN MILLIONS OF DOLLARS)

Source	Total	Federal	State	Local
Total Revenue	1,259,421	660,759	310.828	V
Intergovernmental	184,033	1,804	70,786	111,443
From Federal Government	90,295	—	III	22,427
From state or local government	93,738	1,804	2,918	89,016
Revenue from Own Sources	1,075,388	II	240,042	176,391
General	820,814	487,706	187,373	145,735
Taxes	I	405,714	149,738	94,776
Property	74,969	—	2,949	72,020
Individual and corporate income	407,257	346,688	55,039	5,530
Sales and gross receipts	134,532	48,561	72,751	13,220
Other	33,470	10,465	18,999	4,006
Charges and miscellaneous	170,586	81,992	37,635	50,959
Utility and liquor stores	29,896	—	4,628	25,268
Insurance trust	224,678	171,249	48,041	5,388
Employee and railroad retirement	36,962	6,580	IV	5,260
Unemployment compensation	18,733	162	18,443	128
Old age, disability and health insurance	168,983	164,507	4,476	—

Hypothetical data.

6. What is the value of I in millions of dollars?
   (A) 695,097
   (B) 616,758
   (C) 555,452
   (D) 254,574
   (E) None of the above

7. What is the value of II in millions of dollars?
   (A) 835,346
   (B) 662,563
   (C) 658,955
   (D) 417,433
   (E) None of the above

8. What is the value of III in millions of dollars?
   (A) 73,704
   (B) 68,868
   (C) 67,868
   (D) 67,978
   (E) None of the above

9. What is the value of IV in millions of dollars?
   (A) 43,565
   (B) 29,598
   (C) 25,122
   (D) 22,919
   (E) None of the above

10. What is the value of V in millions of dollars?
   (A) 821,567
   (B) 464,175
   (C) 318,490
   (D) 287,834
   (E) None of the above

TABLE FOR QUESTIONS 11 – 15:

FINANCE COMPANIES—ASSETS AND LIABILITIES: 1970 TO 1980
(IN MILLIONS OF DOLLARS)

Item	1970	1975	1980
Total Receivables	I	85,994	183,341
Consumer Receivables	31,773	40,814	77,460
Retail passenger car paper and others	11,577	13,399	31,950
Retail consumer goods and loans	20,196	27,415	IV
Business Receivables	22,999	39,286	86,067
Wholesale paper and others	14,084	22,012	48,059
Lease paper and others	8,915	17,274	38,008
Other Receivables	2,341	5,894	19,814
Total Liabilities	60,577	III	175,025
Loans and Notes Payable to Banks	7,551	8,617	15,458
Short-term	II	7,900	7,885
Long-term	969	717	7,573
Commercial Paper	22,073	25,905	52,328
Other Debt	30,953	54,194	V

Hypothetical data.

11. What is the value of I in millions of dollars?
    (A) 54,772
    (B) 57,113
    (C) 63,546
    (D) 68,856
    (E) None of the above

12. What is the value of II in millions of dollars?
    (A) 6,582
    (B) 14,522
    (C) 53,026
    (D) 58,236
    (E) None of the above

13. What is the value of III in millions of dollars?
    (A) 62,811
    (B) 88,716
    (C) 94,610
    (D) 97,333
    (E) None of the above

14. What is the value of IV in millions of dollars?
    (A) 45,610
    (B) 47,610
    (C) 47,611
    (D) 54,117
    (E) None of the above

15. What is the value of V in millions of dollars?
    (A) 67,786
    (B) 85,147
    (C) 107,239
    (D) 107,259
    (E) None of the above

Answers and Explanations

1. **(A)** To calculate the total 1979 *Expenditures,* add the 1979 values for *Direct General Expenditures, Utility and Liquor Stores,* and *Insurance Trust Expenditure:* 326,024 + 30,846 + 23,504 = 380,374.

2. **(E)** The correct value (not given as an answer) is calculated by adding the value for *Water and electric* and the value for *Transit and others:* 24,244 + 11,947 = 36,191.

3. **(D)** To calculate the 1981 *Employee retirement costs,* subtract the 1981 value of *Unemployment compensation* from the total *Insurance Trust Expenditure:* 36,582 – 20,887 = 15,695.

4. **(B)** To calculate the value of 1982 *Direct General Expenditures,* add the 1982 values of *Utility and Liquor Stores* and *Insurance Trust Expenditure,* and subtract that sum from the total of 1982 *Expenditures:* 520,966 – (47,970 + 39,466) = 433,530.

5. **(A)** To calculate the percent of total 1982 *Expenditures* represented by *Insurance Trust Expenditures,* add the percents represented by *Direct General Expenditures* and *Utility and Liquor Stores,* and subtract from 100%: 100% – (83.2% + 9.2%) = 7.6%. Alternatively, add the two components of *Insurance Trust Expenditure (Employee retirement and Unemployment compensation):* 3.4% + 4.2% = 7.6%.

6. **(E)** The correct value (not given as an answer) is calculated by subtracting the value for *Charges and miscellaneous* in the TOTAL column from the value for *General* under *Revenue from Own Sources:* 820,814 – 170,586 = 650,228.

7. **(C)** *Federal Revenue from Own Sources* can be calculated by subtracting the value for *Intergovernmental* in the FEDERAL column from the value for *Total Revenue* in the FEDERAL column: 660,759 – 1,804 = 658,955.

8. **(C)** Calculate the value of state revenues *From Federal Government* by subtracting the value of revenues *From state or local government* in the STATE column from the value of *Intergovernmental* revenues in the STATE column: 70,786 – 2,918 = 67,868.

9. **(C)** Calculate the value of state revenues from *Employee and railroad retirement* by subtracting the combined values of *Unemployment compensation* and *Old age, disability, and health insurance* in the STATE column from the value of *Insurance trust:* 48,041 – (18,443 + 4,476) = 25,122.

10. **(D)** To calculate total local revenue, add together LOCAL *Intergovernmental* revenue and *Revenue from Own Sources* in the LOCAL column: 111,443 + 176,391 = 287,834.

11. **(B)** *Total 1970 Receivables* can be calculated by adding the values for 1970 *Consumer Receivables, Business Receivables,* and *Other Receivables:* 31,773 + 22,999 + 2,341 = 57,113.

12. **(A)** The value of 1970 *Short-term* can be calculated by subtracting the value for *Long-term* from the value for *Loans and Notes Payable to Banks:* 7,551 – 969 = 6,582.

13. **(B)** Calculate total 1975 liabilities by adding the value of 1975 *Loans and Notes Payable to Banks, Commercial Paper,* and *Other Debt:* 8,617 + 25,905 + 54,194 = 88,716.

14. **(E)** Calculate the value of 1980 *Retail consumer goods and loans* (not given as an answer) by subtracting the value of 1980 *Retail passenger car paper and others* from 1980 *Consumer Receivables:* 77,460 – 31,950 = 45,510.

15. **(C)** Calculate the value of 1980 *Other Debt* by subtracting the sum of the values of *Loans and Notes Payable to Banks* and *Commercial Paper* from 1980 *Total Liabilities:* 175,025 – (15,458 + 52,328) = 107,239.

The Hour in Review

1. Graph questions involve analyzing the data presented in one of the following kinds of graphs: bar, line, circle, or pictograph.

2. Tabular completion questions require you to fill in the missing data in a table. To arrive at the answer, you must add or subtract the correct entries based on how the other columns are completed.

HOUR 18

Reasoning Problems

What You Will Learn in This Hour

Reasoning problems have become popular on the civil service exam because they pose the sort of problems that must be solved on the job. One popular type of reasoning problem is the work problem, but you may also have to solve a variety of word problems on expenses, wages, productivity, and other on-the-job situations. You'll find examples of all these word problems in this hour, along with strategies for solving them. Here are your goals for this hour:

- Learn to solve work problems.
- Learn to solve other arithmetic reasoning problems.

Solving Work Problems

In work problems, three factors are involved: the number of people working; the time to complete the job, expressed in minutes, hours, or days; and the amount of work done. Work problems follow these rules:

- The number of people working is directly proportional to the amount of work done. The more people on the job, the more work will be done, and vice versa.

- The number of people working is inversely proportional to the time. The more people on the job, the less time it will take to finish it, and vice versa.

- The time expended on a job is directly proportional to the amount of work done. The more time expended on a job, the more work that is done, and vice versa.

Tackling Work Problems

In work problems, you are asked to find a rate, time, or number of workers. Depending on what information you have, you can solve the problem using various formulas, as outlined in this section.

Solving Problems Using Equal Rates

The rate at which a person works is the amount of work he or she can do in a unit of time. If all the workers work at equal rates to complete a job, you can easily find how long it will take any number of the workers to finish the job. Follow these steps:

1. Multiply the number of people by the time to find the amount of time required by one person to complete the job.

2. Divide this time by the number of people required to complete the job to find how long it will take them to finish it.

If four workers each working at the same rate can do a job in 48 days, how long will it take to finish the same job if only three of these workers are able to work on the job?

1. Multiply the number of people by the time: $48 \times 4 = 192$ days. So one worker can do the job in 192 days.

2. Divide this amount by three, the number of workers required: $192 \div 3 = 64$. So three workers can finish the job in 64 days.

In some work problems, the rates, though unequal, can be equalized by comparison. Follow these steps to solve such problems:

1. Determine from the facts how many equal rates there are.

2. Multiply the number of equal rates by the time given.

3. Divide this time by the number of equal rates.

Three workers can do a job in 12 days. Two of the workers work twice as fast as the third. How long would it take one of the faster workers to do the job himself?

1. There are two fast workers and one slow worker, so there are actually five slow workers working at equal rates.

2.   One slow worker will take 12 days × 5 slow workers = 60 days to complete the job.

3.   One fast worker equals two slow workers; therefore, he will take 60 ÷ 2 = 30 days to complete the job.

Solving Problems Using Time

If you're given the various times at which each person in a group can complete a job, you can find the time it will take to do the job if all work together by following these steps:

1.   Invert the time of each person to find how much work each person can do in one unit of time.

2.   Add these reciprocals to find which part of the job all the workers working together can complete in one unit of time.

3.   Invert this sum to find the time it will take all the workers to finish the entire job.

If it takes (A) three days to dig a ditch, whereas (B) can dig it in six days and (C) in 12, how long would it take all three to do the job?

1.   (A) can complete the job in three days; therefore, he can finish $\frac{1}{3}$ of the job in one day. (B) can complete the job in six days; therefore, he can finish $\frac{1}{6}$ of the job in one day. (C) can complete the job in 12 days; therefore, he can finish $\frac{1}{12}$ of the job in one day.

2. $\frac{1}{3} + \frac{1}{6} + \frac{1}{12} = \frac{7}{12}$.

3.   (A), (B), and (C) can finish $\frac{7}{12}$ of the work in one day; therefore, it will take them $\frac{12}{7}$, or $1\frac{5}{7}$, days to complete the job working together.

18

> **Tip**
>
> When given the time it will take one person to finish a job, the reciprocal of that time is how much of the job can be completed in one particular unit of time. For example, if a worker can finish a job in six days, then she can finish $\frac{1}{6}$ of the job in one day. Conversely, the reciprocal of the work done in one unit of time is the time it will take to finish the entire job. For example, if a worker can complete $\frac{3}{7}$ of the work in one day, then he can finish the whole job in $\frac{7}{3}$, or $2\frac{1}{3}$, days.

If you're given the total time it requires a number of people working together to complete a job, and the times of all but one are known, follow these steps to find the missing time:

1. Invert the given times to find how much of the job each worker can complete in one unit of time.

2. Add these reciprocals to find how much of the job can be completed in one unit of time by those workers whose rates are known.

3. Subtract this sum from the reciprocal of the total time to complete the job to find the missing rate.

4. Invert this rate to find the unknown time.

A, B, and C can finish a job in two days. B can finish it in five days, and C can finish it in four days. How long would it take A to finish the job by himself?

1. B can finish the job in five days; therefore, he can complete $\frac{1}{5}$ of the job in one day. C can finish the job in four days; therefore, he can complete $\frac{1}{4}$ of the job in one day.

2. The part of the job that can be completed by B and C together in one day is: $\frac{1}{5} + \frac{1}{4} = \frac{9}{20}$.

3. The total time to complete the job is two days; therefore, all the workers can complete $\frac{1}{2}$ the job in 1 day: $\frac{1}{2} - \frac{9}{20} = \frac{1}{20}$.

4. (A) can complete $\frac{1}{20}$ of the job in one day; therefore, he can finish the whole job in 20 days.

Solving Problems Using All Factors

In some work problems, certain values are given for the three factors: the number of workers, the amount of work done, and the time. Usually you must find the changes that occur when one or two of the factors are given different values.

The best way to solve such problems is to directly make the necessary cancellations, divisions, and multiplications. Try this problem:

If 60 workers can build four houses in 12 months, how many workers, working at the same rate, would be required to build six houses in four months?

In this problem, you can easily see that more workers would be required because more houses must be built in a shorter time:

1. To build six houses instead of four in the same amount of time requires $\frac{6}{4}$ of the number of workers: $\frac{6}{4} \times 60 = 90$.

2.   Because you have four months to complete the job where previously 12 were required, you must triple ($12 \div 4 = 3$) the number of workers: $90 \times 3 = 270$.

Therefore, 270 workers are needed to build six houses in four months.

Workshop: Work Problems

In this workshop, you'll practice solving a variety of work problems. Answers and explanations follow the last question.

Practice Problems

DIRECTIONS: Each question has four suggested answers. Select the correct one.

1.   If 314 clerks filed 6,594 papers in 10 minutes, what is the number filed per minute by the average clerk?

(A) 2

(B) 2.4

(C) 2.1

(D) 2.5

2.   Four men working together can dig a ditch in 42 days. They begin, but one man works only half-days. How long will it take to complete the job?

(A) 48 days

(B) 45 days

(C) 43 days

(D) 44 days

3.   A clerk is requested to file 800 cards. If he can file cards at the rate of 80 cards an hour, the number of cards remaining to be filed after seven hours of work is

(A) 140

(B) 240

(C) 260

(D) 560

4.   If it takes four days for three machines to do a certain job, it will take two machines

(A) 6 days

(B) $5\frac{1}{2}$ days

(C) 5 days

(D) $4\frac{1}{2}$ days

5.   A stenographer has been assigned to place entries on 500 forms. She places entries on 25 forms by the end of half an hour when she is joined by another stenographer. The second stenographer places entries at the rate of 45 an hour. Assuming that both stenographers continue to work at their respective rates of speed, the total number of hours required to carry out the entire assignment is

(A) 5

(B) $5\frac{1}{2}$

(C) $6\frac{1}{2}$

(D) 7

18

6. If in five days a clerk can copy 125 pages, 36 lines each, 11 words to the line, how many pages of 30 lines each and 12 words to the line can he copy in six days?

    (A) 145

    (B) 155

    (C) 160

    (D) 165

7. A and B do a job together in 2 hours. Working alone, A does the job in 5 hours. How long will it take B to do the job alone?

    (A) $3\frac{1}{3}$ hr.

    (B) $2\frac{1}{4}$ hr.

    (C) 3 hr.

    (D) 2 hr.

8. A stenographer transcribes her notes at the rate of one line typed in 10 seconds. At this rate, how long (in minutes and seconds) will it take her to transcribe notes that require seven pages of typing, 25 lines to the page?

    (A) 29 min. 10 sec.

    (B) 17 min. 50 sec.

    (C) 40 min. 10 sec.

    (D) 20 min. 30 sec.

9. A group of five clerks has been assigned to insert 24,000 letters into envelopes. The clerks perform this work at the following rates of speed: Clerk A, 1100 letters an hour; Clerk B, 1450 letters an hour; Clerk C, 1200 letters an hour; Clerk D, 1300 letters an hour; Clerk E, 1250 letters an hour. At the end of two hours of work, Clerks C and D are assigned to another task. From the time that Clerks C and D were taken off the assignment, the number of hours required for the remaining clerks to complete this assignment is

    (A) less than 3 hours.

    (B) 3 hours.

    (C) between 3 and 4 hours.

    (D) more than 4 hours.

10. If a certain job can be performed by 18 workers in 26 days, the number of workers needed to perform the job in 12 days is

    (A) 24

    (B) 30

    (C) 39

    (D) 52

Answers and Explanations

1. (**C**) 6594 papers ÷ 314 clerks = 21 papers filed by each clerk in 10 minutes; 21 papers ÷ 10 minutes = 2.1 papers per minute filed by the average clerk.

2. (**A**) It takes one man 42 × 4 = 168 days to complete the job, working alone. If $3\frac{1}{2}$ men are working (one man works half-days, the other three work full days), the job takes $168 \div 3\frac{1}{2} = 48$ days.

3. (**B**) In seven hours, the clerk files 7 × 80 = 560 cards. Because 800 cards must be filed, there are 800 − 560 = 240 remaining.

4. (**A**) It takes one machine 3 × 4 = 12 days to complete the job. Two machines can do the job in 12 ÷ 2 = 6 days.

5. (**B**) At the end of the first half-hour, there are 500 − 25 = 475 forms remaining. If the first stenographer completed 25 forms in half an hour, her rate is 25 × 2 = 50 forms per hour. The combined rate of the two stenographers is 50 + 45 = 95 forms per hour. The remaining forms can be completed in 475 ÷ 95 = 5 hours. Adding the first half-hour, the entire job requires $5\frac{1}{2}$ hours.

6. (**D**) 36 lines × 11 words = 396 words on each page; 125 pages × 396 words = 49,500 words copied in five days; 49,500 ÷ 5 = 9900 words copied in one day. 12 words × 30 lines = 360 words on each page; 9900 ÷ 360 = $27\frac{1}{2}$ pages copied in one day; $27\frac{1}{2} \times 6 = 165$ pages copied in six days.

7. (**A**) If A can finish the job alone in 5 hours, A can do $\frac{1}{5}$ of the job in one hour. Working together, A and B can complete the job in 2 hours; therefore, in one hour, they finish half the job. In one hour, B alone completes $\frac{1}{2} - \frac{1}{5} = \frac{3}{10}$ of the job. It would take B $\frac{10}{3}$ hours, or $3\frac{1}{3}$ hours, to finish the whole job alone.

8. (**A**) She must type 7 × 25 = 175 lines. At the rate of one line per 10 seconds, the job takes 175 × 10 = 1750 seconds. 1750 seconds ÷ 60 = $29\frac{1}{6}$ minutes, or 29 minutes, 10 seconds.

9. (**B**) All five clerks working together process a total of 1100 + 1450 + 1200 + 1300 + 1250 = 6300 letters per hour. After two hours, they process 6300 × 2 = 12,600 letters. Of the original 24,000 letters, there are 24,000 − 12,600 = 11,400 letters remaining. Clerks A, B, and E working together process a total of 1100 + 1450 + 1250 = 3800 letters per hour. It takes them 11,400 ÷ 3800 = 3 hours to process the remaining letters.

10. (**C**) The job could be completed by one worker in 18 × 26 = 468 days. Completing the job in 12 days requires 468 ÷ 12 = 39 workers.

Solving Arithmetic Reasoning Problems

Arithmetic reasoning problems are word problems that require you to reason out the answer based on the information given. No set formulas must be followed, other than the ones that you've already learned, so the best way to prepare is to practice with several different kinds of reasoning problems.

> **Make Connections**
> Arithmetic reasoning problems often require you to solve problems involving fractions, decimals, percents, ratios, and proportions. Turn back to Hours 15, "Fractions and Decimals," and 16, "Percents, Ratio, and Proportion," to review the rules governing these problems.

Workshop: Reasoning Problems

Here are samples of some of the arithmetic reasoning problems used most often on civil service tests. Answers and explanations follow the last question.

Practice Problems

DIRECTIONS: These questions require you to solve problems formulated in both verbal and numeric form. You will have to analyze a paragraph in order to set up the problem and then solve it. If the exact answer is not given as one of the response choices, you should select choice (E), "None of the above."

1. An investigator rented a car for four days and was charged $200. The car rental company charged $10 per day plus $.20 per mile driven. How many miles did the investigator drive the car?

    (A) 800
    (B) 950
    (C) 1000
    (D) 1200
    (E) None of the above

2. In one federal office, $\frac{1}{6}$ of the employees favored abandoning a flexible work schedule system. In a second office that had the same number of employees, $\frac{1}{4}$ of the workers favored abandoning it. What is the average of the fractions of the workers in the two offices who favored abandoning the system?

    (A) $\frac{1}{10}$
    (B) $\frac{1}{5}$
    → (C) $\frac{5}{24}$
    (D) $\frac{5}{12}$
    (E) None of the above

3. A federal agency had a personal computer repaired at a cost of $49.20. This amount included a charge of $22 per hour for labor and a charge for a new switch that cost $18 before a 10% government discount was applied. How long did the repair job take?

(A) 1 hr. 6 min.

(B) 1 hr. 11 min.

(C) 1 hr. 22 min.

(D) 1 hr. 30 min.

(E) None of the above

4. In a large agency where mail is delivered in motorized carts, two tires were replaced on a cart at a cost of $34 per tire. If the agency had expected to pay $80 for a pair of tires, what percent of its expected cost did it save?

(A) 7.5%

(B) 17.6%

(C) 57.5%

(D) 75.0%

(E) None of the above

5. An interagency task force has representatives from three different agencies. Half of the task force members represent Agency A, one-third represent Agency B, and three represent Agency C. How many people are on the task force?

(A) 12

(B) 15

(C) 18

(D) 24

(E) None of the above

6. It has been established in recent productivity studies that, on the average, it takes a filing clerk two hours and 12 minutes to fill four drawers of a filing cabinet. At this rate, how long would it take two clerks to fill 16 drawers?

(A) 4 hr.

(B) 4 hr. 20 min.

(C) 8 hr.

(D) 8 hr. 40 min.

(E) None of the above

7. It costs $60,000 per month to maintain a small medical facility. The basic charge per person for treatment is $40, but 50% of those seeking treatment require laboratory work at an additional average charge of $20 per person. How many patients per month would the facility have to serve in order to cover its costs?

(A) 1000

(B) 1200

(C) 1500

(D) 2000

(E) None of the above

8. An experimental anti-pollution vehicle powered by electricity traveled 33 kilometers (km) at a constant speed of 110 kilometers per hour (km/h). How many minutes did it take this vehicle to complete its experimental run?

(A) 3

(B) 10

(C) 18

(D) 20

(E) None of the above

18

9. It takes two typists three eight-hour work-
    days to type a report on a word processor.
    How many typists would be needed to
    type two reports of the same length in one
    eight-hour workday?

    (A) 4

    (B) 6

    (C) 8

    (D) 12

    (E) None of the above

10. A clerk is able to process 40 unemploy-
    ment compensation claims in one hour.
    After deductions of 18% for benefits and
    taxes, the clerk's net pay is $6.97 per hour.
    If the clerk processed 1200 claims, how
    much would the government have to pay
    for the work, based on the clerk's hourly
    wage before deductions?

    (A) $278.80

    (B) $255.00

    (C) $246.74

    (D) $209.10

    (E) None of the above

Answers and Explanations

1. **(A)** The investigator rented the car for four days at $10 per day, which is $40; the portion of the total charge expended for miles driven is $200 – $40 = $160. The number of miles driven by the investigator is $160 ÷ $.20 = 800.

2. **(C)** The average of the two fractions is $(\frac{1}{6} + \frac{1}{4}) \div 2 = \frac{5}{24}$.

3. **(D)** The government discount is $18 × 10% = $1.80. The cost of the switch is $18.00 – $1.80 = $16.20. The charge for labor is $49.20 – $16.20 = $33.00. The number of hours worked is $33 ÷ $22 = 1.5 hours, or one hour and 30 minutes.

4. **(E)** The correct answer is not given. The difference between the actual cost of $34 per tire and the expected cost of $40 per tire ($80 ÷ 2) is $6: $6 ÷ $40 = .15, or 15% of the expected cost.

5. **(C)** Obtain the correct answer by computing $\frac{1}{2x} + \frac{1}{3x} + 3 = x$, where x is the total number of task force members; $\frac{1}{2x}$ is the number from Agency A; $\frac{1}{3x}$ is the number from Agency B; and 3 is the number from Agency C. Add the two fractions: $\frac{1}{2x} + \frac{1}{3x} = \frac{5}{6x}$. x (or $\frac{6}{6x}$) $- \frac{5}{6x} = \frac{1}{6x} = 3$. $\frac{1}{6} \times 18 = 3$, so the number of people on the task force is 18.

6. **(E)** The correct answer is not given. First, convert two hours and 12 minutes to 2.2 hours, and then set up a simple proportion: $\frac{2.2}{4} = \frac{x}{16}$. The number of hours it takes one filing clerk to do the job is

2.2 × 16 ÷ 4 = 8.8 hours. If two clerks are filling 16 drawers, the job would be completed in half that time: 4.4 hours, or 4 hours, 24 minutes.

7. **(B)** The basic charge of $40 applies to all patients (x); the additional average charge of $20 applies to only 50% (or $\frac{1}{2}$) of them (.5x). The combined charges—$40 times the total number of patients (40x) plus $20 times $\frac{1}{2}$ the total number of patients (20 × .5x or 10x)—must equal $60,000, the cost of maintaining the medical facility: 40x + 10x = 60,000. Solve for x: 60,000 ÷ 50 = 1200, the number of patients who must be served per month.

8. **(C)** Obtain the correct answer by setting up a simple proportion: $\frac{110 \text{ km}}{60 \text{ min}} = \frac{33 \text{ km}}{x \text{ min}}$ min. 33 × 60 ÷ 110 = 18 min.

9. **(D)** The total number of eight-hour workdays of typing required for the two reports is 3 days × 2 typists × 2 reports = 12 eight-hour workdays of typing. If all of this had to be accomplished in one eight-hour workday, 12 typists would be needed to do the job.

10. **(B)** The clerk's net pay of $6.97 per hour represents 82% of his gross pay (100% – 18% = 82%). The clerk's hourly salary before deductions is $6.97 ÷ 82% = $8.50. The total number of hours of work involved is 1200 forms ÷ 40 forms per hour = 30 hours. The amount the government would have to pay for the work is 30 hours × $8.50 = $255.00.

18

The Hour in Review

1. Work problems involve three factors: the number of people working on a job; the time it takes to complete the job; and the rate of work, or the amount of work that can be completed in one unit of time.

2. Depending on what factors are given in a work problem—the rates of different workers or the time it takes to complete the job—you can solve the problem according to a set formula.

3. Arithmetic reasoning problems require you to reason out the answer based on the variables given. A thorough understanding of the rules governing fractions, decimals, percents, ratios, and proportions is helpful in solving these problems.

Part V

Practice with Sample Exams

HOUR 19

Sample Civil Service Exam 1

What You Will Learn in This Hour

In this hour, you'll take a sample civil service exam. The exam should take you 50 minutes to complete. Use a timer to time the exam, and proceed exactly as you would at the real exam. The exam is broken into two parts:

- Part one of the sample civil service exam: Verbal ability test
- Part two of the sample civil service exam: Clerical ability test

Answer Sheet

Tear out these answer sheets and use them to mark your answers to the sample test that follows. Use a pencil to record your answers exactly as if you were taking the real exam. Be careful of misgridding, erasures, and other mistakes when marking answers.

Verbal Ability Test

1. (A) (B) (C) (D) (E)
2. (A) (B) (C) (D) (E)
3. (A) (B) (C) (D) (E)
4. (A) (B) (C) (D) (E)
5. (A) (B) (C) (D) (E)
6. (A) (B) (C) (D) (E)
7. (A) (B) (C) (D) (E)
8. (A) (B) (C) (D) (E)
9. (A) (B) (C) (D) (E)
10. (A) (B) (C) (D) (E)
11. (A) (B) (C) (D) (E)
12. (A) (B) (C) (D) (E)
13. (A) (B) (C) (D) (E)
14. (A) (B) (C) (D) (E)
15. (A) (B) (C) (D) (E)
16. (A) (B) (C) (D) (E)
17. (A) (B) (C) (D) (E)
18. (A) (B) (C) (D) (E)
19. (A) (B) (C) (D) (E)
20. (A) (B) (C) (D) (E)
21. (A) (B) (C) (D) (E)
22. (A) (B) (C) (D) (E)

23. (A) (B) (C) (D) (E)
24. (A) (B) (C) (D) (E)
25. (A) (B) (C) (D) (E)
26. (A) (B) (C) (D) (E)
27. (A) (B) (C) (D) (E)
28. (A) (B) (C) (D) (E)
29. (A) (B) (C) (D) (E)
30. (A) (B) (C) (D) (E)
31. (A) (B) (C) (D) (E)
32. (A) (B) (C) (D) (E)
33. (A) (B) (C) (D) (E)
34. (A) (B) (C) (D) (E)
35. (A) (B) (C) (D) (E)
36. (A) (B) (C) (D) (E)
37. (A) (B) (C) (D) (E)
38. (A) (B) (C) (D) (E)
39. (A) (B) (C) (D) (E)
40. (A) (B) (C) (D) (E)
41. (A) (B) (C) (D) (E)
42. (A) (B) (C) (D) (E)
43. (A) (B) (C) (D) (E)

44. (A) (B) (C) (D) (E)
45. (A) (B) (C) (D) (E)
46. (A) (B) (C) (D) (E)
47. (A) (B) (C) (D) (E)
48. (A) (B) (C) (D) (E)
49. (A) (B) (C) (D) (E)
50. (A) (B) (C) (D) (E)
51. (A) (B) (C) (D) (E)
52. (A) (B) (C) (D) (E)
53. (A) (B) (C) (D) (E)
54. (A) (B) (C) (D) (E)
55. (A) (B) (C) (D) (E)
56. (A) (B) (C) (D) (E)
57. (A) (B) (C) (D) (E)
58. (A) (B) (C) (D) (E)
59. (A) (B) (C) (D) (E)
60. (A) (B) (C) (D) (E)
61. (A) (B) (C) (D) (E)
62. (A) (B) (C) (D) (E)
63. (A) (B) (C) (D) (E)
64. (A) (B) (C) (D) (E)

65. (A) (B) (C) (D) (E)
66. (A) (B) (C) (D) (E)
67. (A) (B) (C) (D) (E)
68. (A) (B) (C) (D) (E)
69. (A) (B) (C) (D) (E)
70. (A) (B) (C) (D) (E)
71. (A) (B) (C) (D) (E)
72. (A) (B) (C) (D) (E)
73. (A) (B) (C) (D) (E)
74. (A) (B) (C) (D) (E)
75. (A) (B) (C) (D) (E)
76. (A) (B) (C) (D) (E)
77. (A) (B) (C) (D) (E)
78. (A) (B) (C) (D) (E)
79. (A) (B) (C) (D) (E)
80. (A) (B) (C) (D) (E)
81. (A) (B) (C) (D) (E)
82. (A) (B) (C) (D) (E)
83. (A) (B) (C) (D) (E)
84. (A) (B) (C) (D) (E)
85. (A) (B) (C) (D) (E)

19

Clerical Ability Test

1. Ⓐ Ⓑ Ⓒ Ⓓ Ⓔ	31. Ⓐ Ⓑ Ⓒ Ⓓ Ⓔ	61. Ⓐ Ⓑ Ⓒ Ⓓ Ⓔ	91. Ⓐ Ⓑ Ⓒ Ⓓ Ⓔ
2. Ⓐ Ⓑ Ⓒ Ⓓ Ⓔ	32. Ⓐ Ⓑ Ⓒ Ⓓ Ⓔ	62. Ⓐ Ⓑ Ⓒ Ⓓ Ⓔ	92. Ⓐ Ⓑ Ⓒ Ⓓ Ⓔ
3. Ⓐ Ⓑ Ⓒ Ⓓ Ⓔ	33. Ⓐ Ⓑ Ⓒ Ⓓ Ⓔ	63. Ⓐ Ⓑ Ⓒ Ⓓ Ⓔ	93. Ⓐ Ⓑ Ⓒ Ⓓ Ⓔ
4. Ⓐ Ⓑ Ⓒ Ⓓ Ⓔ	34. Ⓐ Ⓑ Ⓒ Ⓓ Ⓔ	64. Ⓐ Ⓑ Ⓒ Ⓓ Ⓔ	94. Ⓐ Ⓑ Ⓒ Ⓓ Ⓔ
5. Ⓐ Ⓑ Ⓒ Ⓓ Ⓔ	35. Ⓐ Ⓑ Ⓒ Ⓓ Ⓔ	65. Ⓐ Ⓑ Ⓒ Ⓓ Ⓔ	95. Ⓐ Ⓑ Ⓒ Ⓓ Ⓔ
6. Ⓐ Ⓑ Ⓒ Ⓓ Ⓔ	36. Ⓐ Ⓑ Ⓒ Ⓓ Ⓔ	66. Ⓐ Ⓑ Ⓒ Ⓓ Ⓔ	96. Ⓐ Ⓑ Ⓒ Ⓓ Ⓔ
7. Ⓐ Ⓑ Ⓒ Ⓓ Ⓔ	37. Ⓐ Ⓑ Ⓒ Ⓓ Ⓔ	67. Ⓐ Ⓑ Ⓒ Ⓓ Ⓔ	97. Ⓐ Ⓑ Ⓒ Ⓓ Ⓔ
8. Ⓐ Ⓑ Ⓒ Ⓓ Ⓔ	38. Ⓐ Ⓑ Ⓒ Ⓓ Ⓔ	68. Ⓐ Ⓑ Ⓒ Ⓓ Ⓔ	98. Ⓐ Ⓑ Ⓒ Ⓓ Ⓔ
9. Ⓐ Ⓑ Ⓒ Ⓓ Ⓔ	39. Ⓐ Ⓑ Ⓒ Ⓓ Ⓔ	69. Ⓐ Ⓑ Ⓒ Ⓓ Ⓔ	99. Ⓐ Ⓑ Ⓒ Ⓓ Ⓔ
10. Ⓐ Ⓑ Ⓒ Ⓓ Ⓔ	40. Ⓐ Ⓑ Ⓒ Ⓓ Ⓔ	70. Ⓐ Ⓑ Ⓒ Ⓓ Ⓔ	100. Ⓐ Ⓑ Ⓒ Ⓓ Ⓔ
11. Ⓐ Ⓑ Ⓒ Ⓓ Ⓔ	41. Ⓐ Ⓑ Ⓒ Ⓓ Ⓔ	71. Ⓐ Ⓑ Ⓒ Ⓓ Ⓔ	101. Ⓐ Ⓑ Ⓒ Ⓓ Ⓔ
12. Ⓐ Ⓑ Ⓒ Ⓓ Ⓔ	42. Ⓐ Ⓑ Ⓒ Ⓓ Ⓔ	72. Ⓐ Ⓑ Ⓒ Ⓓ Ⓔ	102. Ⓐ Ⓑ Ⓒ Ⓓ Ⓔ
13. Ⓐ Ⓑ Ⓒ Ⓓ Ⓔ	43. Ⓐ Ⓑ Ⓒ Ⓓ Ⓔ	73. Ⓐ Ⓑ Ⓒ Ⓓ Ⓔ	103. Ⓐ Ⓑ Ⓒ Ⓓ Ⓔ
14. Ⓐ Ⓑ Ⓒ Ⓓ Ⓔ	44. Ⓐ Ⓑ Ⓒ Ⓓ Ⓔ	74. Ⓐ Ⓑ Ⓒ Ⓓ Ⓔ	104. Ⓐ Ⓑ Ⓒ Ⓓ Ⓔ
15. Ⓐ Ⓑ Ⓒ Ⓓ Ⓔ	45. Ⓐ Ⓑ Ⓒ Ⓓ Ⓔ	75. Ⓐ Ⓑ Ⓒ Ⓓ Ⓔ	105. Ⓐ Ⓑ Ⓒ Ⓓ Ⓔ
16. Ⓐ Ⓑ Ⓒ Ⓓ Ⓔ	46. Ⓐ Ⓑ Ⓒ Ⓓ Ⓔ	76. Ⓐ Ⓑ Ⓒ Ⓓ Ⓔ	106. Ⓐ Ⓑ Ⓒ Ⓓ Ⓔ
17. Ⓐ Ⓑ Ⓒ Ⓓ Ⓔ	47. Ⓐ Ⓑ Ⓒ Ⓓ Ⓔ	77. Ⓐ Ⓑ Ⓒ Ⓓ Ⓔ	107. Ⓐ Ⓑ Ⓒ Ⓓ Ⓔ
18. Ⓐ Ⓑ Ⓒ Ⓓ Ⓔ	48. Ⓐ Ⓑ Ⓒ Ⓓ Ⓔ	78. Ⓐ Ⓑ Ⓒ Ⓓ Ⓔ	108. Ⓐ Ⓑ Ⓒ Ⓓ Ⓔ
19. Ⓐ Ⓑ Ⓒ Ⓓ Ⓔ	49. Ⓐ Ⓑ Ⓒ Ⓓ Ⓔ	79. Ⓐ Ⓑ Ⓒ Ⓓ Ⓔ	109. Ⓐ Ⓑ Ⓒ Ⓓ Ⓔ
20. Ⓐ Ⓑ Ⓒ Ⓓ Ⓔ	50. Ⓐ Ⓑ Ⓒ Ⓓ Ⓔ	80. Ⓐ Ⓑ Ⓒ Ⓓ Ⓔ	110. Ⓐ Ⓑ Ⓒ Ⓓ Ⓔ
21. Ⓐ Ⓑ Ⓒ Ⓓ Ⓔ	51. Ⓐ Ⓑ Ⓒ Ⓓ Ⓔ	81. Ⓐ Ⓑ Ⓒ Ⓓ Ⓔ	111. Ⓐ Ⓑ Ⓒ Ⓓ Ⓔ
22. Ⓐ Ⓑ Ⓒ Ⓓ Ⓔ	52. Ⓐ Ⓑ Ⓒ Ⓓ Ⓔ	82. Ⓐ Ⓑ Ⓒ Ⓓ Ⓔ	112. Ⓐ Ⓑ Ⓒ Ⓓ Ⓔ
23. Ⓐ Ⓑ Ⓒ Ⓓ Ⓔ	53. Ⓐ Ⓑ Ⓒ Ⓓ Ⓔ	83. Ⓐ Ⓑ Ⓒ Ⓓ Ⓔ	113. Ⓐ Ⓑ Ⓒ Ⓓ Ⓔ
24. Ⓐ Ⓑ Ⓒ Ⓓ Ⓔ	54. Ⓐ Ⓑ Ⓒ Ⓓ Ⓔ	84. Ⓐ Ⓑ Ⓒ Ⓓ Ⓔ	114. Ⓐ Ⓑ Ⓒ Ⓓ Ⓔ
25. Ⓐ Ⓑ Ⓒ Ⓓ Ⓔ	55. Ⓐ Ⓑ Ⓒ Ⓓ Ⓔ	85. Ⓐ Ⓑ Ⓒ Ⓓ Ⓔ	115. Ⓐ Ⓑ Ⓒ Ⓓ Ⓔ
26. Ⓐ Ⓑ Ⓒ Ⓓ Ⓔ	56. Ⓐ Ⓑ Ⓒ Ⓓ Ⓔ	86. Ⓐ Ⓑ Ⓒ Ⓓ Ⓔ	116. Ⓐ Ⓑ Ⓒ Ⓓ Ⓔ
27. Ⓐ Ⓑ Ⓒ Ⓓ Ⓔ	57. Ⓐ Ⓑ Ⓒ Ⓓ Ⓔ	87. Ⓐ Ⓑ Ⓒ Ⓓ Ⓔ	117. Ⓐ Ⓑ Ⓒ Ⓓ Ⓔ
28. Ⓐ Ⓑ Ⓒ Ⓓ Ⓔ	58. Ⓐ Ⓑ Ⓒ Ⓓ Ⓔ	88. Ⓐ Ⓑ Ⓒ Ⓓ Ⓔ	118. Ⓐ Ⓑ Ⓒ Ⓓ Ⓔ
29. Ⓐ Ⓑ Ⓒ Ⓓ Ⓔ	59. Ⓐ Ⓑ Ⓒ Ⓓ Ⓔ	89. Ⓐ Ⓑ Ⓒ Ⓓ Ⓔ	119. Ⓐ Ⓑ Ⓒ Ⓓ Ⓔ
30. Ⓐ Ⓑ Ⓒ Ⓓ Ⓔ	60. Ⓐ Ⓑ Ⓒ Ⓓ Ⓔ	90. Ⓐ Ⓑ Ⓒ Ⓓ Ⓔ	120. Ⓐ Ⓑ Ⓒ Ⓓ Ⓔ

19

Verbal Ability Test

85 Questions

> **DIRECTIONS:** Read each question carefully. Select the best answer and darken the proper space on the answer grid. You will have 35 minutes to complete this part of the exam.

1. *Flexible* means most nearly
   (A) breakable
   (B) flammable
   (C) pliable
   (D) weak

2. *Option* means most nearly
   (A) use
   (B) choice
   (C) value
   (D) blame

3. To *verify* means most nearly to
   (A) examine
   (B) explain
   (C) confirm
   (D) guarantee

4. *Indolent* means most nearly
   (A) moderate
   (B) hopeless
   (C) selfish
   (D) lazy

5. *Respiration* means most nearly
   (A) recovery
   (B) breathing
   (C) pulsation
   (D) sweating

6. PLUMBER is related to WRENCH as PAINTER is related to
   (A) brush
   (B) pipe
   (C) shop
   (D) hammer

7. LETTER is related to MESSAGE as PACKAGE is related
   (A) sender
   (B) merchandise
   (C) insurance
   (D) business

8. FOOD is related to HUNGER as SLEEP is related to
   (A) night
   (B) dream
   (C) weariness
   (D) rest

9. KEY is related to TYPEWRITER as DIAL is related to
   (A) sun
   (B) number
   (C) circle
   (D) telephone

19

In questions 10 and 11 and all similar questions, decide which sentence is best with respect to grammar and usage suitable for a formal letter or report.

10. (A) I think that they will promote whoever has the best record.

(B) The firm would have liked to have promoted all employees with good records.

(C) Such of them that have the best records have excellent prospects of promotion.

(D) I feel sure they will give the promotion to whomever has the best record.

11. (A) The receptionist must answer courteously the questions of all them callers.

(B) The receptionist must answer courteously the questions what are asked by the callers.

(C) There would have been no trouble if the receptionist had have always answered courteously.

(D) The receptionist should answer courteously the questions of all callers.

In questions 12–16 and all similar questions, find the correct spelling of the word and darken the proper answer space. If no suggested spelling is correct, darken space (D).

12. (A) collapsible

(B) collapseable

(C) collapseble

(D) None of the above

13. (A) ambigeuous

(B) ambigeous

(C) ambiguous

(D) None of the above

14. (A) predesessor

(B) predecesar

(C) predecesser

(D) None of the above

15. (A) sanctioned

(B) sancktioned

(C) sanctionned

(D) None of the above

16. "Some fire-resistant buildings, although wholly constructed of materials that will not burn, may be completely gutted by the spread of fire through their contents by way of hallways and other openings. They may even suffer serious structural damage by the collapse of metal beams and columns."

The quotation best supports the statement that some fire-resistant buildings

(A) can be damaged seriously by fire.

(B) have specially constructed halls and doors.

(C) afford less protection to their contents than would ordinary buildings.

(D) will burn readily.

17. Civilization started to move ahead more rapidly when people freed themselves of the shackles that restricted their search for the truth.

The paragraph best supports the statement that the progress of civilization

(A) came as a result of people's dislike for obstacles.

(B) did not begin until restrictions on learning were removed.

(C) has been aided by people's efforts to find the truth.

(D) is based on continually increasing efforts.

18. *Vigilant* means most nearly

(A) sensible

(B) watchful

(C) suspicious

(D) restless

19. *Incidental* means most nearly

(A) independent

(B) needless

(C) infrequent

(D) accompanying

20. *Conciliatory* means most nearly

(A) pacific

(B) contentious

(C) obligatory

(D) offensive

21. *Altercation* means most nearly

(A) defeat

(B) concurrence

(C) controversy

(D) vexation

22. *Irresolute* means most nearly

(A) wavering

(B) insubordinate

(C) impudent

(D) unobservant

23. DARKNESS is related to SUNLIGHT as STILLNESS is related to

(A) quiet

(B) moonlight

(C) sound

(D) dark

24. DESIGNED is related to INTENTION as ACCIDENTAL is related to

(A) purpose

(B) caution

(C) damage

(D) chance

25. ERROR is related to PRACTICE as SOUND is related to

(A) deafness

(B) noise

(C) muffler

(D) horn

26. RESEARCH is related to FINDINGS as TRAINING is related to

(A) skill

(B) tests

(C) supervision

(D) teaching

19

27. (A) If properly addressed, the letter will reach my mother and I.

(B) The letter had been addressed to myself and my mother.

(C) I believe the letter was addressed to either my mother or I.

(D) My mother's name, as well as mine, was on the letter.

28. (A) The supervisors reprimanded the typists, whom she believed had made careless errors.

(B) The typists would have corrected the errors had they of known that the supervisor would see the report.

(C) The errors in the typed reports were so numerous that they could hardly be overlooked.

(D) Many errors were found in the reports which they typed and could not disregard them.

29. (A) minieture

(B) minneature

(C) mineature

(D) none of these

30. (A) extemporaneous

(B) extempuraneus

(C) extemperaneous

(D) none of these

31. (A) problemmatical

(B) problematical

(C) problematicle

(D) none of these

32. (A) descendant

(B) decendant

(C) desendant

(D) None of the above

33. The likelihood of America's exhausting its natural resources seems to be growing less. All kinds of waste are being reworked and new uses are constantly being found for almost everything. We are getting more use out of our goods and are making many new byproducts out of what was formerly thrown away.

The paragraph best supports the statement that we seem to be in less danger of exhausting our resources because

(A) economy is found to lie in the use of substitutes.

(B) more service is obtained from a given amount of material.

(C) we are allowing time for nature to restore them.

(D) supply and demand are better controlled.

34. Telegrams should be clear, concise, and brief. Omit all unnecessary words. The parts of speech most often used in telegrams are nouns, verbs, adjectives, and adverbs. If possible, do without pronouns, articles, and copulative verbs. Use simple sentences, rather than complex or compound ones.

The paragraph best supports the statement that in writing telegrams one should always use

(A) common and simple words.

(B) only nouns, verbs, adjectives, and adverbs.

(C) incomplete sentences.

(D) only the words essential to the meaning.

35. To *counteract* means most nearly to

(A) undermine

(B) censure

(C) preserve

(D) neutralize

36. *Deferred* means most nearly
   (A) reversed
   (B) delayed
   (C) considered
   (D) forbidden

37. *Feasible* means most nearly
   (A) capable
   (B) justifiable
   (C) practicable
   (D) beneficial

38. To *encounter* means most nearly to
   (A) meet
   (B) recall
   (C) overcome
   (D) retreat

39. *Innate* means most nearly
   (A) eternal
   (B) well-developed
   (C) native
   (D) prospective

40. STUDENT is related to TEACHER as DISCIPLE is related to
   (A) follower
   (B) master
   (C) principal
   (D) pupil

41. LECTURE is related to AUDITORIUM as EXPERIMENT is related to
   (A) scientist
   (B) chemistry
   (C) laboratory
   (D) discovery

42. BODY is related to FOOD as ENGINE is related to
   (A) wheels
   (B) fuel
   (C) motion
   (D) smoke

43. SCHOOL is related to EDUCATION as THEATER is related to
   (A) management
   (B) stage
   (C) recreation
   (D) preparation

44. (A) Most all these statements have been supported by persons who are reliable and can be depended upon.
   (B) The persons which have guaranteed these statements are reliable.
   (C) Reliable persons guarantee the facts with regards to the truth of these statements.
   (D) These statements can be depended on, for their truth has been guaranteed by reliable persons.

45. (A) The success of the book pleased both the publishers and the authors.
   (B) Both the publisher and they was pleased with the success of the book.
   (C) Neither they or their publisher was disappointed with their success of the book.
   (D) Their publisher was as pleased as them with the success of the book.

46. (A) extercate
   (B) extracate
   (C) extricate
   (D) None of the above

19

47. (A) hereditory

(B) hereditary

(C) hereditairy

(D) None of the above

48. (A) auspiceous

(B) auspiseous

(C) auspicious

(D) None of the above

49. (A) sequance

(B) sequence

(C) sequense

(D) None of the above

50. The prevention of accidents makes it necessary not only that safety devices be used to guard exposed machinery but also that mechanics be instructed in safety rules that they must follow for their own protection, and that the lighting in the plant be adequate.

The paragraph best supports the statement that industrial accidents

(A) may be due to lack of knowledge.

(B) are always avoidable.

(C) usually result from inadequate machinery.

(D) cannot be entirely overcome.

51. The English language is peculiarly rich in synonyms, and there is scarcely a language spoken that has not some representative in English speech. The spirit of the Anglo-Saxon race has subjugated these various elements to one idiom, making not a patchwork, but a composite language.

The paragraph best supports the statement that the English language

(A) has few idiomatic expressions.

(B) is difficult to translate.

(C) is used universally.

(D) has absorbed words from other languages.

52. To *acquiesce* means most nearly to

(A) assent

(B) acquire

(C) complete

(D) participate

53. *Unanimity* means most nearly

(A) emphasis

(B) namelessness

(C) harmony

(D) impartiality

54. *Precedent* means most nearly

(A) example

(B) theory

(C) law

(D) conformity

55. *Versatile* means most nearly

(A) broad-minded

(B) well-known

(C) up-to-date

(D) many-sided

56. *Authentic* means most nearly

(A) detailed

(B) reliable

(C) valuable

(D) practical

57. BIOGRAPHY is related to FACT as NOVEL is related to

(A) fiction

(B) literature

(C) narration

(D) book

58. COPY is related to CARBON PAPER as MOTION PICTURE is related to

(A) theater

(B) film

(C) duplicate

(D) television

59. EFFICIENCY is related to REWARD as CARELESSNESS is related to

(A) improvement

(B) disobedience

(C) reprimand

(D) repetition

60. ABUNDANT is related to CHEAP as SCARCE is related to

(A) ample

(B) costly

(C) inexpensive

(D) unobtainable

61. (A) Brown's & Company employees have recently received increases in salary.

(B) Brown & Company recently increased the salaries of all its employees.

(C) Recently Brown & Company has increased their employees' salaries.

(D) Brown & Company have recently increased the salaries of all its employees.

62. (A) In reviewing the typists' work reports, the job analyst found records of unusual typing speeds.

(B) It says in the job analyst's report that some employees type with great speed.

(C) The job analyst found that, in reviewing the typists' work reports, that some unusual typing speeds had been made.

(D) In the reports of typists' speeds, the job analyst found some records that are kind of unusual.

63. (A) oblitorate

(B) oblitterat

(C) obbliterate

(D) None of the above

64. (A) diagnoesis

(B) diagnossis

(C) diagnosis

(D) None of the above

65. (A) contenance

(B) countenance

(C) countinance

(D) None of the above

19

66. (A) conceivably

(B) concieveably

(C) conceiveably

(D) None of the above

67. Through advertising, manufacturers exercise a high degree of control over consumers' desires. However, the manufacturer assumes enormous risks in attempting to predict what consumers will want and in producing goods in quantity and distributing them in advance of final selection by the consumers.

The paragraph best supports the statement that manufacturers

(A) can eliminate the risk of overproduction by advertising.

(B) distribute goods directly to the consumers.

(C) must depend upon the final consumers for the success of their undertakings.

(D) can predict with great accuracy the success of any product they put on the market.

68. In the relations of humans to nature, the procuring of food and shelter is fundamental. With the migration of humans to various climates, ever new adjustments to the food supply and to the climate became necessary.

The paragraph best supports the statement that the means by which the humans supply their material needs are

(A) accidental.

(B) varied.

(C) limited.

(D) inadequate.

69. *Strident* means most nearly

(A) swaggering

(B) domineering

(C) angry

(D) harsh

70. To *confine* means most nearly to

(A) hide

(B) restrict

(C) eliminate

(D) punish

71. To *accentuate* means most nearly to

(A) modify

(B) hasten

(C) sustain

(D) intensify

72. *Banal* means most nearly

(A) commonplace

(B) forceful

(C) tranquil

(D) indifferent

73. *Incorrigible* means most nearly

(A) intolerable

(B) retarded

(C) irreformable

(D) brazen

74. POLICEMAN is related to ORDER as DOCTOR is related to

(A) physician

(B) hospital

(C) sickness

(D) health

75. ARTIST is related to EASEL as WEAVER is related to

(A) loom

(B) cloth

(C) threads

(D) spinner

76. CROWD is related to PERSONS as FLEET is related to

(A) expedition

(B) officers

(C) navy

(D) ships

77. CALENDAR is related to DATE as MAP is related to

(A) drive

(B) trip

(C) location

(D) vacation

78. (A) Since the report lacked the needed information, it was of no use to them.

(B) This report was useless to them because there were no needed information in it.

(C) Since the report did not contain the needed information, it was not real useful to them.

(D) Being that the report lacked the needed information, they could not use it.

79. (A) The company had hardly declared the dividend till the notices were prepared for mailing.

(B) They had no sooner declared the dividend when they sent the notices to the stockholders.

(C) No sooner had the dividend been declared than the notices were prepared for mailing.

(D) Scarcely had the dividend been declared than the notices were sent out.

80. (A) compitition

(B) competition

(C) competetion

(D) None of the above

81. (A) occassion

(B) occasion

(C) ocassion

(D) None of the above

82. (A) knowlege

(B) knolledge

(C) knowledge

(D) None of the above

83. (A) deliborate

(B) deliberate

(C) delibrate

(D) None of the above

19

84. What constitutes skill in any line of work is not always easy to determine. Economy of time must be carefully distinguished from economy of energy, as the quickest method may require the greatest expenditure of muscular effort and may not be essential or at all desirable.

The paragraph best supports the statement that

(A) the most efficiently executed task is not always the one done in the shortest time.

(B) energy and time cannot both be conserved in performing a single task.

(C) a task is well done when it is performed in the shortest time.

(D) skill in performing a task should not be acquired at the expense of time.

85. It is difficult to distinguish between bookkeeping and accounting. In attempts to do so, bookkeeping is called the art, and accounting the science, of recording business transactions. Bookkeeping gives the history of the business in a systematic matter; and accounting classifies, analyzes, and interprets the facts thus recorded.

The paragraph best supports the statement that

(A) accounting is less systematic than bookkeeping.

(B) accounting and bookkeeping are closely related.

(C) bookkeeping and accounting cannot be distinguished from one another.

(D) bookkeeping has been superseded by accounting.

STOP:
End of Verbal Section

If you finish before time is up, check your work on this part only.
Do not turn to the next part until the signal is given.

Clerical Ability Test

120 Questions

> **DIRECTIONS:** Read each question carefully. Select the best answer and darken the proper space on the answer grid. You will have 15 minutes to complete this part of the exam.
> In questions 1 – 5, compare the three names or numbers, and mark the answers:
> - (A) if ALL THREE names or numbers are exactly ALIKE
> - (B) if only the FIRST and SECOND names or numbers are exactly ALIKE
> - (C) if only the FIRST and THIRD names or numbers are exactly ALIKE
> - (D) if only the SECOND and THIRD names or numbers are exactly ALIKE
> - (E) if ALL THREE names or numbers are DIFFERENT

1.	5261383	5261383	5261338
2.	8125690	8126690	8125609
3.	W. E. Johnston	W. E. Johnson	W. E. Johnson
4.	Vergil L. Muller	Vergil L. Muller	Vergil L. Muller
5.	Atherton R. Warde	Asheton R. Warde	Atherton P. Warde

In questions 6 – 10 and all similar questions, find the correct place for the given name.

6. Hackett, Gerald

    (A)   -

       Habert, James

    (B)   -

       Hachett, J. J.

    (C)   -

       Hachetts, K. Larson

    (D)   -

       Hachettson, Leroy

    (E)   -

7.   Margenroth, Alvin

    (A)   -

       Margeroth, Albert

    (B)   -

       Margestein, Dan

    (C)   -

       Margestein, David

    (D)   -

       Margue, Edgar

    (E)   -

8. Bobbitt, Olivier E.

(A)   -

Bobbitt, D. Olivier

(B)   -

Bobbitt, Olive B.

(C)   -

Bobbitt, Olivia H.

(D)   -

Bobbitt, R. Olivia

(E)   -

9. Mosely, Werner

(A)   -

Mosely, Albert J.

(B)   -

Mosley, Alvin

(C)   -

Mosley, S. M.

(D)   -

Mosley, Vinson N.

(E)   -

10. Youmuns, Frank L.

(A)   -

Youmons, Frank G.

(B)   -

Youmons, Frank H.

(C)   -

Youmons, Frank K.

(D)   -

Youmons, Frank M.

(E)   -

11.   43   (A)   55
       + 32   (B)   65
                                     (C)   66
                                     (D)   75
                                     (E)   None of the above

12.   83   (A)   73
        − 4   (B)   79
                                     (C)   80
                                     (D)   89
                                     (E)   None of the above

13.   41   (A)   281
        × 7   (B)   287
                                     (C)   291
                                     (D)   297
                                     (E)   None of the above

14.   306   (A)   44
        ÷ 6   (B)   51
                                     (C)   52
                                     (D)   60
                                     (E)   None of the above

19

15.   37   (A)   42
       + 15   (B)   52
                                     (C)   53
                                     (D)   62
                                     (E)   None of the above

In questions 16 – 20 and all similar questions, find which one of the suggested answers appears in that question.

									Suggested Answers
16.	6	2	5	K	4	P	T	G	**A** = 4, 5, K, T
17.	L	4	7	2	T	6	V	K	**B** = 4, 7, G, K
18.	3	5	4	L	9	V	T	G	**C** = 2, 5, G, L
19.	G	4	K	7	L	3	5	Z	**D** = 2, 7, L, T
20.	4	K	2	9	N	5	T	G	**E** = None of the above

In questions 21 – 25, compare the three names or numbers, and mark the answer:

- (A) if ALL THREE names or numbers are exactly ALIKE
- (B) if only the FIRST and SECOND names or numbers are exactly ALIKE
- (C) if only the FIRST and THIRD names or numbers are exactly ALIKE
- (D) if only the SECOND and THIRD names or numbers are exactly ALIKE
- (E) if ALL THREE names or numbers are DIFFERENT

21.	2395890	2395890	2395890
22.	1926341	1926347	1926314
23.	E. Owens McVey	E. Owen McVey	E. Owen McVay
24.	Emily Neal Rouse	Emily Neal Rowse	Emily Neal Rowse
25.	H. Merritt Audubon	H. Merriott Audubon	H. Merritt Audubon

26.   Watters, N. O.

     (A)-

       Waters, Charles L.

     (B)-

       Waterson, Nina P.

     (C)-

       Watson, Nora J.

     (D)-

       Wattwood, Paul A.

     (E)-

27.   Johnston, Edward

     (A)-

       Johnston, Edgar R.

     (B)-

       Johnston, Edmond

     (C)-

       Johnston, Edmund

     (D)-

       Johnstone, Edmund A.

     (E)-

28.   Rensch, Adeline

(A)   -

Ramsay, Amos

(B)   -

Remschel, Augusta

(C)   -

Renshaw, Austin

(D)   -

Rentzel, Becky

(E)   -

29.   Schnyder, Maurice

(A)   -

Schneider, Martin

(B)   -

Schneider, Mertens

(C)   -

Schnyder, Newman

(D)   -

Schreibner, Norman

(E)   -

30.   Freedenburg, C. Erma

(A)   -

Freedenberg, Emerson

(B)   -

Freedenberg, Erma

(C)   -

Freedenberg, Erma E.

(D)   -

Freedinberg, Erma F.

(E)   -

31.   Subtract: $68 - 47$

(A) 10

(B) 11

(C) 20

(D) 22

(E) None of the above

32.   Multiply: 50×8

(A) 400

(B) 408

(C) 450

(D) 458

(E) None of the above

33.   Divide: $180 \div 9$

(A) 20

(B) 29

(C) 30

(D) 39

(E) None of the above

34.   Add: $78 + 63$

(A) 131

(B) 140

(C) 141

(D) 151

(E) None of the above

35.   Subtract: $89 - 70$

(A) 9

(B) 18

(C) 19

(D) 29

(E) None of the above

19

									Suggested Answers
36.	9	G	Z	3	L	4	6	N	**A** = 4, 9, L, V
37.	L	5	N	K	4	3	9	V	**B** = 4, 5, N, Z
38.	8	2	V	P	9	L	Z	5	**C** = 5, 8, L, Z
39.	V	P	9	Z	5	L	8	7	**D** = 8, 9, N, V
40.	5	T	8	N	2	9	V	L	**E** = None of the above

In questions 41 – 45, compare the three names or numbers, and mark the answer:

- (A) if ALL THREE names or numbers are exactly ALIKE
- (B) if only the FIRST and SECOND names or numbers are exactly ALIKE
- (C) if only the FIRST and THIRD names or numbers are exactly ALIKE
- (D) if only the SECOND and THIRD names or numbers are exactly ALIKE
- (E) if ALL THREE names or numbers are DIFFERENT

41.	6219354	6219354	6219354
42.	2311.2793	2312793	2312793
43.	1065407	1065407	1065047
44.	Francis Ransdell	Frances Ramsdell	Francis Ramsdell
45.	Cornelius Detwiler	Cornelius Detwiler	Cornelius Detwiler

46. DeMattia, Jessica

(A)   -

    DeLong, Jesse

(B)   -

    DeMatteo, Jessie

(C)   -

    Derby, Jessie S.

(D)   -

    DeShazo, L. M.

(E)   -

47. Theriault, Louis

(A)   -

    Therien, Annette

(B)   -

    Therien, Elaine

(C)   -

    Thibeault, Gerald

(D)   -

    Thiebeault, Pierre

(E)   -

48. Gaston, M. Hubert

(A)   -

Gaston, Dorothy M.

(B)   -

Gaston, Henry N.

(C)   -

Gaston, Isabel

(D)   -

Gaston, M. Melvin

(E)   -

49. SanMiguel, Carlos

(A)   -

SanLuis, Juana

(B)   -

Santilli, Laura

(C)   -

Stinnett, Nellie

(D)   -

Stoddard, Victor

(E)   -

50. DeLaTour, Hall F.

(A)   -

Delargy, Harold

(B)   -

DeLathouder, Hilda

(C)   -

Lathrop, Hillary

(D)   -

LaTour, Hulbert E.

(E)   -

51. Multiply: 62×5

(A) 300

(B) 310

(C) 315

(D) 360

(E) None of the above

52. Divide: $153 \div 3$

(A) 41

(B) 43

(C) 51

(D) 53

(E) None of the above

53. Add: $47 + 21$

(A) 58

(B) 59

(C) 67

(D) 68

(E) None of the above

54. Subtract: $87 - 42$

(A) 34

(B) 35

(C) 44

(D) 45

(E) None of the above

55. Multiply: 37×3

(A) 91

(B) 101

(C) 104

(D) 114

(E) None of the above

19

Suggested Answers

56.	N	5	4	7	T	K	3	Z	**A** = 3, 8, K, N
57.	8	5	3	V	L	2	Z	N	**B** = 5, 8, N, V
58.	7	2	5	N	9	K	L	V	**C** = 3, 9, V, Z
59.	9	8	L	2	5	Z	K	V	**D** = 5, 9, K, Z
60.	Z	6	5	V	9	3	P	N	**E** = None of the above

In questions 61 – 65, compare the three names or numbers, and mark the answer:

- (A) if ALL THREE names or numbers are exactly ALIKE
- (B) if only the FIRST and SECOND names or numbers are exactly ALIKE
- (C) if only the FIRST and THIRD names or numbers are exactly ALIKE
- (D) if only the SECOND and THIRD names or numbers are exactly ALIKE
- (E) if ALL THREE names or numbers are DIFFERENT

61.	6452054	6452654	6452054
62.	8501268	8501268	8501286
63.	Ella Burk Newham	Ella Burk Newnham	Elena Burk Newnham
64.	Jno. K. Ravencroft	Jno. H. Ravencroft	Jno. H. Ravencroft
65.	Martin Wills Pullen	Martin Wills Pulen	Martin Wills Pullen

66. O'Bannon, M. J.

(A)   -

   O'Beirne, B. B.

(B)   -

   Oberlin, E. L.

(C)   -

   Oberneir, L. P.

(D)   -

   O'Brian, S. F.

(E)   -

67.   Entsminger, Jacob

(A)   -

   Ensminger, J.

(B)   -

   Entsminger, J. A.

(C)   -

   Entsminger, Jack

(D)   -

   Entsminger, James

(E)   -

68.   Iacone, Pete R.

(A)   -

Iacone, Pedro

(B)   -

Iacone, Pedro M.

(C)   -

Iacone, Peter F.

(D)   -

Iascone, Peter W.

(E)   -

69.   Sheppard, Gladys

(A)   -

Shepard, Dwight

(B)   -

Shepard, F. H.

(C)   -

Shephard, Louise

(D)   -

Shepperd, Stella

(E)   -

70.   Thackton, Melvin T.

(A)   -

Thackston, Milton G.

(B)   -

Thackston, Milton W.

(C)   -

Thackston, Theodore

(D)   -

Thackston, Thomas G.

(E)   -

71.   Divide: $357 \div 7$

(A) 51

(B) 52

(C) 53

(D) 54

(E) None of the above

72.   Add: $58 + 27$

(A) 75

(B) 84

(C) 85

(D) 95

(E) None of the above

73.   Subtract: $86 - 57$

(A) 18

(B) 29

(C) 38

(D) 39

(E) None of the above

74.   Multiply: 68×4

(A) 242

(B) 264

(C) 272

(D) 274

(E) None of the above

75.   Divide: $639 \div 9$

(A) 71

(B) 73

(C) 81

(D) 83

(E) None of the above

19

Suggested Answers

76.	6	Z	T	N	8	7	4	V	**A** = 2, 7, L, N
77.	V	7	8	6	N	5	P	L	**B** = 2, 8, T, V
78.	N	7	P	V	8	4	2	L	**C** = 6, 8, L, T
79.	7	8	G	4	3	V	L	T	**D** = 6, 7, N, V
80.	4	8	G	2	T	N	6	L	**E** = None of the above

In questions 81 – 85, compare the three names or numbers, and mark the answer:

- (A) if ALL THREE names or numbers are exactly ALIKE
- (B) if only the FIRST and SECOND names or numbers are exactly ALIKE
- (C) if only the FIRST and THIRD names or numbers are exactly ALIKE
- (D) if only the SECOND and THIRD names or numbers are exactly ALIKE
- (E) if ALL THREE names or numbers are DIFFERENT

81.	3457988	3457986	3457986
82.	4695682	4695862	4695682
83.	Sticklund Kanedy	Stricklund Kanedy	Stricklund Kanedy
84.	Joy Harlor Witner	Joy Harloe Witner	Joy Harloe Witner
85.	R. M. O. Uberroth	R. M. O. Uberroth	R. N. O. Uberroth

86. Dunlavey, M. Hilary

(A)   -

    Dunleavy, Hilary G.

(B)   -

    Dunleavy, Hilary K.

(C)   -

    Dunleavy, Hilary S.

(D)   -

    Dunleavy, Hilery W.

(E)   -

87. Yarbrough, Maria

(A)   -

    Yabroudy, Margy

(B)   -

    Yarboro, Marie

(C)   -

    Yarborough, Marina

(D)   -

    Yarborough, Mary

(E)   -

88.   Prouty, Martha

      (A)   -

            Proutey, Margaret

      (B)   -

            Proutey, Maude

      (C)   -

            Prouty, Myra

      (D)   -

            Prouty, Naomi

      (E)   -

89.   Pawlowicz, Ruth M.

      (A)   -

            Pawalek, Edward

      (B)   -

            Pawelek, Flora G.

      (C)   -

            Pawlowski, Joan M.

      (D)   -

            Pawtowski, Wanda

      (E)   -

90.   Vanstory, George

      (A)   -

            Vanover, Eva

      (B)   -

            VanSwinderen, Floyd

      (C)   -

            VanSyckle, Harry

      (D)   -

            Vanture, Laurence

      (E)   -

91.   Add: 28 + 35

      (A) 53

      (B) 62

      (C) 64

      (D) 73

      (E) None of the above

92.   Subtract: 78 − 69

      (A) 7

      (B) 8

      (C) 18

      (D) 19

      (E) None of the above

93.   Multiply: 86 × 6

      (A) 492

      (B) 506

      (C) 516

      (D) 526

      (E) None of the above

94.   Divide: 648 ÷ 8

      (A) 71

      (B) 76

      (C) 81

      (D) 89

      (E) None of the above

95.   Add: 97 + 34

      (A) 131

      (B) 132

      (C) 140

      (D) 141

      (E) None of the above

19

								Suggested Answers
96.	V	5	7	Z	N	9	4	T	**A** = 2, 5, N, Z
97.	4	6	P	T	2	N	K	9	**B** = 4, 5, N, P
98.	6	4	N	2	P	8	Z	K	**C** = 2, 9, P, T
99.	7	P	5	2	4	N	K	T	**D** = 4, 9, T, Z
100.	K	T	8	5	4	N	2	P	**E** = None of the above

In questions 101 – 105, compare the three names or numbers, and mark the answer:

- (A) if ALL THREE names or numbers are exactly ALIKE
- (B) if only the FIRST and SECOND names or numbers are exactly ALIKE
- (C) if only the FIRST and THIRD names or numbers are exactly ALIKE
- (D) if only the SECOND and THIRD names or numbers are exactly ALIKE
- (E) if ALL THREE names or numbers are DIFFERENT

101.	1592514	1592574	1592574
102.	2010202	2010202	2010220
103.	6177396	6177936	6177396
104.	Drusilla S. Ridgeley	Drusilla S. Ridgeley	Drusilla S. Ridgeley
105.	Andrei I. Toumantzev	Andrei I. Tourmantzev	Andrei I. Toumantzov

106. Fitzsimmons, Hugh

(A)   -

Fitts, Harold

(B)   -

Fitzgerald, June

(C)   -

FitzGibbon, Junius

(D)   -

FitzSimons, Martin

(E)   -

107. D'Amato, Vincent

(A)   -

Daly, Steven

(B)   -

D'Amboise, S. Vincent

(C)   -

Daniel, Vail

(D)   -

DeAlba, Valentina

(E)   -

108. Schaeffer, Roger D.

   (A)   -

      Schaffert, Evelyn M.

   (B)   -

      Schaffner, Margaret M.

   (C)   -

      Schafhirt, Milton G.

   (D)   -

      Shafer, Richard E.

   (E)   -

109. White-Lewis, Cecil

   (A)   -

      Whitelaw, Cordelia

   (B)   -

      White-Leigh, Nancy

   (C)   -

      Whitely, Rodney

   (D)   -

      Whitlock, Warren

   (E)   -

110. VanDerHeggen, Don

   (A)   -

      VanDemark, Doris

   (B)   -

      Vandenberg, H. E.

   (C)   -

      VanDercook, Marie

   (D)   -

      vanderLinden, Robert

   (E)   -

111. Add: 75 + 49

   (A) 124

   (B) 125

   (C) 134

   (D) 225

   (E) None of the above

112. Subtract: 69 – 45

   (A) 14

   (B) 23

   (C) 24

   (D) 26

   (E) None of the above

113. Multiply: 36×8

   (A) 246

   (B) 262

   (C) 288

   (D) 368

   (E) None of the above

114. Divide: $328 \div 8$

   (A) 31

   (B) 41

   (C) 42

   (D) 48

   (E) None of the above

115. Multiply: 58×9

   (A) 472

   (B) 513

   (C) 521

   (D) 522

   (E) None of the above

19

Suggested Answers

116.	Z	3	N	P	G	5	4	2	**A** = 2, 3, G, N
117.	6	N	2	8	G	4	P	T	**B** = 2, 6, N, T
118.	6	N	4	T	V	G	8	2	**C** = 3, 4, G, K
119.	T	3	P	4	N	8	G	2	**D** = 4, 6, K, T
120.	6	7	K	G	N	2	L	5	**E** = None of the above

STOP:
End of Clerical Section

HOUR 20

Evaluating Sample Civil Service Exam 1

What You Will Learn in This Hour

In this hour, you will determine how well you did on the sample civil service exam that you took in the last hour. You will calculate your overall score, find the answers to the questions that you missed, and discover any weak areas that you need to review. Do not worry if you do not score as well as you would like. The more you practice, the more your scores will improve. Here are your goals for this hour:

- Evaluate the verbal ability portion of the exam.
- Evaluate the clerical ability portion of the exam.
- Learn how to evaluate yourself.

Scoring the Sample Civil Service Exam

Note that the verbal ability and clerical ability tests are scored differently. The scoring formula for each is explained before that section's answer key. Write your raw score for each portion of the exam on the answer sheet. Mark any questions that you missed for later reference.

Scoring the Verbal Ability Test

The total raw score on the verbal ability portion of the exam consists of the total number of questions that are answered correctly. There is no penalty for wrong answers, and there is no correction made for guessing. No credit, however, is given for any question with more than one answer marked.

Using the following answer key, count the total number of questions that you answered correctly. This is your raw score. The highest possible score is 85.

1.	C	18.	B	35.	D	52.	A	69.	D
2.	B	19.	D	36.	B	53.	C	70.	B
3.	C	20.	A	37.	C	54.	A	71.	D
4.	D	21.	C	38.	A	55.	D	72.	A
5.	B	22.	A	39.	C	56.	B	73.	C
6.	A	23.	C	40.	B	57.	A	74.	D
7.	B	24.	D	41.	C	58.	B	75.	A
8.	C	25.	C	42.	B	59.	C	76.	D
9.	D	26.	A	43.	C	60.	B	77.	C
10.	A	27.	D	44.	D	61.	B	78.	A
11.	D	28.	C	45.	A	62.	A	79.	C
12.	A	29.	D	46.	C	63.	D	80.	B
13.	C	30.	A	47.	B	64.	C	81.	B
14.	D	31.	B	48.	C	65.	B	82.	C
15.	A	32.	A	49.	B	66.	A	83.	B
16.	A	33.	B	50.	A	67.	C	84.	A
17.	C	34.	D	51.	D	68.	B	85.	B

Scoring the Clerical Ability Test

On this portion of the exam, you are penalized for wrong answers. The total raw score is the number of right answers minus one-fourth of the number of wrong answers. (Fractions of one-half or less are dropped.) Calculate your score as follows:

1. Count the number of correct answers that you made according to the following answer key. Do not count any questions with more than one answer marked as correct.

2. Count the number of incorrect answers. Do not count omits as wrong answers, but count double responses as wrong.

3. Multiply the total number of incorrect answers by one-fourth. Drop any fractions of one-half or less.

4. Subtract this number from the total number correct to get the total score. The highest possible score is 120.

For example, if you answered 89 questions correctly and 10 questions incorrectly, and you omitted 21 questions, your total score would be 87 ($\frac{1}{4} \times 10 = 2\frac{1}{2}$; $89 - 2 = 87$).

1.	B	21.	A	41.	A	61.	C	81.	D	101.	D
2.	E	22.	E	42.	A	62.	B	82.	C	102.	B
3.	D	23.	E	43.	B	63.	E	83.	D	103.	C
4.	A	24.	D	44.	E	64.	D	84.	D	104.	A
5.	E	25.	C	45.	A	65.	C	85.	B	105.	E
6.	E	26.	D	46.	C	66.	A	86.	A	106.	D
7.	A	27.	D	47.	A	67.	D	87.	E	107.	B
8.	D	28.	C	48.	D	68.	C	88.	C	108.	A
9.	B	29.	C	49.	B	69.	D	89.	C	109.	C
10.	E	30.	D	50.	C	70.	E	90.	B	110.	D
11.	D	31.	E	51.	B	71.	A	91.	E	111.	A
12.	B	32.	A	52.	C	72.	C	92.	E	112.	C
13.	B	33.	A	53.	D	73.	B	93.	C	113.	C
14.	B	34.	C	54.	D	74.	C	94.	C	114.	B
15.	B	35.	C	55.	E	75.	A	95.	A	115.	D
16.	A	36.	E	56.	E	76.	D	96.	D	116.	A
17.	D	37.	A	57.	B	77.	D	97.	C	117.	B
18.	E	38.	C	58.	E	78.	A	98.	E	118.	B
19.	B	39.	C	59.	D	79.	E	99.	B	119.	A
20.	A	40.	D	60.	C	80.	C	100.	B	120.	E

20

Answer Explanations

You will probably find it helpful to read through all the explanations, both for the questions you missed and for the ones that you answered correctly, to reinforce what you learned in Parts II and III of this book.

Explanations for the Verbal Ability Test

1. **(C)** *Flexible* means "adjustable" or "pliable."

2. **(B)** An *option* is a choice.

3. **(C)** To *verify* is to check the accuracy of or to confirm.

4. **(D)** *Indolent* means "idle" or "lazy."

5. **(B)** *Respiration* is breathing.

6. **(A)** A *brush* is a tool of the *painter's* trade, as a *wrench* is a tool of the *plumber's* trade.

7. **(B)** A *package* transports *merchandise* just as a *letter* transmits a *message*.

8. **(C)** *Sleep* alleviates *weariness* just as *food* alleviates *hunger*.

9. **(D)** The *dial* is an input device of a *telephone*, just as a *key* is an input device of a *typewriter*.

10. **(A)** *Whoever* is the subject of the phrase "whoever has the best record" and is used incorrectly in choice (D). Choices (B) and (C) are wordy and awkward.

11. **(D)** All the other choices contain obvious errors.

12. **(A)** The correct spelling is *collapsible*.

13. **(C)** The correct spelling is *ambiguous*.

14. **(D)** The correct spelling is *predecessor*.

15. **(A)** The correct spelling is *sanctioned*.

16. **(A)** The paragraph presents the problems of fire in fire-resistant buildings. It suggests that the contents of the buildings may burn even though the structural materials themselves do not, and the ensuing fire may even cause the collapse of the buildings. The paragraph does not compare the problem of fire in fire-resistant buildings with that of fire in ordinary buildings, as stated in choice (C).

17. **(C)** The search for truth has speeded the progress of civilization. Choice (B) is incorrect in its statement that "civilization did not begin until…"; rather, civilization moved ahead slowly even before restrictions on learning were removed.

> **Note**
> The directions in the sample exam ask you to choose the best sentence, while in the practice exercises you were asked to choose the incorrect sentence. Reading and following directions carefully is crucial to success on the exam.

18.   **(B)** *Vigilant* means "alert" or "watchful."

19.   **(D)** *Incidental* means "likely to ensue as a chance or minor consequence" or "accompanying."

20.   **(A)** *Conciliatory* means "tending to reconcile" or "to make peace."

21.   **(C)** An *altercation* is a quarrel or a controversy.

22.   **(A)** *Irresolute* means "indecisive" or "wavering."

23.   **(C)** *Stillness* and *sound* are opposites, as are *darkness* and *sunlight*.

24.   **(D)** That which is *accidental* happens by *chance* as that which is *designed* happens by *intention*.

25.   **(C)** A *muffler* reduces *sound* as *practice* reduces *errors*.

26.   **(A)** The desired result of *training* is the development of *skill* as the desired result of *research* is scientific *findings*.

27.   **(D)** Choices (A) and (C) are incorrect in use of the subject form "I" instead of the object of the preposition "me." Choice (B) incorrectly uses the reflexive "myself." Only I can address a letter to myself.

28.   **(C)** All the other choices are quite obviously incorrect.

29.   **(D)** The correct spelling is *miniature*.

30.   **(A)** The correct spelling is *extemporaneous*.

31.   **(B)** The correct spelling is *problematical*.

32.   **(A)** The correct spelling of first choice is *descendant*. An alternate spelling, which is also correct, is *descendent*. A correct spelling is offered among the choices, so (A) is the best answer.

33.   **(B)** In a word, we are preserving our natural resources through recycling.

34.   **(D)** If you omit all unnecessary words, you use only the words essential to the meaning.

35.   **(D)** To *counteract* is to act directly against or to neutralize.

36.   **(B)** *Deferred* means "postponed" or "delayed."

37.   **(C)** *Feasible* means "possible" or "practicable."

38.   **(A)** To *encounter* is to come upon or to meet.

39.   **(C)** *Innate* means "existing naturally" or "native."

40.   **(B)** The *disciple* learns from a *master*, as a *student* learns from a *teacher*.

41.   **(C)** In this analogy of place, an *experiment* occurs in a *laboratory* as a *lecture* occurs in an *auditorium*.

42.   **(B)** *Fuel* powers the *engine* as *food* powers the *body*.

43.   **(C)** *Recreation* occurs in the *theater* as *education* occurs in a *school*.

44.   **(D)** Choice (A) might state either "most" or "all" but not both; choice (B) should read "persons who"; choice (C) should read "with regard to…."

45.   **(A)** Choice (B) is incorrect because it requires the plural verb "were"; choice (C) requires the correlative construction "neither…nor"; choice (D) requires the nominative "they."

46.   **(C)** The correct spelling is *extricate*.

47.   **(B)** The correct spelling is *hereditary*.

20

48. **(C)** The correct spelling is *auspicious*.

49. **(B)** The correct spelling is *sequence*.

50. **(A)** If instruction in safety rules will help to prevent accidents, some accidents must occur because of lack of knowledge.

51. **(D)** The language that has some representative in English speech has had some of its words absorbed into English.

52. **(A)** To *acquiesce* is to give in or to assent.

53. **(C)** *Unanimity* is complete agreement or harmony.

54. **(A)** A *precedent* is an example that sets a standard.

55. **(D)** *Versatile* means "adaptable" or "many-sided."

56. **(B)** *Authentic* means "genuine" or "reliable."

57. **(A)** The information and substance of a *novel* is *fiction*, while the information and substance of *biography* is *fact*.

58. **(B)** *Film* is the medium through which the action of a *motion picture* is projected onto a screen; *carbon paper* is the medium through which a *copy* of words or drawings is transmitted from one piece of paper to another.

59. **(C)** *Carelessness* earns a *reprimand* as *efficiency* merits a *reward*.

60. **(B)** This analogy refers to the marketplace and the law of supply and demand. That which is *scarce* is likely to be *costly*, while that which is *abundant* will be *cheap*.

61. **(B)** In choice (A), the placement of the apostrophe is inappropriate; choices (C) and (D) use the plural, but there is only one company.

62. **(A)** Choices (C) and (D) are glaringly poor. Choice (B) is not incorrect, but choice (A) is far better.

63. **(D)** The correct spelling is *obliterate*.

64. **(C)** The correct spelling is *diagnosis*.

65. **(B)** The correct spelling is *countenance*.

66. **(A)** The correct spelling is *conceivably*.

67. **(C)** Since manufacturers are assuming risks in attempting to predict what consumers will want, their success depends on the ultimate purchases made by the consumers.

68. **(B)** Humans migrate to various climates and adjust the food supply in each climate. The means by which they supply their needs are varied.

69. **(D)** *Strident* means "grating" or "harsh-sounding."

70. **(B)** To *confine* is to limit or to restrict.

71. **(D)** To *accentuate* is to stress, emphasize, or intensify.

72. **(A)** *Banal* means "insipid" or "commonplace."

73. **(C)** One who is *incorrigible* cannot be changed or corrected; the person is irreformable.

74. **(D)** A *doctor* promotes *health* as a *policeman* promotes *order*.

75. **(A)** A *weaver* creates on a *loom* as an *artist* creates on an *easel*.

76. **(D)** Many *ships* make up the *fleet* as many *persons* make up a *crowd*.

77. **(C)** A *calendar* visually represents *dates* as a *map* visually represents *locations*.

78. **(A)** The other choices are quite clearly incorrect.

79. **(C)** Choices (A) and (B) use adverbs incorrectly; choice (D) is awkward and not part of everyday speech.

80. **(B)** The correct spelling is *competition*.

81. **(B)** The correct spelling is *occasion*.

82. **(C)** The correct spelling is *knowledge*.

83. **(B)** The correct spelling is *deliberate*.

84. **(A)** Time and effort cannot be equated. Efficiency must be measured in terms of results.

85. **(B)** The first sentence of the paragraph makes this statement.

20

Explanations for the Clerical Ability Test

1.   **(B)** The third number is different.

> **Tip**
> The choices for this question type remain the same for all questions of this type on the test. Memorizing the answer choices may increase your speed.

2.   **(E)** All three numbers are different.

3.   **(D)** The first name is different.

4.   **(A)** All three names are exactly alike.

5.   **(E)** All three names are different.

6.   **(E)** Hachettson; Hackett

7.   **(A)** Margenroth; Margeroth

12.   **(B)** 79

13.   **(B)** 287

14.   **(B)** 51

15.   **(B)** 52

16.   **(A)** 6 2 **5 K 4** P T G

> **Tip**
> The key to simple arithmetic questions is to avoid careless errors.

8.   **(D)** Bobbitt, Olivia H.; Bobbitt, Olivier E.; Bobbitt, R.Olivia

9.   **(B)** Mosely, Albert J.; Mosely, Werner; Mosley, Alvin.

10.   **(E)** Youmons; Youmuns

11.   **(D)** 75

17.   **(D)** L **4 7 2** T **6** V K

18.   **(E)** The answer cannot be (A) or (B) because there is no **K;** it cannot be (C) or (D) because there is no **2.**

19.   **(B)** G **4 K 7** L **3 5** Z

20.   **(A)** **4 K** 2 9 N **5** T G

> **Note**
> You have not seen this kind of question before, although it should appear similar to the questions in Hour 13, "Clerical Speed and Accuracy." You should be prepared for unfamiliar questions and apply what you have learned to them. The correct answer is the suggested answer whose letters and numbers all appear in the question. You must quickly compare the letters and numbers in the answer choices to those in the questions to find matches.

21. **(A)** All three numbers are exactly alike.

22. **(E)** All three numbers are different.

23. **(E)** All three names are different.

24. **(D)** The first name is different.

25. **(C)** The second name is different.

26. **(D)** Watson; Watters; Wattwood

27. **(D)** Johnston, Edmund; Johnston, Edward; Johnstone, Edmund A.

28. **(C)** Remschel; Rensch; Renshaw

29. **(C)** Schneider, Mertens; Schnyder, Maurice; Schnyder, Newman

30. **(D)** Freedenberg; Freedenburg; Freedinberg

31. **(E)** 21

32. **(A)** 400

33. **(A)** 20

34. **(C)** 141

35. **(C)** 19

36. **(E)** The answer cannot be (A) because there is no **V;** it cannot be (B) or (C) because there is no **5;** it cannot be (D) because there is no **8** or **V.**

37. **(A) L 5 N K 4 3 9 V**

38. **(C) 8 2 V P 9 L Z 5**

39. **(C) V P 9 Z 5 L 8 7**

40. **(D) 5 T 8 N 2 9 V L**

41. **(A)** All three numbers are exactly alike.

42. **(A)** All three numbers are exactly alike.

43. **(B)** The third number is different.

44. **(E)** All three names are different.

45. **(A)** All three names are exactly alike.

46. **(C)** DeMatteo; DeMattia; Derby

47. **(A)** Theriault; Therien

48. **(D)** Gaston, Isabel; Gaston, M. Hubert; Gaston, M. Melvin

49. **(B)** SanLuis; SanMiguel; Santilli

50. **(C)** DeLathouder; DeLaTour; Lathrop

51. **(B)** 310

52. **(C)** 51

53. **(D)** 68

54. **(D)** 45

55. **(E)** 111

56. **(E)** The answer cannot be (A) or (B) because there is no **8;** it cannot be (C) or (D) because there is no **9.**

57. **(B) 8 5 3 V L 2 Z N**

58. **(E)** The answer cannot be (A) or (B) because there is no **8;** it cannot be (C) or (D) because there is no **Z.**

59. **(D) 9 8 L 2 5 Z K V**

60. **(C) Z 6 5 V 9 3 P N**

61. **(C)** The second number is different.

62. **(B)** The third number is different.

63. **(E)** All three names are different.

64. **(D)** The first name is different.

65. **(C)** The second name is different.

66. **(A)** O'Bannon; O'Beirne

67. **(D)** Entsminger, Jack; Entsminger, Jacob; Entsminger, James

68. **(C)** Iacone, Pedro M.; Iacone, Pete R.; Iacone, Peter F.

69. **(D)** Shephard; Sheppard; Shepperd

70. **(E)** Thackston; Thackton

71. **(A)** 51

72. **(C)** 85

73. **(B)** 29

20

74. **(C)** 272

75. **(A)** 71

76. **(D)** 6 Z T N 8 7 4 V

77. **(D)** V 7 8 6 N 5 P L

78. **(A)** N 7 P V 8 4 2 L

79. **(E)** The answer cannot be choice (A) or (B) because there is no **2**; it cannot be choice (C) or (D) because there is no **6**.

80. **(C)** 4 8 G 2 T N 6 L

81. **(D)** The first number is different.

82. **(C)** The second number is different.

83. **(D)** All three names are exactly alike.

84. **(D)** The first name is different.

85. **(B)** The third name is different.

86. **(A)** Dunlavey; Dunleavy

87. **(E)** Yarborough; Yarbrough

88. **(C)** Proutey, Maude; Prouty, Martha; Prouty, Myra

89. **(C)** Pawalek; Pawlowicz; Pawlowski

90. **(B)** Vanover; Vanstory; VanSwinderen

91. **(E)** 63

92. **(E)** 9

93. **(C)** 516

94. **(C)** 81

95. **(A)** 131

96. **(D)** V 5 7 Z N 9 4 T

97. **(C)** 4 6 P T 2 N K 9

98. **(E)** The answer cannot be choice (A) or (B) because there is no **5**; it cannot be choice (C) or (D) because there is no **9**.

99. **(B)** 7 P 5 2 4 N K T

100. **(B)** K T 8 5 4 N 2 P

101. **(D)** The first number is different.

102. **(B)** The third number is different.

103. **(C)** The second number is different.

104. **(A)** All three names are exactly alike.

105. **(E)** All three names are different.

106. **(D)** FitzGibbon; Fitzsimmons; FitzSimons

107. **(B)** Daly; D'Amato; D'Amboise

108. **(A)** Schaeffer; Schaffert

109. **(C)** White-Leigh; White-Lewis; Whitely

110. **(D)** VanDercook; VanDerHeggen; VanderLinden

111. **(A)** 124

112. **(C)** 24

113. **(C)** 288

114. **(B)** 41

115. **(D)** 522

116. **(A)** Z 3 N P G 5 4 2

117. **(B)** 6 N 2 8 G 4 P T

118. **(B)** 6 N 4 T V G 8 2

119. **(A)** T 3 P 4 N 8 G 2

120. **(E)** The answer cannot be choice (A) or (C) because there is no **3**; it cannot be choice (B) or (D) because there is no **T**.

Evaluating Yourself

On your answer sheet, mark the numbers of the questions that you answered incorrectly and check them against the following charts. If you missed several of any question type, you need more practice with that kind of question. Return to the appropriate lesson and review the rules and practice exercises before moving on to the next sample exam.

SELF-EVALUATION CHART: VERBAL ABILITY TEST

Question Type	Question Numbers	Lesson to Review
Grammar and Usage	10–11; 27–28; 44–45; 61–62; 78–79	Hour 3
Spelling	12–15; 29–32; 46–49; 63–66; 80–83	Hour 4
Synonyms	1–5; 18–22; 35–39; 52–56; 69–73	Hour 5
Verbal Analogies	6–9; 23–26; 40–43; 57–60; 74–77	Hour 7
Reading Comprehension	16–17; 33–34; 50–51; 67–68; 84–85	Hour 9

SELF-EVALUATION CHART: CLERICAL ABILITY TEST

Question Type	Question Numbers	Lesson to Review
Alphabetizing and Filing	6–10; 26–30; 46–50; 66–70; 86–90; 106–110	Hour 12
Speed and Accuracy	1–5; 16–25; 36–45; 56–65; 76–85; 96–105; 116–120	Hour 13
Simple Arithmetic	11–15; 31–35; 51–55; 71–75; 91–95; 111–115	Be careful of careless mistakes.

> **Note**
> Do not be discouraged if you did not complete the clerical ability test. You are not expected to answer every question in the time allotted. Remember that although speed is important, accuracy counts more.

20

HOUR **21**

Sample Civil Service Exam 2

What You Will Learn in This Hour

In this hour, you will practice taking another sample civil service exam. The clerical ability portion of this sample exam comes first and is divided into several heavily timed sections, unlike the clerical ability portion of the first sample exam. You will also find different question types on this exam, so read the directions carefully.

This sample exam should take you one hour to complete. Again, you should use a kitchen timer to time the exam—and proceed as if you were taking the actual exam. Here are your goals for this hour:

- Complete Part One of the sample civil service exam: The clerical ability test.
- Complete Part Two of the sample civil service exam: The verbal ability test.

> **Note**
> The answer sheet should be one full page that can be torn out of the book without losing any test questions.

287

Answer Sheet

Tear out these answer sheets and use them to mark your answers to the sample test that
follows. Use a pencil to record your answers, just as you will have to do on the actual test.
Be careful of misgridding, marking the same answer twice, and other common mistakes.

Clerical Ability Test

1. Ⓐ Ⓑ Ⓒ Ⓓ Ⓔ   23. Ⓐ Ⓑ Ⓒ Ⓓ Ⓔ   44. Ⓐ Ⓑ Ⓒ Ⓓ Ⓔ   65. Ⓐ Ⓑ Ⓒ Ⓓ Ⓔ

2. Ⓐ Ⓑ Ⓒ Ⓓ Ⓔ   24. Ⓐ Ⓑ Ⓒ Ⓓ Ⓔ   45. Ⓐ Ⓑ Ⓒ Ⓓ Ⓔ   66. Ⓐ Ⓑ Ⓒ Ⓓ Ⓔ

3. Ⓐ Ⓑ Ⓒ Ⓓ Ⓔ   25. Ⓐ Ⓑ Ⓒ Ⓓ Ⓔ   46. Ⓐ Ⓑ Ⓒ Ⓓ Ⓔ   67. Ⓐ Ⓑ Ⓒ Ⓓ Ⓔ

4. Ⓐ Ⓑ Ⓒ Ⓓ Ⓔ   26. Ⓐ Ⓑ Ⓒ Ⓓ Ⓔ   47. Ⓐ Ⓑ Ⓒ Ⓓ Ⓔ   68. Ⓐ Ⓑ Ⓒ Ⓓ Ⓔ

5. Ⓐ Ⓑ Ⓒ Ⓓ Ⓔ   27. Ⓐ Ⓑ Ⓒ Ⓓ Ⓔ   48. Ⓐ Ⓑ Ⓒ Ⓓ Ⓔ   69. Ⓐ Ⓑ Ⓒ Ⓓ Ⓔ

6. Ⓐ Ⓑ Ⓒ Ⓓ Ⓔ   28. Ⓐ Ⓑ Ⓒ Ⓓ Ⓔ   49. Ⓐ Ⓑ Ⓒ Ⓓ Ⓔ   70. Ⓐ Ⓑ Ⓒ Ⓓ Ⓔ

7. Ⓐ Ⓑ Ⓒ Ⓓ Ⓔ   29. Ⓐ Ⓑ Ⓒ Ⓓ Ⓔ   50. Ⓐ Ⓑ Ⓒ Ⓓ Ⓔ   71. Ⓐ Ⓑ Ⓒ Ⓓ Ⓔ

8. Ⓐ Ⓑ Ⓒ Ⓓ Ⓔ   30. Ⓐ Ⓑ Ⓒ Ⓓ Ⓔ   51. Ⓐ Ⓑ Ⓒ Ⓓ Ⓔ   72. Ⓐ Ⓑ Ⓒ Ⓓ Ⓔ

9. Ⓐ Ⓑ Ⓒ Ⓓ Ⓔ   31. Ⓐ Ⓑ Ⓒ Ⓓ Ⓔ   52. Ⓐ Ⓑ Ⓒ Ⓓ Ⓔ   73. Ⓐ Ⓑ Ⓒ Ⓓ Ⓔ

10. Ⓐ Ⓑ Ⓒ Ⓓ Ⓔ   32. Ⓐ Ⓑ Ⓒ Ⓓ Ⓔ   53. Ⓐ Ⓑ Ⓒ Ⓓ Ⓔ   74. Ⓐ Ⓑ Ⓒ Ⓓ Ⓔ

11. Ⓐ Ⓑ Ⓒ Ⓓ Ⓔ   33. Ⓐ Ⓑ Ⓒ Ⓓ Ⓔ   54. Ⓐ Ⓑ Ⓒ Ⓓ Ⓔ   75. Ⓐ Ⓑ Ⓒ Ⓓ Ⓔ

12. Ⓐ Ⓑ Ⓒ Ⓓ Ⓔ   34. Ⓐ Ⓑ Ⓒ Ⓓ Ⓔ   55. Ⓐ Ⓑ Ⓒ Ⓓ Ⓔ   76. Ⓐ Ⓑ Ⓒ Ⓓ Ⓔ

13. Ⓐ Ⓑ Ⓒ Ⓓ Ⓔ   35. Ⓐ Ⓑ Ⓒ Ⓓ Ⓔ   56. Ⓐ Ⓑ Ⓒ Ⓓ Ⓔ   77. Ⓐ Ⓑ Ⓒ Ⓓ Ⓔ

14. Ⓐ Ⓑ Ⓒ Ⓓ Ⓔ   36. Ⓐ Ⓑ Ⓒ Ⓓ Ⓔ   57. Ⓐ Ⓑ Ⓒ Ⓓ Ⓔ   78. Ⓐ Ⓑ Ⓒ Ⓓ Ⓔ

15. Ⓐ Ⓑ Ⓒ Ⓓ Ⓔ   37. Ⓐ Ⓑ Ⓒ Ⓓ Ⓔ   58. Ⓐ Ⓑ Ⓒ Ⓓ Ⓔ   79. Ⓐ Ⓑ Ⓒ Ⓓ Ⓔ

16. Ⓐ Ⓑ Ⓒ Ⓓ Ⓔ   38. Ⓐ Ⓑ Ⓒ Ⓓ Ⓔ   59. Ⓐ Ⓑ Ⓒ Ⓓ Ⓔ   80. Ⓐ Ⓑ Ⓒ Ⓓ Ⓔ

17. Ⓐ Ⓑ Ⓒ Ⓓ Ⓔ   39. Ⓐ Ⓑ Ⓒ Ⓓ Ⓔ   60. Ⓐ Ⓑ Ⓒ Ⓓ Ⓔ   81. Ⓐ Ⓑ Ⓒ Ⓓ Ⓔ

18. Ⓐ Ⓑ Ⓒ Ⓓ Ⓔ   40. Ⓐ Ⓑ Ⓒ Ⓓ Ⓔ   61. Ⓐ Ⓑ Ⓒ Ⓓ Ⓔ   82. Ⓐ Ⓑ Ⓒ Ⓓ Ⓔ

19. Ⓐ Ⓑ Ⓒ Ⓓ Ⓔ   41. Ⓐ Ⓑ Ⓒ Ⓓ Ⓔ   62. Ⓐ Ⓑ Ⓒ Ⓓ Ⓔ   83. Ⓐ Ⓑ Ⓒ Ⓓ Ⓔ

20. Ⓐ Ⓑ Ⓒ Ⓓ Ⓔ   42. Ⓐ Ⓑ Ⓒ Ⓓ Ⓔ   63. Ⓐ Ⓑ Ⓒ Ⓓ Ⓔ   84. Ⓐ Ⓑ Ⓒ Ⓓ Ⓔ

21. Ⓐ Ⓑ Ⓒ Ⓓ Ⓔ   43. Ⓐ Ⓑ Ⓒ Ⓓ Ⓔ   64. Ⓐ Ⓑ Ⓒ Ⓓ Ⓔ   85. Ⓐ Ⓑ Ⓒ Ⓓ Ⓔ

22. Ⓐ Ⓑ Ⓒ Ⓓ Ⓔ

21

Verbal Ability Test

1. Ⓐ Ⓑ Ⓒ Ⓓ Ⓔ   15. Ⓐ Ⓑ Ⓒ Ⓓ Ⓔ   29. Ⓐ Ⓑ Ⓒ Ⓓ Ⓔ   43. Ⓐ Ⓑ Ⓒ Ⓓ Ⓔ

2. Ⓐ Ⓑ Ⓒ Ⓓ Ⓔ   16. Ⓐ Ⓑ Ⓒ Ⓓ Ⓔ   30. Ⓐ Ⓑ Ⓒ Ⓓ Ⓔ   44. Ⓐ Ⓑ Ⓒ Ⓓ Ⓔ

3. Ⓐ Ⓑ Ⓒ Ⓓ Ⓔ   17. Ⓐ Ⓑ Ⓒ Ⓓ Ⓔ   31. Ⓐ Ⓑ Ⓒ Ⓓ Ⓔ   45. Ⓐ Ⓑ Ⓒ Ⓓ Ⓔ

4. Ⓐ Ⓑ Ⓒ Ⓓ Ⓔ   18. Ⓐ Ⓑ Ⓒ Ⓓ Ⓔ   32. Ⓐ Ⓑ Ⓒ Ⓓ Ⓔ   46. Ⓐ Ⓑ Ⓒ Ⓓ Ⓔ

5. Ⓐ Ⓑ Ⓒ Ⓓ Ⓔ   19. Ⓐ Ⓑ Ⓒ Ⓓ Ⓔ   33. Ⓐ Ⓑ Ⓒ Ⓓ Ⓔ   47. Ⓐ Ⓑ Ⓒ Ⓓ Ⓔ

6. Ⓐ Ⓑ Ⓒ Ⓓ Ⓔ   20. Ⓐ Ⓑ Ⓒ Ⓓ Ⓔ   34. Ⓐ Ⓑ Ⓒ Ⓓ Ⓔ   48. Ⓐ Ⓑ Ⓒ Ⓓ Ⓔ

7. Ⓐ Ⓑ Ⓒ Ⓓ Ⓔ   21. Ⓐ Ⓑ Ⓒ Ⓓ Ⓔ   35. Ⓐ Ⓑ Ⓒ Ⓓ Ⓔ   49. Ⓐ Ⓑ Ⓒ Ⓓ Ⓔ

8. Ⓐ Ⓑ Ⓒ Ⓓ Ⓔ   22. Ⓐ Ⓑ Ⓒ Ⓓ Ⓔ   36. Ⓐ Ⓑ Ⓒ Ⓓ Ⓔ   50. Ⓐ Ⓑ Ⓒ Ⓓ Ⓔ

9. Ⓐ Ⓑ Ⓒ Ⓓ Ⓔ   23. Ⓐ Ⓑ Ⓒ Ⓓ Ⓔ   37. Ⓐ Ⓑ Ⓒ Ⓓ Ⓔ   51. Ⓐ Ⓑ Ⓒ Ⓓ Ⓔ

10. Ⓐ Ⓑ Ⓒ Ⓓ Ⓔ   24. Ⓐ Ⓑ Ⓒ Ⓓ Ⓔ   38. Ⓐ Ⓑ Ⓒ Ⓓ Ⓔ   52. Ⓐ Ⓑ Ⓒ Ⓓ Ⓔ

11. Ⓐ Ⓑ Ⓒ Ⓓ Ⓔ   25. Ⓐ Ⓑ Ⓒ Ⓓ Ⓔ   39. Ⓐ Ⓑ Ⓒ Ⓓ Ⓔ   53. Ⓐ Ⓑ Ⓒ Ⓓ Ⓔ

12. Ⓐ Ⓑ Ⓒ Ⓓ Ⓔ   26. Ⓐ Ⓑ Ⓒ Ⓓ Ⓔ   40. Ⓐ Ⓑ Ⓒ Ⓓ Ⓔ   54. Ⓐ Ⓑ Ⓒ Ⓓ Ⓔ

13. Ⓐ Ⓑ Ⓒ Ⓓ Ⓔ   27. Ⓐ Ⓑ Ⓒ Ⓓ Ⓔ   41. Ⓐ Ⓑ Ⓒ Ⓓ Ⓔ   55. Ⓐ Ⓑ Ⓒ Ⓓ Ⓔ

14. Ⓐ Ⓑ Ⓒ Ⓓ Ⓔ   28. Ⓐ Ⓑ Ⓒ Ⓓ Ⓔ   42. Ⓐ Ⓑ Ⓒ Ⓓ Ⓔ

21

Clerical Ability Test

85 Questions

There are four types of questions in this part of the exam. Each question type has its own set of directions, and each portion is timed separately.

Sequencing

20 Questions

DIRECTIONS: For each question, you are given a name, number, or code, followed by four other names or codes in alphabetical or numerical order. Find the correct space for the given name or number so that it will be in alphabetical and/or numerical order with the others, and mark the letter of that space on your answer sheet. You will have 3 minutes to complete this portion of the exam.

1. | Hackett, Gerald |

    (A) –
        Habert, James
    (B) –
        Hachett, J. J.
    (C) –
        Hachetts, K. Larson
    (D) –
        Hachettson, Leroy
    (E) –

2. | 59233362 |

    (A) –
        58146020
    (B) –
        59233162
    (C) –
        59233262
    (D) –
        5923662
    (E) –

21

3. | MYP-6734 |

(A) –
NYP-6733
(B) –
NYS-7412
(C) –
NZT-4899
(D) –
PYZ-3636
(E) –

4. | Bobbitt, Olivier E. |

(A) –
Bobbitt, D. Olivier
(B) –
Bobbitt, Olive B.
(C) –
Bobbitt, Olivia H.
(D) –
Bobbitt, R. Olivia
(E) –

5. | 00102032 |

(A) –
00120312
(B) –
00120323
(C) –
00120324
(D) –
00200303
(E) –

6. | LPD-6100 |

(A) –
LPD-5865
(B) –
LPD-6001
(C) –
LPD-6101
(D) –
LPD-6106
(E) –

7. Vanstory, George

(A) –
    Vanover, Eva
(B) –
    VanSwinderen, Floyd
(C) –
    VanSyckle, Harry
(D) –
    Vanture, Laurence
(E) –

8. Fitzsimmons, Hugh

(A) –
    Fitts, Harold
(B) –
    Fitzgerald, June
(C) –
    FitzGibbon, Junius
(D) –
    FitzSimons, Martin
(E) –

9. 01066010

(A) –
    01006040
(B) –
    01006051
(C) –
    01016053
(D) –
    01016060
(E) –

10. AAZ-2687

(A) –
    AAA-2132
(B) –
    AAS-4623
(C) –
    ASA-3216
(D) –
    ASZ-5490
(E) –

21

11. | Pawlowicz, Ruth M. |

(A) –
    Pawalek, Edward
(B) –
    Pawelek, Flora G.
(C) –
    Pawlowski, Joan M.
(D) –
    Pawtowski, Wanda
(E) –

12. | NCD-7834 |

(A) –
    NBJ-4682
(B) –
    NBT-5066
(C) –
    NCD-7710
(D) –
    NCD-7868
(E) –

13. | 36270013 |

(A) –
    36260006
(B) –
    36270000
(C) –
    36270030
(D) –
    36670012
(E) –

14. | Freedenburg, C. Erma |

(A) –
    Freedenburg, Emerson
(B) –
    Freedenburg, Erma
(C) –
    Freedenburg, Erma E.
(D) –
    Freedinburg, Erma F.
(E) –

15. | Prouty, Martha |

(A) –
Proutey, Margaret
(B) –
Proutey, Maude
(C) –
Prouty, Myra
(D) –
Prouty, Naomi
(E) –

16. | 58006021 |

(A) –
58006130
(B) –
58097222
(C) –
59000599
(D) –
59909000
(E) –

17. | EKK-1443 |

(A) –
EGK-1164
(B) –
EKG-1329
(C) –
EKK-1331
(D) –
EKK-1403
(E) –

18. | D'Amato, Vincent |

(A) –
Daly, Steven
(B) –
D'Amboise, S. Vincent
(C) –
Daniel, Vail
(D) –
DeAlba, Valentina
(E) –

21

19. | Schaeffer, Roger D. |

(A) –

Schaffert, Evelyn M.

(B) –

Schaffner, Margaret M.

(C) –

Schafhirt, Milton G.

(D) –

Shafer, Richard E.

(E) –

20. | SPP-4856 |

(A) –

PPS-4838

(B) –

PSP-4921

(C) –

SPS-4906

(D) –

SSP-4911

(E) –

Comparisons

30 Questions

DIRECTIONS: In each line across the page are three names, addresses, or codes that are very much alike. Compare the three and decide which ones are EXACTLY alike. On your answer sheet, mark:
- (A) if ALL THREE names, addresses, or codes are exactly ALIKE.
- (B) if only the FIRST and SECOND names, addresses, or codes are exactly ALIKE.
- (C) if only the FIRST and THIRD names, addresses, or codes are exactly ALIKE.
- (D) if only the SECOND and THIRD names, addresses, or codes are exactly ALIKE.
- (E) if ALL THREE names, addresses, or codes are DIFFERENT.

You will have 5 minutes to complete this portion of the exam.

21.	Drusilla S. Ridgeley	Drusilla S. Ridgeley	Drusilla S. Ridgeley
22.	Andrei I. Toumantzev	Andrei I. Tourmantzev	Andrei I. Toumantzov
23.	6-78912-e3e42	6-78912-3e3e42	6-78912-e3e42
24.	86529 Dunwoodie Drive	86529 Dunwoodie Drive	85629 Dunwoodie Drive
25.	1592514	1592574	1592574
26.	Ella Burk Newham	Ella Burk Newnham	Elena Burk Newnham
27.	5416R-1952TZ-op	5416R-1952TZ-op	5416R-1952TZ-op
28.	60646 West Touhy Avenue	60646 West Touhy Avenue	60646 West Touhey Avenue
29.	Mardikian & Moore, Inc.	Mardikian and Moore, Inc.	Mardikian & Moore, Inc.
30.	9670243	9670423	9670423
31.	Eduardo Ingles	Eduardo Inglese	Eduardo Inglese
32.	Roger T. DeAngelis	Roger T. D'Angelis	Roger T. DeAngeles
33.	7692138	7692138	7692138
34.	2695 East 3435 South	2695 East 3435 South	2695 East 3435 South
35.	63qs5-95YT3-001	63qs5-95YT3-001	62qs5-95YT3-001
36.	2789350	2789350	2798350
37.	Helmut V. Lochner	Helmut V. Lockner	Helmut W. Lochner
38.	2454803	2548403	2454803
39.	Lemberger, WA 28094-9182	Lemberger, VA 28094-9182	Lemberger, VA 28094-9182
40.	4168-GNP-78852	4168-GNP-78852	4168-GNP-78852
41.	Yoshihito Saito	Yoshihito Saito	Yoshihito Saito
42.	5927681	5927861	5927681
43.	O'Reilly Bay, LA 56212	O'Reillys Bay, LA 56212	O'Reilly Bay, LA 56212

44.	Francis Ransdell	Frances Ramsdell	Francis Ransdell
45.	5634-OotV5a-16867	5634-Ootv5a-16867	5634-Ootv5a-16867
46.	Dolores Mollicone	Dolores Mollicone	Doloras Mollicone
47.	David C. Routzon	David E. Routzon	David C. Routzron
48.	8932 Shimabui Hwy.	8932 Shimabui Hwy.	8932 Shimabui Hwy.
49.	6177396	6177936	6177396
50.	A8987-B73245	A8987-B73245	A8987-B73245

Spelling

20 Questions

> **DIRECTIONS:** Find the correct spelling of the word and darken the appropriate space on the answer sheet. If none of the spellings is correct, darken space (D). You will have 3 minutes to complete this portion of the exam.

51. (A) anticipate
(B) antisipate
(C) anticapate
(D) None of the above

52. (A) similiar
(B) simmilar
(C) similar
(D) None of the above

53. (A) sufficiantly
(B) suficeintly
(C) sufficiently
(D) None of the above

54. (A) intelligence
(B) inteligence
(C) intellegence
(D) None of the above

55. (A) referance
(B) referrence
(C) referense
(D) None of the above

56. (A) conscious
(B) consious
(C) conscius
(D) None of the above

57. (A) paralell
(B) parellel
(C) parellell
(D) None of the above

58. (A) abundence
(B) abundance
(C) abundants
(D) None of the above

59. (A) corregated
(B) corrigated
(C) corrugated
(D) None of the above

60. (A) accumalation
(B) accumulation
(C) accumullation
(D) None of the above

61. (A) resonance
    (B) resonence
    (C) resonnance
    (D) None of the above

62. (A) benaficial
    (B) benefitial
    (C) beneficial
    (D) None of the above

63. (A) spesifically
    (B) specificially
    (C) specifically
    (D) None of the above

64. (A) elemanate
    (B) elimenate
    (C) elliminate
    (D) None of the above

65. (A) collosal
    (B) colosal
    (C) collossal
    (D) None of the above

66. (A) auxillary
    (B) auxilliary
    (C) auxiliary
    (D) None of the above

67. (A) inimitable
    (B) inimitible
    (C) inimatable
    (D) None of the above

68. (A) disapearance
    (B) dissapearance
    (C) disappearence
    (D) None of the above

69. (A) appelate
    (B) appellate
    (C) apellate
    (D) None of the above

70. (A) esential
    (B) essential
    (C) essencial
    (D) None of the above

Computations

15 Questions

> **DIRECTIONS:** Perform the computation as indicated in the question, and find the answer among the list of alternative responses. If the correct answer is not given among the choices, mark (E). You will have 8 minutes to complete this portion of the exam.

71. 83   (A) 23
    $- 56$ (B) 29
                 (C) 33
                 (D) 37
                 (E) None of the above

72. 15   (A) 22
    $+ 17$ (B) 32
                 (C) 39
                 (D) 42
                 (E) None of the above

21

73.   32   (A) 224
       × 7   (B) 234
                   (C) 324
                   (D) 334
                   (E) None of the above

74.   39   (A) 77
       × 2   (B) 78
                   (C) 79
                   (D) 81
                   (E) None of the above

75.   43   (A) 23
       − 15   (B) 32
                   (C 33
                   (D) 35
                   (E) None of the above

76.   50   (A) 89
       + 49   (B) 90
                   (C) 99
                   (D) 109
                   (E) None of the above

77. 6) 366   (A) 11
                   (B) 31
                   (C) 36
                   (D) 66
                   (E) None of the above

78.   38   (A) 111
       × 3   (B) 113
                   (C) 115
                   (D) 117
                   (E) None of the above

79.   19   (A) 20
       + 21   (B) 30
                   (C) 40
                   (D) 50
                   (E) None of the above

80.   13   (A) 5
       − 6   (B) 7
                   (C) 9
                   (D 11
                   (E) None of the above

81. 6) 180   (A) 29
                   (B) 31
                   (C) 33
                   (D) 39
                   (E) None of the above

82.   10   (A) 0
       × 1   (B) 1
                   (C) 10
                   (D) 100
                   (E) None of the above

83. 7) 287   (A) 21
                   (B) 27
                   (C) 31
                   (D) 37
                   (E) None of the above

84.   12   (A) 21
       + 11   (B) 22
                   (C) 23
                   (D) 24
                   (E) None of the above

85.   85   (A) 19
       − 64   (B) 21
                   (C) 29
                   (D) 31
                   (E) None of the above

Verbal Ability Test

55 Questions

There are four kinds of questions in this part of the exam. Each kind of question has its own set of directions, but the portions containing the different kinds of questions are not separately timed. You will have 50 minutes to complete this portion of the exam.

> **DIRECTIONS:** Questions 1–20 test your ability to follow instructions. Each question directs you to mark a specific number and letter combination on your answer sheet. The questions require your total concentration, because the answers that you are instructed to mark are, for the most part, NOT in numerical sequence (i.e., you would not use Number 1 on your answer sheet to answer Question 1; Number 2 for Question 2; etc.). Instead, you must mark the number and space specifically designated in each test question.

1. Look at the letters below. Draw a circle around the letter that comes first in the alphabet. Now, on your answer sheet, find Number 12 and darken the space for the letter you just circled.

    E   G   D   Z   B   F

2. Draw a line under the odd number below that is more than 5 but less than 10. Find this number on your answer sheet and darken space (E).

    8   10   5   6   11   9

3. Divide the number 16 by 4 and write your answer on the line below. Now find this number on your answer sheet and darken space (A).

    _____

4. Write the letter C on the line next to the left-hand number below. Now, on your answer sheet, darken the space for the number-letter combination you see.

    5 _____   19 _____   7 _____

5. If in any week Wednesday comes before Tuesday, write the number 15 on the line below. If not, write the number 18. Now, on your answer sheet, darken the letter A for the number you just wrote.

    _____

6. Count the number of Bs in the line below and write that number at the end of the line. Now, on your answer sheet, darken the letter D for the number you wrote.

    A D A E B D C A _____

7. Write the letter B on the line with the highest number. Now, on your answer sheet, darken the number-letter combination that appears on that line.

    16 _____   9 _____   20 _____   11 _____

21

8.   If the product of 6 × 4 is greater than the product of 8 × 3, write the letter E on the line below. If not, write the letter C. Now, on your answer sheet, find number 8 and darken the space for the letter you just wrote.

_____

9.   Write the number 2 in the largest circle below. Now, on your answer sheet, darken the space for the number-letter combination in that circle.

10.   Write the letter D on the line next to the number that is the sum of 7 + 4 + 4. Now, on your answer sheet, darken the space for that number-letter combination.

     13 _____   14 _____   15 _____   16 _____   17 _____

11.   If 5 × 5 equals 25, and 5 + 5 equals 10, write the number 17 on the line below. If not, write the number 10. Now, on your answer sheet, darken space (E) for the number you just wrote.

_____

12.   Circle the second letter below. On the line beside that letter, write the number that represents the number of days in a week. Now, on your answer sheet, darken the space for that number-letter combination.

     _____ C _____ D _____ B _____ E

13.   If a triangle has more angles than a rectangle, write the number 13 in the circle below. If not, write the number 14 in the square. Now, on your answer sheet, darken the space for the number-letter combination in the figure that you just wrote in.

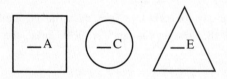

14.   Count the number of Bs below and write that number at the end of the line. Subtract 2 from that number. Now, on your answer sheet, darken space (E) for the number that represents 2 less than the number of Bs in the line.

     B E A D E C C B B B A E B D _____

15.   The numbers below represent morning pick-up times from neighborhood letterboxes. Draw a line under the number that represents the latest pick-up time. Now, on your answer sheet, darken space (D) for the number that is the same as the "minutes" of the time that you underlined.

       9:19 10:16 10:10

16.   If a person who is 6 feet tall is taller than a person who is 5 feet tall and if a pillow is softer than a rock, darken space 11A on your answer sheet. If not, darken space 6B.

17.   Write the fourth letter of the alphabet on the line next to the third number below. Now, on your answer sheet, darken that number-letter combination.

       10 _____   19 _____   13 _____   4 _____

18.   Write the letter B in the box containing the next-to-smallest number. On your answer sheet, darken the space for that number-letter combination.

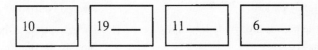

19.   Directly below, you will see three boxes and three words. Write the third letter of the first word on the line in the second box. Now, on your answer sheet, darken the space for that number-letter combination.

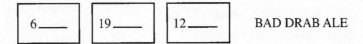

       BAD DRAB ALE

20.   Count the number of points on the figure below. If there are five or more points, darken the space for 6E on your answer sheet. If there are fewer than five points, darken 6A.

21

DIRECTIONS: Each question from 21–40 consists of a sentence written in four different ways. Choose the sentence that is most appropriate with respect to grammar, usage, and punctuation to be suitable for a business letter or report, and darken its letter on your answer sheet. Answer each question in the answer space with the corresponding number.

21. (A) Double parking is when you park your car alongside one that is already having been parked.

(B) When one double parks, you park your car alongside one that is already parked.

(C) Double parking is parking alongside a car already parked.

(D) To double park is alongside a car already parked.

22. (A) This is entirely among you and he.

(B) This is completely among him and you.

(C) This is between you and him.

(D) This is between he and you.

23. (A) As I said, "neither of them are guilty."

(B) As I said, "neither of them are guilty".

(C) As I said, "neither of them is guilty."

(D) As I said, neither of them is guilty.

24. (A) I think that they will promote whoever has the best record.

(B) The firm would have liked to have promoted all employees with good records.

(C) Such of them that have the best records have excellent prospects of promotion.

(D) I feel sure they will give the promotion to whomever has the best record.

25. (A) The receptionist must answer courteously the questions of all them callers.

(B) The receptionist must answer courteously the questions what are asked by the callers.

(C) There would have been no trouble if the receptionist had have always answered courteously.

(D) The receptionist should answer courteously the questions of all callers.

26. (A) Since the report lacked the needed information, it was of no use to them.

(B) This report was useless to them because there were no needed information in it.

(C) Since the report did not contain the needed information, it was not real useful to them.

(D) Being that the report lacked the needed information, they could not use it.

27. (A) The company had hardly declared the dividend till the notices were prepared for mailing.

(B) They had no sooner declared the dividend when they sent the notices to the stockholders.

(C) No sooner had the dividend been declared than the notices were prepared for mailing.

(D) Scarcely had the dividend been declared than the notices were sent out.

28. (A) The supervisors reprimanded the typists, whom she believed had made careless errors.

(B) The typists would have corrected the errors had they of known that the supervisors would see the report.

(C) The errors in the typed reports were so numerous that they could hardly be overlooked.

(D) Many errors were found in the reports which they typed and could not disregard them.

29. (A) "Are you absolutely certain, she asked, that you are right?"

(B) "Are you absolutely certain," she asked, "that you are right?"

(C) "Are you absolutely certain," she asked, "That you are right"?

(D) "Are you absolutely certain", she asked, "That you are right?"

30. (A) He goes only to church on Christmas and Easter.

(B) He only goes to church on Christmas and Easter.

(C) He goes to only church on Christmas and Easter.

(D) He goes to church only on Christmas and Easter.

31. (A) Most all these statements have been supported by persons who are reliable and can be depended upon.

(B) The persons which have guaranteed these statements are reliable.

(C) Reliable persons guarantee the facts with regards to the truth of these statements.

(D) These statements can be depended on, for their truth has been guaranteed by reliable persons.

32. (A) The success of the book pleased both the publishers and authors.

(B) Both the publisher and they was pleased with the success of the book.

(C) Neither they or their publisher was disappointed with the success of the book.

(D) Their publisher was as pleased as them with the success of the book.

33. (A) In reviewing the typists' work reports, the job analyst found records of unusual typing speeds.

(B) It says in the job analyst's report that some employees type with great speed.

(C) The job analyst found that, in reviewing the typists' work reports, that some unusual typing speeds had been made.

(D) In the reports of typists' speeds, the job analyst found some records that are kind of unusual.

34. (A) Every carrier should always have something to throw; not something to throw at the dog but something what will divert its attention.

(B) Every carrier should have something to throw—not something to throw at the dog, but something to divert its attention.

(C) Every carrier should always carry something to throw not something to throw at the dog but something that will divert it's attention.

(D) Every carrier should always carry something to throw, not something to throw at the dog, but, something that will divert its' attention.

21

35. (A) Brown's & Company employees have recently received increases in salary.

    (B) Brown & Company recently increased the salaries of all its employees.

    (C) Recently Brown & Company has increased their employees' salaries.

    (D) Brown & Company have recently increased the salaries of all its employees.

36. (A) If properly addressed, the letter will reach my mother and I.

    (B) The letter had been addressed to myself and my mother.

    (C) I believe the letter was addressed to either my mother or I.

    (D) My mother's name, as well as mine, was on the letter.

37. (A) One of us have to make the reply before tomorrow.

    (B) Making the reply before tomorrow will have to be done by one of us.

    (C) One of us has to reply before tomorrow.

    (D) Anyone has to reply before tomorrow.

38. (A) You have got to get rid of some of these people if you expect to have the quality of the work improve.

    (B) The quality of the work would improve if they would leave fewer people do it.

    (C) I believe it would be desirable to have fewer persons doing this work.

    (D) If you had planned on employing fewer people than this to do the work, this situation would not have arose.

39. (A) The paper we use for this purpose must be light, glossy, and stand hard usage as well.

    (B) Only a light and a glossy, but durable, paper must be used for this purpose.

    (C) For this purpose, we want a paper that is light, glossy, but that will stand hard wear.

    (D) For this purpose, paper that is light, glossy, and durable is essential.

40. (A) This letter, together with the reports, are to be sent to the postmaster.

    (B) The reports, together with this letter, is to be sent to the postmaster.

    (C) The reports and this letter is to be sent to the postmaster.

    (D) This letter, together with the reports, is to be sent to the postmaster.

41. Please consult your office **manual** to learn the proper operation of our copying machine. Manual means most nearly

    (A) labor

    (B) handbook

    (C) typewriter

    (D) handle

42. There is a specified punishment for each **infraction** of the rules. Infraction means most nearly

    (A) violation

    (B) use

    (C) interpretation

    (D) part

43. The order was **rescinded** within the week. Rescinded means most nearly

    (A) revised

    (B) canceled

    (C) misinterpreted

    (D) confirmed

44. If you have a question, please raise your hand to **summon** the test proctor. Summon means most nearly

    (A) ticket

    (B) fine

    (C) give

    (D) call

45. We dared not prosecute the terrorist for fear of **reprisal**. Reprisal means most nearly

    (A) retaliation

    (B) advantage

    (C) warning

    (D) denial

46. The increased use of dictation machines has severely **reduced** the need for office stenographers. Reduced means most nearly

    (A) enlarged

    (B) cut out

    (C) lessened

    (D) expanded

47. Frequent use of marijuana may **impair** your judgment. Impair means most nearly

    (A) weaken

    (B) conceal

    (C) improve

    (D) expose

48. It is altogether **fitting** that the parent discipline the child. Fitting means most nearly

    (A) illegal

    (B) bad practice

    (C) appropriate

    (D) required

21

DIRECTIONS: For questions 49–55, read each paragraph and answer the question that follows it by darkening the letter of the correct answer on your answer sheet. Answer each question in the answer space with the corresponding number.

---

49. A survey to determine the subjects that have helped students most in their jobs shows that typewriting leads all other subjects in the business group. It also leads among the subjects college students consider most valuable and would take again if they were to return to high school.

The paragraph best supports the statement that

(A) the ability to type is an asset in business and in school.

(B) students who return to night school take typing.

(C) students with a knowledge of typing do superior work in college.

(D) success in business is assured those who can type.

50. The Supreme Court's power to invalidate legislation that violates the Constitution is a strong restriction on the powers of Congress. If an Act of Congress is deemed unconstitutional by the Supreme Court, then the Act is voided. Unlike a presidential veto, which can be overridden by a two-thirds vote of the House and the Senate, a constitutional ruling by the Supreme Court must be accepted by the Congress.

The paragraph best supports the statement that

(A) if an Act of Congress is voided, then it has been deemed unconstitutional by the Supreme Court.

(B) if an Act of Congress has not been voided, then it has not been deemed unconstitutional by the Supreme Court.

(C) if an Act of Congress has not been deemed unconstitutional by the Supreme Court, then it is voided.

(D) if an Act of Congress is deemed unconstitutional by the Supreme Court, then it is not voided.

51. Since the government can spend only what it obtains from the people, and this amount is ultimately limited by their capacity and willingness to pay taxes, it is very important that the people be given full information about the full work of the government.

The paragraph best supports the statement that

(A) governmental employees should be trained not only in their own work, but also in how to perform the duties of other employees in their agency.

(B) taxation by the government rests upon the consent of the people.

(C) the release of full information on the work of the government will increase the efficiency of governmental operations.

(D) the work of the government, in recent years, has been restricted because of reduced tax collection.

52. Both the high school and the college should take the responsibility for preparing the student to get a job. Since the ability to write a good application letter is one of the first steps toward this goal, every teacher should be willing to do what he can to help the student learn to write such letters.

The paragraph best supports the statement that

(A) inability to write a good letter often reduces one's job prospects.

(B) the major responsibility of the school is to obtain jobs for its students.

(C) success is largely a matter of the kind of work the student applies for first.

(D) every teacher should teach a course in the writing of application letters.

53. Direct lighting is the least satisfactory lighting arrangement. The desk or ceiling light with a reflector that diffuses all the rays downward is sure to cause a glare on the working surface.

The paragraph best supports the statement that direct lighting is least satisfactory as a method of lighting chiefly because

(A) the light is diffused, causing eyestrain.

(B) the shade on the individual desk lamp is not constructed along scientific lines.

(C) the working surface is usually obscured by the glare.

(D) direct lighting is injurious to the eyes.

54. "White collar" is a term used to describe one of the largest groups of workers in American industry and trade. It distinguishes those who work with the pencil and the mind from those who depend on their hands and the machine. It suggests occupations in which physical exertion and handling of materials are not primary features of the job.

The paragraph best supports the statement that "white collar" workers are

(A) not so strong physically as those who work with their hands.

(B) those who supervise workers handling materials.

(C) all whose work is entirely indoors.

(D) not likely to use machines as much as are other groups of workers.

21

55. In large organizations, a standardized, simple, inexpensive method of giving employees information about company policies and rules, as well as specific instructions regarding their duties, is practically essential. This is the purpose of all office manuals of whatever type.

The paragraph best supports the statement that office manuals

(A) are all about the same.

(B) should be simple enough for the average employee to understand.

(C) are necessary to large organizations.

(D) act as constant reminders to the employee of his duties.

HOUR 22

Evaluating Sample Civil Service Exam 2

What You Will Learn in This Hour

In this hour, you will determine how you did on the second sample civil service exam. You will calculate your overall score, find the answers to the questions that you missed, and discover any weak areas that you need to review. Here are your goals for this hour:

- Learn how to calculate your score.
- Learn how to evaluate the clerical ability portion of the exam.
- Learn how to evaluate the verbal ability portion of the exam.
- Learn how to evaluate yourself.

Scoring the Sample Civil Service Exam

Your score on this sample exam is based solely on the number of questions that you answered correctly. Wrong answers have no effect on the score. The two parts are timed and administered in two separate units, but they are not scored separately. There is no clerical ability score and no verbal ability score; rather, there is only a single exam score.

To determine your raw score, count all of your correct answers on the full exam based on the following answer keys. The highest possible score is 140.

Answer Key for Sample Exam 2

Clerical Ability Test

1.	E	18.	B	35.	B	52.	C	69.	B
2.	D	19.	A	36.	B	53.	C	70.	B
3.	A	20.	C	37.	E	54.	A	71.	E
4.	D	21.	A	38.	C	55.	D	72.	B
5.	A	22.	E	39.	D	56.	A	73.	A
6.	C	23.	C	40.	A	57.	D	74.	B
7.	B	24.	B	41.	A	58.	B	75.	E
8.	D	25.	D	42.	C	59.	C	76.	C
9.	E	26.	E	43.	C	60.	B	77.	E
10.	C	27.	A	44.	C	61.	A	78.	E
11.	C	28.	B	45.	D	62.	C	79.	C
12.	D	29.	C	46.	B	63.	C	80.	B
13.	C	30.	D	47.	E	64.	D	81.	E
14.	A	31.	D	48.	A	65.	D	82.	C
15.	C	32.	E	49.	C	66.	C	83.	E
16.	A	33.	A	50.	A	67.	A	84.	C
17.	E	34.	A	51.	A	68.	D	85.	B

Verbal Ability Test

1.	D	12.	B	23.	D	34.	B	45.	A
2.	C	13.	D	24.	A	35.	B	46.	C
3.	E	14.	A	25.	D	36.	D	47.	A
4.	A	15.	D	26.	A	37.	C	48.	C
5.	C	16.	D	27.	C	38.	C	49.	A
6.	E	17.	E	28.	C	39.	D	50.	B
7.	D	18.	A	29.	B	40.	D	51.	B
8.	C	19.	D	30.	D	41.	B	52.	A
9.	E	20.	B	31.	D	42.	A	53.	C
10.	B	21.	C	32.	A	43.	B	54.	D
11.	A	22.	C	33.	A	44.	D	55.	C

Answer Explanations

Again, read through all the answer explanations, both for the questions you missed and for the ones that you answered correctly. This will help you review what you have previously learned.

Clerical Ability Test

1. **(E)** Hachettson; Hackett

2. **(D)** 59233262; 59233362; 59233662

3. **(A)** MYP-6734; NYP-6733

4. **(D)** Bobbitt, Olivia H.; Bobbitt, Olivier E.; Bobbitt, R. Olivia

5. **(A)** 00102032; 00120312

6. **(C)** LPD-6001; LPD-6100; LPD-6101

7. **(B)** Vanover; Vanstory; VanSwinderen

8. **(D)** FitzGibbon; Fitzsimmons; Fitz-Simons

9. **(E)** 01016060; 01066010

10. **(C)** AAS-4623; AAZ-2687; ASA-3216

11. **(C)** Pawelek; Pawlowicz; Pawlowski

12. **(D)** NCD-7710; NCD-7834; NCD-7868

13. **(C)** 36270000; 36270013; 36270030

14. **(A)** Freedenburg, C. Erma; Freedenburg, Emerson

15. **(C)** Proutey, Maude; Prouty, Martha; Prouty, Myra

16. **(A)** 58006021; 58006130

17. **(E)** EKK-1403; EKK-1443

18. **(B)** Daly; D'Amato; D'Amboise

19. **(A)** Schaeffer; Schaffert

20. **(C)** PSP-4921; SPP-4856; SPS-4906

21. **(A)** All three names are exactly alike.

22. **(E)** All three names are different: Toumantzev; Tourmantzev; Toumantzov

23. **(C)** The middle number is different: 6-78912-3e3e42

24. **(B)** The last address is different: 85629 Dunwoodie Drive

25. **(D)** The first number is different: 1592514

26. **(E)** All three names are different: Ella Burk Newham; Ella Burk Newnham; Elena Burk Newnham

27. **(A)** All three codes are exactly alike.

28. **(B)** The last address is different: 60646 West Touhey Avenue

29. **(C)** The second name is different: Mardikian and Moore, Inc.

30. **(D)** The first number is different: 9670243

31. **(D)** The first name is different: Ingles (missing the final "e")

32. **(E)** All three names are different: DeAngelis; D'Angelis; DeAngeles

33. **(A)** All three numbers are exactly alike.

34. **(A)** All three addresses are exactly alike.

35. **(B)** The third number is different: 62qs5-95yT3-001.

36. **(B)** The last number is different: 2798350

37. **(E)** All three names are different: Helmut V. Lochner; Helmut V. Lockner; Helmut W. Lochner

38. **(C)** The second number is different: 2548403

39. **(D)** The first address is different: Lemberger, WA 28094-9182

40. **(A)** All three codes are exactly alike.

41. **(A)** All three names are exactly alike.

42. **(C)** The second number is different: 5927861

43. **(C)** The second address is different: O'Reillys Bay, LA 56212

44. **(C)** The second name is different: Frances Ramsdell

45. **(D)** The first code is different: 5634-OotV5a-16867

46. **(B)** The last name is different: Doloras

47. **(E)** All three names are different: David C. Routzon; David E. Routzon; David C. Routzron

48. **(A)** All three addresses are exactly alike.

49. **(C)** The second number is different: 6177936

50. **(A)** All three codes are exactly alike.

51. **(A)** The correct spelling is *anticipate*.

52. **(C)** The correct spelling is *similar*.

53. **(C)** The correct spelling is *sufficiently*.

54. **(A)** The correct spelling is *intelligence*.

55. **(D)** The correct spelling is *reference*.

56. **(A)** The correct spelling is *conscious*.

57. **(D)** The correct spelling is *parallel*.

58. **(B)** The correct spelling is *abundance*.

59. **(C)** The correct spelling is *corrugated*.

60. **(B)** The correct spelling is *accumulation*.

61. **(A)** The correct spelling is *resonance*.

62. **(C)** The correct spelling is *beneficial*.

63. **(C)** The correct spelling is *specifically*.

64. **(D)** The correct spelling is *eliminate*.

65. **(D)** The correct spelling is *colossal*.

22

66. **(C)** The correct spelling is *auxiliary*.

67. **(A)** The correct spelling is *inimitable*.

68. **(D)** The correct spelling is *disappearance*.

69. **(B)** The correct spelling is *appellate*.

70. **(B)** The correct spelling is *essential*.

71. **(E)** 27

72. **(B)** 32

73. **(A)** 224

74. **(B)** 78

75. **(E)** 28

76. **(C)** 99

77. **(E)** 61

78. **(E)** 114

79. **(C)** 40

80. **(B)** 7

81. **(E)** 30

82. **(C)** 10

83. **(E)** 41

84. **(C)** 23

85. **(B)** 21

Verbal Ability Test

1. **(D)** This answer goes with question 6. There is one B on the line, choice (D) is correct.

2. **(C)** This answer goes with question 9. The largest circle is around the letter C, so choice (C) is correct.

3. **(E)** This answer goes with question 14. There are five Bs in the line, and $5 - 2 = 3$.

4. **(A)** This answer goes with question 3. $16 \div 4 = 4$.

5. **(C)** This answer goes with question 4. The left-hand number is 5.

6. **(E)** This answer goes with question 20. There are five points on a star, so choice (E) is correct.

7. **(D)** This answer goes with question 12. The second letter is D, and the number of days in a week is seven, so choice (D) is correct.

8. **(C)** This answer goes with question 8. $6 \times 4 = 24$ and $8 \times 3 = 24$, so 6×4 is not greater than 8×3.

9. **(E)** This answer goes with question 2. 9 is the only odd number listed that is greater than 5 and less than 10, so choice (E) is correct.

10. **(B)** This answer goes with question 18. The next-to-smallest number listed is 10.

11. **(A)** This answer goes with question 16. It is true that a 6-foot-tall person is taller than a 5-foot-tall person and that a pillow is softer than a rock.

12. **(B)** This answer goes with question 1. Of the letters listed, the one that comes first in the alphabet is B.

13. **(D)** This answer goes with question 17. The fourth letter in the alphabet is D, and the third number listed is 13.

14. **(A)** This answer goes with question 13. It is not true that a triangle has more angles than a rectangle, so you should have written 14 beside letter A, which is enclosed by a square.

15. **(D)** This answer goes with question 10. $7 + 4 + 4 = 15$, so choice (D) is correct.

16. **(D)** This answer goes with question 15. The latest time is 10:16.

17. **(E)** This answer goes with question 11. It is true that $5 \times 5 = 25$ and $5 + 5 = 10$.

18. **(A)** This answer goes with question 5. Wednesday never comes before Tuesday, so you should have written down the number 18.

19. **(D)** This answer goes with question 19. The third letter in the first word is D, and the second box contains the number 19.

20. **(B)** This answer goes with question 7. The highest number listed is 20.

Note

You have not seen this kind of question before. It tests your ability to read directions carefully and follow them exactly, a necessity for succeeding on any civil service exam. If you made any errors, go back and reread the questions that you missed more carefully.

---

21. **(C)** Choice (A) has two grammatical errors: when to introduce a definition; and the unacceptable verb form is already having been parked. Choice (B) incorrectly shifts subjects from one to you. Choice (D) does not make sense.

22. **(C)** Choices (A) and (B) are incorrect because only two persons are involved in the statement; between is used when there are only two, and among is reserved for three or more. Choices (A) and (D) use the pronoun he; the object of a preposition, in this case, between, must be in the objective case, him.

23. **(D)** Punctuation aside, both (A) and (B) incorrectly place the verb in the plural, are; neither is a singular indefinite pronoun and requires a singular verb. The choice between (C) and (D) is more difficult, but this is a simple statement and not a direct quote.

24. **(A)** Whoever is the subject of the phrase, whoever has the best record; hence, choice (A) is the correct answer and choice (D) is wrong. Both choices (B) and (C) are wordy and awkward.

25. **(D)** All of the other choices contain obvious errors.

26. **(A)** Choice (B) uses the plural verb were with the singular subject information. Choices (C) and (D) are colloquial and incorrect even for informal speech; they have no place in business writing.

27. **(C)** Choices (A) and (B) use adverbs incorrectly. Choice (D) is awkward and not part of everyday speech.

28. **(C)** Choices (B) and (D) are obviously incorrect. In choice (A), the pronoun who should be the subject of the phrase, who had made careless errors.

29. **(B)** Only the quoted material should be enclosed by quotation marks, so choice (A) is incorrect. Only the first word of a sentence should begin with a capital letter, so choices (C) and (D) are wrong. In addition, only the quoted material itself is a question; the entire sentence is a statement. Therefore, the question mark must be placed inside the quotes.

30. **(D)** Choices (A), (B), and (C) imply that he stays in church all day on Christmas and Easter and goes nowhere else. In addition, choice (C) splits the infinitive awkwardly. In choice (D), the modifier only is correctly placed to tell us that the only times he goes to church are on Christmas and Easter.

31. **(D)** Choice (A) might state that most or all but not both. Choice (B) should read persons who. Choice (C) should read with regard to….

32. **(A)** Choice (B) is incorrect because it requires the plural verb were. Choice (C) requires the correlative construction neither…nor. Choice (D) requires the nominative they.

33. **(A)** Choices (C) and (D) are glaringly poor. Choice (B) is not incorrect, but choice (A) is far better.

34. **(B)** Choice (A) incorrectly uses a semicolon to separate a complete clause from a sentence fragment; it also incorrectly uses *what* in place of *that*. Choice (C) is a run-on sentence that also misuses an apostrophe—*it's* is the contraction for it is, not the possessive of it. Choice (D) uses commas indiscriminately; it also misuses the apostrophe.

35. **(B)** In choice (A), the placement of the apostrophe is inappropriate. Choices (C) and (D) use the plural, but there is only one company.

36. **(D)** Choices (A) and (C) are incorrect in use of the subject form I instead of the object of the preposition me. Choice (B) incorrectly uses the reflexive myself; only I can address a letter to myself.

37. **(C)** Choice (A) incorrectly uses the plural verb form have with the singular subject one. Choice (B) is awkward and wordy. Choice (D) incorrectly changes the subject from one of us to anyone.

38. **(C)** Choice (A) is wordy. In choice (B), the correct verb should be have in place of leave. In choice (D), the word arose should be arisen.

39. **(D)** The first three sentences lack parallel construction. All of the words that modify paper must appear in the same form.

40. **(D)** The phrase, together with…, is extra information and not a part of the sentence; therefore, choices (A) and (B) contain errors of agreement. Choice (C) also presents subject-verb disagreement, but in this case, the compound subject, indicated by the conjunction and, requires a plural verb.

41. **(B)** Even if you do not recognize the root "manu" as meaning "hand" and relating directly to handbook, you should have no trouble getting this question right. If you substitute each of the choices in the sentence, you will see that only one makes sense.

42. **(A)** Within the context of the sentence, punishment for use, interpretation, or part of the rules does not make sense. Since it is reasonable to expect punishment for negative behavior with relation to the rules, violation, which is the meaning of infraction, is the proper answer.

43. **(B)** The prefix "re," meaning "back" or "again," should help narrow your choices to (A) or (B). To rescind is to take back or to cancel.

44. **(D)** First eliminate choice (C) since it does not make sense in the sentence. Your experience with the word summons may be with relation to tickets and fines, but tickets and fines have nothing to do with asking questions while taking a test. Even if you are unfamiliar with the word summon, you should be able to choose call as the best synonym in this context.

45. **(A)** Reprisal means "injury done for injury received," or "retaliation."

46. **(C)** To reduce is to make smaller or lessen.

47. **(A)** To impair is to make worse, to injure, or to weaken.

48. **(C)** Fitting in this context means "suitable" or "appropriate."

49. **(A)** The survey showed that of all subjects, typing helped most in business. It was also considered valuable by college students in their schoolwork.

50. **(B)** You can infer the answer from the information in the second sentence, which states that if an Act of Congress has been deemed unconstitutional, then it is voided. In choice (B), we are told that an Act of Congress is not voided; therefore, we can conclude that it has not been deemed unconstitutional by the Supreme Court.

51. **(B)** According to the paragraph, the government can spend only what it obtains from the people. The government obtains money from the people by taxation. If the people are unwilling to pay taxes, the government has no source of funds.

52. **(A)** Step one in the job application process is often the application letter. If the letter is not effective, the applicant will not move on to the next step, and job prospects will be greatly lessened.

53. **(C)** The second sentence of the paragraph states that direct lighting causes glare on the working surface.

54. **(D)** While all of the answer choices are likely to be true, the answer suggested by the paragraph is that "white collar" workers work with their pencils and their minds, rather than with their hands and machines.

55. **(C)** All the paragraph says is that office manuals are a necessity in large organizations.

Evaluating Yourself

Since there is only a single exam score, your performance on any single question type does not matter. In order to earn a high score, however, you must do well on all parts of the exam. Using the following self-evaluation charts, check how many of each question type you missed to gauge your performance on that question type. Then, concentrate your efforts toward improvement in the areas with which you had the most difficulty. It will be worth your while to return to the chapter indicated and review.

SELF-EVALUATION CHART: CLERICAL ABILITY TEST

Question Type	Question Numbers	Lesson to Review
Alphabetizing and Filing	1–20	Hour 12
Clerical Speed and Accuracy	21–50	Hour 13
Spelling	51–70	Hour 4
Computations	71–85	(Watch out for careless errors)

SELF-EVALUATION CHART: VERBAL ABILITY TEST

Question Type	Question Numbers	Lesson to Review
Following Written Instructions	1–20	(Read and follow instructions carefully)
English Grammar and Usage	21–40	Hour 3
Synonyms	41–48	Hour 5
Reading Comprehension	49–55	Hour 9

Use the following chart to find out where your total score falls on a scale from Poor to Excellent.

SCORE RATING CHART

	Excellent	Good	Average	Fair	Poor
Score	125–140	109–124	91–108	61–90	0–6

Hour **23**

Municipal Office Aide Sample Exam

What You Will Learn in This Hour

In this hour, you will take a third sample civil service exam. This sample exam is a bit different from the last two. It is based on civil service exams given by cities, rather than being based on the federal exams. This will help you practice taking different kinds of exams, so you can prepare for all possible situations. Here is your goal for this hour:

- Complete the sample exam.

Answer Sheet

Tear out this answer sheet and use it to mark your answers to the sample test that follows. Use a pencil to record your answers exactly as you will do on the actual test. Be sure to time yourself when taking the exam and stop when time is up, just as if you were taking the actual civil service exam. The exam should take you one hour to complete.

23

1. Ⓐ Ⓑ Ⓒ Ⓓ Ⓔ	21. Ⓐ Ⓑ Ⓒ Ⓓ Ⓔ	41. Ⓐ Ⓑ Ⓒ Ⓓ Ⓔ
2. Ⓐ Ⓑ Ⓒ Ⓓ Ⓔ	22. Ⓐ Ⓑ Ⓒ Ⓓ Ⓔ	42. Ⓐ Ⓑ Ⓒ Ⓓ Ⓔ
3. Ⓐ Ⓑ Ⓒ Ⓓ Ⓔ	23. Ⓐ Ⓑ Ⓒ Ⓓ Ⓔ	43. Ⓐ Ⓑ Ⓒ Ⓓ Ⓔ
4. Ⓐ Ⓑ Ⓒ Ⓓ Ⓔ	24. Ⓐ Ⓑ Ⓒ Ⓓ Ⓔ	44. Ⓐ Ⓑ Ⓒ Ⓓ Ⓔ
5. Ⓐ Ⓑ Ⓒ Ⓓ Ⓔ	25. Ⓐ Ⓑ Ⓒ Ⓓ Ⓔ	45. Ⓐ Ⓑ Ⓒ Ⓓ Ⓔ
6. Ⓐ Ⓑ Ⓒ Ⓓ Ⓔ	26. Ⓐ Ⓑ Ⓒ Ⓓ Ⓔ	46. Ⓐ Ⓑ Ⓒ Ⓓ Ⓔ
7. Ⓐ Ⓑ Ⓒ Ⓓ Ⓔ	27. Ⓐ Ⓑ Ⓒ Ⓓ Ⓔ	47. Ⓐ Ⓑ Ⓒ Ⓓ Ⓔ
8. Ⓐ Ⓑ Ⓒ Ⓓ Ⓔ	28. Ⓐ Ⓑ Ⓒ Ⓓ Ⓔ	48. Ⓐ Ⓑ Ⓒ Ⓓ Ⓔ
9. Ⓐ Ⓑ Ⓒ Ⓓ Ⓔ	29. Ⓐ Ⓑ Ⓒ Ⓓ Ⓔ	49. Ⓐ Ⓑ Ⓒ Ⓓ Ⓔ
10. Ⓐ Ⓑ Ⓒ Ⓓ Ⓔ	30. Ⓐ Ⓑ Ⓒ Ⓓ Ⓔ	50. Ⓐ Ⓑ Ⓒ Ⓓ Ⓔ
11. Ⓐ Ⓑ Ⓒ Ⓓ Ⓔ	31. Ⓐ Ⓑ Ⓒ Ⓓ Ⓔ	
12. Ⓐ Ⓑ Ⓒ Ⓓ Ⓔ	32. Ⓐ Ⓑ Ⓒ Ⓓ Ⓔ	
13. Ⓐ Ⓑ Ⓒ Ⓓ Ⓔ	33. Ⓐ Ⓑ Ⓒ Ⓓ Ⓔ	
14. Ⓐ Ⓑ Ⓒ Ⓓ Ⓔ	34. Ⓐ Ⓑ Ⓒ Ⓓ Ⓔ	
15. Ⓐ Ⓑ Ⓒ Ⓓ Ⓔ	35. Ⓐ Ⓑ Ⓒ Ⓓ Ⓔ	
16. Ⓐ Ⓑ Ⓒ Ⓓ Ⓔ	36. Ⓐ Ⓑ Ⓒ Ⓓ Ⓔ	
17. Ⓐ Ⓑ Ⓒ Ⓓ Ⓔ	37. Ⓐ Ⓑ Ⓒ Ⓓ Ⓔ	
18. Ⓐ Ⓑ Ⓒ Ⓓ Ⓔ	38. Ⓐ Ⓑ Ⓒ Ⓓ Ⓔ	
19. Ⓐ Ⓑ Ⓒ Ⓓ Ⓔ	39. Ⓐ Ⓑ Ⓒ Ⓓ Ⓔ	
20. Ⓐ Ⓑ Ⓒ Ⓓ Ⓔ	40. Ⓐ Ⓑ Ⓒ Ⓓ Ⓔ	

Municipal Office Aide Exam

50 Questions

> **DIRECTIONS:** Choose the best answer to each question and mark its letter on the answer sheet. You will have one hour to complete the exam.

23

1. In order to maintain office coverage during working hours, your supervisor has scheduled your lunch hour from 1 p.m. to 2 p.m., and your coworker's lunch hour is from 12 p.m. to 1 p.m. Lately, your coworker has been returning late from lunch each day. As a result, you do not get a full hour, since you must return to the office by 2 p.m. Of the following, the best action for you to take first is to

   (A) explain to your coworker in a courteous manner that his or her lateness is interfering with your right to a full hour for lunch.

   (B) tell your coworker that his or her lateness must stop, or you will report him or her to your supervisor.

   (C) report your coworker's lateness to your supervisor.

   (D) leave at 1 p.m. for lunch, whether your coworker has returned or not.

2. Assume that, as an office worker, one of your jobs is to open mail sent to your unit, read the mail for content, and send the mail to the appropriate person for handling. You accidentally open and begin to read a letter marked "personal" addressed to a coworker. Of the following, the best action for you to take is

   (A) report to your supervisor that your coworker is receiving personal mail at the office.

   (B) destroy the letter so that your coworker doesn't know you saw it.

   (C) reseal the letter and place it on the coworker's desk without saying anything.

   (D) bring the letter to your coworker and explain that you opened it by accident.

3. Suppose that in evaluating your work, your supervisor gives you an overall good rating, but states that you sometimes turn in work with careless errors. The best action for you to take would be to

   (A) ask a coworker who is good at details to proofread your work.

   (B) take time to do a careful job, paying more attention to detail.

   (C) continue working as usual since occasional errors are to be expected.

   (D) ask your supervisor if he or she would mind correcting your errors.

DIRECTIONS: Questions 4–8 consist of a sentence that may or may not be an example of good English. The underlined parts of each sentence may be correct or incorrect. Examine each sentence, considering grammar, punctuation, spelling, and capitalization. If the English usage in the underlined parts of the sentence given is better than any of the changes in the underlined words suggested in options (B), (C), or (D), choose option (A). If the changes in the underlined words suggested in options (B), (C), or (D) would make the sentence correct, choose the correct option. Do not choose an option that will change the meaning of the sentence.

4. This manual <u>discribes the duties performed</u> by an office aide.

(A) Correct as is

(B) describe the duties performed

(C) discribe the duties performed

(D) describes the duties performed

5. There <u>weren't no</u> paper in the supply closet.

(A) Correct as is

(B) weren't any

(C) wasn't any

(D) wasn't no

6. The new employees left <u>there</u> office to attend a meeting.

(A) Correct as is

(B) they're

(C) their

(D) thier

7. The office worker started working at <u>8;30 a.m.</u>

(A) Correct as is

(B) 8:30 a.m.

(C) 8;30 A,M.

(D) 8:30 AM.

8. The <u>alphabet, or A to Z sequence are</u> the basis of most filing systems.

(A) Correct as is

(B) alphabet, or A to Z sequence, is

(C) alphabet, or A to Z, sequence are

(D) alphabet, or A too Z sequence, is

23

> **DIRECTIONS:** Questions 9–13 have two lists of numbers. Each list contains three sets of numbers. Check each of the three sets in the list on the right to see if they are the same as the corresponding set in the list on the left. Mark your answers as follows:
> - (A) if NONE of the sets in the right list is the SAME as those in the left list
> - (B) if ONLY ONE of the sets in the right list is the SAME as those in the left list
> - (C) if ONLY TWO of the sets in the right list are the SAME as those in the left list
> - (D) if ALL THREE sets in the right list are the SAME as those in the left list

9.   7143592185   7143892185
        8344517699   8344518699
        9178531263   9178531263

10. 2572114731   257214731
        8806835476   8806835476
        8255831246   8255831246

11. 331476853821   331476858621
        6976658532996   6976655832996
        3766042113715   3766042113745

12. 8806663315   880663315
        74477138449   74477138449
        211756663666   211756663666

13. 990006966996   99000696996
        53022219743   53022219843
        4171171117717   4171171177717

DIRECTIONS: Questions 14–16 have two lists of names and addresses. Each list contains three sets of names and addresses. Check each of the three sets in the list on the right to see if they are the same as the corresponding set in the list on the left. Mark your answers as follows:
- (A) if NONE of the sets in the right list is the SAME as those in the left list
- (B) if ONLY ONE of the sets in the right list is the SAME as those in the left list
- (C) if ONLY TWO of the sets in the right list are the SAME as those in the left list
- (D) if ALL THREE sets in the right list are the SAME as those in the left list

14.   Mary T. Berlinger   Mary T. Berlinger
           2351 Hampton St.   2351 Hampton St.
           Monsey, N.Y. 20117   Monsey, N.Y. 20117

           Eduardo Benes   Eduardo Benes
           473 Kingston Avenue   473 Kingston Avenue
           Central Islip, N.Y. 11734   Central Islip, N.Y. 11734

           Alan Carrington Fuchs   Alan Carrington Fuchs
           17 Gnarled Hollow Road   17 Gnarled Hollow Road
           Los Angeles, California 91635   Los Angeles, California 91685

15.   David John Jacobson   David John Jacobson
           178 35 St. Apt. 4C   178 53 St. Apt. 4C
           New York, N.Y. 00927   New York, N.Y. 00927

           Ann-Marie Calonella   Ann-Marie Calonella
           7243 South Ridge Blvd.   7243 South Ridge Blvd.
           Bakersfield, California 96714   Bakersfield, California 96714

           Pauline M. Thompson   Pauline M. Thomson
           872 Linden Ave.   872 Linden Ave.
           Houston, Texas 70321   Houston, Texas 70321

16.   Chester LeRoy Masterton   Chester LeRoy Masterson

 B   152 Lacy Rd.   152 Lacy Rd.
           Kankakee, Ill. 54532   Kankakee, Ill. 54532

           William Maloney   William Maloney
           S. LaCrosse Pla.   S. LaCross Pla.
           Wausau, Wisconsin 52146   Wausau, Wisconsin 52146

           Cynthia V. Barnes   Cynthia V. Barnes
           16 Pines Rd.   16 Pines Rd.
           Greenpoint, Mississippi 20376   Greenpoint, Mississippi 20376

23

DIRECTIONS: You are to answer questions 17–20 solely on the basis of the information contained in the following passage:

Duplicating is the process of making a number of identical copies of letters, documents, etc., from an original. Some duplicating processes make copies directly from the original document. Other duplicating processes require the preparation of a special master, and copies are then made from the master. Four of the most common duplicating processes are stencil, fluid, offset, and Xerox.

In the stencil process, the typewriter is used to cut the words into a master, called a stencil. Drawings, charts, or graphs can be cut into the stencil using a stylus. As many as 3,500 good-quality copies can be reproduced from one stencil. Various grades of finished paper from inexpensive mimeograph to expensive bond can be used.

The fluid process is a good method of copying from 50 to 125 good-quality copies from a master, which is prepared with a special dye. The master is placed on the duplicator, and special paper with a hard finish is moistened and then passed through the duplicator. Some of the dye on the master is dissolved, creating an impression on the paper. The impression becomes lighter as more copies are made, and once the dye on the master is used up, a new master must be made.

The offset process is the most adaptable office duplicating process because this process can be used for making a few copies or many copies. Masters can be made on paper or plastic for a few hundred copies or on metal plates for as many as 75,000 copies. By using a special technique called photo-offset, charts, photographs, illustrations, or graphs can be reproduced on the master plate. The offset process is capable of producing large quantities of fine, top-quality copies on all types of finished paper.

The Xerox process reproduces an exact duplicate from an original. It is the fastest duplicating method because the original material is placed directly on the duplicator, eliminating the need to make a special master. Any kind of paper can be used. The Xerox process is the most expensive duplicating process; however, it is the best method of reproducing small quantities of good-quality copies of reports, letters, official documents, memos, or contracts.

17. The offset process is the most adaptable office duplicating process because
    (A) it is the quickest duplicating method.
    (B) it is the least expensive duplicating method.
    (C) it can produce a small number or a large number of copies.
    (D) a softer master can be used over and over again.

18. Which one of the following duplicating processes uses moistened paper?
    (A) Stencil
    (B) Fluid
    (C) Offset
    (D) Xerox

19. The fluid process would be the best process to use for reproducing
    (A) five copies of a school transcript.
    (B) 50 copies of a memo.
    (C) 500 copies of a form letter.
    (D) 5,000 copies of a chart.

20. Which one of the following duplicating processes does not require a special master?
    (A) Fluid
    (B) Xerox
    (C) Offset
    (D) Stencil

DIRECTIONS: For questions 21–23, select the choice that is closest in meaning to the underlined word.

---

21. A central file eliminates the need to retain duplicate material. The word retain means most nearly
    (A) keep
    (B) change
    (C) locate
    (D) process

22. Filing is a routine office task. Routine means most nearly
    (A) proper
    (B) regular
    (C) simple
    (D) difficult

23. Sometimes a word, phrase, or sentence must be deleted to correct an error. Deleted means most nearly
    (A) removed
    (B) added
    (C) expanded
    (D) improved

Code Table

T	M	V	D	S	P	R	G	B	H
1	2	3	4	5	6	7	8	9	0

DIRECTIONS: The code table above shows 10 letters with matching numbers. For questions 24–28, there are three sets of letters. Each set of letters is followed by a set of numbers that may or may not match their correct letters according to the code table. For each question, check all three sets of letters and numbers and mark your answer as follows:

- (A) if NO PAIRS are CORRECTLY MATCHED
- (B) if only ONE PAIR is CORRECTLY MATCHED
- (C) if only TWO PAIRS are CORRECTLY MATCHED
- (D) if ALL THREE PAIRS are CORRECTLY MATCHED

23

24. DSPRGM   456782
    MVDBHT   234902
    HPMDBT   062491

25. BVPTRD   936184
    GDPHMB   807029
    GMRHMV   827032

26. MGVRSH   283750
    TRDMBS   174295
    SPRMGV   567283

27. SGBSDM   489542
    MGHPTM   290612
    MPBMHT   269301

28. TDPBHM   146902
    VPBMRS   369275
    GDMBHM   842902

DIRECTIONS: In each of the questions 29–32, the names of four people are given. For each question, choose as your answer the one of the four names given that should be filed first according to the usual system of alphabetical filing of names.

29. (A) Howard J. Black
    (B) Howard Black
    (C) J. Howard Black
    (D) John H. Black

30. (A) Theodora Garth Kingston
    (B) Theadore Barth Kingston
    (C) Thomas Kingston
    (D) Thomas T. Kingston

31. (A) Paulette Mary Huerta
    (B) Paul M. Huerta
    (C) Paulette L. Huerta
    (D) Peter A. Huerta

32. (A) Martha Hunt Morgan
    (B) Martin Hunt Morgan
    (C) Mary H. Morgan
    (D) Martine H. Morgan

33. Which one of the following statements about proper telephone usage is not always correct? When answering the telephone, you should

    (A) know who you are speaking to.

    (B) give the caller your undivided attention.

    (C) identify yourself to the caller.

    (D) obtain the information the caller wishes before you do your other work.

34. Assume that, as a member of a Worker's Safety Committee in your agency, you are responsible for encouraging other employees to follow correct safety practices. While you are working on your regular assignment, you observe an employee violating a safety rule. Of the following, the best action for you to take first is to

    (A) speak to the employee about safety practices and order him or her to stop violating the safety rule.

    (B) speak to the employee about safety practices and point out the safety rule he or she is violating.

    (C) bring the matter up in the next committee meeting.

    (D) report this violation of the safety rule to the employee's supervisor.

35. Assume that you have been temporarily assigned by your supervisor to do a job that you do not want to do. The best action for you to take is

    (A) discuss the job with your supervisor, explaining why you do not want to do it.

    (B) discuss the job with your supervisor and tell him or her that you will not do it.

    (C) ask a coworker to take your place on this job.

    (D) do some other job that you like; your supervisor may give the job you do not like to someone else.

23

DIRECTIONS: You are to answer questions 36–38 solely on the basis of the information contained in the following passage:

The city government is committed to providing a safe and healthy work environment for all city employees. An effective agency safety program reduces accidents by educating employees about the types of careless acts that can cause accidents. Even in an office, accidents can happen. If each employee is aware of possible safety hazards, the number of accidents on the job can be reduced.

Careless use of office equipment can cause accidents and injuries. For example, file cabinet drawers that are filled with papers can be so heavy that the entire cabinet could tip over from the weight of one open drawer.

The bottom drawers of desks and file cabinets should never be left open, since employees could easily trip over open drawers and injure themselves.

When reaching for objects on a high shelf, an employee should use a strong, sturdy object such as a stepstool to stand on. Makeshift platforms made out of books, papers, or boxes can easily collapse. Even chairs can slide out from underfoot, causing serious injury.

Even at an employee's desk, safety hazards can occur. Frayed or cut wires should be repaired or replaced immediately. Typewriters or computers that are not firmly anchored to the desk or table could fall, causing injury.

Smoking is one of the major causes of fires in the office. A lighted match or improperly extinguished cigarette thrown into a wastebasket filled with paper could cause a major fire with possible loss of life. Most companies prohibit smoking inside the office building. If it is permitted to smoke indoors, ashtrays should be used. Smoking is particularly dangerous in offices where flammable chemicals are used.

---

36. The goal of an effective safety program is to

   (A) reduce office accidents.

   (B) stop employees from smoking on the job.

   (C) encourage employees to continue their education.

   (D) eliminate high shelves in offices.

37. Desks and file cabinets can become safety hazards when

   (A) their drawers are left open.

   (B) they are used as wastebaskets.

   (C) they are makeshift.

   (D) they are not anchored securely to the floor.

38. Smoking is especially hazardous when it occurs

(A) near exposed wires.

(B) in a crowded office.

(C) in an area where flammable chemicals are used.

(D) where books and papers are stored.

39. Assume that you are assigned to work as a receptionist and your duties are to answer phones, greet visitors, and do other general office work. You are busy with a routine job when several visitors approach your desk. The best action to take is to

(A) ask the visitors to have a seat and assist them after your work is completed.

(B) tell the visitors that you are busy and they should return at a more convenient time.

(C) stop working long enough to assist the visitors.

(D) continue working and wait for the visitors to ask you for assistance.

40. Assume that your supervisor has chosen you to take a special course during working hours to learn a new payroll procedure. Although you know that you were chosen because of your good work record, a coworker who feels that he or she should have been chosen has been telling everyone in your unit that the choice was unfair. Of the following, the best way to handle this situation first is to

(A) suggest to the coworker that everything in life is unfair.

(B) contact your union representative in case your coworker presents a formal grievance.

(C) tell your supervisor about your coworker's complaints and let him or her handle the situation.

(D) tell the coworker that you were chosen because of your superior work record.

DIRECTIONS: You are to answer questions 41–45 solely on the basis of the information contained in the following passage:

The telephone directory is made up of two books. The first book consists of the introductory section and the alphabetical listing of names section. The second book is the classified directory (also known as the Yellow Pages). Many people who are familiar with one book do not realize how useful the other can be. The efficient office worker should become familiar with both books in order to make the best use of this important source of information.

The introductory section gives general instructions for finding numbers in the alphabetical listing and classified directory. This section also explains how to use the telephone company's many services, including the operator and information services; gives examples of charges for local and long-distance calls; and lists area codes for the entire country. In addition, this section provides a useful postal ZIP code map.

The alphabetical listing of names section lists the names, addresses, and telephone numbers of subscribers in an area. These guide names indicate the first and last name to be found on that page. "Telltales" help locate any particular name quickly. A cross-reference spelling is also given to help locate names that are spelled several different ways.

City, State, and Federal Government agencies are listed in the blue pages of the alphabetical book under the major government heading. For example, an agency of the Federal Government would be listed under "United States Government."

The classified directory, or Yellow Pages, is a separate book. In this section are advertising services, public transportation line maps, shopping guides, and listings of businesses arranged by the type of product or services they offer. This book is most useful when looking for the name or phone number of a business when all that is known is the type of product offered and the address, or when trying to locate a particular type of business in an area. Businesses listed in the classified directory can usually be found in the alphabetical listing of names section. When the name of the business is known, you will find the address or phone number more quickly in the alphabetical listing of names section.

41. Advertising services would be found in the

(A) introductory section.

(B) alphabetical listing of names section.

(C) classified directory.

(D) information services.

42. According to the information in the passage for locating government agencies, the Information Office of the Department of Consumer Affairs of New York City government would be alphabetically listed first under

(A) "I" for Information Office.

(B) "D" for Department of Consumer Affairs.

(C) "N" for New York City.

(D) "G" for government.

43. When the name of a business is known, the quickest way to find the phone number is to look in the

(A) classified directory.

(B) introductory section.

(C) alphabetical listing of names section.

(D) advertising service section.

44. The quickest way to find the phone number of a business when the type of service a business offers and its address are known is to look in the

(A) classified directory.

(B) alphabetical listing of names section.

(C) introductory section.

(D) information service.

45. What is a "telltale"?

(A) An alphabetical listing

(B) A guide name

(C) A map

(D) A cross-reference listing

46. Assume that your unit ordered 14 staplers at a total cost of $30.20, and each stapler cost the same amount. The cost of one stapler was most nearly

(A) $1.02.

(B) $1.61.

(C) $2.16.

(D) $2.26.

47. Assume that you are responsible for counting and recording licensing fees collected by your department. On a particular day, your department collected in fees 40 checks in the amount of $6 each; 80 checks in the amount of $4 each; 45 $20 bills; 30 $10 bills; 42 $5 bills; and 186 $1 bills. The total amount in fees collected on that day was

(A) $1,406.

(B) $1,706.

(C) $2,156.

(D) $2,356.

48. Assume that you are responsible for your agency's petty cash fund. During the month of February, you pay out seven subway fares at $1.25 each and one taxi fare for $7.30. You pay out nothing else from the fund. At the end of February, you count the money left in the fund and find three $1 bills, four quarters, five dimes, and four nickels. The amount of money you had available in the petty cash fund at the beginning of February was

(A) $4.70.

(B) $11.35.

(C) $16.05.

(D) $20.75.

49. Assume that you are assigned to sell tickets at a city-owned ice skating rink. An adult ticket costs $3.75, and a children's ticket costs $2. At the end of the day, you find that you have sold 36 adult tickets and 80 children's tickets. The total amount of money you collected for that day was

(A) $285.50.

(B) $295.00.

(C) $298.75.

(D) $301.00.

50. If each office worker files 487 index cards in one hour, how many cards can 26 office workers file in one hour?

(A) 10,662

(B) 12,175

(C) 12,662

(D) 14,266

HOUR 24

Evaluating the Municipal Office Aide Sample Exam

What You Will Learn in This Hour

In this hour, you will determine how you did on the sample municipal office aide exam. You will calculate your overall score, find the answers to the questions that you missed, and discover any weak areas that you need to review. Here are your goals for this hour:

- Calculate your score.
- Find explanations for the correct answers.
- Learn how to evaluate yourself.

Scoring the Sample Exam

All of the questions on this exam count as one point each. You are not penalized for incorrect answers or skipped questions. To score the exam, count the number of questions that you answered correctly according to the following answer key. This number equals your raw score. The highest possible score is 50.

Answer Key

1.	A	11.	A	21.	A	31.	B	41.	C
2.	D	12.	D	22.	B	32.	A	42.	C
3.	B	13.	A	23.	A	33.	D	43.	C
4.	D	14.	C	24.	C	34.	B	44.	A
5.	C	15.	B	25.	A	35.	A	45.	B
6.	C	16.	B	26.	D	36.	A	46.	C
7.	B	17.	C	27.	A	37.	A	47.	C
8.	B	18.	B	28.	D	38.	C	48.	D
9.	B	19.	B	29.	B	39.	C	49.	B
10.	C	20.	B	30.	B	40.	C	50.	C

Answer Explanations

1. **(A)** The first step is to discuss the problem with your coworker. Remember that calm, polite discussion is almost always the correct answer when given as a choice.

2. **(D)** Obviously, the best thing to do is to be honest with your coworker and to deliver the letter.

3. **(B)** The best solution is to work on the areas that your supervisor has told you need improvement so that you can do a better job. If you're committing many careless errors, you need to be more careful when doing your work.

8. **(B)** The alphabet—singular—is. The phrase or A to Z sequence is extra information about the alphabet, so it is enclosed by commas. Too means "also" or "excessive" and is the incorrect spelling of to.

9. **(B)** The numbers in the first and second sets are different: 7143592185 and 7143892185; 8344517699 and 8344518699.

10. **(C)** The numbers in the first set are different: 2572114731 and 257214731.

11. **(A)** None of the sets is alike: 331476853821 and 331476858621;

> **Note**
> Questions 1–3 and all similar questions are judgment questions. They rely on your common sense and good judgment in interpersonal relations.

4. **(D)** The subject of the sentence, the manual, is singular, so the verb must be singular as well. The correct spelling is describes.

5. **(C)** Paper is a singular noun taking the singular verb wasn't. The construction weren't no constitutes an unacceptable double negative.

6. **(C)** Their is the possessive. They're is the contraction for they are. There refers to a place. Choice (D) is a misspelling.

7. **(B)** The correct way to express time is 8:30 a.m. Alternatively, 8:30 A.M. is also correct, but it is not one of the choices.

6976658532996 and 6976655832996; 3766042113715 and 3766042113745.

12. **(D)** All of the sets are exactly alike.

13. **(A)** None of the sets is alike: 990006966996 and 99000696996; 53022219743 and 53022219843; 4171171117717 and 4171171177717.

14. **(C)** The ZIP codes in the third set are different: Los Angeles, California 91635 and Los Angeles, California 91685.

15. **(B)** The first and third sets are different: 178 35 St. Apt. 4C and 178 53 St. Apt. 4C; Pauline M. Thompson and Pauline M. Thomson.

16. **(B)** The first and second sets are different: Chester LeRoy Masterton and Chester LeRoy Masterson; S. LaCrosse Pla. and S. LaCross Pla.

17. **(C)** See the first sentence of the fourth paragraph.

18. **(B)** See the second sentence of the third paragraph.

19. **(B)** In choices (C) and (D), the numbers are too high for the fluid process. Five copies would be most efficiently reproduced by the Xerox process without preparing a master.

20. **(B)** See the second sentence of the last paragraph.

21. **(A)** To retain is to hold or to keep.

22. **(B)** A routine is a course of action that is followed regularly.

23. **(A)** To delete is to strike out or to remove.

24. **(C)** The second set is incorrectly coded: MVDBHT–234902 (should be 1).

25. **(A)** No sets are correctly coded: BVPTRD–936184 (should be 7); GDPHMB–807029 (should be 46); GMRHMV–827032 (should be 23).

26. **(D)** All three sets are correctly coded.

27. **(A)** No sets are correctly coded: SGBSDM–489542 (should be 5); MGHPTM–290612 (should be 8); MPBMHT–269301 (should be 2).

28. **(D)** All three sets are correctly coded.

29. **(B)** The correct alphabetization is: Black, Howard; Black, Howard J.; Black, J. Howard; Black, John H.

30. **(B)** The correct alphabetization is: Kingston, Theadore Barth; Kingston, Theadora Garth; Kingston, Thomas; Kingston, Thomas T.

31. **(B)** The correct alphabetization is: Huerta, Paul M.; Huerta, Paulette L.; Huerta, Paulette Mary; Huerta, Peter A.

32. **(A)** The correct alphabetization is: Morgan, Martha Hunt; Morgan, Martin Hunt; Morgan, Martine H.; Morgan, Mary H.

33. **(D)** You must always identify yourself, find out to whom you are speaking, and be courteous to the caller, but sometimes a return call could give information at a later hour or date.

34. **(B)** The first thing to do is speak to the employee who may not even be aware of the rule.

35. **(A)** Be "up front" with your supervisor. Refusing to do a distasteful task or trying to hand it off to someone else is not proper business procedure.

36. **(A)** See the second sentence of the first paragraph.

37. **(A)** See the third paragraph.

38. **(C)** See the last sentence of the last paragraph.

39. **(C)** A receptionist receives visitors.

40. **(C)** No matter how you approach the co-worker, you are likely to create ill feeling. Let your supervisor handle this tricky office morale problem.

41. **(C)** See the second sentence of the last paragraph.

42. **(C)** See the fourth paragraph.

43. **(C)** See the last sentence of the last paragraph.

44. **(A)** See the third sentence of the last paragraph.

45. **(B)** See the second sentence of the third paragraph.

46. **(C)** $30.20 ÷ 14 = $2.157; round up to $2.16.

47. **(C)** 40 checks × $6 = $240; 80 checks × $4 = $320; 45 bills × $20 = $900; 30 bills × $10 = $300; 42 bills × $5 = $210; 186 bills × $1 = $186; $240 + $320 + $900 + $300 + $210 + $186 = $2,156.

48. **(D)** 7 subway fares × $1.25 = $8.75; 1 taxi fare × $7.30 = $7.30; $8.75 + $7.30 = $16.05, the total amount spent during the month. 3 dollar bills = $3; 4 quarters = $1; 5 dimes = $.50; 4 nickels = $.20; $3 + $1 + $.50 + $.20 = $4.70, the total amount left at the end of the month. $16.05 + $4.70 = $20.75, the total amount at the beginning of the month.

49. **(B)** 36 adults × $3.75 = $135; 80 children × $2 = $160; $135 + $160 = $295.

50. **(C)** 487 cards × 26 workers = 12,662.

24

Evaluating Yourself

Since there is only a single exam score, your performance on any single question type does not matter. In order to earn a high score, however, you must do well on all parts of the exam. Using the following self-evaluation chart, check how many of each question type you missed to gauge your performance on that question type. Then, concentrate your efforts toward improvement in the areas with which you had the most difficulty. It will be worth your while to return to the chapter indicated and review.

SELF-EVALUATION CHART

Question Type	Question Numbers	Lesson to Review
Judgment	1–3, 33–35, 39–40	Hour 10
English Grammar and Usage; Spelling	4–8	Hours 3 and 4
Clerical Speed and Accuracy	9–16	Hour 13
Reading Comprehension	17–20, 36–38, 41–45	Hour 9
Synonyms	21–23	Hour 5
Coding	24–28	Hour 13
Alphabetizing and Filing	29–32	Hour 12
Decimals	46–49	Hour 15
Work Problems	50	Hour 18

Appendices

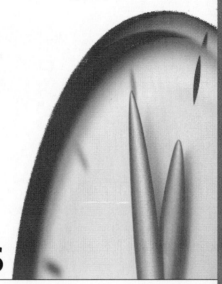

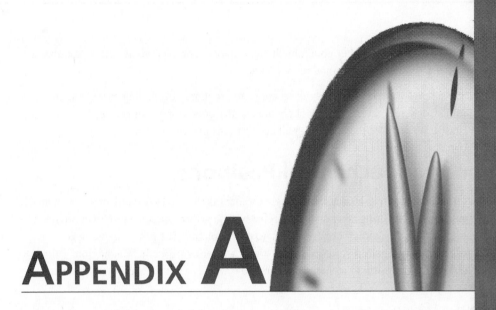

APPENDIX A

Selected Jobs in the Federal Service

This appendix describes the different kinds of jobs available in the federal government, along with typical duties, salary levels, and requirements of those positions. Use this appendix to discover the range of available positions and determine those in which you might be interested.

Clerical Positions

Nearly half the jobs in the federal civil service are clerical, and the government's demand for clerical workers often exceeds the supply. Agencies have not been able to fill all the positions for competent stenographers, typists, office machine operators, and file clerks.

In government, the title "clerk" describes more positions than it does in private industry. For instance, an editor or a writer may be called an editorial clerk, a purchasing agent with fairly important responsibilities may be called a purchasing clerk, or an accountant may be called a cost accounting clerk.

The following are some other government clerical jobs: correspondence clerk, shorthand reporter, mail clerk, file clerk, and record clerk.

Clerical salaries have risen sharply in recent years, probably exceeding average salaries for similar jobs in private industry. There are usually good opportunities for advancement, and clerical jobs can be the start of a real career in the government.

Labor and Mechanical Positions

Most people do not realize that the U.S. government is the largest employer of mechanical, manual, and laboring workers in the country. The government is more than offices. It is also factories, shipyards, shops, docks, and power plants. The government makes battleships, runs irrigation systems, and operates a printing office in Washington. There are more than one million mechanical and manual workers in the federal government.

Apprentices

The government hires fully qualified mechanics, artisans, and laborers, but several agencies conduct their own apprenticeship training programs for young people who want to learn a trade. Apprentices are employed in Navy yards, arsenals, other Department of Defense (DOD) establishments, and the Government Printing Office. There are apprenticeship training programs in many occupations, among them carpenter, coppersmith, electrician, electronics mechanic, glass apparatus maker, instrument maker, machinist, painter, plumber, refrigeration and air-conditioning mechanic, sheet-metal worker, toolmaker, and welder.

Apprenticeships usually last four years, or eight 6-month periods, made up of approximately 1,025 shop and school hours. There are no educational requirements, but the applicant must take a written test. The minimum age for apprentices is usually 18. There is no maximum age limit.

When an apprentice has finished the prescribed period of training, he or she is promoted to the status of artisan, regardless of age. Advancement comes regularly to the apprentice who completes service satisfactorily. There is no hard and fast pay scale for all apprentices. The apprentice pay rate is usually set in ratio to the journeyman pay in the trade.

Skilled and Semiskilled Positions

The full list of skilled and semiskilled jobs in the government probably includes every kind of job in this class. The following is just a selection of positions in federal establishments: woodworker, aircraft mechanic, metalsmith, radio mechanic, mason, toolmaker, machinist, radio and electronics mechanic, radar mechanic, water plant operator, automotive mechanic, locksmith, cook, gardener, butcher, blacksmith, munitions handler, freight handler, and laundry helper.

The government usually follows the custom of the trade. Most, but not all, positions are paid at hourly rates, and often skill sets the rate of pay. In some cases, the government pays on a piecework basis. Overtime is on a time-and-a-half basis, rather than at straight time, as in jobs of other types.

Skilled and semiskilled craft positions are also open on a full-time, annual-salary basis. Some typical positions of this kind include the following: electrician, plumber, carpenter, painter, operating engineer, office appliance technician, and photographer.

Unskilled Positions

Thousands of positions in the government service are open to those with no skills or with only a small amount of training. The following are just a selection:

- Housekeeping aides (restricted to veterans)
- Kitchen helpers (restricted to veterans)
- Janitors
- Messengers (restricted to veterans)
- Elevator operators
- General laborers
- Custodial laborers
- Laundry workers
- Mess attendants (restricted to veterans)
- Storekeeping clerks

Professional and Administrative Positions

Many professional and administrative positions are available in government agencies, including the following: personnel management, computer science, general administration, economics, Social Security administration, management analysis, tax collection, electronic data processing, budget management, park ranger activities, statistics, investigation, procurement and supply, housing management, archival science, adjudication and other quasi-legal work, and food and drug inspection. Passing a civil service exam is required for many of these positions. The exam generally measures a candidate's aptitude for the position and ability to be trained, rather than prior knowledge of the position's duties.

> **Note**
> Some agencies offer a limited number of what are, perhaps, the most coveted assignments—management internships. Specifically planned programs are designed to develop employees with unusual promise as future administrators. Persons considered for these internships must pass additional tests of greater difficulty.

Legal Positions

Legal positions range from higher-grade positions that require full professional legal training to those in the lower grades, requiring legal training but little or no experience. They include attorneys and clerkships.

Attorneys

Attorney positions are filled on a more subjective basis than most civil service jobs and are based mainly on the attorney's achievements in law school, the scored resume, interviews, and recommendations from politicians, college professors, and other influential people.

Attorneys should apply directly to the particular government agency where they want to work. The Office of Personnel Management (OPM) ordinarily does not maintain lists of federal agencies that may want to employ attorneys. Each federal agency is responsible for determining the qualifications of attorneys who apply, as well as for making the appointments in accordance with appropriate standards.

Congressional committees also use lawyers to investigate, question witnesses, gather evidence, and write reports. The lawyer who wants that kind of job should make the acquaintance of political leaders and cultivate the party leaders in a position to hand out such posts. Keeping posted on Congressional events and following up on the creation of special committees is also important.

> **Tip**
> If you are an attorney who would like to work for the federal government, you should keep up with news of agencies and bureaus as they are formed. Getting in at start-up offers the most opportunities for employment and advancement. Colleagues who are already in federal employment are a great source of information about new openings.

Federal Clerkships

Federal clerkships are perhaps the most eagerly sought short-term legal positions. All federal judges are allotted at least two law clerks. A clerkship runs from one to two years, during which the clerk does legal research, writes briefs, and assists at various tasks in the office of the judge. A clerkship is excellent legal training and offers the clerk an opportunity to make lifelong contacts in both the legal and political worlds.

Various factors enter into winning a federal clerkship: the prestige of the law school; law school grades; publications; honors; the desire of the judge for "balance" among the clerks in terms of gender, race, and geography; the interview; and the enthusiasm and standing of those who recommend the applicant.

> **Note**
> Federal judges, federal district attorneys (DAs), and assistant DAs are appointed by the President. Patronage is an important factor in getting these positions. The advice of senators and representatives and the local party political leaders pretty much decides who gets the job.

A

Investigative and Law Enforcement Positions

The highly publicized Federal Bureau of Investigation (FBI) is only one federal agency that enforces the law. A dozen agencies employ law enforcement officers for jobs that range from guarding property and patrolling borders to the most highly technical intelligence operations, including the following: Department of Justice (DOJ), State Department, Treasury Department, Postal Service, Army Department, Navy Department, Nuclear Regulatory Commission, Food and Drug Administration (FDA), Securities and Exchange Commission (SEC), and the Customs Bureau.

The work of law enforcement officers and investigators is dramatic, but it is often arduous and dangerous as well. Federal law enforcement frequently requires long absences from home and operating under trying physical conditions. In some of the security positions, the training is as tough as that given to commando units in the armed forces.

Most of the posts naturally have stiff physical requirements, calling for well-proportioned, healthy, agile persons. Eyesight and hearing requirements are higher than for most other federal jobs, and candidates must have full use of their arms and legs. Speech defects, scars, blemishes, or other defects that might interfere with the appointee's duties will cause rejection.

The positions described in this section represent the law enforcement and investigation positions in the federal service.

FBI Special Agent

The FBI has been given the authority to hire its own personnel. In addition to its agents, it hires clerical and specialized personnel. Applications may be filed at any time and may be obtained from the Director, Federal Bureau of Investigation, Washington D.C., or from any of the Bureau's offices, located in most larger cities.

The special agent enforces federal law, investigates its violations, gathers evidence for prosecution, checks the background of individuals, and traces criminals. The work extends from enforcing antitrust laws to tracing bribes to uncovering evidence of espionage. There are five entrance programs for FBI Special Agent's under which applicants can qualify: law, accounting, foreign language, science, and modified.

Applicants must be citizens between the ages of 23 and 37 and meet high educational requirements. They also must qualify on batteries of written and oral exams that measure emotional stability, resourcefulness, interpersonal and communication skills, and the ability to apply analytical methods to work assignments. Since Special Agents must be able to use firearms and defensive tactics, each applicant must pass a rigid physical examination, be capable of strenuous physical exertion, and have excellent hearing and eyesight. Before hiring, the FBI conducts an extensive background and character investigation.

Securities Investigator

Securities investigators examine the financial statements of national securities exchanges, brokers, and investment advisers to determine their financial condition and compliance with the regulations of the SEC. They also conduct investigations of fraud.

Securities investigator positions require, at minimum, three years general accounting experience and two to three years specialized auditing, investigative, or administrative experience in the securities field—which is generally known in the trade as "back office" experience. Applicants do not have to take a written test but are rated primarily on the quality, scope, and responsibility of their experience. Salaries start at grades GS-9 to GS-11.

Treasury Enforcement Agent

Treasury enforcement agents enforce laws under the jurisdiction of the Treasury Department. Positions are located in the following enforcement arms of the Treasury: Bureau of Alcohol, Tobacco, and Firearms (ATF); Bureau of Engraving and Printing; Customs Service; IRS Criminal Investigation Division and Internal Security Division; and Secret Service. Duties range from surveillance and undercover work to presenting evidence to government prosecutors and testifying in court.

Experience in dealing with groups and in criminal investigation, four years of college study, membership in the Bar, or a CPA certificate may be required. Applicants have to take the Treasury Enforcement Agent examination. Starting salaries range from grades GS-5 to GS-7.

IRS Agent

Internal Revenue Service (IRS) agents examine and audit the accounting books and records of individuals, partnerships, fiduciaries, and corporations to determine their correct federal tax liabilities. These positions require a minimum of four years of college with concentration in accounting, three years of comparable experience, or a Certified Public Accountant (CPA) certificate. Applicants without a CPA certificate or accounting degree must take a written test on accounting principles. Starting salaries range from grades GS-5 to GS-7.

IRS Special Agent

Special agents in the IRS investigate criminal violations of federal tax laws, make recommendations with respect to criminal prosecution, prepare technical reports, and assist the U.S. Attorney in preparing cases for trial. Three years of experience in commercial accounting, a law degree, or extensive accounting education is required. Applicants must also take the Treasury Enforcement Agent examination. Starting salaries range from GS-5 to GS-7.

Correctional Officer

Correctional officers supervise, safeguard, and train inmates in federal prisons. Those who start out as correctional officers often advance to supervisory and administrative positions in such fields as custody, education, vocational training, skilled trades, social services, parole, recreation, culinary service, accounting, and farm activities. Applicants must be

U.S. citizens, have comparable experience or education, have excellent character backgrounds, remain cool in emergencies, and have good morals, patience, and a capacity for leadership. There are strict vision, hearing, physical, and age requirements. Salaries start at grade GS-6.

Guard

Guards patrol premises to prevent trespassing, fire, theft, damage, or vandalism. They also protect the occupants of the buildings from outside annoyances and interferences, control traffic, and perform other duties. No experience is required for the entry-level positions. Physical, hearing, and vision requirements are strict. All applicants must take a written test of reading comprehension and ability to follow oral directions. Salaries start at grade GS-2 to GS-3 with more experience.

Inspector Positions

Inspection work is related to investigation. Inspectors see that building construction, elevators, fire escapes, plumbing, and other projects comply with regulations. They test weights and measures and act to enforce sanitary, food and drug, and public health laws. A government inspector may also check public works, playgrounds, street lighting and overhead lines, transportation, or public-safety devices.

Safety Inspector

The safety inspector enforces the Interstate Commerce Commission's motor carrier safety regulations. Safety inspectors advise transportation companies in the development of safety activities, accident prevention plans, and driver education, inspect motor vehicles, investigate accidents, and work with state agencies. Two years experience investigating highway accidents, inspecting motor vehicles, conducting hearings on traffic violations, maintaining motor carrier fleets, or important work on highway safety programs is required. Work as a traffic officer, motor vehicle dispatcher, or insurance claims adjuster does not qualify. Applicants are rated entirely on the basis of a written test. Salary is grade GS-5 at entrance.

Patent Examiner

The patent examiner performs professional scientific and technical work in examining applications for U.S. patents. The examiner evaluates an invention, determines if it will perform as claimed, uncovers any previous knowledge comparable to the invention, and determines whether the application and its claimed invention meets all legal requirements. All applicants must have a bachelor's degree or higher degree in professional engineering or science and are rated on the extent and quality of their relevant experience and training. A test is not required. Starting salaries range from grades GS-5 to GS-13.

Medical Positions

With the growth of social services in the past 50 years, the government has developed a need for physicians, medical researchers, nurses, dentists, and similar workers. The growth of psychiatric concepts, the development of occupational therapy, the public demand that veterans who need medical care should have it—all of these factors demand a force of medical practitioners working for the government.

Medical researchers study bacteriological warfare, hunt for protection against the effects of radioactivity, and prepare new vaccines, serums, and other biological products. Other medical jobs involve inspecting laboratories, testing pharmaceuticals, running public relations campaigns, examining those entering the public service, caring for Native Americans on reservations, administrating hospitals, and straight medical work from the care of colds to the most complex plastic surgery.

The Veterans' Administration (VA) employs the most medical workers in peacetime. The Army and Navy have medical and dental corps, which, of course, grow enormously during war. Other agencies that need medical workers are the Public Health Service, the FDA, the Children's Bureau of the Department of Health, and the Bureau of Indian Affairs (BIA) of the Interior Department. American physicians also accompany our missions in the Foreign Service. Many federal agencies employ nurses in the in-house medical facilities that they maintain for their employees. Nurses also serve in U.S. hospitals and serve as consultants to state health departments on programs to control tuberculosis and venereal disease.

This section describes some medical positions in the federal service.

Medical Officer

Medical officers occupy positions in the Public Health Service, FDA, Children's Bureau, Department of Health, BIA, VA, and many other federal agencies. Medical officers determine whether medicines are labeled properly. They conduct extensive research in maternal and child health and in services to physically and/or mentally challenged children. They serve in Native American hospitals and as district physicians in small government dispensaries. They have the opportunity of working in teaching hospitals in the federal service that are approved by the American Medical Association (AMA). There they obtain a wide variety of medical experience, particularly in the field of tropical diseases. They also inspect vessels and airplanes entering ports, harbors, and airfields and examine aliens entering the U.S.

Professional Nurse

Professional nurses serve in hospitals on Native American reservations, Army hospitals, and Navy hospitals. Most available positions are in Public Health Service hospitals located in major port cities and at the Clinical Center at the National Institutes of Health (NIH). Public health nursing consultants are employed in the Children's Bureau, where they work with state agencies. Positions range from staff nurse through nurse consultant and divison chief.

Applicants for all professional nurse positions must have completed a full nursing course. They must also be currently registered as professional nurses in the U.S. For positions in grades GS-6 and higher, they must have had specialized professional experience appropriate to the position. The entrance salary for a staff nurse is GS-5 to GS-7 and for a head nurse is GS-7 to GS-9. The pay of public-health nurse positions is from GS-7 to GS-9 at entrance. Nurse consultant positions pay GS-11 to GS-13.

Dental Assistant

Dental assistants receive and prepare patients, assist the dentist in both non-surgical and surgical dentistry, and may perform dental X-ray or prosthetic work. They also keep records of appointments, examinations, treatments, and supplies. Applicants must have had two years of dental assistant experience, including one year of specialization in restoration, dental X-raying, or dental prosthetics. Dental assistant courses may be substituted for experience. No written test is required. Salaries start at grade GS-4.

Dental Hygienist

Dental hygienists give oral prophylaxis to patients in hospitals and clinics. They conduct oral hygiene educational programs and instruct hospital and clinic personnel in the oral hygiene maintenance techniques. Applicants for all grades must be currently licensed to practice as dental hygienists in the U.S. Applicants for GS-4 and higher positions must have successfully completed a full course of dental hygiene and/or have comparable experience. No written test is required. Applicants are judged on the extent and quality of their educational experience and on personal qualities.

Other Medical and Nursing Positions

Other government positions in the medical and nursing fields include medical technician, laboratory helper, X-ray technician, occupational therapist, orthopedic technician, dental technician, and veterinarian. Entrance salaries for these positions range from grades GS-3 to GS-14.

Economics and Statistics Positions

The complexities of modern government require the services of people who "understand figures." Hardly an activity exists in any department that does not demand the work of an accountant, statistician, economist, or mathematician. Every citizen knows of the work done by the IRS. Statisticians in the Census Bureau prepare data for businesses and keep facts on the ups and downs of business. Other statisticians work with scientists, collecting and analyzing statistical reports that are frequently the basis of long-range national policy. They work on problems dealing with production, marketing, distribution, taxation, and other economic questions.

Accountants and budget examiners go over the dollars and cents spent by various departments, submit estimates, and sometimes cut spending programs. They make up payrolls, work on retirement mathematics, and examine the books of stock exchange firms. They study the background of bankruptcies, audit the books of public utility companies, and check into the financial conditions of banks. In another sphere, they may analyze the fiscal policy of the U.S. and determine methods of adapting that policy to the economic needs of the country. They make up the nation's budget and suggest appropriations for all government activities.

Mathematicians work with scientists in all of their activities, from plotting the course of planets to devising formulas in atomic physics. They work with engineers building bridges, solve equations about heat conduction or electrical circuits, make computations to predict weather, and determine the path of missiles and the intensity of earthquakes.

The "figures" people are so important that it is not an overstatement to say that modern government could not function without them. The Department of Agriculture, Tennessee Valley Authority, Department of Labor, National Labor Relations Board, Census Bureau, Treasury Department, and SEC are only some of the agencies that need workers with mathematics or economics backgrounds. As the government grows more complex, the need for qualified people will increase.

Some typical government positions in these fields are explained in this section.

A

Accounting Assistant

The duties of this position vary, depending on the agency. For GS-5 positions, applicants must meet one of the following requirements: study in accounting above the high school level, progressive experience, a combination of both, or a CPA certificate. For GS-7 positions, applicants must meet the requirements for GS-5 plus additional graduate study or experience in professional accounting. Applicants qualifying based on education or a CPA certificate do not take an exam. Salaries start in the GS-5 to GS-7 range.

Accountant and Auditor

Accountants and auditors collect and evaluate data, maintain and examine records, plan new accounting systems and revise old ones, prepare statements, examine transactions to determine accuracy and legality, and analyze financial reports. These positions require a high degree of professional accounting experience and/or education. Salaries range from the GS-9 grade through the GS-15 grade at entrance.

Revenue Officer

Revenue officers collect delinquent taxes and secure delinquent tax returns. They investigate and analyze business situations, negotiate agreements to satisfy tax obligations, enforce tax law, and perform related work. Preferably, applicants should have taken college courses in subjects such as accounting, business administration, business economics, finance, and law. Starting salaries range from the GS-5 to the GS-7 levels.

Tax Technician

Tax technicians represent the IRS in consulting with taxpayers to identify and explain tax issues and to determine the correct tax liability. An exam may be used to fill tax technician positions. Preferably, applicants should have studied accounting, business administration, business economics, finance, or law in college. Starting salaries range from the GS-5 to GS-7 levels.

Statistician

Statisticians provide professional consultation requiring the application of statistical theory and techniques in a variety of fields, including social, natural, and physical sciences and administration. Applicants must have a bachelor's degree in mathematics and statistics. They must also have had from two to three years professional experience. No written test is given. Salaries range from grades GS-9 through GS-15.

Economist

Economists research economic phenomena, interpret economic data, prepare reports on economic facts and activities, investigate and evaluate reports for their economic implications, and consult with government policymakers. Applicants are rated on the amount and quality of their experience, education, and training. Salaries start at grade GS-9 and range from GS-11 through GS-15.

Management Analyst

The management analyst's work includes evaluating administrative systems and facilities for the management and control of government operations and developing new or improved procedures, systems, and organization structures. Applicants must have had several years of experience or graduate study (depending on the grade applied for) in such fields as tabulation and machine accounting, forms control, records management, or budgetary preparation and presentation. They must also pass a written exam. Salaries start at grades GS-9 to GS-12.

Budget Examiner

Budget examiners survey government programs, review budgets, and present budgets to the proper authorities. They are often responsible for the development and operation of systems for reporting work performed and funds expended. Requirements and salary levels for this position are similar to those for the management analyst.

Teaching and Library Positions

Although teaching is primarily a function of state and local government, the federal government employs teachers and educators for a number of services. With the new emphasis on vocational guidance, opportunities for qualified teachers in the federal service have increased. Pay rates compare favorably with those of larger cities.

Among the agencies that employ teachers and educators are the BIA, the VA, the Department of Agriculture, and the Department of Education. The BIA alone employs more than 1,200 teachers. In the VA, there is informal class teaching and individual instruction, and teachers assist in arranging correspondence courses. A number of teaching positions are also available abroad. The Department of Health uses highly trained education experts to work with colleges, universities, and state educational systems in setting up educational programs. Among the other teaching jobs in the federal service are educational research, in-service training work in all agencies, and playground and recreation directing.

A

Almost every federal agency has a librarian who takes care of the agency's reading and reference materials. Agencies that service the public with such information, such as the Departments of Agriculture and Commerce, use many libraries. In Washington, librarians assist federal employees by giving them reference materials and by doing research for them. Branches of the VA have libraries that offer limited opportunities for trained librarians.

The largest number of librarians is employed in the Library of Congress. The jobs there are diverse and complex—locating books and documents, looking for facts for Congress members, working on major research projects, and writing reports that sometimes influence national policies. Employees of the Library of Congress are not under the civil service. Applicants should write directly to the Director of the Library in Washington, D.C.

The following are some of the teaching and library posts available in the federal service.

Bureau of Indian Affairs

The Bureau of Indian Affairs (BIA) is responsible for the education of Native American children who are not educated by public schools in states where they live and for a program of adult education that can bridge the gap between life on the reservation and mainstream, contemporary America. The BIA operates 254 schools, serving more than 50,000 students. Adult education aids more than 31,000 Native Americans in 303 communities. Arizona, New Mexico, Alaska, North Dakota, and South Dakota have the largest concentration of Native American schools, although some educators are needed each year in California, Oklahoma, Oregon, Utah, Kansas, Florida, Mississippi, Montana, North Carolina, and Louisiana. Classroom teachers and guidance counselors are especially needed.

Most BIA schools are located in isolated, rural places more than 30 miles from the nearest city. The work involved in combating physical isolation, as well as physical and emotional poverty, demands dedication, imagination, and strength—but it can be very rewarding.

Agency for International Development

The Agency for International Development (AID) administers America's foreign aid program in the developing countries of Asia, Africa, and Latin America. Since the progress of a developing country hinges on the ability of its people to learn the skills by which they can support and govern themselves, education plays an important part in that program. AID educators work with local officials on projects ranging from selecting textbooks to setting up educational television. They also help plan educational programs that meet the needs for particular areas and train people of that area to run the programs themselves.

AID hires advisers in the fields of elementary education, higher education, human resources development, teacher education, trade-industrial education, and vocational education. Classroom teaching alone does not provide the experience needed, and positions usually require advanced degrees and several years of administrative and program responsibility.

For jobs with AID, write to:

Chief, Talent Search
Office of Personnel and Manpower
Agency for International Development
Washington, D.C. 20523

Department of Defense

Did you know that the ninth-largest American school system lies entirely outside the continental United States? Schools in 27 foreign countries are set up by the Department of Defense (DOD) to provide education for children of overseas military and civilian personnel. More than 167,000 dependents attend 292 such schools around the world. The largest single group of educators—7,100 of them—works for the government in this system. Jobs in the DOD schools correspond to those in any large American school system, including positions such as administrators, counselors, classroom teachers, teachers of the physically and mentally challenged, teachers of special subjects, and librarians. Teaching experience is required.

Working with the DOD school system offers the chance to live and travel in a foreign country while pursuing a career. For jobs with DOD Overseas Dependents Schools, contact your local U.S. Employment Service office.

Federal Correctional Institutions

Far from the hardened master-criminal stereotype, the average inmate in a federal prison is under 30 years old, has a fifth-grade education, and is serving time for auto theft. Educational programs within the system are aimed at helping inmates succeed at a second chance at useful citizenship. Academic programs range from remedial reading for functional illiterates to instruction at the high-school level. Vocational training is aimed at providing marketable skills, including work as dental technicians, computer training, welding, masonry, small engine repair, and auto repair. The Bureau of Prisons also employs educators in the fields of library work, arts and crafts, recreation, guidance, supervisory and administrative work, occupational therapy, and research and development.

Department of Education

The Office of Education (OE) links federal education programs with state and local agencies, colleges and universities, international education organizations, and professional associations. Its role has many facets, ranging from school desegregation under the Civil Rights Act to administering funds for library construction, from researching education for physically and/or mentally challenged children to compiling statistics, from consulting services to adult and vocational education programs.

While OE is involved in so many phases of education, it has virtually no opportunities for classroom teachers as such. The need is for experienced professionals, including college and university presidents and deans, department heads, administrators, research scholars, staff assistants, vocational and technical specialists, counseling and testing experts, and curriculum specialists. If you meet these qualifications, you will find the broad scale of OE programs interesting and stimulating.

> **Note**
> Each year, OE hires young people with bachelor's and master's degrees who are not educators as such. As a recent college graduate, you can put your general education background to work in an administrative capacity in many of the programs at OE.

Public Health Education

The public health educator specializes in getting health facts accepted and used. The work represents a rare blend of specific training and the ingenuity needed to communicate and work with a wide variety of groups of people. For those few who meet the professional standards, it is a challenging, relatively new field for educators in government.

Education Research and Program Specialist

These specialists may perform any of the following duties: appraising educational practices here and abroad; planning, conducting, and evaluating surveys and research; publishing educational articles and bulletins; consulting with local, state, national, or international bodies; and planning and administering grants in aid. Fields of specialization include elementary, vocational, school administration, guidance, and international education.

Applicants must have a college degree in education and extensive experience in administration, research, or other activities in the field of education. For jobs at the GS-14 and higher grades, the applicant must have made significant contributions to education and earned outstanding recognition in his or her field. No written exam is required; rather, candidates are judged on background and experience. Salaries range from grades GS-9 to GS-15.

Librarian

The work of librarians involves acquisitions, cataloging, and classification, reference, and bibliography in federal libraries. As many of the libraries are highly specialized, the work often lies in one field. At the higher levels, librarians may assume complete charge of a large library, organize and direct the activities of a division in a large library, or serve as consulting specialists to research personnel.

Depending upon the grade of the position, applicants must have a bachelor's degree with significant study in library science, a higher degree in library science, and/or equivalent experience. Some applicants are required to take a written test. Salaries range from grades GS-5 through GS-15.

Library Assistant

The duties of the library assistant include stack maintenance, book and bindery preparation, circulation work, making additions to serial, shelf-list, and catalog records, arranging interlibrary loans, compiling lists of books, answering reference questions, checking in and routing periodicals, and comparable work. GS-5 positions involve supervising library assistants in lower grades.

Depending on the grade applied for, from one to three years experience and/or undergraduate study is required. Two thirds of this experience must have been specialized. A written exam consisting of alphabetizing, arithmetic, and verbal ability questions is given. Competitors for grade GS-5 positions are also required to take a test of supervisory judgment. Salaries start at grades GS-3 to GS-5.

Archives Assistant

Archives assistants work in receiving, sorting, filing, classifying, and indexing noncurrent records and documents, searching for, charging out, and providing information as requested, and packing, sorting, and preserving noncurrent records. At the GS-5 level, many positions involve supervisory duties. Depending on the grade applied for, from one to three years of experience and/or undergraduate study in history, government, political science, sociology, economics, or public administration is required. The basis of rating and salary range is similar to that for library assistants.

Social Work Positions

In recent times, a new grouping of government activities built around certain basic needs of the people (i.e., social security, elderly and unemployment insurance, and various welfare projects) has become prevalent. The federal government takes a hand in the dissemination of nutrition and health education, publishes cookbooks, and advises on the proper care of babies. It grants aid to states for dealing with people suffering from emotional and psychological problems, and to some extent aids these people directly. Much of this work is performed by trained social workers. This section examines the duties and qualifications required for one of these positions.

Social Worker—Corrections

Social workers work in correctional institutions to develop personal histories of new inmates, prepare progress reports on their adjustment both within the institution and in the outside environment, explain rules, policies, and decisions to prisoners, plan with them regarding parole and release, and advise them about personal and family problems. They make recommendations to prison administration regarding prisoners' special needs and requests, and they are responsible for the detention of prisoners assigned to them. Social workers at grade GS-7 work as trainees, while those at grade GS-9 work with a large degree of independence.

Applicants for GS-7 positions must have had five years of experience in social casework, including one year of correctional work or an equivalent bachelor's degree. Applicants with a master's degree in social work are eligible for GS-9 positions. No written test is required. Applicants are rated on the extent and quality of their experience. Salaries range from grades GS-7 to GS-9.

Science and Engineering Positions

Scientific research and development is carried out in 25 federal departments and agencies, principally in the laboratories of the Departments of the Army, Navy, and Air Force; National Aeronautics and Space Administration (NASA); Department of Agriculture; National Bureau of Standards; Department of the Interior; Federal Aviation Agency (FAA); NIH; and VA. Recently, employment conditions in the federal service for scientists have radically improved. Now there are more than 71,000 employees in science and 116,000 in engineering, constituting 11.5 percent of the white-collar workforce.

Within the framework of government-wide personnel laws and policies, agency and laboratory directors maintain a creative environment by providing privileges and recognition for their scientific personnel, such as the following: encouraging staff members to attend meetings of professional societies and to publish in professional journals, giving them credit lines on official publications of the laboratory, giving them the freedom to teach and serve as consultants on the outside and to write books, maintaining a liberal patent policy, providing reasonable flexibility of working hours, establishing meaningful professional titles, and encouraging coworkers of different grades to consider themselves colleagues, not bosses and subordinates.

The scientific and engineering jobs listed in this section are only a small portion of those that exist.

Chemists

For GS-5 positions, a bachelor's degree in chemistry or experience in the field of chemical engineering is required. For grades GS-5 through GS-12, no written test is required. Applicants' qualifications are rated by subject specialists and determined by evaluation of experience, education, and training. Salaries range from grades GS-5 to GS-15, depending on experience.

Physicists

Physicists work in one or more of the branches of physical science, conducting or assisting in technical projects and applying scientific knowledge to the solution of problems. For GS-5 positions, a bachelor's degree with a concentration in physics is required. For grades GS-7 through GS-15, applicants must meet additional experience requirements. Applicants' qualifications are judged from a review of their experience, education, and training. Salaries start at grades GS-5 through GS-15.

Engineers

Engineering fields include agricultural, civil, electrical, electronic, mining, and others. All applicants must have a bachelor's degree in engineering or an equivalent combination of engineering education and experience. They must also have passed the Engineer-in-Training Examination, participated in certain specialized courses, or have demonstrable professional stature. Superior academic achievement, creative research or development, or extensive graduate work may qualify applicants for higher positions. All applicants are rated on experience, education, and training. Starting salaries range from grades GS-5 to GS-15.

Engineering Drafters

Engineering drafters use calculations and drafting instruments to make working drawings, assemblies, and layouts of various types of equipment. For all grades, applicants must meet specific experience and/or education requirements. Experience may be in working as a cartographic, engineering, or statistical drafter, or experience in skilled and mechanical trades and related scientific and engineering technician occupations. Competitors for GS-2 and GS-3 positions are rated on a written test. Competitors for GS-4, GS-5, and GS-7 positions are rated on the extent and quality of their education, experience, and training relevant to the position. The rating is based on the application and sample engineering drafting work.

Engineering Aid—Highway

Engineering aides assist with highway location surveys, highway construction, and minor inspection of highway or bridge construction. Applicants must have had one-and-a-half years total experience or equivalent education in engineering, drafting, mathematics and/ or the physical sciences. Competitors are rated on the extent and quality of their education, experience, and training. Salaries start at the GS-3 level.

Geologists

Typical duties of geologists involve geological mapping, making and recording field observations, collecting samples for laboratory analysis, identifying and studying samples, compiling and interpreting data, making special studies, and preparing professional scientific and economic reports for publication. Applicants must have a bachelor's degree with a concentration in geology and related sciences or an equivalent combination of education and professional experience. A graduate degree, superior academic achievement, professional work experience combined with this education, or creative investigation or research contributions may qualify the applicant for higher grades. No written test is required. All ratings are based on an evaluation of experience, education, and training. Salaries range from GS-9 to GS-15.

Metallurgists

For GS-5 positions, a four-year college course including metallurgy study is required. For GS-7 positions, additional professional experience or graduate study is required. Applicants are rated based on an evaluation of their education and experience. Salaries start at grades GS-5 and GS-7.

Research Psychologists

The types of work covered under this heading include experimental and physiological psychology, personnel measurement and evaluation, social psychology, and engineering psychology. Depending on the grade applied for, applicants must have had professional experience and/or graduate study. No written exam is required. Applicants are rated on an evaluation of their personal and professional qualifications. Starting salaries range from grades GS-9 to GS-15.

Forestry, Agriculture, and Conservation Positions

A

Two departments of the government—Agriculture and Interior—employ experts on soil, forestry, and water resources. Although the work they do is often difficult and sometimes dangerous, those who hold these positions express a real love for the tasks they perform. The pay is not always high, but it has been increasing. As the nation learns how vital it is to conserve and improve its natural resources, these jobs should grow in importance. Occupational experts believe that jobs in forestry, agriculture, and conservation are "good bets" in coming years.

The tasks performed by government workers in agriculture, horticulture, soil science, conservation, and farming include the following: development of agriculture techniques and products, inspecting farm products, care of trees, experimental landscape gardening, soil research, testing fruits, vegetables, trees, and shrubs, dairy sanitation and efficiency studies, determining the mineral, water, and agricultural resources of public lands, control and prevention of soil erosion, moisture conservation, research to bring about rapid reforestation, experimental farming, grazing research, care, breeding, and feeding of farm and dairy animals, research to conserve forests and to use their products, and the economics of all these subjects.

Agricultural Managers

Agricultural managers perform a broad range of functions in carrying out credit and technical assistance programs for rural communities. The work involves crop and livestock production, preparation and marketing of products, and supporting financial, management, rural housing, and community resource development activities. A bachelor's degree in farm, livestock, or ranch management; agricultural economics; agricultural education; agronomy; husbandry; agricultural engineering; general agriculture; horticulture; or other related area is required.

Agronomists

Agronomists perform research on the fundamental principles of plant, soil, and related sciences, as they apply this information to crop breeding and production, conservation, propagation and seed production, ground maintenance, and plant adaptation and varietal testing. A bachelor's degree in the basic plant sciences (botany, plant taxonomy, plant ecology, plant breeding or genetics, microbiology, or soil science) and/or in agronomic subjects (plant breeding, crop production, or soil and crop management) is required.

Forestry Specialists

These specialists work to develop, conserve, and protect natural forest resources. They also manage those resources, including timber, forage, watersheds, wildlife, and land, to meet present and future public needs. Research work involves development of new, improved, or more economic scientific instruments and the techniques necessary to perform such work. A diversified college degree in forestry is required. Supplemental professional experience may also be required for some administrative positions.

Husbandry Specialists

These specialists develop and improve methods of breeding, feeding, nutrition, and management of poultry and livestock and the quality of meat, poultry, and dairy products. A college degree in the basic biological and agricultural sciences is required, with a concentration in animal sciences.

Plant Quarantine and Pest Control Specialists

These specialists apply knowledge of the biological and plant sciences, the transportation and shipping industries, and quarantine techniques to the establishment and enforcement of plant quarantines, the government of the movement of injurious plant pests, or to the survey, detection, identification, control, or eradication of plant pests. College course work in any combination of the following is required: entomology, botany, plant pathology, nematology, horticulture, mycology, invertebrate zoology, or closely related fields.

Range Conservationists

Range conservationists take inventory of, improve, protect, and manage rangelands and related grazing lands. They also regulate grazing on public rangelands, develop cooperative relationships with range users, assist landowners with planning and applying range conservation programs, develop technical standards and specifications, conduct research on the principles underlying rangeland management, and develop new-and-improved instruments and techniques. College course work in the plant, animal, and soil sciences and natural resources management is required.

Soil Conservationists

Soil conservationists coordinate work in soil, water, and resource conservation programs to bring about sound land use and improve the quality of the environment. A bachelor's degree in soil conservation or closely related agricultural or natural resource sciences is required.

Soil Science Specialists

These specialists study soils from the standpoint of their morphology, genesis, and distribution, their interrelated physical, chemical, and biological properties and processes, their relationships to climactic, physiographic, and vegetative influence, and their adaptation to use and management in agriculture.

Wildlife Biologists

Wildlife biologists work to conserve and manage wildlife and to establish and apply the biological principles and techniques necessary for the conservation and management of wildlife.

Wildlife Refuge Managers

These specialists develop management and operation plans for bird and game refuges, see that the wildlife is properly protected, and work with individuals, organizations, and the general public on refuge and related wildlife management programs. College course work in zoology, mammalogy, ornithology, animal ecology, or wildlife management and/or botany is required.

Zoologists

Zoologists research parasitic and nonparasitic organisms affecting plants and domestic and wild animals, pathology, epidemiology, immunology, physiology, and host relationships, and biological, physical, and chemical control. A college degree in biological science, including course work in zoology and the related animal sciences, is required.

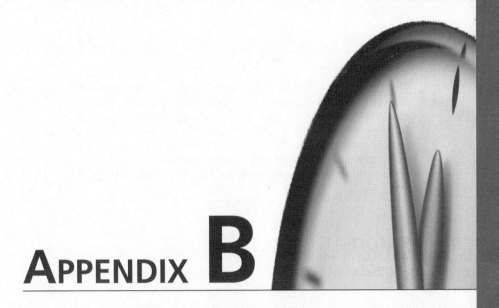

APPENDIX **B**

Selected State and Municipal Positions

Nearly all states and municipalities use trained business, technical, and professional employees in a variety of fields. College graduates who have prepared for such positions are encouraged to step directly from the classroom into state and municipal service at the bottom rung of any one of the many career ladders in its numerous departments, institutions, and agencies. This appendix describes some of these entry-level positions, which are generally filled competitively by civil service exams.

> **Note**
> Civil service law usually requires that when a vacancy higher than the entrance
> level is to be filled, the appointment must be made, if possible, by promoting
> those holding positions in a lower grade in the department, office, or institu-
> tion where the vacancy exists. This law increases opportunities for the advance-
> ment of those employees who come into civil service at the lowest rung of the
> career ladder and emphasizes the importance of the recruitment of well-
> trained, intelligent personnel in these entry-level positions.

Clerical Positions

Clerical support staff is employed through state and municipal government. Clerks
perform a variety of administrative and clerical duties necessary to run state and local
government. Often, applicants must pass a written clerical and verbal abilities test to
become eligible for these positions. For more advanced positions, a typing or stenography
test, higher education, or professional experience may also be required.

The following are some examples of clerical jobs in state and local government:

- Messengers sort and carry mail, documents, or other materials between offices or
  buildings.
- Clerks perform basic clerical duties, such as gathering and providing information,
  sorting, filing, and checking materials.
- Clerk-typists perform typing and clerical duties, such as providing information,
  composing short letters and memos, sorting, filing, and checking materials.
- Clerk-stenographers take dictation and transcribe notes. Other duties may include
  typing, providing information, composing letters and memos, sorting, and filing
  materials.
- Secretary-typists perform secretarial duties, which usually involve typing correspondence, reports, and statistical material while acting as a secretary to one or more
  employees.
- Executive secretaries perform highly responsible secretarial work as staff assistants
  to executive directors. They may also supervise a small clerical staff.
- Library assistants perform clerical work in a library, such as maintaining files and
  records, sorting and shelving books, and checking materials for accuracy.

Computer-related Positions

Computers are steadily becoming more important in all branches of the civil service, and for many functions of state and municipal governments, they are now essential. The duties of computer personnel vary with the size of the installation, the type of equipment used, and the policies of the employer. As computer usage grows in government organizations, so will the need for computer professionals and related occupations.

Computer-related positions often require related experience, vocational training, and/or a college degree in computer science, in addition to passing the civil service exam. Applicants for some positions may also be given a performance test, or the written test may include computer-related questions to ascertain applicants' technical knowledge.

The following are some typical computer-related jobs in state and local government:

- Data entry machine operators operate a variety of data-entry equipment, entering information from various source documents onto magnetic tape, disks, or into a computer. They may also verify information, operate auxiliary equipment, and perform editing and coding tasks.

- Computer operator trainees are trained to monitor and control the operation of data-processing equipment in conformance with programmed instructions. They may also operate peripheral equipment, such as disk and tape drives and printers.

- Computer operators monitor and control computers in compliance with instructions describing each computer application. They also operate magnetic tape and disk drives, printers, and other peripheral devices. In some installations, they may confer with programmers or system analysts on procedural matters and problems.

- Computer specialists in applied programming have highly complex technical or supervisory responsibilities involved in the development and maintenance of applications and systems for use in the operation of a large or medium-size computer installation. They conduct feasibility studies, write reports, prepare specifications for systems and programs, evaluate the work of subordinates, and perform related duties.

- Computer specialists in database administration have technical or supervisory responsibilities for the design, implementation, enhancement, and maintenance of database management systems. They have a wide range of duties that can include maintaining software, providing on-the-job training, and ensuring data security.

- Computer programmers prepare detailed instructions to adapt various operations to data processing, prepare input and output layouts and block diagrams to show the sequence of computations for the solution of problems on computers and peripheral equipment, and use programming languages to develop machine instructions for data manipulations.

B

Financial Positions

Officials in government must have updated financial information to make important decisions. Accountants and auditors prepare, analyze, and verify financial reports that furnish that kind of information. In addition, government accountants and auditors maintain and examine the records of government agencies and audit private businesses and individuals whose dealings are subject to government regulations.

These positions often require higher education in accounting, economics, finance, banking, or related subjects, as well as professional experience or a valid Certified Public Accountant (CPA) license. The written test may include questions on accounting principles and practices, reviewing financial records, interpreting financial written material, analyzing accounting systems, and related areas. Some higher-level positions are judged based on education and experience and do not require a written exam.

Law Enforcement Positions

Law enforcement in America is fragmented and specialized. There are some 40,000 separate law enforcement agencies representing municipal, county, state, and federal governments. Highly trained police officers are found in both large and small cities. Of the more than 17,000 cities in the U.S., 55 have populations exceeding a quarter of a million, and those employ about one-third of all police personnel. Of the law enforcement units at the state level, two of the best-known are the state police and the highway patrol. State police engage in a full range of law enforcement activities, including criminal investigation. Highway patrol units are concerned almost entirely with traffic control and enforcement and have limited general police authority.

Municipal Police Officers

Applicants typically must meet age and medical requirements, have a high school diploma or have served in the armed forces, and have a character suited for police work. Applicants must pass a written exam that tests for the abilities required for success as a police officer. The questions on the exam test mental abilities, such as interpreting rules and regulations, verbal reasoning, number series, table interpretation, and reading comprehension. Some positions may require unique skills, such as an Emergency Medical Technician certificate or fluency in a foreign language.

State Troopers

State troopers are often required to work on a rotating shift basis, be available for duty 24 hours a day, work on holidays, and work in inclement weather. They can be transferred anywhere in the state. Applicants must be able to use a firearm and perform strenuous tasks.

The basic requirements include U.S. citizenship, state residency, passing a background investigation, meeting age limits, possessing a high school diploma, passing a medical exam, and meeting vision and hearing standards. Conviction of a felony, an unsatisfactory driving record, or conviction of driving while under the influence of alcohol or drugs can serve as a basis for disqualification. Applicants must also pass a written test pertaining to accuracy of observation and memory and ability to read and comprehend reports, manuals, and laws. They must also pass an oral appraisal exam assessing communication skills and a physical performance test.

First-year employees are trained in the knowledge and skills required to function independently as a law enforcement officer. They must complete a basic police training curriculum of law enforcement course work and physical training. For the rest of the training period, they accompany experienced troopers on patrols to detect or prevent traffic and criminal law violations, investigate complaints, and provide a variety of related services to the public.

Correction Officers

Correction officers are charged with the safekeeping of people who have been arrested and are awaiting trial or who have been convicted of a crime and are sentenced to serve time in a correctional institution. They maintain order within the prison, enforce rules and regulations, and often supplement the counseling that inmates receive from mental-health professionals.

Entry-level correctional work is of a training nature. Trainees participate in formal courses to develop the skills and techniques for the proper supervision and custody of inmates. Training covers areas like law, sociology, psychology, counseling, firearms, and crisis prevention and intervention. Work assignments are routinely performed under senior officer supervision and include maintaining security and order, monitoring inmate movement, inspecting grounds and buildings, and searching for contraband.

Candidates must be state residents, meet age limits, and pass a written and oral test, an employment interview, a physical fitness test, a medical exam, and psychological tests. The written exam tests observation and memory, associative memory, and reading comprehension. The oral test determines job interest, poise and self-confidence, the ability to organize and express thoughts, and problem-solving abilities.

B

Firefighting Positions

Every year, fires take thousands of lives and destroy property worth billions of dollars. Firefighters help protect the public against this danger.

During duty hours, firefighters must be prepared to respond to a fire and handle any emergency that arises. Because firefighting is dangerous and complicated, it requires organization and teamwork. At every fire, firefighters perform specific duties assigned by an officer. They may connect hose lines to hydrants, operate a pump, or position ladders. Their duties may change several times while the team is in action. They may rescue victims and administer emergency medical aid, ventilate smoke-filled areas, operate equipment, and salvage the contents of buildings. Some firefighters operate fire apparatuses, ambulances, emergency rescue vehicles, and fireboats. Between alarms, they have classroom training, and they clean and maintain equipment, conduct practice drills, and participate in physical-fitness exercises.

Most fire departments are also responsible for fire prevention. They provide specially trained personnel to inspect public buildings for conditions that might cause a fire. They may check building plans, the number and working condition of fire escapes and fire doors, the storage of flammable materials, and other possible hazards. In addition, firefighters educate the public about fire prevention and safety measures. They frequently speak on the subject before school assemblies and civic groups.

Basic requirements include a high school diploma, a valid state motor vehicle driver's license, age and height limits, vision standards, and proof of good character. Applicants must take a written exam that tests ability to learn and perform the work of a firefighter. The exam may include questions on understanding job information, applying laws, rules, and regulations to job situations, recognizing appropriate behavior, understanding mechanical devices, and remembering the details of a floor layout. In addition, there is a physical test.

Investigative Positions

The range of activities performed by modern state and municipal authorities means that they have a great need for information—hence the need for investigators. Investigators have a wide variety of functions: to examine claims for benefits or compensation to ensure that they are valid and conform with regulations, to gather evidence of fraud and other wrongdoing to be used in legal actions, and to discover violations of rules and regulations.

Investigative positions often require related experience, such as police work, insurance investigation, private investigation, or federal or military investigation. Higher education may be substituted for experience. Applicants must also take a written exam that tests for knowledge, skills, and abilities in areas like reasoning, interviewing and investigative techniques, evaluating information and evidence, understanding and interpreting written material, and preparing written material. Higher-level positions may not require a written exam; rather, those applicants are judged on education and experience alone.

The following are some typical investigative positions:

- Investigators examine violations of tax-liability laws and violations of miscellaneous rules and regulations of various sate or local agencies. They may also determine applicants' qualifications for civil service employment.

- Compensation claims investigators investigate workers' compensation and disability benefits claims.

- Unemployment insurance investigators investigate fraud by claimants or employers and cases of employee misconduct, determine employee status and claimant eligibility, and investigate related employment cases. Trainees in this position receive on-the-job training while performing the duties of the job.

Legal Positions

The legal activities of many government departments require the services of attorneys of various grades. Lawyers in the office of the Attorney General handle a great deal of important state legal work. In addition to these are many legal positions, some under specialized titles, that are filled from open-competitive civil service lists. The state offers opportunities for legally trained employees to rise to highly responsible, well-paid positions.

In state and municipal government, legal assistants, under the direction of staff attorneys, are responsible for compiling and organizing documentation, preparing legal documents and forms, logging information, and preparing correspondence and subpoenas. They respond to inquiries and complaints, track cases, ensure that deadlines are met, and maintain calendars. They also conduct research into legal matters, analyze materials, prepare and maintain files, record and monitor the status of legislation, and gather materials and summaries of legislation pertinent to the agency.

Legal assistant positions require a degree in paralegal studies or legal specialty training. Written exams for legal assistants test abilities in areas like record-keeping and preparing written material in a legal context, understanding and interpreting legal material, and conducting research into legal matters.

B

Social Welfare Positions

Those involved in the social welfare field are community troubleshooters. Through direct counseling, referral to other services, or policymaking and advocacy, they help individuals, families, and groups cope with their problems. Those in the area of planning and policy help people understand how social systems operate and propose ways to bring about needed change in institutions such as health services, housing, and education. Among the major helping professions, a tradition of concern for the poor and disadvantaged characterizes and distinguishes social work.

Often, a higher degree is required of these positions, such as a bachelor's or master's degree in social work, social sciences, health sciences, or psychology. Related professional experience also counts heavily. When working with inmates, applicants may have to pass an investigative screening, be trained in using firearms, and meet physical and medical standards. Written exams, when given, test for understanding of social issues, effective interviewing skills, development and maintenance of client records, characteristics, behavior, and problems of human behavior and the disabled, methods of investigating child abuse, understanding laws and regulations, preparing written material, and the principles and practices of social casework.

Health-related Positions

With the continuing growth of social services, state and local governments increasingly need physicians, medical researchers, nurses, and similar workers. The growth of psychiatric concepts, the development of occupational therapy, and the increasing demands that an aging population will place on society in general and the health-care industry in particular—all of these factors demand a force of health-care practitioners working for the government at the state and local levels, as well as at the federal level.

Nurses, physician's assistants, physical therapists, occupational therapists, pharmacists, and dental hygienists in the employ of the government must have a current license to practice. Additional experience or a higher degree may be required for some positions. For many positions, no written exam is given; instead, candidates are judged on experience and training. For lower-level positions, the written exam may test abilities to read medical charts, complete forms, write reports, record data, work with patients, know laboratory principles and practices, and to recognize basic principles of health care, biology, or chemistry.

Engineering Positions

Engineers design machines, processes, systems, and structures. They apply scientific and mathematical theories and principles to solve practical technical problems. In state and local government, most work in one of the more than twenty-five specialties recognized by professional societies. Electrical, mechanical, civil, industrial, chemical, and aerospace engineering are the largest specialties. Although many engineers work in design and development, others work in testing, production, operations, and maintenance.

Besides specialized higher education and related experience, other requirements may be mathematical skills, drawing skills, and familiarity with architectural design and drafting. For many positions, no written test is given; rather, candidates are judged on their educational backgrounds and professional experiences. Written tests, when given, generally measure mechanical knowledge and ability, as well as shop, safety, and conservation practices.

Mechanical Positions

Most mechanics acquire their skills on the job under the supervision of experienced workers. Increasingly, formal mechanic training acquired in high school, vocational or technical school, community or junior college, or in the armed forces is an asset to those entering mechanical or repair careers. Often, prior experience is required. The civil service exam tests mechanical knowledge related to the vacant position.

Custodial and Service Positions

B

This section lists some examples of the wide range of custodial and service occupations available in state and local government. Many of these positions require no formal education, qualification, or experience, but a written exam testing the ability to understand instructions, arithmetic ability, and mechanical knowledge is given. Physical exams may be required for some positions.

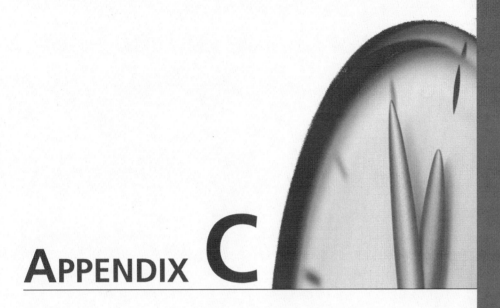

APPENDIX C

Senior Office Typist Sample Exam

This appendix gives you one more sample exam with which to practice. This exam is quite a bit longer than the ones you took previously. It should take you three hours to complete. It is based on the civil service exams given by the court system for clerical positions, and so it will give you the opportunity to practice with different kinds of questions. At the end of this appendix are the answer explanations and evaluation information for the sample exam.

Answer Sheet

Tear out this answer sheet and use it to mark your answers to the sample test that follows. Use a pencil to record your answers, just as you will do on the actual test.

1. Ⓐ Ⓑ Ⓒ Ⓓ Ⓔ	26. Ⓐ Ⓑ Ⓒ Ⓓ Ⓔ	51. Ⓐ Ⓑ Ⓒ Ⓓ Ⓔ	76. Ⓐ Ⓑ Ⓒ Ⓓ Ⓔ
2. Ⓐ Ⓑ Ⓒ Ⓓ Ⓔ	27. Ⓐ Ⓑ Ⓒ Ⓓ Ⓔ	52. Ⓐ Ⓑ Ⓒ Ⓓ Ⓔ	77. Ⓐ Ⓑ Ⓒ Ⓓ Ⓔ
3. Ⓐ Ⓑ Ⓒ Ⓓ Ⓔ	28. Ⓐ Ⓑ Ⓒ Ⓓ Ⓔ	53. Ⓐ Ⓑ Ⓒ Ⓓ Ⓔ	78. Ⓐ Ⓑ Ⓒ Ⓓ Ⓔ
4. Ⓐ Ⓑ Ⓒ Ⓓ Ⓔ	29. Ⓐ Ⓑ Ⓒ Ⓓ Ⓔ	54. Ⓐ Ⓑ Ⓒ Ⓓ Ⓔ	79. Ⓐ Ⓑ Ⓒ Ⓓ Ⓔ
5. Ⓐ Ⓑ Ⓒ Ⓓ Ⓔ	30. Ⓐ Ⓑ Ⓒ Ⓓ Ⓔ	55. Ⓐ Ⓑ Ⓒ Ⓓ Ⓔ	80. Ⓐ Ⓑ Ⓒ Ⓓ Ⓔ
6. Ⓐ Ⓑ Ⓒ Ⓓ Ⓔ	31. Ⓐ Ⓑ Ⓒ Ⓓ Ⓔ	56. Ⓐ Ⓑ Ⓒ Ⓓ Ⓔ	81. Ⓐ Ⓑ Ⓒ Ⓓ Ⓔ
7. Ⓐ Ⓑ Ⓒ Ⓓ Ⓔ	32. Ⓐ Ⓑ Ⓒ Ⓓ Ⓔ	57. Ⓐ Ⓑ Ⓒ Ⓓ Ⓔ	82. Ⓐ Ⓑ Ⓒ Ⓓ Ⓔ
8. Ⓐ Ⓑ Ⓒ Ⓓ Ⓔ	33. Ⓐ Ⓑ Ⓒ Ⓓ Ⓔ	58. Ⓐ Ⓑ Ⓒ Ⓓ Ⓔ	83. Ⓐ Ⓑ Ⓒ Ⓓ Ⓔ
9. Ⓐ Ⓑ Ⓒ Ⓓ Ⓔ	34. Ⓐ Ⓑ Ⓒ Ⓓ Ⓔ	59. Ⓐ Ⓑ Ⓒ Ⓓ Ⓔ	84. Ⓐ Ⓑ Ⓒ Ⓓ Ⓔ
10. Ⓐ Ⓑ Ⓒ Ⓓ Ⓔ	35. Ⓐ Ⓑ Ⓒ Ⓓ Ⓔ	60. Ⓐ Ⓑ Ⓒ Ⓓ Ⓔ	85. Ⓐ Ⓑ Ⓒ Ⓓ Ⓔ
11. Ⓐ Ⓑ Ⓒ Ⓓ Ⓔ	36. Ⓐ Ⓑ Ⓒ Ⓓ Ⓔ	61. Ⓐ Ⓑ Ⓒ Ⓓ Ⓔ	86. Ⓐ Ⓑ Ⓒ Ⓓ Ⓔ
12. Ⓐ Ⓑ Ⓒ Ⓓ Ⓔ	37. Ⓐ Ⓑ Ⓒ Ⓓ Ⓔ	62. Ⓐ Ⓑ Ⓒ Ⓓ Ⓔ	87. Ⓐ Ⓑ Ⓒ Ⓓ Ⓔ
13. Ⓐ Ⓑ Ⓒ Ⓓ Ⓔ	38. Ⓐ Ⓑ Ⓒ Ⓓ Ⓔ	63. Ⓐ Ⓑ Ⓒ Ⓓ Ⓔ	88. Ⓐ Ⓑ Ⓒ Ⓓ Ⓔ
14. Ⓐ Ⓑ Ⓒ Ⓓ Ⓔ	39. Ⓐ Ⓑ Ⓒ Ⓓ Ⓔ	64. Ⓐ Ⓑ Ⓒ Ⓓ Ⓔ	89. Ⓐ Ⓑ Ⓒ Ⓓ Ⓔ
15. Ⓐ Ⓑ Ⓒ Ⓓ Ⓔ	40. Ⓐ Ⓑ Ⓒ Ⓓ Ⓔ	65. Ⓐ Ⓑ Ⓒ Ⓓ Ⓔ	90. Ⓐ Ⓑ Ⓒ Ⓓ Ⓔ
16. Ⓐ Ⓑ Ⓒ Ⓓ Ⓔ	41. Ⓐ Ⓑ Ⓒ Ⓓ Ⓔ	66. Ⓐ Ⓑ Ⓒ Ⓓ Ⓔ	91. Ⓐ Ⓑ Ⓒ Ⓓ Ⓔ
17. Ⓐ Ⓑ Ⓒ Ⓓ Ⓔ	42. Ⓐ Ⓑ Ⓒ Ⓓ Ⓔ	67. Ⓐ Ⓑ Ⓒ Ⓓ Ⓔ	92. Ⓐ Ⓑ Ⓒ Ⓓ Ⓔ
18. Ⓐ Ⓑ Ⓒ Ⓓ Ⓔ	43. Ⓐ Ⓑ Ⓒ Ⓓ Ⓔ	68. Ⓐ Ⓑ Ⓒ Ⓓ Ⓔ	93. Ⓐ Ⓑ Ⓒ Ⓓ Ⓔ
19. Ⓐ Ⓑ Ⓒ Ⓓ Ⓔ	44. Ⓐ Ⓑ Ⓒ Ⓓ Ⓔ	69. Ⓐ Ⓑ Ⓒ Ⓓ Ⓔ	94. Ⓐ Ⓑ Ⓒ Ⓓ Ⓔ
20. Ⓐ Ⓑ Ⓒ Ⓓ Ⓔ	45. Ⓐ Ⓑ Ⓒ Ⓓ Ⓔ	70. Ⓐ Ⓑ Ⓒ Ⓓ Ⓔ	95. Ⓐ Ⓑ Ⓒ Ⓓ Ⓔ
21. Ⓐ Ⓑ Ⓒ Ⓓ Ⓔ	46. Ⓐ Ⓑ Ⓒ Ⓓ Ⓔ	71. Ⓐ Ⓑ Ⓒ Ⓓ Ⓔ	
22. Ⓐ Ⓑ Ⓒ Ⓓ Ⓔ	47. Ⓐ Ⓑ Ⓒ Ⓓ Ⓔ	72. Ⓐ Ⓑ Ⓒ Ⓓ Ⓔ	
23. Ⓐ Ⓑ Ⓒ Ⓓ Ⓔ	48. Ⓐ Ⓑ Ⓒ Ⓓ Ⓔ	73. Ⓐ Ⓑ Ⓒ Ⓓ Ⓔ	
24. Ⓐ Ⓑ Ⓒ Ⓓ Ⓔ	49. Ⓐ Ⓑ Ⓒ Ⓓ Ⓔ	74. Ⓐ Ⓑ Ⓒ Ⓓ Ⓔ	
25. Ⓐ Ⓑ Ⓒ Ⓓ Ⓔ	50. Ⓐ Ⓑ Ⓒ Ⓓ Ⓔ	75. Ⓐ Ⓑ Ⓒ Ⓓ Ⓔ	

C

Senior Office Typist Exam

95 Questions

DIRECTIONS: Select the best answer from the choices given and mark its letter on your answer sheet. The exam is divided into several sections, but they are timed together. You will have 3 hours to complete the exam.

Spelling

DIRECTIONS: For Questions 1–10, choose the word that is correctly spelled.

1. (A) apellate
    (B) appelate
    (C) appeallate
    (D) appellate

2. (A) presumption
    (B) presoumption
    (C) presumsion
    (D) presumptsion

3. (A) litigiant
    (B) litigent
    (C) litigant
    (D) litigint

4. (A) committment
    (B) commitment
    (C) comittment
    (D) comitment

5. (A) affidavid
    (B) afidavis
    (C) affidavit
    (D) afidavit

6. (A) arraign
    (B) arrain
    (C) arreign
    (D) areign

7. (A) cumalative
    (B) cummuletive
    (C) cummalative
    (D) cumulative

8. (A) sevarance
    (B) severance
    (C) severence
    (D) severants

9. (A) adjurnment
    (B) adjuornment
    (C) ajournment
    (D) adjournment

10. (A) comenced
    (B) commentced
    (C) commenced
    (D) commensced

11. (A) Punishment must be a planned part of a comprehensive program of treating delinquency.
    (B) It is easier to spot inexperienced check forjers than other criminals.
    (C) Even young vandals and hooligans can be reformed if given adequate attention.
    (D) No error.

12. (A) The court officer does not have the authority to make exceptions.
    (B) Usually the violations are the result of illegal and dangerous driving behavior.
    (C) The safety division is required to investigate if the dispatcher files a complaint.
    (D) No error.

13. (A) Comic books that glorify the criminal have a distinct influence in producing young criminals.
    (B) Some of the people behind bars are innocent people who have been put there by mistake.
    (C) Educational achievment is closely associated with delinquency.
    (D) No error.

14. (A) Disciplinary action is most effective when it is taken promptly.
    (B) Release on "personal recognizance" refers to release without bail.
    (C) Parole violators forfeit their freedom.
    (D) No error.

15. (A) Some responsibilities take precedence over preservation of evidence.
    (B) Objects should not be touched unless there is some compelling reason.
    (C) The detension system works unfairly against people who are single and un employed.
    (D) No error.

16. (A) Evidence is inmaterial if it does not prove the truth of a fact at issue.
    (B) Without qualms, the offender will lie and manipulate others.
    (C) If spectators become disorderly, the court officer may threaten to cite them for contempt of court.
    (D) No error.

17. (A) Under certain conditions, circumstantial evidence may be admissible.
    (B) Just because evidence is circumstantial does not mean that it is irrelevant.
    (C) An aggressive offender may appear to be very hostile.
    (D) No error.

18. (A) A victim of assault may want to take revenge.
    (B) The result of the trial was put in doubt when the prosecuter produced a surprise witness.
    (C) The court officer must maintain order and decorum in the courtroom.
    (D) No error.

19. (A) A person whose accident record can be explained by a <u>correctable</u> physical defect cannot be called "accident-prone."

    (B) A <u>litigant</u> should not be permitted to invoke the aid of technical rules.

    (C) Refusal to <u>waive</u> immunity automatically terminates employment.

    (D) No error.

20. (A) Court employees may be fired for <u>malfeasance</u>.

    (B) A common tactic used by defense lawyers is <u>embarrassment</u> of the witness.

    (C) The criminal justice system may be called an "<u>adversary</u> system."

    (D) No error.

Grammar

> **DIRECTIONS:** For questions 21–27, choose the sentence that is grammatically incorrect.

21. (A) One of us had to reply before tomorrow.

    (B) All employees who had served from 40 to 51 years were retired.

    (C) The personnel office takes care of employment, dismissals, and etc.

    (D) We often come across people with whom we disagree.

22. (A) The jurors have been instructed to deliver a sealed verdict.

    (B) The court may direct the convict to be imprisoned in a county penitentiary instead of a state prison.

    (C) Conveying self-confidence is displaying assurance.

    (D) He devotes as much, if not more, time to his work than the rest of the employees.

23. (A) In comparison with that kind of pen, this kind is more preferable.

    (B) The jurors may go to dinner only with the permission of the judge.

    (C) There was neither any intention to commit a crime nor any injury incurred.

    (D) It is the sociological view that all weight should be given to the history and development of the individual.

24. (A) The supervisor makes the suggestions for improvement, not the employee.

    (B) Violations of traffic laws and illegal and dangerous driving behavior constitutes bad driving.

    (C) Cynics take the position that the criminal is rarely or never reformed.

    (D) The ultimate solution to the housing problem of the hardcore slum does not lie in code enforcement.

C

25. (A) No crime can occur unless there is a written law forbidding the act or omission in question.

    (B) If one wants to prevent crime, we must deal with the possible criminals before they reach the prison.

    (C) One could reasonably say that the same type of correctional institution is not desirable for the custody of all prisoners.

    (D) When you have completed the report, you may give it to me or directly to the judge.

26. (A) The structure of an organization should be considered in determining the organization's goals.

    (B) Complaints are welcomed because they frequently bring into the open conditions and faults in service that should be corrected.

    (C) The defendant had a very unique alibi, so the judge dismissed the case.

    (D) Court officers must direct witnesses to seats when the latter present themselves in court to testify.

27. (A) The clerk promptly notified the judge of the fire for which he was highly praised.

    (B) There is justice among thieves; the three thieves divided the goods equally among themselves.

    (C) If he had been notified promptly, he might have been here on time.

    (D) Though doubt may exist about the mailability of some matter, the sender is fully liable for law violation if such matter should be non-mailable.

DIRECTIONS: For questions 28–34, choose the sentence that is grammatically correct.

---

28. (A) In high-visibility crimes, it is apparent to all concerned that they are criminal acts at the time when they are committed.

    (B) Statistics tell us that more people are killed by guns than by any kind of weapon.

    (C) Reliable persons guarantee the facts with regards to the truth of these statements.

    (D) The errors in the typed report were so numerous that they could hardly be overlooked.

29. (A) She suspects that the service is not so satisfactory as it should be.

    (B) The court officer goes to the exhibit table and discovered that Exhibit B is an entirely different document.

    (C) The jurors and alternates comprise a truly diverse group.

    (D) Our aim should be not merely to reform lawbreakers but striking at the roots of crime.

30. (A) Close examination of traffic accident statistics reveal that traffic accidents are frequently the result of violations of traffic laws.

(B) If you had planned on employing fewer people than this to do the work, this situation would not have arose.

(C) As far as good looks and polite manners are concerned, they are both alike.

(D) If a murder has been committed with a bow and arrow, it is irrelevant to show that the defendant was well acquainted with firearms.

31. (A) An individual engages in criminal behavior if the number of criminal patterns which he or she has acquired exceeds the number of non-criminal patterns.

(B) Every person must be informed of the reason for their arrest unless arrested in the actual commission of a crime.

(C) The one of the following motorists to which it would be most desirable to issue a summons is the one which was late for an important business appointment.

(D) The officer should glance around quickly but with care to determine whether his entering the area will damage any evidence.

32. (A) The typist would of corrected the errors had she realized that the supervisor would see the report.

(B) If the budget allows, we are likely to reemploy anyone whose training fits them to do the work.

(C) Since the report lacked the needed information, it was of no value to me.

(D) There would have been no trouble if the receptionist would have always answered courteously.

33. (A) Due to the age of the defendant, the trial will be heard in Juvenile Court and the record will be sealed.

(B) Calculate the average amount stolen per incident by dividing the total value by the amount of offenses.

(C) The combination to the office safe is known only to the chief clerk and myself.

(D) Hearsay is evidence based on repeating the words told by another but is not based on personal observation or knowledge.

34. (A) A court officer needs specific qualifications that are different than those required of police officers.

(B) Understanding how one's own work contributes to the effort of the entire agency indicates an appreciation for the importance of that job.

(C) If only one guard was assigned to the jury room, the chances of wrongdoing would be heightened.

(D) One should not use an improved method for performing a task until you have obtained approval of the supervisor.

Clerical Checking

> **DIRECTIONS:** For questions 35–50, compare the name/address/number listings in all three columns. Then mark your answers as follows:
> - (A) if the listings in ALL THREE columns are exactly ALIKE.
> - (B) if only the listings in the FIRST and THIRD columns are exactly ALIKE.
> - (C) if only the listings in the FIRST and SECOND columns are exactly ALIKE.
> - (D) if the listings in ALL THREE columns are DIFFERENT.

35.

John H. Smith	John H. Smith	John H. Smith
238 N. Monroe Street	238 N. Monroe Street	238 N. Monroe Street
Phila., PA 19147	Phila, PA 19147	Phila., PA 19147
176-54-326	176-54-326	176-54-326
5578-98765-33	5578-98765-33	5578-98765-33

36.

Evan A. McKinley	Evan A. McKinley	Evan A. McKinley
2872 Broadway	2872 Broadway	2872 Broadway
East Amherst, NY 14051	East Amherst, NY 14051	East Amherst, NV 14051
212-883-5184	212-883-5184	212-883-5184
9803-115-6848	9083-115-6848	9803-115-6848

37.

Luigi Antonio Cruz, Jr.	Luigi Antonio Cruz, Jr.	Luigi Antonio Cruz, Jr.
2695 East 3435 South	2695 East 3435 South	2695 East 3435 South
Salt Lake City, UT 84109	Salt Lake City, UT 84109	Salt Lake City, UT 84109
801-485-1563, x.233	801-485-1563, x.233	801-485-1563, x.233
013-5589734-9	013-5589734-9	013-5589734-9

38.

Educational Records Inst.	Educational Records Inst.	Educational Records Inst.
P.O. Box 44268a	P.O. Box 44268a	P.O. Box 44286a
Atlanta, Georgia 30337	Atlanta, Georgia 30337	Atlanta, Georgia 30337
18624-40-9128	18624-40-9128	18624-40-9128
63qs5-95YT3-001	63qs5-95YT3-001	63qs5-95YT3-001

39.

Sr. Consultant, Labor Rel.	Sr. Consultant, Labor Rel.	Sr. Consultant, Labor Rel.
Benner Mgmt. Group	Banner Mgmt. Group	Benner Mgmt. Group
86408 W. 3rd Ave.	86408 W. 3rd Ave.	84608 W. 3rd Ave.
Trowbridge, MA 02178	Trowbridge, MA 02178	Trowbridge, MA 02178
617-980-1136	617-980-1136	617-980-1136

40.

Marina Angelika Salvis	Marina Angelika Salvis	Marina Angelika Salvis
P.O.B. 11283 Gracie Sta.	P.O.B. 11283 Gracie Sta.	P.O.B. 11283 Gracie Sta.
Newtown, PA 18940-0998	Newtown, PA 18940-0998	Newtown, PA 18940-0998
215-382-0628	215-382-0628	215-382-0628
4168-GNP-78852	4168-GNP-78852	4168-GNP-78852

41. Durham Reichard, III   Durham Reichard, III   Durham Reichard, III
     8298 Antigua Terrace   8298 Antigua Terrace   8298 Antigua Terrace
     Gaithersburg, MD 20879   Gaithersburg, MD 20879   Gaithersberg, MD 20879
     301-176-9887-8   301-176-9887-8   301-176-9887-8
     0-671-843576-X   0-671-843576-X   0-671-843576-X

42. L. Chamberlain Smythe   L. Chamberlain Smythe   L. Chamberlain Smythe
     Mardikian & Moore, Inc.   Mardikian and Moore, Inc.   Markdikian & Moore, Inc.
     Cor. Mott Street at Pell   Cor. Mott Street at Pell   Cor. Mott Street at Pell
     San Francisco, Calif.   San Francisco, Calif.   San Francisco, Calif.
     58312-398401-25   58312-398401-25   58312-398401-25

43. Ramona Fleischer-Chris   Ramona Fleisher-Chris   Ramona Fleischer-Chris
     60646 West Touhy Avenue   60646 West Touhy Avenue   60646 West Touhey Avenue
     Sebastopol, CA 95472   Sebastopol, CA 95472   Sepabstopol, CA 95472
     707-998-0104   707-998-0104   707-998-0104
     0-06-408632-0   0-06-408632-0   0-06-408632-0

44. George Sebastian Barnes   George Sebastian Barnes   George Sebastian Barnes
     Noble/Encore/Dalton   Noble/Encore/Dalton   Noble/Encore/Dalton
     43216 M Street, NE   43216 M. Street, NE   43216 M Street, NE
     Washington, DC 20036   Washington, DC 20036   Washington, DC 20036
     202-222-1272   202-222-1272   202-222-1272

45. Baldwin Algonquin, III   Baldwin Algonquin, III   Baldwin Algonquin, III
     2503 Bartholemew Way   2503 Bartholemew Way   2503 Bartholomew Way
     Lemberger, VA 28094-9182   Lemberger, VA 28094-9182   Lemberger, VA 28094-9182
     9-1-303-558-8536   9-1-303-558-8536   9-1-303-558-8536
     683-64-0828   683-64-0828   683-64-0828

46. Huang Ho Cheung   Huang Ho Cheung   Huang Ho Cheung
     612 Gallopade Gallery, E.   612 Gallopade Gallery, E.   612 Gallopade Gallery, E.
     Seattle, WA 98101-2614   Seattle, WA 98101-2614   Seattle, WA 98101-2614
     001-206-283-7722   001-206-283-7722   001-206-283-7722
     5416R-1952TZ-op   5416R-1952TZ-op   5416R-1952TZ-op

47. Hilliard H. Hyacinth   Hilliard H. Hyacinth   Hilliard H. Hyacinth
     86529 Dunwoodie Drive   86529 Dunwoodie Drive   85629 Dunwoodie Drive
     Kanakao, HI 91132   Kanakao, HI 91132   Kanakao, HI 91132
     808-880-8080   808-880-8080   808-880-8080
     6-78912-e3e42   6-78912-3e3e42   6-78912-e3e42

C

48.   Anoko Kawamoto   Anoko Kawamoto   Anoko Kawamoto
      8932 Shimabui Hwy.   8932 Shimabui Hwy.   8932 Shimabui Hwy.
      O'Reilly Bay, LA 56212   O'Reillys Bay, LA 56212   O'Reilly Bay, LA 56212
      713-864-7253-4984   713-864-7253-4984   713-864-7253-4984
      5634-Ootv5a-16867   5634-Ootv5a-16867   5634-Ootv5a-16867

49.   Michael Chrzanowski   Michael Chrzanowski   Michael Chrzanowski
      312 Colonia del Valle   312 Colonia del Valle   312 Colonia del Valle
      4132 ES, Mexico DF   4132 ES, Mexico DF   4132 ES, Mexico D.F.
      001-45-67265   001-45-67265   001-45-67265
      A8987-B73245   A8987-B73245   A8987-B73245

50.   Leonard Wilson-Wood   Leonard Wilson-Wood   Leonard Wilson-Wood
      6892 Grand Boulevard, W.   6892 Grand Boulevard, W.   6892 Grand Boulevard, W.
      St. Georges South, DE   St. Goerges South, DE   St. Georges South, DE
      302-333-4273   302-333-4273   302-333-4273
      0-122365-3987   0-122365-3987   0-122365-3987

Office Record Keeping

DIRECTIONS: Study the information given in the tables and combine the information as indicated. Answer questions 51–65 in accordance with the information on the tables. You are NOT permitted to use a calculator to arrive at totals.

DAILY LOG OF CASES

Monday

Judge	Date Filed	Sum at Issue	Disposition	Award
Baron	6/5/91	$9,500	Adjourned	X
Lee	4/2/92	$20,000	Dismissed	X
Conlon	12/8/90	$12,000	Settled	X
Ramos	3/31/92	$5,500	Settled	X
Lee	10/8/91	$10,000	Dismissed	X
Jones	1/5/92	$14,000	Found for plaintiff	$15,000
Baron	5/1/93	$7,600	Adjourned	X

Tuesday

Judge	Date Filed	Sum at Issue	Disposition	Award
Ramos	2/2/92	$3,000	Found for plaintiff	$3,375
Amati	8/6/92	$8,000	Dismissed	X
Moro	4/8/91	$11,500	Found for plaintiff	$9,000
Jones	11/17/90	$12,000	Adjourned	X
Conlon	12/4/90	$4,500	Adjourned	X
Amati	6/12/91	$2,000	Settled	$15,000

Wednesday

Judge	Date Filed	Sum at Issue	Disposition	Award
Conlon	1/7/93	$10,000	Dismissed	X
Baron	5/3/92	$5,000	Adjourned	X
Ramos	6/22/91	$7,500	Found for plaintiff	$6,000
Moro	2/15/93	$22,000	Settled	X
Lee	9/7/92	$8,000	Settled	X
Conlon	11/30/90	$16,000	Found for plaintiff	$17,250
Amati	7/10/92	$10,000	Found for plaintiff	$10,850

Thursday

Judge	Date Filed	Sum at Issue	Disposition	Award
Jones	5/18/92	$7,500	Found for plaintiff	$6,000
Amati	3/6/91	$9,250	Settled	X
Conlon	3/31/92	$6,000	Adjourned	X
Moro	8/28/91	$12,000	Adjourned	X
Conlon	10/30/90	$4,600	Found for plaintiff	$5,000

Friday

Judge	Date Filed	Sum at Issue	Disposition	Award
Lee	4/12/92	$6,000	Adjourned	X
Baron	1/28/93	$9,500	Dismissed	X
Ramos	7/17/92	$28,000	Found for plaintiff	$20,000
Amati	12/2/91	$15,000	Settled	X
Lee	2/21/92	$8,000	Found for plaintiff	$8,625
Moro	5/9/91	$22,000	Settled	X
Baron	8/25/91	$11,000	Dismissed	X
Jones	11/4/90	$5,500	Settled	X

C

DAILY BREAKDOWN OF CASES

	Mon.	Tue.	Wed.	Thurs.	Fri.	Total
Case Status						
Dismissed	2	1	1	0	2	6
Adjourned						
Settled						
Found for Plaintiff						
Total Cases						
Cases Filed by Year						
1990	1	2	1	1	1	6
1991						
1992						
1993						
Total Cases						

SUMMARY OF CASES

Judge	Dismissed	Adjourned	Settled	Found for Plaintiff	Total
Amati	1		3	1	5
Baron					
Conlon					
Jones					
Lee					
Moro					
Ramos					

51. The judge scheduled to hear the greatest number of cases in this week was

(A) Amati.

(B) Lee.

(C) Conlon.

(D) Ramos.

52. The judge who determined no cash awards in this week was

(A) Moro.

(B) Jones.

(C) Baron.

(D) Lee.

53. How many judges were assigned to hear more than one case in one day?

(A) 1

(B) 2

(C) 3

(D) 4

54. In how many cases was the sum finally awarded lower than the sum at issue?

(A) 2

(B) 3

(C) 4

(D) 5

55. How many of the cases filed in 1990 were dismissed?

(A) 0

(B) 1

(C) 2

(D) 3

56. Of the cases adjourned, the greatest number were filed in

(A) 1990.

(B) 1991.

(C) 1992.

(D) 1993.

57. Which two judges were scheduled to sit on only three days?

(A) Jones and Baron

(B) Baron and Lee

(C) Lee and Moro

(D) Ramos and Jones

58. In which month were the greatest number of cases filed?

(A) February

(B) May

(C) August

(D) November

59. The total amount of money awarded on Wednesday was

(A) $33,500

(B) $34,100

(C) $35,300

(D) $45,000

60. The total amount of money awarded by Jones was

(A) $39,000

(B) $21,500

(C) $21,000

(D) $17,500

61. The amount at issue in the cases that were adjourned on Thursday was

(A) $12,100

(B) $18,000

(C) $21,350

(D) $29,250

62. When the amount of an award is greater than the sum at issue, the higher award represents an additional sum meant to cover plaintiff's costs in the suit. The total amount awarded this week to cover costs was

(A) 4,800

(B) 9,000

(C) 3,500

(D) 17,500

63. If all the plaintiffs who filed cases in 1993 were awarded exactly the sums for which they sued, they would have received a total of

(A) $41,500

(B) $45,100

(C) $48,600

(D) $49,100

64. The total amount awarded to plaintiffs who filed their cases in 1990 was

(A) $1,650

(B) $20,600

(C) $22,250

(D) $22,650

65. Comparing cases filed in 1991 with cases filed in 1992,

(A) four more of the 1991 cases were settled than 1992 cases.

(B) two fewer 1992 cases were settled than 1991 cases.

(C) an equal number of cases was settled from the two years.

(D) three more of the 1991 cases were settled than 1992 cases.

Reading, Understanding, and Interpreting Written Material

> **DIRECTIONS:** Questions 66 – 95 are based on the following passages. Each passage contains several numbered blanks. Read the passage once quickly to get the overall idea. Below each passage are listed sets of words numbered to match the blanks. Read the passage through a second time more slowly, and choose the word from each set that makes the most sense both in the sentence and in the total paragraph.

A large proportion of people __66__ bars are __67__ convicted criminals, __68__ people who have been arrested and are being __69__ until __70__ trials in __71__. Experts have often pointed out that this __72__ system does not operate fairly. For instance, a person who can afford to pay bail usually will not get locked up. The theory of the bail system is that the person will make sure to show up in court when he or she is supposed to; __73__, bail will be forfeited—the person will __74__ the __75__ that was put up. Sometimes a person __76__ can show that he or she is a stable __77__ with a job and a family will be released on "personal recognizance" (without bail). The result is that the well-to-do, the __78__, and the family men can often __79__ the detention system. The people who do wind up in detention tend to __80__ the poor, the unemployed, the single, and the young.

66. (A) under
    (B) at
    (C) tending
    (D) behind

67. (A) always
    (B) not
    (C) hardened
    (D) very

68. (A) but
    (B) and
    (C) also
    (D) although

69. (A) hanged
    (B) freed
    (C) held
    (D) judged

70. (A) your
    (B) his
    (C) daily
    (D) their
71. (A) jail
    (B) court
    (C) fire
    (D) judgment
72. (A) school
    (B) court
    (C) detention
    (D) election
73. (A) otherwise
    (B) therefore
    (C) because
    (D) then
74. (A) save
    (B) spend
    (C) lose
    (D) count
75. (A) wall
    (B) money
    (C) front
    (D) pretense

76. (A) whom
    (B) which
    (C) what
    (D) who
77. (A) citizen
    (B) horse
    (C) cleaner
    (D) clown
78. (A) handsome
    (B) athletic
    (C) employed
    (D) alcoholic
79. (A) survive
    (B) avoid
    (C) provide
    (D) institute
80. (A) become
    (B) help
    (C) be
    (D) harm

___81___ acts are classified according to ___82___ standards. One is whether the ___83___ is major or minor. A major offense, such as murder, would be ___84___ a felony, ___85___ a minor offense, such as reckless driving, would be considered a misdemeanor. ___86___ standard of classification is the specific kind of crime committed. Examples are burglary and robbery, which are ___87___ often used incorrectly by individuals who are ___88___ aware of the actual ___89___ as defined by law. A person who breaks ___90___ a building to commit a ___91___ or other major crime is ___92___ of burglary, while robbery is the felonious taking of an individual's ___93___ from his person or ___94___ his immediate ___95___ by the use of violence or threat.

81. (A) People's
    (B) Criminal
    (C) Felonious
    (D) Numerous

82. (A) decent
    (B) published
    (C) community
    (D) several

83. (A) crime
    (B) act
    (C) offender
    (D) standard

84. (A) labeled
    (B) convicted
    (C) executed
    (D) tried

85. (A) moreover
    (B) because
    (C) whereas
    (D) hence

86. (A) Gold
    (B) Juried
    (C) Another
    (D) My

87. (A) crimes
    (B) terms
    (C) verdicts
    (D) sentences

88. (A) sometimes
    (B) very
    (C) not
    (D) angrily

89. (A) difference
    (B) definitions
    (C) crimes
    (D) victims

90. (A) down
    (B) into
    (C) apart
    (D) from

91. (A) felony
     (B) burglary
     (C) robbery
     (D) theft
92. (A) accused
     (B) convicted
     (C) freed
     (D) guilty
93. (A) life
     (B) liberty
     (C) property
     (D) weapon

94. (A) throughout
     (B) in
     (C) by
     (D) for
95. (A) lifetime
     (B) home
     (C) presence
     (D) concern

Scoring the Sample Exam

Each question is equally weighted. Give yourself one point for each correct answer, as determined by the following answer key. Incorrect or blank answers do not count against you. The highest possible score is 95.

Answer Key

1.	D	20.	D	39.	D	58.	B	77.	A
2.	A	21.	C	40.	A	59.	B	78.	C
3.	C	22.	D	41.	C	60.	C	79.	B
4.	B	23.	A	42.	B	61.	B	80.	C
5.	C	24.	B	43.	D	62.	D	81.	B
6.	A	25.	B	44.	B	63.	D	82.	D
7.	D	26.	C	45.	C	64.	C	83.	A
8.	B	27.	A	46.	A	65.	B	84.	A
9.	D	28.	D	47.	D	66.	D	85.	C
10.	C	29.	C	48.	B	67.	B	86.	C
11.	B	30.	D	49.	C	68.	A	87.	B
12.	D	31.	A	50.	A	69.	C	88.	C
13.	C	32.	C	51.	C	70.	D	89.	A
14.	D	33.	A	52.	C	71.	B	90.	B
15.	C	34.	B	53.	D	72.	C	91.	D
16.	A	35.	B	54.	C	73.	A	92.	D
17.	D	36.	D	55.	A	74.	C	93.	C
18.	B	37.	A	56.	C	75.	B	94.	B
19.	D	38.	C	57.	B	76.	D	95.	C

Answer Explanations

1. **(D)** The correct spelling is *appellate.*

2. **(A)** The correct spelling is *presumption.*

3. **(C)** The correct spelling is *litigant.*

4. **(B)** The correct spelling is *commitment.*

5. **(C)** The correct spelling is *affidavit.*

6. **(A)** The correct spelling is *arraign.*

7. **(D)** The correct spelling is *cumulative.*

8. **(B)** The correct spelling is *severance.*

9. **(D)** The correct spelling is *adjournment.*

10. **(C)** The correct spelling is *commenced.*

11. **(B)** The correct spelling is *forgers.*

12. **(D)** None of the words is *misspelled.*

13. **(C)** The correct spelling is *achievement.*

14. **(D)** None of the words is *misspelled.*

15. **(C)** The correct spelling is *detention.*

16. **(A)** The correct spelling is *immaterial.*

17. **(D)** None of the words is *misspelled.*

18. **(B)** The correct spelling is *prosecutor.*

19. **(D)** None of the words is misspelled.

20. **(D)** None of the words is misspelled.

21. **(C)** There should be no *and* before the etc. at the end of a series of words.

22. **(D)** This is an incomplete comparison. It should read, "He devotes as much as, if not more, time to his work than the rest of the employees."

23. **(A)** More preferable is a redundancy; preferable alone is quite adequate.

24. **(B)** The compound subject, violations …and… behavior, requires the plural form of the verb constitute.

25. **(B)** This sentence shifts point of view midstream. It could read either, If one wants to prevent crime, one must deal…, or, If we want to prevent crime, we must deal….

26. **(C)** Unique means that there is only one; therefore, the word can take no qualifier.

27. **(A)** This is an ambiguous statement. Was the judge praised for the fire? Was the clerk praised for the fire? It would be better to say, The clerk was highly praised for promptly notifying the judge of the fire.

28. **(D)** Sentence (A) reads as if all concerned are criminal acts. Since guns are a kind of weapon, sentence (B) would have to read, "…than any other kind of weapon." In sentence (C), regards is the wrong word; the word required is regard.

29. **(C)** In sentence (A), the idiomatic form is as satisfactory. Sentence (B) confuses two verb tenses in the same sentence; it would be correct to say that the court officer went …and discovered…. Sentence (D) requires a parallel construction, either reforming and striking or to reform and to strike.

30. **(D)** In sentence (A), examination, being singular, requires the singular verb, reveals. The correct form of sentence (B) is …would not have arisen. As for sentence (C), the word alike obviously includes both, so the word both is redundant.

C

31. **(A)** In sentence (B), every person is singular and therefore must be informed of the reason for his or her arrest. In sentence (C), a motorist is a person, not a thing, so use to whom and who rather than to which and which. Sentence (D) requires the parallelism of quickly but carefully.

32. **(C)** Sentence (A) requires the auxiliary verb *have* in place of the incorrect *of*. In sentence (B), anyone is singular, so the referent pronoun must also be singular: ...whose training fits him or her to do the work. The construction of sentence (D) is awkward; if the receptionist had always answered is sufficient and accurate.

33. **(A)** Sentence (D) is wordy and clearly wrong. In sentence (B), what is meant is the number of offenses. In sentence (C), we need a simple objective case pronoun: ...is known only to the chief clerk and me.

34. **(B)** In sentence (A), the correct idiomatic form is different from. Sentence (C) requires a subjunctive form because the statement is contrary to fact: If only one guard were.... Sentence (D) shifts point of view; for consistency, the pronoun throughout may be either one or you.

35. **(B)** There is a difference in the second column: Phila., PA 19147 and Phila, PA 19147

36. **(D)** All three columns are different: East Amherst, NY 14051 and East Amherst, NV 14051 (third column); 9803-115-6848 and 9083-115-6848 (second column)

37. **(A)** All three columns are alike.

38. **(C)** There is a difference in the third column: P.O. Box 44268a and P.O. Box 44286a

39. **(D)** All three columns are different: Benner Mgmt. Group and Banner Mgmt. Group (second column); 86408 W. 3rd Ave. and 84608 W. 3rd Ave. (third column)

40. **(A)** All three columns are alike.

41. **(C)** The third column is different: Gaithersburg, MD 20879 and Gaithersberg, MD 20879

42. **(B)** The second column is different: Mardikian & Moore, Inc. and Mardikian and Moore, Inc.

43. **(D)** All three columns are different: Ramona Fleischer-Chris and Ramona Fleisher-Chris (second column); 60646 West Touhy Avenue and 60646 West Touhey Avenue (third column)

44. **(B)** The second column is different: 43216 M Street, NE and 43216 M. Street, NE

45. **(C)** The third column is different: 2503 Bartholemew Way and 2503 Bartholomew Way

46. **(A)** All three columns are alike.

47. **(D)** All three columns are different: 86529 Dunwoodie Drive and 85629 Dunwoodie Drive (third column); 6-78912-e3e42 and 6-78912-3e3e42 (second column)

48. **(B)** The second column is different: O'Reilly Bay, LA 56212 and O'Reillys Bay, LA 56212

49. **(C)** The third column is different: 4132 ES, Mexico DF and 4132 ES, Mexico D.F.

50. **(A)** All three columns are alike.

51. **(C)** Conlon was scheduled to hear 6 cases: 1 on Monday, 1 on Tuesday, 2 on Wednesday, and 2 on Thursday. Amati and Lee were scheduled for 5 cases apiece, and Ramos was only scheduled for 4.

52. **(C)** Of the cases Baron was scheduled to hear, 3 were adjourned (2 on Monday and 1 on Wednesday) and 2 were dismissed (on Friday), so he didn't give any cash awards. Jones gave cash awards in 2 cases, and Moro and Lee gave cash awards in 1 case each.

53. **(D)** Lee and Baron were both scheduled for 2 trials on Monday and Friday, Amati was scheduled for 2 on Tuesday, and Conlon was scheduled for 2 on Wednesday and Thursday, for a total of 4 judges.

54. **(C)** On Tuesday, Moro awarded $9,000 in a suit for $11,500; on Wednesday, Ramos awarded $6,000 in a suit for $7,500; on Thursday, Jones awarded $6,000 in a suit for $7,500; and on Friday, Ramos awarded $20,000 in a suit for $28,000, for a total of 4 cases.

55. **(A)** Of the 6 cases filed in 1990, 2 were settled (1 on Monday and 1 on Friday), 2 were adjourned (both on Tuesday), and 2 were adjudicated (1 on Wednesday and 1 on Thursday). None was dismissed.

56. **(C)** 3 of the 1992 cases were adjourned: 1 on Wednesday, 1 on Thursday, and 1 on Friday. Only 1 1993 case was adjourned, and 2 each of 1990 and 1991 cases were adjourned.

57. **(B)** Lee and Baron each sat on Monday, Wednesday, and Friday. Jones sat on Monday, Tuesday, Thursday, and Friday. Moro sat on Tuesday, Wednesday, Thursday, and Friday. Ramos sat on Monday, Tuesday, Wednesday, and Friday.

58. **(B)** 4 cases were filed in May (see the tables for Monday, Wednesday, Thursday, and Friday). 3 cases were filed in each of February, August, and November.

59. **(B)** $6,000 + $17,250 + $10,850 = $34,100

60. **(C)** $15,000 (on Monday) + $6,000 (on Thursday) = $21,000

61. **(B)** $6,000 (Conlon's first case) + $12,000 (Moro's case) = $18,000

62. **(D)** $15,000 − $14,000 = $1,000 (Jones on Monday); $3,375 − $3,000 = $375 (Ramos on Tuesday); $15,000 − $2,000 = $13,000 (Amati on Wednesday); $17,250 − $16,000 = $1,250 (Conlon on Wednesday); $10,850 − $10,000 = $850 (Amati on Wednesday); $5,000 − $4,600 = $400 (Conlon on Thursday); $8,625 − $8,000 = $625 (Lee on Friday); $1,000 + $375 + $13,000 + $1,250 + $850 + $400 + $625 = $17,500

63. **(D)** $7,600 (filed on 5/1/93 and heard on Monday) + $10,000 (filed on 1/7/93 and heard on Wednesday) + $22,000 (filed on 2/15/93 and heard on Wednesday) + $9,500 (filed on 1/28/93 and heard on Friday) = $49,100

64. **(C)** On Wednesday, Conlon awarded $17,350 in a 11/30/90 case; on Thursday, Conlon awarded $5,000 in a 10/30/90 case; $17,350 + $5,000 = $22,250

65. **(B)** Four 1991 cases were settled—on Tuesday, Thursday, and Friday; only 2 1992 cases were settled.

66. **(D)** People are generally said to be behind bars.

67. **(B)** The second part of the sentence should lead you to choose the contrasting word not.

68. **(A)** Again, a contrasting word, but, fits best.

69. **(C)** The word that makes the most sense in the context of the sentence is held.

C

70. **(D)** Since people is plural, you must choose the plural possessive, their.

71. **(B)** Trials are generally held in court.

72. **(C)** The paragraph is discussing jailing of people awaiting trial, a form of detention.

73. **(A)** Reading the two parts of the sentence shows that you need a contrasting word, otherwise.

74. **(C)** To forfeit bail, as stated earlier in the sentence, means that you lose your money.

75. **(B)** Since bail is a set amount of cash, money is the best choice here.

76. **(D)** Since the pronoun refers to a person, you must choose who.

77. **(A)** The only choice that makes sense is citizen.

78. **(C)** As stated earlier—a stable citizen with a job—people who are employed can often avoid the detention system.

79. **(B)** Since these people are released on personal recognizance, they avoid the detention system.

80. **(C)** Be makes the most sense in the context of the sentence.

81. **(B)** A quick reading of the paragraph reveals that it is discussing criminal acts.

82. **(D)** Again, reading over the paragraph reveals that it is discussing more than one, or several, standards.

83. **(A)** Since the previous sentence was discussing criminal acts, crime is the best choice here.

84. **(A)** Labeled fits best in the context of the sentence.

85. **(C)** Major and minor offenses are being contrasted here, so choose the contrasting word, whereas.

86. **(C)** This sentence discusses a second standard, so the best choice is another.

87. **(B)** This sentence is talking about definitions, so terms is the best choice.

88. **(C)** Since the terms are used incorrectly, the people who use them are not aware of their legal definitions.

89. **(A)** This sentence is clearly discussing the difference between the two terms.

90. **(B)** Typically, a person breaks into a building.

91. **(D)** Eliminate felony for one of the more specific terms. Since this part of the sentence is defining robbery, you can't reuse that term, and you already know that a burglary isn't the same thing as a robbery. Therefore, the best choice is theft.

92. **(D)** When a person commits the crime of burglary, he or she is guilty of burglary.

93. **(C)** Robbery generally means taking someone's property.

94. **(B)** In fits the context of the sentence best.

95. **(C)** You can eliminate home—you already know that that's a burglary. The only other choice that makes sense is presence.

Evaluating Yourself

In order to earn a high score, however, you must do well on all parts of the exam. Using the following chart, check how many of each question type you missed to gauge your performance on that kind of question. Then, concentrate your efforts toward improvement in the areas with which you had the most difficulty; it will be worth your while to return to the indicated chapter and review.

SELF-EVALUATION CHART

Question Type	Question Numbers	Lesson to Review
Spelling	1–20	Hour 4
English Grammar and Usage	21–34	Hour 3
Clerical Speed and Accuracy	35–50	Hour 13
Tabular Completions	51–65	Hour 17
Effective Expression	66–95	Hour 8

C

Jump Start Your Civil Service Career.

Whether you're trying to pass a qualifying exam or looking for a new job, ARCO's extensive line of Civil Service books can help you get the wheels in motion.

24 Hours to the Civil Service Exams
Twenty-four one-hour lessons covering the qualifying exam for federal, state, and municipal positions.

American Foreign Service Officer Exam
Covers both the written exam and oral assessment.

Clerical Exams
Practice for landing clerical jobs in the government and private sector.

Emergency Dispatcher/ 911 Operator Exam
Features 2 full-length practice exams for a position in an emergency assistance control center.

Court Officer Exam
Training for the qualifying exams for positions as bailiffs, senior court officers, and court clerks.

Federal Jobs
A directory of entry-level jobs in every important federal agency

Mechanical Aptitude & Spatial Relations Tests
Practice questions and review for exams measuring mechanical aptitude, symbol reasoning, and spatial relations.

THOMSON

ARCO

To order:
Visit www.petersons.com and receive a 20% discount
Call 800-338-3282 or visit your local bookstore